Sermons

to

The Spiritual Man

SERMONS TO THE SPIRITUAL MAN

William G. T. Shedd

Solid Ground Christian Books
Birmingham, Alabama

SOLID GROUND CHRISTIAN BOOKS
PO Box 660132, Vestavia Hills, AL 35266
205-443-0311
sgcb@charter.net
http://www.solid-ground-books.com

Sermons to the Spiritual Man

by William G.T. Shedd

Taken from the 1972 edition by Banner of Truth Trust

Published by Solid Ground Christian Books

Classic Reprints Series

First printing December 2003

ISBN: 1-932474-22-6

Manufactured in the United States of America

PREFATORY NOTE

THIS volume is complementary to another, published in 1871, under the title of "Sermons to the Natural Man." In the earlier volume, the author aimed to address the human conscience. In this, he would speak to the Christian heart. The former supposed original and unpardoned sin, and endeavored to produce the consciousness of it. The latter supposes forgiven and indwelling sin, and would aid in the struggle and victory over it. The writer has had evidence, both from this country and from abroad, that theological sermonizing and the close application of truth are not so unwelcome and unpopular, as they are sometimes represented to be. This encourages him to hope that the present volume, which takes a wider range, and brings to view the experiences and aspirations of the regenerate believer, may find a yet larger class of sympathetic readers. At the same time, the author is well aware that both volumes are out of all keeping with some existing tendencies in the religious world. But these tendencies are destined to disappear, whenever the blind guides shall cease to lead the blind, and honest self-knowledge shall take the place of self-flattery and religious delusion. That this will happen, is as certain as that the Holy Spirit has not forsaken the world for which God incarnate died, but will, in His own way, again search and illumine the human soul, as in "the times of refreshing from the presence of the Lord."

UNION THEOLOGICAL SEMINARY, NEW YORK,
April 15, 1884.

CONTENTS

CONTENTS

SERMONS.

———•———

SERMON I.

RELIGIOUS MEDITATION.

PSALM civ. 34.—" My meditation of Him shall be sweet."

THERE is no being with whom man stands in such close and important relations as with the invisible God, and yet there is no being with whom he finds it so difficult to have communication. The earth he can see and touch. His fellow-man he can look in the eye and speak to. But "no man hath seen God at any time." Century after century passes by, and the Highest utters no voice that is audible to the outward ear. Thousands and millions of human supplications are sent up to Him who dwells in the heavens, but the heavens are not rent, no deity comes down, and no visible sign is made. The skies are silent. The impenetrable vail between man's body and God's spirit is not withdrawn even for an instant.

As this continues to be the case generation after generation, and century after century, it is natural that those who know of nothing but an external and visible communication between themselves and their Maker should become sceptical concerning his actual existence. Like the pagan idolater, they demand a God who can be seen and handled. Like him, too, they hanker after prodigies and wonders, and desire to be put into palpable communication with the Celestial Powers. " This generation seeketh after a sign." It is not surprising, consequently, that the natural man, finding no response to his passionate and baffled attempts to penetrate the invisible and eternal by the method of the five senses, falls into unbelief, and concludes in his heart that a deity who never shows himself has no real being.

Thus the natural tendency of all men who hold no prayerful and spiritual communication with their Maker is to atheism, so long as they live in a world where he makes no external displays of his person and his presence. A time is indeed coming, when an outward vision of God will break upon them so palpable and evident that they will call upon the rocks and mountains to cover them from it ; but until that time they are liable to a scepticism which often renders it difficult, even when they make some efforts to the contrary, to believe that there is a God.

But the child of God—the believing, the spiritual, the prayerful man—is delivered from this atheism. For he knows of an intercourse with his Maker, which, though unattended by signs and wonders, by palpability and tangibility for the bodily senses, is as real and convincing as anything outward or visible can be. He has experienced the forgiveness of sin, and found the disquieting remorse of his soul displaced by the peace of God in his conscience, and the love of God in his heart. He has known the doubts and fears of a sick bed to give way before God's inward assurance of mercy and acceptance. He has been in a horror of great mental darkness, and into that black void of his soul God has suddenly made a precious promise, or a comforting truth of his word, to shine out clear, distinct, and glittering, like a star shooting up into a midnight sky. He has had love, and peace, and joy, and the whole throng of devout and spiritual affections, flow in currents through his naturally hard and parched soul, at the touch of a Spirit, at the breath of a Being, not of earth or of time. And perhaps more convincing than all, he has offered up prayers and supplications, with strong crying and tears, for a strength that was not in himself but which he must get or die, for a blessing that his hungry famine-struck soul must obtain or be miserable, and has been heard in that he feared. Thus the Christian's belief in the Divine existence is a vital one. In a higher sense than that of the poet, it is "felt in the blood, and felt along the heart." It is part and particle of his consciousness, waning only as his religious experience wanes, and dying only when that deathless thing shall die.

Yet there are fluctuations in the Christian's faith and sense of God. He needs to school and train himself in this reference. God himself has appointed instrumentalities by which to keep the knowledge of himself pure, clear, and bright in the souls of his children, "until the day break and the shadows flee away;" and among them is the habit of devout reflection upon his being and attributes.

The uses of *religious meditation* upon God, to which we are urged by both the precept and the example of the Psalmist, may be indicated in the three following propositions: 1. Meditation upon God is a lofty and elevating act, because God is infinite in his being and perfections. 2. It is a sanctifying act, because God is holy in his nature and attributes. 3. It is a blessed act of the mind, because God is infinitely blessed, and communicates of his fulness of joy to all who contemplate it.

I. In the first place, meditation upon God is a high and

elevating mental act, because of the immensity of the Object. "Behold the heaven of heavens cannot contain thee," said the awe-struck Solomon. "God is a most pure spirit, immutable, immense," says the Creed. Reflection upon that which is infinite tends of itself to enlarge and ennoble. Meditation upon that which is immense produces a lofty mood of mind. This is true even of merely material immensity. He who often looks up into the firmament, and views the great orbs that fill it, and the great movements that take place in it, will come to possess a spirit akin to this material grandeur—for the astronomical spirit is a lofty one—while he who keeps his eyes upon the ground, and looks at nothing but his little plot of earth, and his own little life with its little motions, will be apt to possess a spirit grovelling like the things he lives among, and mean like the dirt he treads upon. Says the thoughtful and moral Schiller:[1] "The vision of unlimited distances and immeasurable heights, of the great ocean at his feet and the still greater ocean above him, draws man's spirit away from the narrow sphere of sense, and from the oppressive stricture of physical existence. A grander rule of measurement is held out to him in the simple majesty of Nature, and environed by her great forms he can no longer endure a little and narrow way of thinking. Who knows how many a bright thought and heroic resolve, which the student's chamber or the academic hall never would have originated, has been started out by this lofty struggle of the soul with the great spirit of Nature; who knows whether it is not in part to be ascribed to a less frequent intercourse with the grandeur of the material world, that the mind of man in cities more readily stoops to trifles, and is crippled and weak, while the mind of the dweller

---

[1] Ueber das Erhabene.

beneath the broad sky remains open and free as the firmament under which it lives."[1]

But if this is true of the immensity of Nature, much more is it of the immensity of God. If the sight of the heavens and the stars, of the earth and the vast seas, has a natural tendency to elevate and ennoble the human intellect, much more will the vision granted only to the pure in heart—the vision of the infinite Being who made all these things—exalt the soul above all the created universe. For the immensity of God is the immensity of mind. The infinity of God is an infinity of truth, of purity, of justice, of mercy, of love, and of glory. When the human intellect perceives God, it beholds what the heaven of heavens does not possess and cannot contain. His grandeur and plenitude is far above that of material creation; for he is the source and the free power whence it all came. The magnificence and beauty of the heavens and earth are the work of his fingers; and there is nothing which the bodily sense can apprehend, by day or by night, however sublime and glorious it may be, that is not infinitely inferior to the excelling, transcending glory of God.

It is one of the many injuries which sin does to man, that it degrades him. It excludes him from the uplifting vision of the Creator, and causes him to expend his mental force upon inferior objects—upon money, houses, lands, titles, and "the bubble reputation." Sin imprisons man within narrow limitations, and thus dwarfs him. And it is one of the consequences of his regeneration that he is enabled to soar again into the realm of the Infinite, and

---

[1] In a similar strain Cicero remarks: "Est animorum ingeniorumque naturale quoddam quasi pabulum consideratio contemplatioque naturæ: erigimur; elatiores fieri videmur; humana despicimus; cogitantesque supera atque cœlestia, hæc nostra, ut exigua et minima, contemnimus."
—*Academicæ Quæstiones*, II., 41.

behold unlimited perfection, and thereby regain the dignity he lost by apostasy. For it is a moral and spiritual difference that marks off the hierarchies of heaven from the principalities of hell. Rational beings rise in grade and glorious dignity by virtue of their character. But this character is intimately connected with the clear, unclouded contemplation of God. It is the beatific vision that renders the archangels so lofty. And it is only through a spiritual beholding of God that man can reascend to the point but little lower than the angels, and be crowned again with glory and honor.

II. In the second place, meditation upon God is a *sanctifying* act, because God is holy and perfect in his nature and attributes. The meditation of which the Psalmist speaks in the text is not that of the schoolman, or the poet, but of the devout, saintly, and adoring mind. That meditation upon God which is "sweeter than honey and the honey-comb" is not speculative, but practical. That which is speculative and scholastic springs from curiosity. That which is practical flows from love. This is the key to this distinction, so frequently employed in reference to the operations of the human mind. All merely speculative thinking is inquisitive, acute, and wholly destitute of affection for the object. But all practical thinking is affectionate, sympathetic, and in harmony with the object. When I meditate upon God because I love him, my reflection is practical. When I think upon God because I desire to explore him, my thinking is speculative. None, therefore, but the devout and affectionate mind truly meditates upon God; and all thought upon that Being which is put forth merely to gratify the curiosity and pride of the human understanding forms no part of the Christian habit and practice which we are recommending. Man in every age has endeavored "by searching to find out God." He has striven almost convulsively to fathom the abyss of the Deity, and discover the deep things of the Creator. But because it was from the love of knowledge rather than from the love of God, his efforts have been both unprofitable and futile. He has not sounded the abyss, neither has his heart grown humble, and gentle, and tender, and pure. His intellect has been baffled, and, what is yet worse, his nature has not been renovated. Nay, more, a weariness and a curse has come into his spirit, because he has put the comprehension of an object in the place of the object itself; because, in his long struggle to understand God, he has not had the first thought of loving and serving him.

There is, indeed, for the created mind, no true knowledge of the Creator but a practical and sanctifying knowledge. God alone knows the speculative secrets of his own being. The moral and holy perfections of the Godhead are enough, and more than enough, for man to meditate upon. "The secret things belong unto the Lord our God," said Moses to the children of Israel, "but those things which are revealed belong unto us, and to our children forever, that we may *do* all the words of his law."

True meditation, thus proceeding from filial love and sympathy, brings the soul into intercourse and communion with its object. Devout and holy reflection upon God introduces man into the divine presence, in a true and solid sense of these words. Such a soul shall know God as the natural man does not, and cannot. "Judas saith unto him, not Iscariot, Lord, how is it that thou wilt manifest thyself unto us, and not unto the world? Jesus answered, and said unto him, If a man love me, he will keep my words: and my Father will love him, and we will *come* unto him and make our *abode* with him." In the hour of spiritual and affectionate musing upon the character and attributes of God—and especially upon their manifestation in the Person and Work of Christ—there is a positive impression upon the heart, directly from God. In what other mode can we get near to the Invisible One, here upon earth, than by some mental act or process? In what other way than by prayer and meditation can we approach God? We cannot see him with the outward eye. We cannot touch him with the hand. We cannot draw nigh to him with a body of flesh and blood. In no way, here below, can we have intercourse with God, except "in spirit." He is a pure Spirit, and that part of us which has to do with him is the spirit within us. And in this mode of existence, the only ordinary medium of communication between the divine and the human spirit is thought and prayer. God, with all the immensity of his being, and all the infinitude of his perfections, is virtually non-existent for that man who does not meditate and who never prays. For so long as there is no medium of intercourse there is no intercourse. The power of thought and of spiritual supplication is all that God has given us in this life whereby we may approach him, and be impressed by his being and attributes. Eye hath not seen him; the ear cannot hear him. Nothing but the invisible can behold the invisible. Here upon earth, man must meet God in the depths of his soul, in the privacy of his closet, or not at all.

The Christian life is so imperfect here below, that it is unsafe to set it up as a measure of what is possible under the covenant of grace. The possibilities and capacities of the Christian religion are by no means to be estimated by the stinted draughts made upon them by our unfaithfulness and unbelief. Were we as meditative and prayerful as was Enoch, the seventh from Adam, we, like him, should "walk with God." This was the secret of the wonderful spirituality and unearthliness that led to his translation. Is there upon earth to-day any communion between man and God superior to that between the patriarchal mind and the Eternal? Men tell us that the ancient church was ignorant, and that it cannot be expected that Seth and Enoch and David should be possessed of the vast intelligence of the nineteenth century. But show me the man among the millions of our restless and self-conceited civilization who walks with God as Enoch did, and who meditates upon that glorious Being all the day and in the night watches as David did—show me a man of such mental processes as these, and I will show you one whose shoe latchets, even in intellectual respects, the wisest of our savans is not worthy to stoop down and unloose. No scientific knowledge equals, either in loftiness or in depth, the immortal vision of the saint and seraphim. And were we accustomed to such heavenly contemplation and musing, the "fire would burn" in our hearts as it did in that of the Psalmist, and our souls would "pant" after God. God would be real to our feelings, instead of being a mere abstraction for our understandings. We should be conscious of his presence with a distinctness equal to that with which we feel ·the morning wind, and should see his glory as clearly as we ever saw the sun at noonday. With as much certainty as we know the sky to be overhead, and underneath the solid ground, should we be certain that "God is, and is the rewarder of them that diligently seek him." There would be contact. "I want," said Niebuhr, wearied with seeking and not finding, "I want a God who is heart to my heart, spirit to my spirit, life to my life." Such is God to every soul that loves him, and meditates because it loves.

True meditation, then, being practical, and thereby bringing the subject of it into communion with the object of it, is of necessity sanctifying. For the object is Infinite

Holiness and Purity. It is he in whom is centred and gathered and crowded all possible perfections. And can our minds muse upon such a Being and not become purer and better? Can we actually and affectionately commune with the most perfect and high God in the heavens and not become sanctified? The spirit of a man takes its character from the themes of its meditation. He who thinks much upon wealth becomes avaricious; he whose thoughts are upon earthly glory becomes ambitious; and he whose thoughts are upon God becomes godlike.

III. In the third place, meditation upon God is a *blessed* act of the mind, because God himself is an infinitely blessed being, and communicates of his fulness of joy to all who contemplate it. Mere thinking, in and of itself, is not sufficient to secure happiness. Everything depends upon the quality of the thought, and this again upon the nature of the object upon which it is expended. There are various kinds and degrees of mental enjoyment, each produced by a particular species of mental reflection; but there is no thinking that gives rest and satisfaction and joy to the soul, but thinking upon the glorious and blessed God. All other thought ultimately baffles and tires us. Heaven comes into the human mind not through poetry, or philosophy, or science, or art—not through any secular knowledge—but through religion. When a man thinks of his wealth, his houses, his friends, or his country, though he derives a sort of pleasure from so doing, yet it is not of such a grave and solid species as to justify its being denominated "bliss." No thought that is expended upon the creature, or upon any of the creaturely relations, can possibly produce that "sober certainty of waking bliss" which constitutes heaven. If it can, why is not man a blessed spirit here on earth? If it can, why is it that man in all his movements and strivings never reaches a final centre, at which he is willing to say to his soul: "This is enough; this is all; here stand and remain forever?" Man is constantly thinking upon the things of earth, and if they have the power to awaken calm and contented thought, and to induce a permanent and perfect joy, why is he so restless and unhappy? And why does he become the more wearied and soured, the more intensely he thinks and toils?

But there is higher and nobler thought than that of trade and politics. Man can meditate upon purely intellectual themes. He can expend intense reflection upon the mysteries and problems of his own mind, and of the Eternal Mind. He can put forth an earnest and graceful effort of his powers within the province of beautiful letters and fine art. But does even such an intellectual, and, so far as it goes, such an elevating meditation as this produce and preserve genuine tranquillity and enjoyment? Are poet and philosopher synonymous with saint and angel? Is the learned man necessarily a happy one? Look through the history of literary men, and see their anxious but baffled research, their eager but fruitless inquiry, their acute but empty speculation, their intense but vain study, and you will know that the wise man spake true when he said, "He that increaseth knowledge increaseth sorrow." Hear the sigh of the meditative Wordsworth:

> "Me this unchartered freedom tires;
> I feel the weight of chance desires;
> My hopes no more must change their name,
> I long for a repose that ever is the same."

No, all thought which does not ultimately come home to God in practical, filial, and sympathetic communion, is incapable of rendering the soul blest. The intellect may find a kind of pleasure in satisfying its inquisitive and proud desire " to be as gods, knowing good and evil," but the heart experiences no peace or rest, until by a devout and religious meditation it enters into the fulness of God and shares in his eternal joy.

And here again, as in the former instance, our personal experience is so limited and meagre that the language of Scripture, and of some saints on earth, seems exaggerated and rhetorical. Says the sober and sincere apostle Paul —a man too much in earnest, and too well acquainted with the subject, to overdraw and overpaint—" Eye hath not seen, nor ear heard, neither have entered into the heart of man, the things which God hath prepared for them that love him." There is a strange unearthly joy, when a pure and spiritual mind is granted a clear view of the divine perfections. It rejoices with a joy unspeakable and full of glorying. All finite beauty, all created glory, is but a shadow in comparison. The holy mind rapt in contemplation says with Augustine : " When I love God, I do not love the beauty of material bodies, nor the fair harmony of time, nor the brightness of the light so gladsome to our eyes, nor sweet melodies of varied songs, nor the fragrant smell of flowers and perfumes and spices ; not manna nor honey. None of these do I love, when I love my God. And yet I love a kind of melody, a kind of fragrance, and a kind of food, when I love my God—the light, the melody, the fragrance, and the food of the inner man : when there shineth into my soul what space cannot contain, and there soundeth what time beareth not away, and there smelleth what breathing disperseth not, and there tasteth what eating diminisheth not. This is it which I love, when I love my God." '

We find it difficult, with our sluggish and earthly tem-

---

¹ Confessions, X., 6.

per, to believe all this, and to sympathize with it. Yet it is simple naked truth and fact. There is a heaven, whether we reach it or not. There is a beatific vision of God, whether it ever dilate and enrapture our eyes or not. God is infinite blessedness and glory, and no good being can behold him without partaking of it. As he gazes, he is changed into the same image from glory to glory. The more clear and full his vision, the more overwhelming and boundless is the influx of heaven into him. We may know something of this here on earth. The more we meditate upon God and divine things, the happier shall we become in our own minds. There are at this moment, upon this cursed and thistle-bearing earth, some meek and gentle spirits whose life of prayer and holy communion streaks the heavens with bars of amber, and apparels everything in heavenly light. And the more this divine pleasure enters the soul, the more will it hunger and thirst after it. For this is the *summum bonum;* this is the absolute delight. This never satiates. This never wearies. This joy in the vision of God has the power to freshen and invigorate while it runs through the fibres of the heart; and therefore, even amidst the most ecstatic and satisfying visions of heaven, the blessed still cry : "My soul pants after thee, O God, as the hart pants after the water-brook; my heart and my flesh cries out for the living God."

Never will our minds reach a state in which they will really be at rest, and never will they put forth an activity which they will be willing to have eternal, until they acquire the mental habits of the holy angels. In the saints' everlasting rest, there is an unintermittent contemplation and sight of God. Who of us is ready for it? Who of us is certain that he will not turn away, when he finds that this, and this alone, is the heaven of which he has heard

so much. Who of us has such a holy frame and such a
spiritual sympathy with God, that every deeper descent
into that abyss of holiness and purity will reveal new sights
of joy, and start out new feelings of wonder and love?
Who of us can be happy in heaven? For this open vision
of God, this sight of him face to face, this beatific contemplation of his perfections, is the substance of paradise, the
jasper foundation of the city of God.

We have thus seen that religious meditation upon God
and divine things elevates, sanctifies, and blesses. But
though this Christian habit produces such great and good
fruits, there is probably no duty that is more neglected.
We find it easier to read our Bible, than to ponder upon it;
easier to listen to preaching, than to inwardly digest it;
easier to respond to the calls of benevolence and engage in
external service in the church, than to go into our closets.
And is not this the secret of the faint and sickly life in our
souls? Is not this the reason why we live at a poor dying
rate? Think you that if we often entered into the
presence of God and obtained a realizing view of things
unseen and eternal, earthly temptation would have such a
strong power over us as it does? Think you that if we
received every day a distinct and bold impression from the
attributes of God, we should be so distant from him in
our hearts? Can we not trace our neglect of duty, our
lukewarm feelings, and our great worldliness of heart, to
our lack of the vision of God?

The success of a Christian mainly depends upon a uniform and habitual communion with his God and Redeemer. No spasmodic resolutions into which he may be
exasperated by the goadings of conscience can be a substitute for it. If holy communion and prayer are interrupted, he will surely fall into sin. In this world of
continual temptation and of lethargic consciences, we need

to be awakened and awed by the serene splendor of God's
holy countenance. But we cannot behold that amidst the
vapors and smoke of every-day life. We must go into
our closets and "shut the door, and pray to our Father
who seeth in secret." Then shall we know how power to
resist temptation comes from fellowship with God. Then
shall we know what a sabbath that soul enjoys, which,
with open eye, looks long and steadily at the Divine
perfections. With what a triumphant energy, like that of
the archangel trampling on the dragon, does Moses come
down from the Mount into the life of conflict and trial.
With what a vehement spiritual force does a holy mind
resist evil, after it has just seen the contrast between evil
and God. Will the eagle that has soared above the
earth in the free air of the open firmament of heaven, and
has gazed into the sun with an undazzled eye, endure to
sink and dwell in the dark cavern of the owl and the bat?
Then will the spirit which has seen the glorious light of
the divine countenance endure to descend and grovel in
the darkness and shame of sin.

It should, therefore, be a diligent and habitual practice
with us, to meditate upon God and divine things. Time
should be carefully set apart and faithfully used for this
sole purpose. It is startling to consider how much of our
life passes without any thought of God ; without any distinct and filial recognition of his presence and his character. And yet how much of it might be spent in sweet
and profitable meditation. The avocations of our daily
life do not require the whole of our mental energy and reflection. If there were a disposition ; if the current of
feeling and affection set in that direction ; how often
could the farmer commune with God in the midst of his
toil, or the merchant in the very din and press of his business. How often could the artisan send his thoughts and his

ejaculations upward, and the work of his hands be none
the worse for it. " What hinders," says Augustine,[1] " what
hinders a servant of God while working with his hands,
from meditating in the law of the Lord, and singing unto
the name of the Lord most high ? As for divine songs, he
can easily say them even while working with his hands,
and like as rowers with a boat-song, so with godly melody
cheer up his very toil." But the disposition is greatly
lacking. If there were an all-absorbing affection for God
in our hearts, and it were deep joy to see him, would not
this " sweet meditation " of the Psalmist be the pleasure
of life, and all other thinking the duty—a duty performed from the necessity that attaches to this imperfect
mode of existence, rather than from any keen relish for
it ? If the vision of God were glorious and ravishing to
our minds, should we not find them often indulging
themselves in the sight, and would not a return to the
things of earth be reluctant ? Would not thought upon
God steal through and suffuse all our other thinking, as
sunset does the evening sky, giving a pure and saintly hue
to all our feelings, and pervading our entire experience ?
So it works in other provinces. The poet Burns was so
deeply absorbed in the visions, aspirations, and emotions
of poetry, that the avocations of the farmer engrossed
but little of his mind, and it has been said of him,
that " though his hand was on the plough his heart
was with the muse." Were the Christian as much absorbed in the visions, aspirations, and emotions of religion, it would be said of him, too : " His hand is on
the plough, but his heart is with his God ; his head is in
his worldly business, but his heart is with his God."

Finally, let us be urged up to the practice of this duty

---

[1] De Opere Monachorum, XVII.

by a consideration which has most force, it is true, for un-renewed men who know nothing of the Christian expe-rience, but which still has much strength for us if we consider our remaining sin and the slender amount of our intercourse with God. We still find it too difficult to delight in God. It is still not so easy and pleasant as it ought to be to walk with God. Notwithstanding our vocation and our expectation, it is still too difficult for us to be happy in heaven. It is in this reference that the subject we have been considering speaks with great emphasis. Let us remember that a foundation for heaven in our own minds is requisite in order to the enjoyment of the heaven that is on high.[1] That rational being who does not practise the meditations and enjoy the experiences of heaven, will not be at home there, and, therefore, will not go there. Every being goes to " his own place." Is it supposable that a soul that never here on earth con-templated the Divine character with pleasure, will see that character in eternity, in peace, and joy? Is it sup-posable that a human spirit filled with self-seeking and worldliness, and wholly destitute of devout and adoring meditations, will be taken among seraphim and cherubim when taken out of time? Is that world of holy con-templation the proper place for a carnal mind filled through and through with only earthly and selfish thoughts? Can the sensual Dives be happy in the bosom of Abraham? God is not mocked, neither can a man cheat and impose upon his own soul when in eternity. Every one will then be brought to his individuality. He will know then, if not

---

[1] " A human being," says Channing, " who has lived without God, and without self-improvement, can no more enjoy heaven than a moulder-ing body lifted from the tomb and placed amidst beautiful prospects, can enjoy the light through its decayed eyes, or feel the balmy air which blows away its dust."—Sermon on Immortality.

before, what he does really love and what he does really loathe. And if in that other world there be only a pretended and hollow affection for God, with what a sigh and long-drawn moan will the wretched being fling down the harp with which he vainly tries to sing the heavenly song. For whatsoever a man thinks of with most relish here in time, he shall think of with most relish in eternity. He who loves to think of wealth, and fame, and sensual pleasure, and loathes to think of God, and Christ, and heavenly objects, shall think of wealth, and fame, and sensual pleasure in eternity, where all such thinking is "the worm that dieth not, and the fire that is not quenched." But he who, in any degree, loves to think of God and Christ, and abhors to think of sin in all its forms, shall think of God and Christ in eternity—where all such thought is music, and peace, and rest.

The destination of every man in another world may be inferred and known from the general tenor of his thoughts in this. He who does not love to think upon a particular class of subjects here will not love to think upon them there. The mere passage from time to eternity can no more alter a man's likes or dislikes in this respect than the passage of the Atlantic can alter them. And that rational spirit, be it human, angelic, or arch-angelic, which in eternity cannot take positive delight in contemplating God, but recoils from all such contemplation, is miserable and lost, though it tread the golden streets and hear the rippling murmurs of the river of the water of life. But if our meditation upon God is sweet here, it will be sweeter in eternity. And then our blessedness will be certain and secure ; for no spirit, human, angelic, or arch-angelic, can by any possibility be made unblest in any part of God's vast dominions, if it really finds joy in the contemplation of the ever-present God.

SERMON II.

CHRISTIAN MODERATION.

PROVERBS xvi. 32.—"He that is slow to anger is better than the mighty; and he that ruleth his spirit than he that taketh a city."

THE book of Proverbs is the best of all manuals for the formation of a well-balanced mind. The object of Solomon in composing it seems to have been to furnish to the church a summary of rules and maxims by which the Christian character, having been originated by regeneration, should then be educated and made symmetrical. We do not, therefore, go to this portion of Scripture so much for full and definite statements of the distinguishing doctrines of revealed religion, as for those wise and prudential canons whereby we may reform extravagance, prune down luxuriance, and combine the whole variety of traits and qualities into a harmonious and beautiful unity. We do not find in this part of the Bible careful and minute specifications of the doctrine of the trinity, of the apostasy of mankind, of the incarnation of the Son of God, of vicarious atonement, regeneration and justification. They are hinted at, it is true—as when the Eternal Wisdom is spoken of as being with the Lord " in the beginning of his way, before his works of old; as one brought up with him, daily his delight, and rejoicing always before him." (Prov. viii. 22, 30.) Here we have the same doctrine, germinally, with that of the Apostle John, when he affirms that the Eternal Word, or Reason, " in the beginning was with God, and was God." And what are such assertions, as that " there is not a just man upon earth that doeth good and sinneth not " (Eccl. vii. 20), and such questions as, " Who can say, I have made my heart clean, I am pure from my sin " ? (Prov. xx. 9), but an indirect statement of the doctrine of human depravity ? Still it is not the main purpose of Solomon, in those two books of the inspired canon which go under the name of Proverbs and Ecclesiastes, to particularly enunciate the evangelical system ; but rather to set forth those principles of ethics, and religious prudence, which must always follow in the train of evangelical religion. It is reserved for other portions of the Bible—for the Gospels and the Epistles—to make the fundamental statements, and lay the foundations of Christian character ; while it remains for the wise Preacher to follow up with those teachings which serve to develop and beautify it. The book of revelation is, in this way, like the book of nature. The scientific naturalist does not claim that everything in nature is upon a dead level in respect to intrinsic worth and importance—that a bit of charcoal is just as valuable as a bit of diamond ; that a lily is just as high up the scale of creation as a man. But he does claim that one is as much the work of creative power as the other, and in its own sphere and place is as indispensable to the great sum total of creation as is the other. And so, too, the scientific theologian does not claim that everything in the Bible is upon a dead level in respect to intrinsic value—that the book of Esther is as important for purposes of regeneration and conversion as is the Epistle to the Romans—but he does claim that both alike are the product of Divine inspiration ; that both alike are a portion of that Word of God, that sum-total of revealed truth upon which, as a whole, the kingdom of God in the earth is to be founded and built up. Had the book of Esther been lost out of the canon, it would not have been so great a detriment to the church as the loss of the Gospel of John, or of the Epistle to the Romans. If the missionary were allowed to carry only a single fragment of Scripture into a heathen population, and were compelled to make his choice between the book of Proverbs or the Gospel of St. Matthew, he would undoubtedly select the latter. Not, however, because one is less trustworthy than the other; but because one contains more of the doctrinal material which the missionary employs in laying the foundation of the church; because it gives more information concerning the Lord Jesus Christ and the way of salvation than does the other. The book of Proverbs, as we have remarked, was composed not so much for the purpose of originating a holy character, as of shaping and polishing it; and for this purpose it is indispensable, and for this purpose it was inspired. And hence in missionary fields, as well as in the church at large, the wise maxims and well-grounded ethics of Solomon will always follow up the evangelical truths and doctrines of the Apostle John, and the Apostle Paul.

" He that is slow to anger is better than the mighty; and he that ruleth his spirit than he that taketh a city." In this concise sententious "proverb," the wise man describes and recommends a certain kind of temper which should be possessed and cherished by the people of God. We purpose, in the first place, briefly to describe this temper; in the second place, to mention some of the obstacles that oppose its formation; and in the third place, to point out the true source and root of it.

The temper that is recommended in the text, to say it in a word, is *Christian moderation.* St. Paul urges the same thing with Solomon, when he writes to the

Philippians: "Let your moderation be known unto all men;" when he writes to the Thessalonians: "Let us watch and be sober;" and when he writes to Titus, that "the grace of God which bringeth salvation hath appeared to all men, teaching us that denying ungodliness and worldly lusts, we should live soberly, righteously, and godly in this present world."

I. In defining, in the first place, the *nature* of this temper and disposition, it is evident that a man who is "slow to anger," and who "ruleth his spirit," is characterized by sobriety and equanimity. He is never driven to extremes, in any direction. For anger is one of the most vehement of emotions, and he who can control it can control anything, can "take a city." Hence this particular passion is selected as the specimen. He who reins in his own impulsive wrath with such a strong and firm rein that it never gets the mastery over him, will find it no difficult task to rule and regulate the whole brood of passions which have their nest in corrupt human nature. Such a man is even-tempered, in the deepest sense. Such a man stands in just and proper relations to both worlds. He lives with contentment here upon earth, and at the same time lays up treasure in heaven. He does not drown himself in worldly lusts, like a voluptuary, and neither does he kill out all human sympathies, like an ascetic. He uses this world as not abusing it in either direction. He does not abuse the good things of this life, by an immoderate indulgence in them, or an immoderate desire and toil after them; and he does not abuse the legitimate enjoyments of this existence, by a fanatical contempt and rejection of them altogether. He is not so absorbed in the things of time and sense, as to lose sight of eternal realities; neither is he so monkishly indifferent to the interests and objects of this life, as to be either a drone or a malcontent. He responds to all the reasonable and proper demands of domestic, social, and civil existence, while yet he never becomes so extreme in his attachment, and so enslaved to them, that it costs him murmurings and bitter pangs to be called away from these circles into the immediate presence of God.

This is indeed a wonderful temper to be attained by so ill-governed, so passionate, impulsive, and unbalanced a creature as man. It is no wonder that such a well-poised and symmetrical character as this floated as an unattainable ideal before the minds of the better pagan philosophers. This is the famous "temperance" which meets the scholar so continually in the writings of Plato and Aristotle—that golden mean between the extremes of passion and apathy which the philosopher strives to reach. "Quietly reflecting"—says Plato—"on the madness and ungovernable passions of the multitude, and attending to his own affairs, like a man sheltered under a wall in a storm of dust and foam borne along on the wind, by which he sees all about him overwhelmed in disorder, such an one is content to pass his life free from violence and passion, and to effect his exit hence with good hopes, cheerful and serene."[1] This is his description of the moderation, the equanimity, the temperance of the philosophic mind. But in other places this thoughtful pagan confesses that this golden mean is never reached here upon earth, either by the philosopher or the common man. He compares the soul to a pair of horses—one of them erect, finely formed, with high neck, aquiline nose, white-colored, black-eyed, a lover of honor and temperance and true glory, driven without the whip, by word of command and voice only; the other crooked, thick set, clumsily put together, with

---

[1] Republic, VI., 495.

strong neck, short throat, flat face, black color, gray-eyed, addicted to insolence and swaggering, scarcely obedient to whip and spur together.¹ These two opposing creatures, according to him, represent the present condition of the human soul. There are aspirations that would lead it upward, but there are appetites that drag it downward. The white horse would pursue the path of honor and excellence; but the black horse draws away from the path, and plunges madly downward. And the black horse is the strongest. The appetite is too mighty for the resolution. There is an infinite aspiration, and an infinitesimal performance. Such is the mournful confession of the greatest thinker outside of the pale of revelation ; and if a Plato could dis-cover and teach to future generations the corruption and helplessness of human nature, what shall we say of those teachers under the full light of revelation, who would have us believe that there is no corruption in man but such as can be eradicated by man himself, and who would dispense with the evangelical means and methods of heal-ing and salvation.

II. And this brings us to consider, in the second place, some of the *obstacles* that oppose the formation of such a Christian sobriety and moderation. They spring from two general sources—the sense, and the mind. They are partly physical, and partly intellectual obstacles.

1. In the first place, this Christian sobriety and modera-tion is opposed by the appetites and passions of the *body*. St. Paul, speaking of man before regeneration, says, " When we were in the flesh, the motions [passions] of sins which were by the law did work in our members, to bring forth fruit unto death." It is one of the effects of apostasy, that human nature is corrupted upon the physical side of it, as

---

¹ Phædrus, XXV., 3.

well as upon the mental and moral side. "Original sin," as the Westminster creed affirms, "is the corruption of the *whole* nature." The bodily appetites are very different now from what they would have been, had man remained in his original and holy condition. When Adam came from the hand of the Creator, his physical nature was pure and perfect. All of his appetites and sensibilities were in just proportion, and were exactly balanced and harmonized. The original and holy Adam was no glutton, and no voluptuary. Every appetite of the body was even-tempered, never reaching beyond the just limits, and going as far, and only as far, as the healthy and happy condition of the organism required. Probably the brute creation approaches nearer to the original Adam, in this particular of a sound physical organization, than do his degenerate posterity. How comparatively moderate all the physical appetites are, in the low sphere of the dumb animals.[1] The ox and the horse, for example, having satisfied the healthy and natural cravings of hunger, demand nothing further. They never gorge themselves to a surfeit, and they seek no stimulants. The range of their appetite is narrow. A few grasses, with the pure flowing water to drink, meet all their wants. But man's physical appetites are multitudinous, and, what is yet worse, they are exorbitant. They are continually reaching out beyond the proper limits, and beyond what the organism requires, and bring his higher intellectual and moral nature into subjection to themselves. The history of human civilization is to a great extent the history of human luxury; and the history of human luxury is the history of bodily appetites growing more and more inordinate, and growing by what they feed upon. The very civilization of which we hear so much, and

---

[1] Compare Plutarch: On Natural Affection toward one's Offspring.

which is so often represented as the unmixed glory of the human race, the evidence and record of its advance toward perfection, is in one of its aspects the record of its shame, and the evidence of its apostasy. For it brings to view the corruption of human nature upon the physical side. It reveals acquired and unnatural appetites, fed and satiated by ingenious supplies. The whole industry and energy of entire classes of laborers and artisans is employed in ministering to extreme cravings, and unhealthy wants, that could have no existence if human nature were possessed of that physical sobriety and moderation which the Bible enjoins, or even of that temperance which the Greek philosopher praised and recommended.

That which is true of man generally, is true of the individual. There are great obstacles to that well-regulated temper which Solomon recommends in the text, arising from flesh and sense. There is no need of entering into any detail, for every man's own consciousness will testify that every day, and every hour, "the body of this death," this "vile body," as St. Paul denominates it, stands in opposition to that calm and equable frame of soul which is "slow to anger." The corruption of nature is constantly showing itself in a rush to an extreme. The natural appetites, which were implanted in order to preserve the body from weakness and decay, and which in their original and pure condition were aids to virtue and holy living— these very appetences, now extreme and disordered, are strong temptations to sin, and the very worst obstacles to holiness. "How is the gold become dim! How is the most fine gold changed!" All that part of our being which connects us with this glorious outer world, and which was originally intended to subserve our spiritual interests, and to assist in preparing us for a final blessed destination, has by apostasy become subservient to our destruction.

The physical appetites which in their pure state, as seen in holy Adam and in the sinless humanity of our Blessed Lord, contributed directly to a well-regulated and well-governed frame of the soul, now tend directly to throw it off its equilibrium, and to fill it with restlessness and dissatisfaction—to make it a troubled sea whose waters cast up mire and dirt.

2. But again, in the second place, this Christian sobriety and moderation meets with an obstacle in man's disordered *mental* nature. The prophet Isaiah, in describing human sinfulness, remarks that the "whole head is sick." The apostasy of Adam has affected the nobler and higher part of man, as well as his lower and meaner part. The disorder that now prevails in his intellectual and moral nature opposes his most earnest endeavors to be "slow to anger," and to "rule his spirit." Consider, for instance, how lawless and ungoverned is the human imagination. This is a faculty of a high order, and by it man is capable of "thoughts that wander through eternity." But as it now exists in fallen man, it is the source of the most wayward and perverse mental action. It fills the soul with extravagant conceits, greedy desires, unreal joys, and unreal sorrows. The believer is commanded by the Apostle Paul, to "cast down imaginations, and every high thing that exalts itself against the knowledge of God, and to bring every thought into captivity to the obedience of Christ." But he finds it one of his most difficult tasks, because the disorder and the lawlessness are so very far within him. It is in some respects easier to control the physical appetites than to rule an inflamed and extravagant fancy. That youth, for example, who has stimulated his imagination by the immoderate and long-continued reading of fiction, has a harder task before him, in some particulars, than the drunkard or the debauchee. He has

introduced extravagance and lawlessness into a faculty which in its best condition is liable to waywardness, and he discovers, when he attempts to undo his own work, that he has a life-long labor before him. How many there are, in this age of voracious and indiscriminate novel-reading, who will tell us that they have ruined their intellects by their folly; that they have lost the power of sober, concatenated thinking; that they are carried along passively by the currents of fanciful imaginings that surge and dash within them; that they have no rule of their own minds, and whenever the temptation presents they are swift to wrath, and every other impulsive passion.

Again, the human understanding itself—that comparatively cool and unimpassioned part of the human soul—opposes obstacles to Christian sobriety and moderation. A man's purely intellectual conclusions and convictions may be so one-sided and extreme as to spoil his temper. Fanaticism in every age furnishes examples of this. The fanatic is generally an intellectual person. He is vehement and extreme, not for the sake of a vice or a pleasure, but for the sake of an opinion or a doctrine. His ungoverned temper does not commonly spring out of sensual appetites and indulgences. On the contrary, his blood is usually cold and thin, and his life abstemious and ascetical. But his passion runs to his brain. He holds an intellectual opinion or an intellectual conviction that is but a half-truth, with a spasmodic energy; and the consequence is, that he is swift to anger, and reckless of consequences in that direction. No large and comprehensive vision, and no moderate and well-balanced temper, is possible when passion has in this manner worked its way into the understanding. Every age of the world affords examples of this kind. How many individual Christians, and how many individual churches, have lost their Christian sobriety and their charitable moderation, because they have "leaned to their own understanding," and as a consequence their understanding acquired a leaning and lost its equipoise.

From these sources, then, we find obstacles issuing that oppose the formation of that temper which the Apostle Paul has in view when he says: "Let your moderation be known to all men," and which Solomon recommends when he says: "He that is slow to anger is better than the mighty, and he that ruleth his spirit than he that taketh a city." Our corrupt physical nature, and our disordered mental constitution, are continually drawing us aside from that true golden mean between all extremes which should ever be before the eye of a Christian, and which he must attain in order to enter the world where everything is symmetrical and harmonious, like the character of God himself.

III. We are, therefore, led to inquire, in the third place, for the true *source* of this Christian temperance and moderation. Such a spirit as we have been speaking of must have its root in *love*. The secret of such an even temper is charity; the "charity that suffereth long and is kind, that vaunteth not itself, is not puffed up, seeketh not her own, thinketh no evil." No man can have this large-minded, comprehensive, and unshaken equilibrium, who does not love God supremely and his neighbor as himself. We have already noticed that the wise pagan thinkers had an idea of some such well-balanced temper and spirit. They were painfully conscious of the passionateness of the human soul, and its inclination to rush into extremes—extremes of physical license, and extremes of intellectual license. But they knew no method of curing the evil, and they never cured it. And there was a good reason. They could not generate holy love in their own hearts, or in the hearts of others. The human heart is carnal, and thereby at enmity with God; it is selfish, and thereby at enmity with man. So long as this is the character of man, it is impossible for him to be "slow to anger" and to "rule his spirit." The physical appetite will be constantly breaking over its proper limits, the imagination will be lawless, and the understanding proud and opinionated. But the instant the enmity ceases and the charity begins, the selfish passionateness and license disappear. You cannot rule your impulsive spirit, you cannot curb and control your lawless appetites, by a mere volition. You cannot bring all your mental and physical powers into equilibrium by a dead lift. The means is not adequate to the end. Nothing but the power of a new affection; nothing but the love of God shed abroad in your heart, and the love of Christ sweetly swaying and constraining you, can permanently and perfectly reduce all the restlessness and recklessness of your nature to order and harmony. And this can do it. There is something strangely powerful and transforming in love. It is not limited in its influence to any one part of the soul, but it penetrates and pervades the whole of it, as quicksilver penetrates the pores of gold. A conception is confined to the understanding; a volition stops with the will; but an affection like heavenly charity diffuses itself through the entire man. Head and heart, reason, will, and imagination, are all modified by it. The revolutionizing effect of this feeling within the sphere of human relations is well understood. When the romantic passion is awakened, it expels for the time being all others, and this period of human life takes its entire tone and color from the affection. Even the clown becomes gentle and chivalrous under its influence.[1] But this is vastly more true of the spiritual and heavenly love. When this springs up in the soul, all the thoughts, all the purposes, all

---

[1] See Dryden's Cymon and Iphigenia.

the passions, and all the faculties of the soul are changed by it. And particularly is its influence seen in rectifying the disorder and lawlessness of the soul. Heavenly charity cannot be resisted. Pride melts away under its warm breath; selfishness disappears under its glowing influence; anger cannot stand before its gentle force. Whatever be the form of sin that offers resistance, it inevitably yields before "love unfeigned; love out of a pure heart." "Charity never faileth," says the Apostle Paul. "Love conquers all things," says the pagan Ovid.

Our subject, then, teaches the necessity of the *new birth*. It corroborates our Lord's declaration: "Except a man be born again, he cannot see the kingdom of God." For, how is this heavenly affection, which is to subdue and quell all the passion and wrath of human nature, to be generated? It is "not born of blood, or of the will of the flesh, or of the will of man, but of God." There may be outward self-control, without any inward self-government. It is not enough that we do not exhibit our anger and our passion. It must be eradicated. It is not enough that we rein in a restive spirit. The very spirit itself must become mild and gentle. It is a weary, and in the end a profitless, effort which that man puts forth, who attempts to obey such an injunction as that of Solomon in the text, without laying his foundation deep in a renovated nature. In the opening of the discourse, we alluded to the fact that the ethics of Solomon must follow after the evangelical doctrines of the Gospels and the Epistles. In like manner, the cultivation of a symmetrical and beautiful moderation of both the bodily appetites and the mental passions, in order to be successful, must be preceded by a change of heart. Otherwise there is nothing but the austere and ungenial attempt of a moralist to perform a repulsive task. Love—holy and heavenly charity—must be generated, and then under its spontaneous and happy impulse it will be comparatively easy to rectify the remaining corruption, and repress the lingering excesses and extremes of appetite and passion. When the Apostle John had become so far advanced in years, that he could no longer exhibit the fire and force of that earlier period when he was one of the sons of thunder, he caused himself to be carried into the assemblies of the Christians, and in weak and faltering accents said: "Children, love one another; children, love one another." This tradition of the Early Church accords well with the tone and teachings of those three Epistles which were among the last utterances of the last of the apostles. Heavenly charity, after a life prolonged nearly one hundred years, had become the dominant affection of the soul. And how almost impossible it would have been to have ruffled that heavenly temper! How easy it was for him to rule his spirit! How slow to anger must he have become! In the days of his early discipleship, St. John was swift to wrath, and upon one occasion sought to persuade the serene and compassionate Redeemer to command the lightnings to come down from the sky, and consume the Samaritan village that would not receive him. But in the last days of his apostleship and his pilgrimage, he had breathed in the kind and compassionate spirit of his Master, and his utterance was a very different one.

That which St. John needed is needed by human nature always and everywhere. We are not better than he. There are in every man the same inordinate passions, and the same need of a radical transformation. He became a changed creature, the lion was converted into the lamb, through faith in Jesus Christ—by an act of trust and confidence in the Divine Redeemer. His own words are: "Whosoever believeth that Jesus is the Christ—is *born of*

God: and whatsoever is born of God overcometh the world, and this is the victory that overcometh the world, even our faith. We know that whosoever is born of God sinneth not; but he that is begotten of God keepeth himself, and that wicked one toucheth him not. And we know that the Son of God is come, and hath given us an understanding, that we may know him that is true; and we are in him that is true, even in his son Jesus Christ. This is the true God and eternal life." Here is positive affirmation and asseveration. "We *know*." It is the utterance of a personal experience, and an infallible inspiration.

Confide then in the Son of God. Put your eternal destiny into His hands. Do not look down into the dark deep well of your own helplessness and guilt for pardon and purification, but look up for these into the infinitude and grace of Him "in whom dwells all the fulness of the God head bodily." That look is faith; and faith is salvation.

SERMON III.

THE SUPREME EXCELLENCE OF GOD.

MATTHEW xix. 16, 17.—"And behold, one came, and said unto him, Good Master, what good thing shall I do, that I may have eternal life ? And he said unto him, Why callest thou me good ? there is none good but one, that is God."

THE eternal Son of God knew perfectly what was in every man who came unto him in the days of his flesh. With far more accuracy and certainty than man can read the character in the expression of the eye, or in the features of the face, did the omniscient Redeemer read the character of the very soul itself, in its inward expression and lineaments. Hence his answers to questions always had reference to the disposition and temper of the questioner. "Our Saviour Christ," says Lord Bacon, "not being like man, who knows man's thoughts by his words, but knowing men's thoughts immediately, he never answered their words, but their thoughts." Thus, when the chief priests and elders of the people came unto him as he was teaching, and asked by what authority he did so, and who gave him the authority, knowing that this question was not put from any sincere desire to learn the truth respecting himself and his works, but from a wish to work him evil, he answered their question by asking them a question regarding the baptism of John—a question which, however they answered it, would condemn their past treatment of John, and their present refusal to acknowledge himself to be the Messiah of whom John was the forerunner. Again, when one asked the question, "Are there few to be saved?" our Lord, knowing that an idle curiosity had prompted it, answered by saying, "Strive to enter in at the strait gate; for many, I say unto you, will seek to enter in, and shall not be able." So, also, in the answer of the Saviour to the young man who had come asking, "What good thing shall I do that I may have eternal life?" reference is had to the state of the young man's opinions. Our Lord knew that this youth did not look upon the person whom he was addressing as God manifest in the flesh, but as a wise human teacher in the things of the law; and that he applied to him not as the Truth itself, and the Life itself, but only as knowing, perhaps, some portion of infinite truth, and as being able, perhaps, to point out the way to eternal life. Hence our Lord begins his reply by inquiring, "Why callest thou me *good?*" Instead of first correcting the young man's erroneous view of the nature and character of the person to whom he was speaking, he proceeds as if it were a true one. "You consider me to be a mere man; why do you call any mere man good? Why do you address a creature as the Holy One? There is none good but one, that is God."

By this reply the Saviour intended to bring into the light the main error of the young man—the opinion, namely, that any man is good in and of himself. He desired to awaken in him a sense of sin, so that the self-righteous youth might be delivered from his pride and self-satisfaction, and be led to look away from himself and his own works to God, the source and ground of all goodness; and more particularly to that Mediator between God and man who then and there stood before him.

This text, then, invites us to contemplate the *pre-emi-*

nence of the Divine excellence over that of creatures, and
to draw some inferences from the fact. What, then, are
the senses in which "there is none good but one, that is
God ?"

I. In the first place, God is the only *necessarily* good
Being. We naturally shrink from applying the conception
of necessity to a free spirit; but it is because we associate
with it the notion of external compulsion. God is not
forced to be holy by an agency outside of himself, and
other than his own; and it is not in this sense that he is
necessarily good.

But there is a necessity that has its foundation in the
nature and idea of a thing, as when we say that a triangle
necessarily has three sides. We say that God is necessarily
existent, not because he is forced to exist by something out
of himself, but because the idea of an infinite and absolutely perfect Being implies necessity of being. A being
who once did not exist, and who may become extinct, is a
finite and imperfect being, and consequently not God. In
like manner God is necessarily holy, because the conception of infinite excellence excludes the possibility of apostasy and sin which attaches to finite virtue. Infinite holiness is immutable, and therefore infinite sinfulness is
impossible. God's will is one with his reason in such a
mode that the supposition of a schism and conflict between
the two contradicts the idea of God. In the case of a finite
creature, we can conceive of a conflict between the constitutional and the executive faculties without any altera-
tion in the grade of existence; but if the infinite Creator
fall into collision with himself, he is no longer infinite.
Man's will may come into hostility to his conscience, and
he still remain human. Angels may fall, and still be
angels. Both continue in the same relative grade of existence as before the change—that of a finite and mutable

creature. But if a schism and conflict should be introduced into the Godhead, and he should fall into collision
with himself, he would by that single fact prove himself
to belong to a changeable and finite grade of being. It
could not be said of him : " Thou art the same from everlasting to everlasting. With thee there is no variableness,
neither shadow of turning." At such a catastrophe, hell
from beneath would be moved with a more profound
amazement than that which greeted the fallen Lucifer,
and with a more awful surprise than heart can conceive of
there would burst from all the ranks of limited and mutable intelligences the utterance : "Art thou, the Eternal,
become like one of us?" The unique and transcendent
perfection, then, of an infinite Being precludes the possibility of his becoming finite in any respect—and to become
evil is to become finite ; nay, more, is to become weak, and
miserable, and guilty.

But not only does the idea of the Deity imply his necessary excellence, it is implied also in his position and relationships. From the very nature of these, the divine will
cannot be divorced from the divine reason and come into
hostility to it. " God cannot be tempted," says St. James,
and there cannot be sin without temptation. There is
nothing greater and better than the Infinite that can be an
inducement to apostasy. When man apostatized, there was
something above him which he was reaching out after.
He desired to become " as gods." He expected to attain
a higher position. But God is already God—infinite, self-
sufficing, and blessedly self-satisfied. There is nothing
higher than himself to reach after. No motive to sin can
assail the Supreme, and therefore sin is impossible to him.
In order to be tempted, God was compelled to become incarnate, and assume a finite, temptable nature.

Will and reason, then, in God are one and inseparable,

and he is necessarily good in the same sense that he is necessarily existent. There is no compulsion from without, but the necessity is implied in the idea of the Being. God's pure and perfect nature is the law and principle of God's pure and perfect character. Should the two become contrary and hostile, the Infinite would become finite, the Creator would become a creature. There is none good, then, but God, in the sense that if he becomes evil he loses his grade of being. The divine excellence, therefore, is as necessary and immutable as the divine existence. Does God cease to be holy, he ceases to be deity.

II. In the second place, God is the only *originally* good Being. All rational creatures, if they are good, derive their goodness. They are not good in and of themselves as the ultimate source. They look up to a yet better Being, and confess that they are only reflections of a splendor and glory that is above them. Hence the finite mind *adores ;* but the infinite mind never does or can. Hence the angel lifts up his eye in the beatific vision, that his soul may rest upon a deeper and firmer virtue than his own. Hence the man prays and supplicates for an excellence that is not aboriginal and necessarily connected with his own being. But God *is* goodness, not merely has it. God *is* love, not merely has it. God *is* light, not merely has it. Will and reason are identical in him. He is not excellent because his nature derives excellence from another's nature, but because it is infinite excellence itself. Righteousness is not so much a particular attribute of God as it is his essential quality ; the supporter of his attributes, that which is the substrate of them all, that which penetrates them and makes them fair, lovely, and perfect. As the earth is at once the bearer and nourisher of all trees and fruits, and by its genial influence and nurture makes them pleasant to the eye and good for food, so righteous-

ness is the underlying ground of all the attributes of God.
Righteousness imparts to the divine justice its serène and
awful beauty. Righteousness regulates the divine mercy,
and prevents it from becoming mere indulgence. Righteousness enters into all the natural attributes of Jehovah, and renders his omnipotence, and omnipresence—his
otherwise soulless and characterless traits—worthy of love
and reverence. The Platonists speak of an original light
that is the source of all the light of the sun and stars—a
light that is pureness itself, and gives to the sun its dazzle
and to the stars their sparkle. So righteousness is the
aboriginal rectitude from which all the qualities of
Jehovah derive their worth and perfection, and of which
all finite virtue is the faint reflection.

III. In the third place, God is the only *self-subsistently*
good Being. His excellence does not depend upon the will
and power of any other than himself. All created spirits,
as we have already hinted, must look to God for the existence and perpetuity of righteousness within themselves;
but God looks only to himself that he may be righteous.
As he is self-subsistent in his being, so he is in his char-
actèr. The divine will needs no strengthening in order to
its continuing holy, because it is already an infinite force.
Its energy is omnipotent, and we have seen that it is so
blended and one with the divine reason that a separation
and antagonism is conceivable only upon the supposition
that God ceases to be infinite. The goings forth of the
divine will are without variableness or shadow of turning.
From eternity to eternity the decisions and determinations
of God are but the efflux of the divine essence, and participate in the immanent and necessary characteristics of the
divine constitution. The triune God, therefore, is independently good. Though the finite creation should all aposta-
tize and become evil, yet God remains the same Holy One

for ever. Man is affected by the fall of man; angels are seduced from their allegiance by angels; God alone is unmoved and unaffected by all the change and apostasy of creation. In the calm air of his own eternity he exists unchangeably holy, because of a self-sufficient and self-sustaining power; while angels and men fall away from holiness and from him, and introduce sin and death into the universe.

IV. And this leads naturally to the fourth position, that God is the only *immutably* good Being. This is a glorious truth for every created mind that is good, and desires to remain so. The Supreme Being is unchangeably excellent. The infinitude of his nature places him beyond all the possibilities, contingencies, and hazards of finite existence. All the created universe may fall from goodness, but God is no part of the universe. He created all the worlds from nothing, and whatever they may be or do does not in the least affect his nature and attributes. God is the Being from whom other beings fall away into sin and misery. As the essence of God would not be affected in the least if the entire substance of the universe should be annihilated, or if it had never been made from nothing, so the moral excellence of God would not be diminished in the slightest manner though all the creatures of his power should plunge into the abyss of evil. Amidst the sin of a world, and in opposition to the kingdom and prince of evil, God remains immutably holy, and by the intrinsic and eternal immaculateness of his character is entitled to deal out an eternal judgment, and a righteous retribution, upon every soul that doeth evil. Though he sees in his universe much iniquity, yet he is of purer eyes than to look upon it with any indulgence. Though sin has been the product of the will of man for six thousand years, yet his moral anger burns with the same steady and dreadful intensity against it now, as when Adam heard the voice of the Lord God walking in the garden in the cool of the day, and was afraid, and hid himself. The same spiritual excellence in God which caused the flood to destroy the old wicked world, and which rained fire and brimstone upon filthy Sodom and Gomorrah, causes him to be displeased with the wicked this day, and every day.

Now, there is something indescribably cheering and strengthening in this truth and fact. As we look abroad over the world and see how full of sin it is; as we reflect upon the limited and feeble nature of all finite spirits, though they be in the highest range of the heavenly hierarchies; as we consider the liability of everything within the sphere of creation to undergo changes and fluctuations; it imparts a serene joy and a calm strength to the soul to lift up the eye to the eternal hills, and to remember that above all this sphere of finiteness and limitation and sin there dwells One Being who is the same from everlasting to everlasting, and who is not under any possibilities or liabilities of change either in his existence or his character. For the very thought that God might possibly become like his creatures; that he of whom his own word asserts "it is impossible that he should lie," should yet be false to his own nature and to his word; that he, to whom the seraphim in their trisagion, their thrice-repeated and intensely emphasized "holy," ascribe an inherent and necessary perfection, should yet become vile like the worms of his footstool—the thought, we say, that the Supreme Being, the first cause and last end of all other beings and things, might possibly become unholy and unworthy, sends a shrinking and a shudder through the human soul. All sense of safety and security disappears, and the mind feels that there is no difference between finite and Infinite ; between the creature and the Creator. Both alike are liable

to the contingency of apostasy. Both alike may grovel in
the dust. Nay, rather, let us fall back upon the immutability and intrinsic unchangeableness of the Divine character, and with an upward-looking eye say with one of the
loftiest and lowliest of human spirits : "Lord, I have
viewed the universe over in which thou hast set me; I
have tried how this thing and that thing will fit my spirit,
and the design of my creation; and can find nothing in
which to rest, for nothing here doth itself rest; but such
things as please for awhile, in some degree, vanish and flee
as shadows before me. Lo, I come to thee, the Eternal
Being, the Spring of Life, the Centre of Rest, the Stay of
the Creation ; I join myself to thee ; with thee I will lead
my life and spend my days, with whom I aim to dwell
forever, expecting, when my little, finite, fluctuating time
is over, to be taken up ere long into thy Eternity." [1]
    Thus is it true, that "there is none good but one, that
is God." There is but one Being in whom righteousness
and holiness are necessary, aboriginal, self-subsistent, and
immutable.
    But who of us worthily apprehends this great truth ?
Who of us sees with the crystal clearness of a seraph's
vision that God's excellence is transcendent; that, compared with his immaculateness, angelic purity is not pure,
and the stainless heavens are not clean ? Did we with
open vision behold the infinite excellence of the Creator,
we should be awed like the prophet Isaiah when the pillars
of the temple moved at the voice of the wing-veiled
seraphim, and the house was filled with smoke. And if
our minds were pure, we should pass by all the holiness
and excellence of the creature, and gaze steadfastly upon
the increate and underived excellence of Jehovah, and by

---

[1] Howe : Vanity of Man as Mortal.

thus gazing we should be changed into the same image from glory to glory in an endless succession. But we languish, we perish, from lack of vision.

That we may be moved to seek the vision granted to the pure in heart, let us now attend to some of the conclusions flowing from the truth that " there is none good but one, that is God."

1. In the first place, then, if God alone is supremely good, he alone is to be *glorified* and *adored*. Goodness is intrinsically worthy to be magnified and extolled. Righteousness is fitted to awaken ascriptions of blessing, and honor, and thanksgiving, and glory, and dominion, and power. This accounts for the hallelujahs of heaven. There is a quality in the increate and transcending excellence of the most high God that dilates the holy mind, and renders it enthusiastic. Hence the saints on high are made vocal and lyrical by the vision of God's moral perfection, and they give vent to their emotions in " the sevenfold chorus of hallelujahs and harping symphonies." There is much of this in the experience of the Psalmist. He beholds the divine excellence, and glories in it. It is a species of humble and holy boasting of the greatness and glory of Jehovah. " My soul shall make her boast in the Lord ; O magnify the Lord with me, and let us exalt his name together. In God we boast all the day long, and praise thy name forever." There is that in the divine character which, while it abases the creature in reference to his own personal character and merits, exalts and sublimes him in reference to the excellence of his Maker. This is that unearthly vision which visits the soul of the dying, and makes his voice ring like a clarion in his proclamation and heralding of what God is. " Praise him" —said the dying Evarts, one of the coolest, and calmest, and most judicial of minds, in his ordinary mood, and in

reference to all finite things—"praise him in a way you know not of."

This inward glorying in the attributes of God is the great duty and ultimate end of man. Man's chief end is to glorify God. Obedience itself, or the performance of an outward service, is second in rank to this inward service of worship, when the soul is absorbed and lost in admiration of the divine perfections. All that the creature can do for God is little or nothing ; and the Almighty certainly does not need the labor and toil of any of his creatures. But the service is a greater one when the soul acknowledges what God is and does. In this instance, the human agency acquires an added dignity and value from the side of Divinity ; even as sin becomes an infinite evil because of its reference to God. The recognition of the divine excellence, and the inward adoration that accompanies it, is the last accomplishment of the Christian life ; and it is this which crowns, and completes, and thereby ends, the Christian race and the Christian fight.

Such a feeling as this cannot properly go out toward any being but the Supremely Good. The secondary recipients from the primary source can never be the objects of glory and exaltation. Saint-worship is irrational. For there is none supremely good but one, and none but the Supreme deserves the exaltation. As there is but one life in nature, and the individual tree or plant is alive because it partakes of it, so there is but one Eternal Excellence, and individual spirits are excellent because they participate in it. God alone, therefore, is worthy to receive all the glory, and all the extolling, and all the magnifying that belongs to excellence. To unfold the illustration—when the naturalist looks upon the tree or the plant, he does not ascribe the beauty of its form and foliage, and the richness of its fruit, to that single isolated individual specimen, but to the great general life in nature which produced it; to that vast vegetative power which God has impressed upon nature. In like manner when we see moral excellence in the creature, we do not ascribe the glory and praise to the individual, but to that Spirit of Good, the Holy Spirit, who produced it in him. Neither men nor angels are worthy to be magnified and extolled, because their virtue is not aboriginal. The really good man or angel refers his character to God, and is filled with abhorrence at the thought of glorifying himself, or of being glorified for it. And there is no sin that so grieves him as his propensity to a detestable self-idolatry. When Paul and Barnabas, after healing the cripple, heard that the priest of Jupiter had brought oxen and garlands unto the gates, and was about to offer sacrifice with the people unto them as unto gods come down in the likeness of men, they rent their clothes and ran in among the people, crying out, and saying, "Sirs, why do ye these things? We also are men of like passions with you." In like manner does every finite spirit that really partakes of the Divine excellence recoil at the thought of ascriptions of praise unto himself, and says unto those who would forget the Creator in the excellence of the creature, "Why marvel ye at me? or why look ye so earnestly on me, as though by my own ultimate power or holiness I am holy?" Whatever, then, we may think of man, and however we may regard him, to God alone belong glory, and honor, and thanksgiving, and blessing, and dominion, and power.

2. Secondly, if God alone is supremely good, it is *sin*, and the very essence of sin, not to glorify him.

The ultimate form of moral evil consists in worshipping the creature, and not exalting and adoring the Creator. We can often reduce one form of transgression into another. Theft is a species of selfishness—an attempt to gratify personal desires at the expense of another's interest. Ambition is a kind of rebellion—an endeavor to overleap the limits which have been prescribed to the individual by his Maker. And so it is easy to generalize almost every transgression, and find its root in a wider and deeper principle of evil. But what generalization is wider and deeper than the indisposition to worship and magnify God in the heart? Hence the apostle Paul, after particularizing the sins of the heathen, gathers and concentrates the substance of all their sin and guilt in the one fact, "that when they knew God, they glorified him not as God"; that "they worshipped the creature more than the Creator." And in another place, when he would exhibit the universal and generic quality in the sin of man, he strengthens his affirmation that "all have sinned," by the additional clause, "and come short of the glory of God." This is an indictment to which every man must plead guilty, and which stops the mouth of him who is "willing to justify himself." For who has worshipped and served the eternal God, in his body and spirit which are His, as that Being is worthy to be worshipped? Who of the sons of men has not come short in this respect? One of the Greek words for sin signifies to fail of hitting the mark by reason of the arrow's not coming up to the target. If this be the idea and visual image of sin, who of us is not a sinner?

There are some advantages, and there are also some disadvantages, in looking upon sin as consisting in disobeying particular commandments; in not keeping this or that separate precept; in swearing, or lying, or stealing. We must begin with this, but we must not end with it. If we stop at this point, we run the hazard of becoming self-righteous. We are in danger of presuming that because we do not lie, or swear, or steal, we are morally perfect.

In the beginning of the Christian life, the eye is naturally and properly fixed upon those separate acts of transgression upon which we can put our finger—that more external part of our sinfulness which it is our first and easiest duty to put away. But we soon learn, if we are progressive, that all these particular transgressions are but different modes in which the great and primitive sin of human nature manifests itself; are only varied exhibitions of that disinclination and aversion to glorify God, and extol him in the heart, which is the ultimate and original sin of man. He, therefore, who does not, after putting away swearing, lying, and stealing, look down a little lower into his heart, and detect the yet subtler ramifications of his corruption, will be likely to degenerate into a mere moralist, instead of becoming one of those spiritually-minded Christians who become more lowly, and humble, and broken-hearted, as they become more and more upright and obedient in their external conduct. The biographies of men like Leighton and Edwards must ever be a mystery, and a self-contradiction, to those who do not see that the very essence and inmost quality of sin consists in the lack of a heart to magnify the Lord, and to exalt his holy name. Read the diaries of such men, and witness their moaning in secret over the vileness of their hearts; hear the outbursting expression that "the sin is infinite upon infinite;" and then think of the pure and saintly course of their lives, when those lives are tried by the tests of external and single commandments, and does it not seem strange and paradoxical? These men were not hypocrites. No one can suspect them of this. But were they not self-deceived and mistaken? So some critics say, who judge of human character by the more superficial and outward criteria.

The key to the difficulty is found in the fact, that for such men as Leighton and Edwards the substance and in-

most quality of sin had come to be this continual failure to glorify God in the heart, in a manner worthy of
God's infinite excellence. Their character in this particular they felt to be imperfect. They were sinners in this
respect. When they prayed, their prayers were defective
from a lack of full faith in God's being and readiness to
bless; and this was coming short of God's glory. When
they praised and worshipped, their emotions and utterances were far below God's worthiness and desert; and
this was coming short of God's glory. When they obeyed
the statutes and commandments of God, it was not with
that totality and completeness of service which is due to
such a perfect and excellent Being; and this was to come
short of the Divine glory. They could not say, as did the
only perfect man that ever lived upon earth: "I have
glorified thee on the earth: I have finished the work thou
gavest me to do." And their apprehension of the sinfulness of this falling short of the chief end of man's creation was as painful as that which accompanies an ordinary
Christian's sense of guilt when he violates some particular
commandment of the decalogue. They had passed beyond the more common forms of sin, because they had, in
a great measure, overcome and subdued them. A class of
temptations which assail us, on our low position and with
our low degree of spirituality, had little or no influence
with them; and hence we wonder that their expressions
of contrition and self-loathing should be so intense. We
think that if our lives could but reach the pitch of excellence to which they attained, there would be but little
cause for the shame and lamentation which now accompanies our review of our daily walk and conversation. But
with them we should discover that in respect to sin, as in
respect to hell itself, "in every deep there is a lower deep."
The supreme excellence of God, and the spirituality of

his law, would dawn more and more upon our minds; the sense of our obligation, as his creatures, to magnify and glorify him in every act and every element of our existence, would grow stronger and stronger; our consciousness of failure to render this perfect homage and fealty would become deeper and deeper; and thus, while our obedience of particular and single commandments was becoming more and more punctilious and uniform, our feeling of defect at the fountain-head of character would become more and more poignant and self-abasing. We should see, as we had not before, that the very core and essence of moral evil consists in " worshipping and serving the creature more than the Creator." We should understand that there is no sin so wearing and wearisome as human egotism—as man's inveterate unwillingness to sink self, and renounce all idolatry, in the humble and adoring recognition of God's infinite perfection. We should understand, and sympathize with, that low and penitential refrain which mingles with the jubilant music of all the saintly spirits in the history of the Church.

Endeavor, then, to get into this mood and frame of mind. Be impressed with the greatness, goodness, and glory of God. Let the Divine attributes encompass you like an atmosphere. Then you will put away all pride and vain-glory, and can say in the language of that exquisite psalm: " Lord, my heart is not haughty, nor mine eyes lofty; neither do I exercise myself in great matters, or in things too high for me. Surely I have behaved and quieted myself as a child that is weaned of his mother; my soul is even as a weaned child."

SERMON IV.

THE FATHERHOOD OF GOD.

LUKE xvi. 25.—"But Abraham said, Son, remember that thou in thy life-time receivedst thy good things, and likewise Lazarus evil things, but now he is comforted, and thou art tormented."

AT first sight, it appears singular that the unbelieving and impenitent Dives, in the very place of retribution, should be addressed by Abraham "the father of believers" by the endearing title of "son." This word, however, as employed in the Scriptures, has more than one signification. It may denote only the benevolent and kindly relation existing between the Creator and the creature, as when the apostle Paul quotes approvingly the sentiment of the pagan poet: "We are his offspring;" or as when St. Luke, tracing up the genealogy of Christ to the beginning of creation, calls Adam the "son of God." And it may also mark merely the relation of dependence and inferiority, in some particular, existing between man and man. In such connections as these, the term does not necessarily imply any real filial feeling on the part of the so-called son, or teach that the one to whom it is applied is in affectionate and childlike sympathy with the one who applies it. Joshua, for instance, addresses the guilty Achan, who had stolen the Babylonish garment and the wedge of gold, with this endearing title. "My son, give, I pray thee, glory to the Lord God of Israel, and make confession unto him; and tell me now what thou hast done; hide it not from me." Achan was not a son in feeling, and in truth. He loved neither God, nor Joshua the servant of God. Hence, notwithstanding this employment of the epithet, "Joshua and all Israel with him took Achan, the son of Zerah, and the silver, and the garment, and the wedge of gold, and his sons, and his daughters, and his oxen, and his asses, and his sheep, and his tent, and all that he had, and stoned him with stones, and burned them with fire." In like manner, in the text, Abraham who had been called "father" by the sinful Dives—"Father Abraham, have mercy upon me"—addresses the guilty creature of God as son: "Son, remember that thou in thy life-time receivedst thy good things, and likewise Lazarus evil things; but now he is comforted, and thou art tormented."

The phraseology employed in this parable of our Lord, together with such a use of the term "son" as that made by Joshua in reference to Achan, throws light upon the doctrine of the *Fatherhood of God.* It is of the utmost consequence that we make no mistake respecting this important truth. In what sense, then, is God the Father of all men; and in what sense is he not the Father of all men? For it is clear that God does not sustain the same relation in every respect to all mankind equally and alike. He is not the Father of Judas Iscariot and Nero, in the identical sense in which he is of the apostle John and archbishop Leighton. He is not the Father of an impenitent Messalina, in the same way that he is of a broken-hearted Magdalen. For in the former case there is no affectionate filial feeling; and God, by his prophet Malachi, says to any and every man who would use the endearing term while at the same time he does not cherish the appropriate emotions: "A son honoreth his father;

if then I be a father, where is mine honor?" If the children of men, if any class of creatures, presume to denominate the Eternal One their Father, certainly they should evince their sincerity by the exercise of the correspondent sentiment.

I. In answering the first question, we remark that God is the Father of all men indiscriminately and without exception, in that he is their *Creator.* The author of any being or thing is naturally denominated its father. "Have we not one father? Hath not one God created us?" (Mal. ii. 10). "Hath the rain a father? And who hath begotten the drops of the dew?" (Job xxxviii. 28). When the devil "speaketh a lie, he speaketh of his own"—of what he himself has invented and made—"for he is a liar, and the father of it" (John viii. 44). "Every good gift, and every perfect gift, is from above, and cometh down from the Father of lights"—the originating author of all illumination, physical or mental (James i. 17). "To find the Maker and Father of the universe," says Plato, "is a difficult task" (Timaeus, 28). In this sense, God is the Father of all men indiscriminately. The hardened transgressor who is to be sent to everlasting perdition, and the penitent believer who is to be raised to heights of glory, here stand upon the same plane. They are of that "one blood" of which God made all mankind; and there is no difference between them. They are alike his "offspring," and he is alike their Father. This is the common basis upon which all creatures appear. The rich and the poor, the saint and the sinner here meet together, and the Lord is equally the Maker and providential Father of them all.

Such a common relationship as this to the Divine providence and benevolence justifies the use of the word "father" in a secondary and qualified meaning. God, because he created the human soul, is profoundly interested in it. He does not and cannot hate any substance that he has made. That rational and immortal spirit which he originated from nothing, and endowed with attributes resembling his own, is very dear to him as its maker. This is evinced by the care which he takes of it. He maintains it in being by a positive act of omnipotence, and he is continually supplying its multiplied wants. Were it not for his perpetual benevolence and oversight, the soul and body of man would sink into non-existence, or be overwhelmed by suffering and pain. Now, such an interest in the constitutional structure of his creatures on the part of God, justifies his calling himself " the Father of the spirits of all flesh." And every human being, whatever his moral character, is an object of benevolent and paternal concern to his maker. Even when he is transgressing the Divine law, the Divine hand that made him holds him in existence, crowns his life with blessings, makes the sun to shine upon him, and the rain to fall upon his broad acres, as if he were a child in the high and tender meaning of the word.

II. But while this is so, and should awaken sorrow in every man for his rebellion and ingratitude, it is nevertheless a fact that God is not the Father of all men indiscriminately in the highest and fullest sense of the term— their Father by *redemption* and *adoption.*

For man in his unrenewed state is an enemy of God. "The carnal mind is enmity against God" (Rom. viii. 7). We are "by nature children of wrath" (Eph. ii. 3). This is the attitude in which, by reason of apostacy, man stands towards his kind and benevolent Creator. And this attitude is incompatible with the relation of father and child in the full, tender, and affectionate meaning of these terms. With such an inimical feeling in the heart, it is impossible to cry, "Abba, Father!" An enemy of God cannot sincerely say, "Our Father which art in heaven." Hence the apostle describes the change that is made by regeneration, in the following language: "Ye have not received the spirit of bondage again to fear; but ye have received the spirit of adoption whereby we cry Father, Father. The spirit itself beareth witness with our spirit that we are the children of God." Previously to this, the parties have been estranged from each other. Sinful man fears his holy Maker, and his holy Maker frowns upon sinful man. And these words are to be taken in their strict meaning upon both sides. It is a false view that represents God as really complacent towards every man irrespective of his character, and that it is only the creature's groundless fear that stands in the way of a pleasant and happy intercourse. God really and truly makes a difference in his own mind and feeling between the man that obeys and confides in him, and the man who disobeys and distrusts him. He is positively displeased with the transgressor of his law, and the reconciliation which is effected by the atonement of Christ is mutual. God's holiness is reconciled to man, and man is reconciled to God. When a penitent sinner trusts in the expiatory sacrifice of Jesus Christ, then the triune God becomes his Father in the high and endearing signification of the term, and the man becomes a child of God in the same signification. The relation which is now established between the parties is not merely that of the creature to the Creator—a relation that does not necessarily involve love and obedience—but there is mutual affection, and delightful intercourse and communion. On the evening of the night in which Chalmers was summoned instantaneously from earth to heaven, he was overheard while walking in his garden uttering in earnest and affectionate tones: "My Father, O my heavenly Father." This is childhood in the full sense; and this is the Divine fatherhood in its blessed truth and reality. "As many as are led by the spirit of God, they are the sons of God" (Rom. viii. 14). "I have often found," says Bunyan, "that when I can say but this word *Father*, it doth me more good than if I called him by any other Scripture name. It is worth your noting, that to call God by this title was rare among the saints in Old Testament times. Seldom do you find him called by this name—no, sometimes not in three or four books; but now, in New Testament times, he is called by no name so often as this, both by the Lord Jesus himself, and by the apostles afterwards. Indeed, the Lord Jesus was he that first made the name common among the saints, and that taught them, both in their discourse, their prayers, and their writings, so much to use it; it being more pleasing to God, and discovering more plainly our interest in God, than any other expression. For by this one name, we are made to understand that all our mercies are the offspring of God, and that we also that are called are his children by adoption." [1]

Having thus briefly explained the senses in which God is and is not the Father of all men, we turn to deduce some practical lessons from the subject.

1. In the first place, we see how it is possible for God to be both a *Father* and a *Judge* at one and the same time, and to both *love* and *abhor* simultaneously. The reader of the Bible observes sometimes with perplexity, that God is represented as looking upon man with two wholly diverse emotions. The Scriptures seem to be self-contradictory. Sometimes God appears as yearning over man in compassion; and sometimes as consuming him with the blast of the breath of his nostrils. Sometimes his utter-

---

[1] Bunyan: Come, and Welcome, to Jesus Christ.

ance is: "Turn ye, turn ye, for why will ye die? As I live, saith the Lord God, I have no pleasure in the death of the wicked. The Lord doth not afflict willingly nor grieve the children of men." And sometimes the declaration is: "Thou hatest all workers of iniquity. God is angry with the wicked every day. Who may stand in thy sight when once thou art angry! Who knoweth the power of thine anger! Even according to thy fear so is thy wrath. The wrath of God is revealed from heaven against all unrighteousness. He that believeth not the Son shall not see life; but the wrath of God abideth on him." How can these two feelings co-exist in one and the same Being, towards one and the same person? How can blessing and cursing proceed out of the same mouth? How can the same fountain send forth both sweet waters and bitter? Must we not assume that one or the other of these declarations is figurative, and in this way harmonize the Bible with itself?

In the light of the distinction between God as the benevolent creator and preserver of all men—their providential Father in the general sense, and God as the redeeming and reconciled Father of penitent believers—their Father in the special sense, we find the clue to the difficulty. The kindly and benevolent feeling of the general paternity may co-exist with the holy displeasure of the righteous Judge. Even an imperfect man is capable of such a double emotion. A kind earthly father, or a gentle mother, may be filled with most intense displeasure at the hardened wickedness and profligacy of a child, and yet at the same time would gladly lay down life to secure his repentance and eternal welfare. By reason of the father's or the mother's moral excellence and resemblance to God, there can be nothing but abhorrence of the child's sin; and if the parent should be informed from an infallible source that the child would never repent, but would continue a hardened and wilful transgressor through all eternity, he would not only acquiesce in the judgment of God that banished him from heaven, but would say with all the holy, "Amen: so it must be, so it should be." For sin is an evil and a terrible thing, and even the dearest earthly ties cannot induce a holy and spiritual mind to approve of it, or desire that it should escape the merited punishment. And yet that parent is ready for any self-sacrifice that would deliver the rebellious and transgressing child from sin, and the penalty of sin. He says with David over the dead body of his wicked son: "O my son Absalom! my son, my son Absalom! would God I had died for thee, O Absalom, my son, my son!" And, with David, he never presumes to question the righteousness of the divine procedure in the punishment of a hardened transgressor, even though that transgressor be bone of his bone and flesh of his flesh.

The feeling of displeasure with which God regards sin belongs to his pure and perfect nature, and it is impossible for him to exist without it. It is no more optional with him to abhor iniquity, than it is to be omnipotent or omnipresent. God must, from his very nature and idea, be all-powerful, and in every place; and for the same reason he must react against evil wherever it exists. But at the same time he has no malice in his nature. He wishes well to every creature whom he has made. He cherishes a benevolent, and in this sense a paternal feeling towards every rational spirit. Even a little sparrow does not fall dead to the ground without his taking an interest in it; and certainly, then, he cannot be inspired with any malicious or unkind emotion toward the rational and immortal spirits who are of more value than many sparrows. The Creator can feel a natural and necessary abhorrence of the sinner's sin, while yet he feels an infinite compassion for the sinner's soul. Says Augustine: "It is written, 'God commendeth his love towards us, in that while we were yet sinners Christ died for us.' He loved us, therefore, even when in the exercise of enmity against him we were working iniquity. And yet it is said with perfect truth: 'Thou hatest, O Lord, all workers of iniquity.' Wherefore, in a wonderful and divine manner he both hated and loved us at the same time. He hated us as being different from what he had made us; but as our iniquity had not entirely destroyed his work within us, he could at the same time, in every one of us, hate what we had done, and love what he had created."

God loves man as a creature, while he is angry with him as a sinner. He takes a deep and tender interest in the soul which he has made and keeps in existence, while he is filled with a deep displeasure at the sin which is in that soul. Where is the inconsistency in the simultaneous existence of these two emotions? Each is exercised towards its proper object. The love goes out towards the soul as such; and the wrath goes out towards the sin as such. The sin is in the soul and cannot be separated from it except by the substitution of holiness in its place. If, then, any man retains the sinfulness of his soul, he must not expect that God's general benevolence and providential paternity will nullify his holiness; that his interest in the workmanship of his hands will overcome his regard for truth and righteousness, and induce him to let sin go unpunished. The providential paternity of God, and the universal sonship of man, are consistent with the punishment of incorrigible and hardened depravity.

2. In the second place, we learn from this subject, that it is our duty to exercise the *same feelings* towards the soul of man, and the sin of man, that God does.

We are commanded to imitate God in his moral perfections. "Be ye holy for I am holy. Be ye perfect as your Father in heaven is perfect." We cannot obey these injunctions without sympathizing with God in his benevolent love for the human soul, and his holy disapprobation of human sinfulness. And this sympathy should be seen first in reference to ourselves, and then in regard to others. We have no right to treat other souls differently from our own. Religion must begin at home, and hence while we cherish a rational love for our own souls, we should at the same time sternly condemn and abhor our own personal sin. A man should both love and hate himself. While he says: "Skin for skin, yea, all that I have I will give for my life," he should also say, "I abhor myself." While he is deeply anxious for his own well-being here and hereafter, he should sympathize with his holy Maker in abominating the iniquity of his own heart. These two feelings are not incompatible. Nay, we never begin to love ourselves aright, until we begin to condemn and hate our sins.

And, certainly, if we deal in this manner with our own souls and our own sins, we are entitled to deal in this manner with the souls and sins of others. As we mingle in society and come in contact with our fellow-creatures and our fellow-sinners, we ought to feel the same desire that God does for their soul's welfare, and the same abhorrence which he feels for their soul's sin. No malice, no envy, no ill-will, towards any creature of God should ever rise within us. We ought to wish well to the whole rational universe. Such was the angelic song: "Peace on earth, and good will to men." As creatures simply, and not taking their sinfulness into account, we should love all men indiscriminately, and desire their happiness in time and eternity. But when we leave out this characteristic, and contemplate any man as an antagonist of God, and a bitter enemy of that holy and perfect Being, we should be filled with a righteous displeasure, and desire his punishment. We should say with David : " Do not I hate them, O Lord, that hate thee? I hate them with perfect hatred : I count them mine enemies " (Ps. cxxxix. 21, 22).

And if we have done all this in reference to ourselves personally, mankind will not complain if we subject them to the same tests, and treat them in the same manner. Nay, more, we shall do them good by our impartiality and sincerity. If we really love their souls, they will let us hate their sins. If we labor and pray, that as creatures of God, and capable of eternal purity and joy, they do not go down to perdition, they will not object to the severest denunciation of their iniquity.

It is the duty of the Church to sympathize with God in all his feelings towards a world lying in wickedness. Christians must not be inspired with any mere sentimentalism in reference to the sins and sorrows of man, for God is not. With him they must look with a clear, impartial eye, and remember that wherever there is suffering in the universe of God, there is sin. These sorrows of humanity are the consequence of the guilt of humanity, and when we look upon them, either in our own case or that of others, we are to say : "Just and righteous art thou, O God, in all this punitive infliction. Man has transgressed, and therefore he suffers. Death hath passed upon all men, because all have sinned." And on the other hand, we are to sympathize with God in his tender concern for the soul, as distinguished from the sin. We are to see in every fellow-man a spark of the Divine intelligence ; a partaker, as St. Peter says, of a divine nature ; an immortal spirit similar to the Eternal Spirit, and destined to live forever. We are to remember that such an essence as this is worth saving; that it is an infinite loss when it goes to perdition, and that no sacrifice is too great to save it. God, who looks into the nature of things, saw its value, and shrank not from the most costly sacrifice. He spared not his own Son, but gave him up in order that the soul, the rational deathless nature of man, might be saved.

What an increase of power would be imparted to the Church, if every member of it were filled with these two emotions, pure and simple, which dwell in the bosom of God. There would be no self-indulgence in sin, and no weak and fond indulgence of sin in others. The eye would be single, solemn, piercing, holy. A healthy conscience would brace up and strengthen the entire man, and he would go forth into the world, a terror to evil-doers, and a praise to them who do well. And at the same time, this Christian would be a very tender-hearted creature. He would feel the worth of every soul in itself, abstracted from the sin that is in it. His heart would yearn towards it, as an emanation from God, and an immortal thing for which Christ died. His works would follow his faith, and he would labor and pray for its welfare, with a solemnity, a persistence, and a holy earnestness, that would certainly receive the Divine approbation and blessing.

3. In the third place, this subject furnishes a *test* of a renewed and spiritual mind.

A worldly mind is selfish in its love, and selfish in its hatred. It is displeased with sin when it interferes with its own enjoyment, and it is pleased with righteousness when it promotes its own happiness. If the worldling loses something in his own mind, body, or estate, by the theft or the lie of a transgressor, he inveighs bitterly against these particular sins. And if he is the gainer in his worldly circumstances by the industry, honesty, or godliness of a Christian man, he is profuse in his praise of these virtues and graces. But he does not love holiness for its own intrinsic excellence, neither does he hate sin because of its abstract odiousness. If the sins of his fellow-men would promote his selfish purposes, he would encourage them, and be highly displeased at any attempt to check or remove them. His character and feelings are exactly the reverse of those of God. He has no love for the soul of his fellow-man as the workmanship of the Creator, and no abhorrence of his sin as an evil thing in itself and under all circumstances. He cares not what becomes of the immortal part of his fellow-creature. He never toils or prays for its welfare. And his feelings towards the sins of a fellow-creature depend entirely upon how his interests are affected by them. Terrible as is the fact, it is nevertheless a fact, that the selfishness of the natural heart hesitates not to sacrifice the very soul, the very being itself, of a fellow-creature, in order to attain its own purposes. Alexander and Napoleon, in the prosecution of their plans, used the bodies and minds of millions of their fellow-men as the potter uses the passive clay. And how many there are, in narrower circles than those of the conqueror and the monarch, who do the same thing, and are madly rushing to the same condemnation.

But not so with the true child of God. He loves the soul, and hates the sin. His feeling in each instance is pure, spiritual, disinterested. He loves his own soul and abhors his own sin. And he does by others as he does by himself. He is not displeased with the transgressions of men merely because they injure his private interests. He would gladly suffer that loss, if thereby he could secure their repentance and reformation. He abhors their iniquity for its own intrinsic quality, as God abhors it. His hatred of moral evil is spiritual, disinterested, holy, like that of his Father in heaven, with whom he sympathizes, and for whose honor he is jealous. And his love for the welfare of every man indiscriminately partakes of the same spirituality. He is ready to toil, give of his substance, and pray for the salvation of fellow-creatures whom he never saw, and never will see, until he stands with them at the judgment seat. He needs no introduction in order to take an interest in a lost man. The heathen in the heart of China or of Africa lie with as much weight upon his heart and conscience, as do the impenitent in his own neighborhood. Worldly men sometimes wonder, and sometimes scoff, at the interest which the Church of God is taking in the millions of paganism who are thousands of miles away from them. They tell us that the heathen are at our own doors, and regard this great endeavor to obey the last command of Christ to preach the gospel to every creature, as quixotic and visionary. But they feel no Divine love for man as the image of God; as a creature who came from the same plastic hand that they came from; as an immortal spirit possessing the same properties and qualities that they are possessed of; and above all, as the object of the same Divine pity in the blood of Christ by which they themselves must be saved, if saved at all. They have no fellow-feeling with their race ; and what is yet more, they have no sympathy with God the Redeemer of man.

It is obvious that this is a very searching and a very accurate test of Christian character. It is possible to cherish a religiousness that is so selfish, so destitute of warm and disinterested love for human welfare, as to deserve condemnation. This is the weak side, this is the great defect, in some very interesting phases of religious character. Look at the mediæval monk and his severe spiritual experiences. He is constantly occupied with the salvation of his soul. He thinks of nothing else, and lives for nothing else. And yet in finding his life he loses it. All these experiences are a refined form of self-love. He has merely transferred his self-seeking from time to eternity. What he needs is, to love others as he loves himself; to break out from his seclusion and preach the gospel to his fellow-men. Having freely received, he should freely give. Those are truthful and discriminating remarks which the historian of Latin Christianity makes respecting the famous treatise on the "Imitation of Christ," in which this species of piety finds its finest and most winning delineation. "Its sole, single, exclusive object," he says, " is the purification, the elevation of the individual soul, of the man absolutely isolated from his kind, of the man dwelling alone in solitude in the hermitage of his own thoughts ; with no fears or hopes, no sympathies of our common nature: he has absolutely withdrawn and secluded himself not only from the cares, the sins, the trials, but from the duties, the connections, the moral and religious fate of the world. Never was misnomer so glaring, if justly considered, as the title of the book, the 'Imitation of Christ.' That which distinguishes Christ, that which distinguishes Christ's apostles, that which distinguishes Christ's religion—the love of *man*—is entirely and absolutely left out. Had this been the whole of Christianity, our Lord himself (with reverence be it said) had lived like an Essene, working out or displaying his own sinless perfection by the Dead Sea: neither on the mount, nor in the temple, nor even on the cross. The apostles had dwelt entirely on the internal emotions of their own souls, each by himself; St. Peter still by the lake Gennessaret, St. Paul in the desert of Arabia, St. John in Patmos. Christianity had been without any exquisite precept for the purity, the happiness of

social or domestic life ; without self-sacrifice for the good
of others ; without the higher Christian patriotism, devotion on evangelic principles to the public weal; without
even the devotion of the missionary for the dissemination
of gospel truth ; without the humbler and gentler daily
self-sacrifice for relatives, for the wife, the parent, the
child. Christianity had never soared to be the civilizer of
the world. ' Let the world perish, so the single soul can
escape on its solitary plank from the general wreck,' such
had been its final axiom." [1]

4. In the fourth place, we learn from this subject, how
sad must be the *final condition* of those who never become the "dear children" of God, and to whom God is
not a Father in the high and endearing sense of these
terms.

It is a frequent remark, that a blessing or a privilege
when abused or perverted becomes the greatest of curses.
And so it is in this instance. If we pervert and abuse the
relation which as creatures we sustain to our Creator—if
we live upon his bounty, and yet rebel against his authority
—the fact that we are his offspring will only increase our
condemnation. This paternal interest which God takes in
us as his workmanship—this care, this protection, this
providence which guards and guides us every day—if it
be accompanied with no suitable feeling and action upon
our part, will only result in a severer punishment. Unless
by faith and repentance we come to be more than the creatures of God ; unless we become children and he becomes
a Father in the full and blessed sense, our God and Father
in Christ; there is no peace or joy possible for us. It will
be no source of comfort to remember that he is the providential Father of all spirits by creation. The devils them-

---

[1] Milman : Latin Christianity, Book XIV., Chap. iii.

selves share in this general fatherhood and benevolence of the Supreme Being. There is no malice in the Eternal Mind toward the arch-fiend himself. That fallen and wicked spirit is as dependent as he ever was upon the sustaining providence of the Most High. He is as much as ever the offspring of the Almighty. In this sense, he is still a son of the Highest. But this only renders him the more intensely guilty and unhappy. He has abused, and he is still and ever abusing the Divine benevolence, the Divine beneficence, the Divine providence, the Divine paternity. He has no filial feeling towards the Universal Parent, and therefore God is not *his* God and Father. He never says: "Our Father, hallowed be thy name. Thy kingdom come. Thy will be done." And so it is and must be in every instance of this kind. It is precisely so with the impenitent, the unfilial, the alienated man. Unless the prodigal returns to his original relations, the fact that by creation God is his Father will render his condemnation more just and righteous, and his condition more wretched. It will be embittered by the reflection, that from first to last God was good and kind to him; that he never in the least injured the dependent creature whom he called into being; that he never felt the least ill-will towards him, but on the contrary cared for him, and did him good all the days of his life—in short, that he exercised towards him all the paternal feeling that was possible in the case. But there is one phase of a father's feeling which it is impossible for God to exhibit in such an instance as this. The creature has become his enemy. He opposes his will to that of God; his carnal mind is not subject to the law of God. The tender and affectionate feeling of a father cannot be manifested under such circumstances. All that God can do in this case is to continue to exhibit his general benevolence and providential fatherhood, with the desire that it may soften the hard heart, and that "the goodness of God may lead to repentance." But if it all fails, if the creature to the end abuses this kindness and persists in his enmity and hatred, then the benevolent Creator must assume his function of Judge, and when the final day arrives must sentence this wicked and impenitent offspring of his to everlasting perdition, as he has sentenced the rebellious angels before him.

Lay, then, this truth to heart. God cannot be a Father to any man who cannot from the fulness of his heart cry unto him, "My Father." His entreaty by his prophet is: "Wilt thou not from this time cry unto me, My Father, be thou the guide of my youth." This entreaty, though primarily addressed to the young, is intended for all. God desires to be more than our Creator. He is not content with bestowing these temporal and providential blessings with which he is crowning our life. He desires to impart the richer gifts of his grace. He would give not merely his gifts, but Himself to his creatures. But the creature repulses him. How many a man is at this very moment saying to his Maker: "Give me wealth, give me health, give me worldly ease and pleasure, give me intellectual power and fame, give me political influence and sway in the land, but do not give me Thyself." Is such a heart as this fitted for the world of light and love? Is this the utterance of a child? Can God be a dear Father to such an one? It is impossible from the nature of the case.

Lay, not, then the flattering unction to your soul, that the universal fatherhood of God is sufficient to secure your eternal welfare. That is a great and glorious truth, but if you never get beyond it in your religious experience, to the doctrine of the special and endearing fatherhood of God in Christ, it will minister to your condemnation and everlasting woe. Seek, then, to enter into a truly filial relation with your Maker. Rest not until you have made your peace with God's holiness and justice by his blood of atonement, and then you will "know with all saints the height and depth" of his fatherly love in Christ, "which passeth knowledge."

SERMON V.

THE FUTURE VISION OF GOD.

2 CORINTHIANS, iv. 18.—"The things which are not seen are eternal."

THERE is a difference between things that are not seen, and things that are invisible. An object may not be seen at this particular moment, or under the present circumstances, and yet it may come into sight hereafter, or under a different set of surroundings. But an object that is strictly invisible cannot be seen either now or hereafter; from the present point of view, or from any conceivable position whatsoever. There are stars in the heavens that have never yet been observed by any human eye, but which can be brought into view by a higher power of the telescope. They are unseen, but they do not belong to the class of absolute invisibilities. But the spiritual essence of God, and the immaterial substance of the human soul, are strictly invisible. Not only are they not seen as yet, but they never will be seen by any vision whatsoever.

This distinction is marked by the apostle Paul, and indicated by the difference in the phraseology which he employs. In the text, he uses the same form of words (μὴ βλεπόμενα) with that employed in Hebrews xi. 1, where it is affirmed that faith is "the evidence [conviction] of things not seen" (οὐ βλεπομένων). In this latter instance the writer refers to objects that are not visible now, but which will be visible hereafter. " Faith," he says, " is the conviction of things not seen " in the present, but to be seen in the future. He cites in illustration the case of Noah. The flood had not yet come and was a " thing not seen," when the patriarch exercised the act of faith ; but it afterward came, and was both visible and tangible. But when St. Paul, in Rom. i. 20, declares that " the invisible things of God, from the creation of the world, are clearly seen, being understood by the things that are made, even his eternal power and godhead," he employs a different word (ἀόρατα) which denotes that these things are intrinsically invisible. The eternal power and godhead—the Divine essence itself, with its inherent attributes—cannot be seen with the bodily eye. It can only be " understood," that is, illustrated and interpreted, " by the things that are made."

The text, then, leads us to contemplate those objects which we do not see now, but which we shall see hereafter. It does not call us to a metaphysical investigation of those things which are absolutely beyond the reach of finite cognition, because they are intrinsically invisible and incomprehensible ; but it invites us to examine those realities which we do not now see, or which at least we see through a glass darkly, but which we shall hereafter see, and see face to face.

The first and greatest of these realities is *God.* After what we have remarked concerning the Divine essence, it will of course be understood that we do not mean to teach that we shall comprehend the mystery of the Godhead in the future life. " No man hath seen God at any time." No finite intelligence whatever, be it man or angel, can penetrate the inscrutable abyss of the Divine nature. This is an absolute invisibility, and neither in this world nor the next will the created mind comprehend it. But there is a *manifestation* of God, whereby he puts himself into relation and communication with his creatures, so that they may know him sufficiently to glorify and enjoy him. The apostle John alludes to this, when, after saying that no man hath seen the invisible and unsearchable God at any time, he adds, "The only begotten God who is in the bosom of the Father, he hath declared him." In the incarnation of the second trinitarian Person, the deity steps out, as it were, from behind the thick clouds and darkness that veil him from the human intelligence, and shows himself. Think of the difference that has been made in man's knowledge of God, by the Word's becoming flesh and dwelling among us. Compare the view of God which is enjoyed by all who have the four Gospels in their hands, with that which was granted to the wisest and most reflecting of the heathen. The little child in the Sabbath-school knows more of the being and attributes, and particularly of the purposes of the Most High, than Plato himself. For Christ, the God-Man, stands before his infantile vision "the brightness of the Father's glory, and the exact image of his person;" so that the deity possesses for this little child's mind in a Christian land a reality, a distinctness, an excellence, and a beauty, that never was revealed to the most serious, the most capacious, and the most highly disciplined intelligence of pagan antiquity. In the incarnate Word, that "unknown God" whom Paul alluded to on Mars hill, whom the philosophers of Athens were ignorantly worshipping, and after whom they were blindly groping if haply they might find him, assumes a corporeal human presence. He breaks through the sky, he bursts the dim ether, and stands out like the sun on the edge of the horizon a sublime and glorious Form. We see his face, alas! marred more than any man; we hear his voice. He is Immanuel—God with us. I tell you that many sages and philosophers, many kings and prophets, have desired to see those things which the little child now sees, and have not seen them; to hear those things which the little child now hears, and have not heard them.

But the future manifestation of God that is to be made in heaven is yet more impressive and refulgent than this. The tabernacling of God in the flesh, eighteen centuries ago, was only preparatory to the great final manifestation of himself to his Church in the world of light; and glorious as was the former, yet far more glorious will be the latter. " For even that which was made glorious had no glory in this respect, by reason of the glory that excelleth. For if that which is done away was glorious, much more that which remaineth is glorious " (2 Cor. iii. 10, 11). Christ upon earth in his state of humiliation was indeed glorious; but Christ upon the mediatorial throne, still clothed in human nature but in his estate of exaltation, is far more glorious.

It is not for us to say in what particulars God will be manifested to the blessed on high, whereby his presence will be far more impressive than it was in the theophanies of the Old Dispensation, or even in the earthly incarnation of the New. But we know the fact from the teaching of Scripture. The appearance of Jehovah to Abraham, when he was in Mesopotamia, before he dwelt in Charran; to Moses in the burning bush, and on Mount Sinai; to the child Samuel in the dim recesses of the temple; to Isaiah when he saw the Lord sitting upon a throne high and lifted up, and his train filled the temple; and last of all, the actual residence of this second Person of the Trinity on the plains of Palestine, and among the hills of Judea— all these graduated and growing revelations of the deity fall short of that which shall be in the future world. For the future world is the final one. All the preparatory steps and stages in the religious education of the Church; all the gradual and growing revelations that have been employed to bring man into nearer and nearer communication with the unseen God ; will have accomplished their purpose. The last wall of separation between the finite and the infinite Spirit will have been broken down ; man and God will meet face to face, and know even as they are known. Hence the last manifestation must be the crowning one. In heaven, God assumes a form more glorious and distinct than he has before assumed upon earth. He puts himself into a relation to human creatures that will influence them, and affect them, more profoundly and vividly than ever before.

There is one proof of this to which we invite attention. It is the fact that the heavenly world is a world of perfect worship ; and perfect worship supposes a resplendent manifestation and clear vision of the Object of worship.

We see the operation of this principle in the idolatries of the world. The pagan requires some visible form before which he can bow down, and to which he can address his prayers. His error and his sin does not lie in the fact that he craves an object to worship, but in the fact that he selects a wrong object. No creature can offer prayer or praise to a nonentity ; and the idolater is following a legitimate and constitutional conviction of the human mind, when he seeks some being, real or imaginary, toward whom his religious aspirations may go out, and upon whom they may terminate. He cannot pray into the air. His words need to strike upon some object, and rebound to him in an answer All this is natural and proper. But his error consists in substituting an image of gold and silver, or the sun, moon, and stars, or the forces of nature, for the Invisible Spirit. Rejecting that idea of an "eternal power and Godhead" which

St. Paul asserts to be innate in every man, and to be
" clearly seen and understood by the things that are
made," the idolater betakes himself to the notions of his
fancy, which are more in accordance with his vile affections. Leaving his reason, he takes lessons in theology
from his imagination. " Becoming vain in their imaginations, their foolish heart was darkened; professing themselves to be wise, they became fools, and changed the
glory of the incorruptible God into an image made like to
corruptible man, and to birds, and four-footed beasts, and
creeping things." Not, then, in seeking an object of worship, but in substituting a false for the true one, does the
sin and folly of the idolater consist. There must be an
object, in order to any worship.

We find this same principle operating in the minds of
believers themselves. What a craving there oftentimes is
in the heart of a child of God, to behold the Being whom
he has worshipped so long, but whom he has never seen.
It is true that he enjoys many aids to his faith and worship. The history of all these Divine manifestations to
the patriarchs, and prophets, and apostles, is before him,
and he reads it often and again. Still more, the story of
the incarnation, and of the residence of God the Son here
upon earth, he peruses over and over. These place the
object of worship very plainly before him, in comparison
with the dimness of natural religion, and the darkness of
idolatry. Nevertheless, he desires a fuller manifestation
than this, and looks forward to one in the future. He
sees through a glass darkly, though living under the light
of revelation ; and says with David, "I shall be satisfied
[only] when I awake in Thy likeness." "If," says Richard Baxter, " an angel from heaven should come down on
earth to tell us all of God that we would know, and might
lawfully desire and ask him, who would not turn his

back upon libraries, and universities, and learned men,
to go and discourse with such a messenger? What travel
should I think too far, what cost too great, for one hour's
talk with such a messenger?" This is the utterance of that
holy man when he was standing upon the borders of eternity, and was about to go over into the "everlasting rest"
whose felicity he has described so well. This is one of his
"Dying Thoughts," and from it we see how ardently he
desired to behold God, the great Object of worship, face
to face. He had worshipped him long, and he had loved
him long. He had enjoyed a clearer mental vision, probably, than is granted to most believers. And yet he is not
satisfied. With the Psalmist he cries out: "As the hart
panteth after the water brooks, so panteth my soul after
thee, O God. My soul thirsteth for God, for the living
God: when shall I come and appear before God?"

Now from these facts in the human constitution, and in
the Christian experience, we infer that there will be a
full and unclouded vision of God in the future life. This
is one of those "eternal things" which are not seen as
yet, but which will be seen hereafter. For the future
world is the world where worship reaches its perfection;
and therefore it must be the world where the Object of
worship shines out like the sun. The Scripture figures
and representations imply this. "I saw a great white
throne," says St. John, "and him that sat on it, from
whose face the earth and the heaven fled away, and there
was found no place for them. And I saw the dead, small
and great, stand before God." In this description of the
last judgment, the creature and the Creator meet face to
face. Who can doubt, from this statement, that when the
books are opened and the final reckoning is made, the
phenomenal appearance of the Deity will be far more
startling and striking than any previous manifestation that

he has made. "Behold he cometh with clouds; and every eye shall see him, and they also which pierced him." Here we are told that the human eye looks directly into the Divine eye. There is even a specification of individuals. That Roman soldier who pierced the side of the Lord of Glory on Mount Calvary with his spear, will, in the day of doom, see that same Eternal One as distinctly as he saw him when nailed to the cross. These passages relate to the eternal judgment, and imply an immediate manifestation of God then and there; a direct vision of him, face to face. But with equal plainness do the representations of St. John respecting the eternal worship teach the same truth. "I saw," he says, " no temple in the heavenly Jerusalem; for the Lord God Almighty, and the Lamb, are the temple of it. And the city had no need of the sun, neither of the moon to shine in it, for the glory of God did lighten it, and the Lamb is the light thereof. And his servants see his face, and his name is in their foreheads." It is not possible, as we have before remarked, to imagine or describe this glorious and final theophany. We cannot draw a picture of that resplendent Form before which the heavenly hosts bow in reverence and love. And all such attempts to go beyond what is written are presumptuous. The Italian painters sometimes do this; and even our own Milton, in some of his attempts to delineate the state and glory of the Eternal God, not only shows a faltering pinion, but derogates from the Divine honor. The subject is beyond human powers. Even the pen of inspiration could not convey to such faculties as those of man, and particularly to such an earthly-minded creature as he is, an adequate and full idea of the " excellent glory." Nevertheless, there is such a glory; there is such a transcendant manifestation of the great Object of worship. And it is for us to think of it as we do of a star, or a sun, that is not yet within the range of our vision. We have no doubt that Sirius is this moment shining with a brilliancy beyond conception; that he is throwing out beams into universal space that glitter and gleam beyond any light that ever was on sea or land. We do not now see that star; our eyes are not now blinded by its intolerable brightness. But there are eyes that behold it; and if it should be brought within the range of our vision, we should be forced to shield our orbs from its glare. Just so is it with the celestial manifestation of God. It does not now strike upon our vision, because we are upon earth. It is one of the "eternal things" which are not seen as yet. But it is none the less a reality. The star is shining in full effulgence within its own sphere; and there are creatures who behold and adore. "Beloved, now are we the sons of God, and it doth not appear what we shall be; but we know that when he shall appear, we shall be like him, for we shall see him as he is." [1]

For it will not be possible to offer unto God a perfect worship, until we see him as the angels and the spirits of just men made perfect see him. Even here upon earth, the fervency of our love and praise depends upon the clearness with which we behold the Divine perfections. When our spiritual perception is dim, our worship is faint; but when we are granted, in the sanctuary or in the closet, some unusual views of our Maker and Redeemer, our languid affections are quickened. Worship, as we have repeatedly remarked, depends upon a sight of the Object of worship; and it rises or sinks as that comes into our view, or recedes from it. The Persian Fire-Worshippers adored the sun. So long as that luminary was below the horizon they were silent, and offered no worship; but

---

[1] On the beatific vision, see Augustine's City of God, Book XXII. Chap. xxix.

when the first streaks of light and the first bars of crimson
began to appear in the morning sky, they began to kindle
in their own minds.   Yet their worship did not reach its
height, until

> " Right against the eastern gate
> The great sun began his state,
> Robed in flames and amber light."

So is it with Christian worship.   Here upon earth we
see some faint streaks of the Divine glory, and we offer
some faint and imperfect adoration.   But when the full-
orbed glory of God shall rise upon our clear and purged
vision in another world, our anthems will be like those of
the heavenly host.   Here upon earth, our praise is to
some degree an effort.   We study, and we toil, to give
unto God the glory due unto his name.   And this is right.
For here, in time, our religion must be to some extent a
race and a fight.   There are obstacles to a perfect service
which arise from our own indwelling sin, and from the
unfavorable circumstances in which we are placed in a
world like this.   And among these unfriendly circumstances is the fact, that here in time God does not reveal
himself in the fulness of his glory.   We see him through
a glass darkly.   But when we shall " come and appear before God"; when we shall behold the Object of worship
precisely as he is, it will cost us no effort to worship him.
Our adoration will become spontaneous and irrepressible.
For the Object itself prompts the service.   We shall not
need to urge our hearts up to the anthem.   They will be
drawn out by the magnetic attraction, the heavenly beauty
of the Divine Nature.

We have thus considered one of those eternal realities
which are not seen as yet.   We have meditated upon that
special manifestation which God makes of himself to the
worshippers in the upper sanctuary.   Guided by the state-

ments of Scripture, which are also confirmed by the instinctive desires of the renewed heart, as well as by the constitutional workings of the human mind, we have seen that the great object of our love and our worship will not always be seen through a glass darkly. The Christian will one day behold God face to face. Man was originally made to live in the immediate presence of his Maker. The account that is given us in the opening chapters of Genesis shows that Adam's intercourse with God was much like that which the angels enjoy. And is it reasonable to suppose that when the Creator had produced a creature in his own likeness, and had endowed him with holiness and knowledge, and made him capable of a blessed companionship with himself, he would then have thrust him away from his presence and shut him out of his communion? In the pagan mythology, Saturn devours his own children; but that glorious and blessed Being "of whom the whole family in heaven and earth is named," delights to communicate the fulness of his own joy to his offspring. Nothing but apostasy and rebellion have interrupted this primeval intercourse between man and God. When guilty Adam heard the voice of the Lord God walking in the garden in the cool of the day, he hid himself. Previously to this, that voice had had no terrors for him. When, therefore, the restoration shall have taken place, and man shall have been reinstated in his original condition, the old intercourse will be resumed. The same direct vision, the same social converse, the same condescending manifestation, will be granted and enjoyed. "I heard a great voice out of heaven, saying, Behold, the tabernacle of God is with men, and he will dwell with them, and they shall be his people, and God himself shall be with them, and be their God."

In concluding the examination of this passage of Scripture up to this point—for other important points still remain to be considered—we remark, that it is the duty of the Christian to live in *hope* of the full vision of God in heaven. The apostle Paul, after saying that "the whole creation groaneth and travaileth in pain together" —in other words, that there seems to be, even in the material world, a craving expectation of something higher and better—adds, that even those "who have the first fruits of the Spirit groan within themselves, waiting for the adoption, that is to say, the redemption of the body" from death and corruption. And everywhere in his Epistles, he represents the true believer as living in hope. "We are saved by hope," he says, "but hope that is seen is not hope; for what a man seeth, why doth he yet hope for?"

This hope extends, of course, to everything comprehended in the Christian life and experience. It is a hope that temptation will one day wholly cease; that trials and sorrows will all disappear; that sin will be entirely cleansed from the soul, and that perfect peace and joy will be its portion. But our subject directs our thoughts to a single particular—to the hope, namely, that we shall one day behold God face to face. That good and gracious Being whom we have never seen; whose very existence we have held to by an act of pure faith without sight; who has never spoken a word to us that was audible by the outward ear; who has never given us any visible sign or evidence of his existence—that Being to whom we have committed our eternal interests, and our eternal destiny, without having either seen his shape or heard his voice; to whom we have lifted up our hearts in the hour of affliction, and in the watches of the night, while yet no visible ray has emanated from his throne and his presence; to whom in his temple, and in our own closets, we have endeavored to render a reverential homage and service, though we have had no visible object to bow down before—that invisible, inaudible, intangible, and utterly unsearchable Spirit, we shall one day behold face to face. It is not the intention or the desire of our God to keep his children forever at this remote distance from him. He cannot wisely make such miraculous manifestations of himself to his Church in every age, as he has made to them in some ages; and he cannot appear in celestial glory here in these fogs and vapors of earth. A perpetual miracle would defeat its own end. The rejecters of the truth connected with the miracle would soon become accustomed to it, as they did under the miraculous dispensation; "for though Christ had done so many miracles before them, yet they believed not on him" (John xii. 37). And even the partially-sanctified people of God themselves would receive a fainter and fainter impression from it. The celestial manifestation of God is therefore in reserve, and we must hope and wait for it. Let us, therefore, as Moses did, "endure as seeing him who is invisible." For we shall not be called to endure forever. There is a time coming when faith shall be turned into sight; when that star whose beams have never yet fallen upon our vision, but which has all the while been shining in its glory, shall break through the dusky air, and we shall see it, and rejoice in its everlasting radiance and gleam.

> " Then ' Glory to the Father, to the Son,
> And to the Holy Spirit,' rings aloud
> Throughout all Paradise; that with the song
> The spirit reels, so passing sweet the strain.
> And what it sees is equal ecstasy:
> One universal smile it seems of all things;
> Joy past compare; gladness unutterable;
> Imperishable life of peace and love;
> Exhaustless riches, and unmeasured bliss." [1]

[1] Dante: Paradise, XXVII. 1-9.

SERMON VI.

GOD THE STRENGTH OF MAN.

Psalm lxxxiv. 5.—"Blessed is the man whose strength is in Thee."

Power and enjoyment are reciprocally related to each other. "To be weak is to be miserable," said Satan to Beelzebub, as they lay weltering in the floods of tempestuous fire, after their expulsion from heaven; and it is a truth, though falling from satanic lips. He who is filled with a sense of weakness and danger is unhappy; but he who is conscious of inward power and security is blest. It is a universal fact that the enjoyment of any being is proportioned to his strength, and partakes of the nature of it. If his is an inferior and uncertain strength, his is an inferior and uncertain happiness. If his confidence is in his health and his wealth, then his enjoyment is of an earthly nature, and will endure only while he lives upon earth. If his is a superior and permanent strength, his is a superior and permanent enjoyment. If the strength of a man is the eternal God, and the immutable truth that is settled in heaven; if it is in spiritual and heavenly objects; then his happiness is heavenly, and will endure forever.

The Divine Word, however, throws all these lower species out of the account, and calls no man strong unless his strength is in God; no creature happy unless he reposes unwaveringly upon his Father in heaven. And this judgment of the Word of God is true altogether. For ought that pleasure to be denominated by so expressive a term as *blessedness*, which depends upon the fragile objects of sense and time, and which ceases altogether when the soul passes into another world? Does that man know anything of true mental peace and satisfaction who merely buys and sells and gets gain? Has he anything of heaven in his experience who makes himself his own end and his own strength, and finds in the hour of real trial—of affliction and of death, when flesh and heart fail—that God is not the strength of his heart and his portion forever? The Bible does not look upon man and his happiness with man's weak eye. It takes its stand in the skies, far above the little theatre of this existence, and looks with the all-surveying glance of God. It contemplates man as an immortal creature who must live forever; who needs communion with God, and love to him and from him, and trust in him, in order that the long eternity of his existence may have something to repose upon, and not be an unsupported aching void in which there is not a moment of genuine happiness, not a single element of peace. Consequently in giving an opinion and estimate, the Scriptures pay little attention to this short life of threescore years and ten. They measure by eternity. Man may deem himself happy if he can obtain what this life offers, but the Bible calls him miserable—nay, calls him a fool—because the time is very near when this whole earthly life itself will terminate. Man calls himself happy if he can grasp and cling to the objects of this world ; but the Word of God asserts that he is really wretched, because this world will soon be melted with fervent heat. Man flatters himself that all is well with him while he gratifies the flesh, and feeds the appetites of his corrupt nature ; but

God asserts in thunder-tones that all is ill with him, because his spirit is not fed with the bread that cometh down
from heaven. God is on the throne, and looks down upon
all the dwellers upon the face of the earth, and from his
calm seat sees all their hurried, busy, and little movements
—like those of ants upon the ant-hill—and he knows, and
in his Word affirms, that however much they may seem to
enjoy in their low sphere, and in their grovelling pursuits,
they are nevertheless possessed of nothing like solid good
in any degree, unless they look up to him from amidst the
stir and dimness of earth, for a participation in the holiness and happiness of their Creator. He knows and
affirms, that no man whose strength is not in Him, whose
supports and portion are merely temporal and earthly, is
blessed.

Man is a creature of time, and sustains relations in it.
He is also a creature made for eternity, and sustains corresponding relations. Let us then look at him in these
two different worlds, that we see how he is blessed in them
both if his strength is in God; and how he is unblest in
them both if his strength is not in God.

I. In the first place, man is in *time*, and in an earthly
and transient state of being; how will he be unblest in
this life if his strength is not in God, and how will he be
blest in this life if his strength is in God?

If man is ever to be happy without God, it must be in
some such world as this. It must be in a material world,
where it is possible to banish the thought of God and of responsibility, and find occupation and a species of enjoyment
in other beings and objects. If a creature desires to be happy
away from God, and in opposition to his commandment, he
must accomplish it before he goes into a spiritual world;
he must effect it amidst these visible and temporal scenes.
This is his only opportunity. No sinful creature can be

happy for a moment in the life to come. He must therefore obtain before he dies all the enjoyment he will ever obtain. Like Dives, he must receive all his "good things" here. If man can ever dispense with the help and favor of God, and not feel his need of him, it must be when he is fully absorbed in the cares and interests of this life, and when he can centre his affections on father and mother, on houses and lands. Standing within this sphere, he can, if ever, be without God and not be miserable. For he can busy his thoughts, and exert his faculties, and send forth his affections, and thus find occupation away from his Creator. And hence it is, that there is so much of sinful pleasure in this life, while there is none of it in the next. In this material world a man can make himself his own end of living, and not be constantly wretched. But in the spiritual world where God and duty must be the principal subjects of reflection, no man can be supremely selfish without being supremely miserable. Take therefore your sinful enjoyment in this life—ye who hanker after this kind of pleasure—for it is impossible to find any of it in the next life. "Rejoice, O young man, in the days of thy youth, and let thy heart cheer thee in the days of thy youth, and walk in the ways of thine heart, and in the sight of thine eyes: but know thou that for all these things God will bring thee into judgment."

Still, even this life, with all its sinful enjoyment, is not a blessed life for a worldly man. There is a heaven-wide difference between earthly pleasure and blessedness. The worldling sees dark days and sad hours, when he is compelled to say, even in the midst of all that this life gives him: "I am not a blessed being; I am not peaceful and free from apprehension; I am not right with God. And I know that I never shall be, in this line of life. Heaven is impossible for me, until I love God more than I

love myself and the world." All serious reflection tends
to destroy the happiness of such a man. He cannot commune an instant with his own heart, without beginning to
feel wretched. Thinking makes him miserable. He has
fastened his affections, which can really find no rest but in
an infinite good, upon gold, honor, and pleasure. But he
knows in his reflecting moments that his gold will perish,
and if it did not, that he must ultimately grow weary of
it. He knows that worldly honor and sensual enjoyment
will flee away from his dying bed; and that even if they
did not, they could be no solace to him in that awful crisis
of the soul. He knows in these honest and truthful hours
that the *chief* good is not his, because he has not made
God his strength and portion. And although, because of
his alienation from God and servile fear of him, and his
dislike of the warfare with selfishness and sin which the
gospel requires, he may rush away even further than ever
from God, and cling with yet more intensity to the objects
of this life, he is nevertheless attended with an obscure
feeling that all is not well with his soul. That old and
solemn question : "Is it well with thy soul ? " every now
and then peals through him, and makes him anxious. But
what kind of pleasure is that which can thus be interrupted ? How can you call a being blessed who is standing
upon such a slippery place ? A man needs to feel not only
happy, but *safely* happy—happy upon solid and immov-
able grounds—in order to be truly happy. Probably
Dives himself sometimes had a dim intimation of the
misery that was to burst upon him when he should stand
before God. Probably every worldly man hears these
words said to him occasionally from the chambers of his
conscience : " You are comparatively at ease now, but this
ease cannot be permanent. You know, or may know, that
you will have no source of peace in death and the judg-

ment. Your portion is not in God, and therefore you cannot rest upon him when flesh and heart fail."

But there are other objects in this world in which man endeavors to find strength and happiness, besides gold and honor and sensual pleasure. He seeks it in the delights of home, and in the charities and sympathies of social life. And we grant that the enjoyment which these bestow upon him is great. But it is not the greatest, and it is not *eternal*. Christ has said: "He that loveth father and mother, son or daughter, more than me, is not worthy of me, and cannot be my disciple." This affirmation of our Saviour has its ground in the nature of the human spirit, and its relation to God. However much we may love our kindred and friends, they cannot take the place of God; they cannot be an object of supreme affection. However much, in our idolatrous fondness, we may try to make them our hope and portion, we shall discover sooner or later that they cannot meet the higher and eternal demands of our complex being—that they cannot satisfy that immortal part which God intended should find its strength and blessedness in him alone. There are capabilities of worship and adoration and heavenly service given us by creation, and they ought to be awakened, renovated, set in action, and met by their appropriate object—God only wise, God over all blessed forever. Conscience, moreover, the law of our moral existence, is solemn in its command: "Thou shalt love the Lord thy God with all thy heart, and all thy might." It forbids us to live solely and absorbingly in the lower sphere of social relations, and bids us to soar above and expend our choicest affection upon the Father of spirits—the Infinite One whose we are, and whom we are bound to serve. The original constitution of our souls interferes with the attempt to be happy in the social and domestic circles without God; and although conscience cannot conquer our folly and our sin, it can and does disquiet and harass our minds.

But even if man could be perfectly happy in the strength and solace springing from his domestic and social relations, he would be so but for a short time. The enjoyment coming from them is continually fluctuating. The lapse of years produces great modifications of the family, even here upon earth. The child grows up to manhood, and the parent passes into old age. The child becomes a parent himself, and is engrossed in new relations and cares; while the parent dies more and more to earthly ties, and when his spirit returns to God who gave it he is done with earth and all its interests. In the kingdom of God they neither marry nor are given in marriage, but are as the angels of God. These temporal earthly relationships of father and son, wife and child, cannot, therefore, be relied upon as the *everlasting* foundation of trust and joy. They are merely preparatory to the higher relationships which we must sustain in a future life, or be miserable.

Furthermore, even in this life they are continually breaking up. Death comes. Friend after friend is continually departing, and the grief at the loss is as poignant as the joy in the possession. The happiness that is dependent upon even a true and tried friend is transient and uncertain. It lasts not long, for the grave removes him from our eyes, and we are left to mourn. The world that was bright because he was in it, has grown dark because he has left it. We turn away in brokenness of heart, and feel in these sad moments, if at no other time, that we need a more abiding Friend; that we need that friendship of God by which earthly friendships are consecrated and ennobled; that we need him for the strength of our heart when he putteth lover and friend far from us. And as we leave the lesser circle of kindred and friends, and look forth into that of society around us, we find that there is continual change. If our happiness is entirely dependent upon the world around us, and we have made its interests and pursuits our main support, we discover that the world itself has no permanency. One generation goes and another comes. Where is the generation that crowded these streets, transacting business and absorbed in earthly pursuits, fifty years ago? All that whirl is hushed in death; and fifty years hence, the same inquiry will be put respecting the noise and bustle that now roars and chokes in these avenues of business and pleasure. Man and man's life is the shadow of a shadow. Everything in him and about him is in a perpetual flux toward eternity, and the immediate presence of God. He cannot, if he would, stop the course of that upon which he has made his happiness to depend, but is hurried along into a mode of existence where there is no change, and but one engrossing Object, even God himself. Can strength, peaceful strength, be predicated of us, then, if we have no standing-place but that which is every instant gliding like quicksand from under our feet? Can true happiness be affirmed of our souls, if their supreme good is in that which is leaving us every day, and which we shall leave entirely behind us when we die?

We have thus seen that it cannot be said : "Blessed is the man whose strength is in wealth, or in reputation, or in pleasure, or in kindred and friends, or in the interests and pursuits of social and civil life." That it can be said of man even in this transient and sorrowful life, and amidst these unsatisfying and fleeting relationships: " Blessed is the man whose strength is in God," needs but little proof. " Thou wilt keep him in perfect peace whose soul is stayed on Thee," is the affirmation of one who knew by his own personal experience. " Great peace have all they that love thy law," says one who tried it for himself. He whose supreme strength is in God will be happy in any relation that he sustains, and in any world in which God may please to put him. He who is strong in the Lord, and has him for his portion, cannot be made miserable. If he should be sent on an errand to the spirits in hell, he would go fearlessly, and there would be nothing in that world of woe that could disturb his holy and affectionate trust in God. A man whose heart is fixed, trusting in the Lord, is absolutely independent of the whole creation. His wealth may take wings and fly away; but the cheering presence of his Maker and Saviour is in his heart still. Worldly good he may, or may not have; but the approbation of God destroys all regard for it, and all sense for it, even as the sunlight by its bright effulgence annihilates moonlight and starlight. He may be very happy in his domestic and social relations; but this happiness will have its deeper foundation and source in God. It will not be a forbidden enjoyment that never goes beyond the earthly objects of his affection, and centres solely and supremely in the wife or the child. As a father or a son, as a neighbor or a citizen, he will look up to his Heavenly Father—to his Father in Christ, "of whom the whole family on earth and heaven is named"—as the blessed ground of all these relationships, and in whose glory they should all be merged. Therefore, amidst all change which is incident to them, he will be unmoved, because God is immutable; he will be strong as they reveal their weakness and perishing nature, because his primal strength is in God; and he will be blessed as the sources of his earthly enjoyment fail, because God is his chief good.

It is because man's hope and strength are not in God, that his enjoyment of created good is so unsatisfactory and uncertain. "Godliness hath the promise of the life that

now is, as well as that which is to come;" and if all men
were godly, the earth would be fairer around them, and
more full of promise and of hope. The elder Edwards
thus describes the change which came over the visible
material world after his conversion, and as his sense of
divine things increased; "The appearance of everything
was altered; there seemed to be, as it were, a calm sweet
cast, or appearance of divine glory in almost everything.
God's excellency, his wisdom, his purity and love, seemed
to appear in everything; in the sun, and moon, and stars;
in the clouds and blue sky; in the grass, flowers, trees;
in the water, and all nature; which used greatly to fix my
mind. I often used to sit and view the moon for continuance; and in the day, spent much time in viewing the
clouds and sky, to behold the sweet glory of God in these
things; in the meantime singing forth with low voice, my
contemplations of the Creator and Redeemer. And scarce
anything among all the works of nature was so sweet to
me as thunder and lightning; formerly nothing had been
so terrible to me. Before, I used to be uncommonly terri-
fied with thunder, and to be struck with terror when I saw
a thunder-storm rising; but now, on the contrary, it re-
joiced me. I felt God, so to speak, at the first appearance
of a thunder-storm; and used to take the opportunity, at
such times, to fix myself in order to view the clouds, and
see the lightning play, and hear the majestic and awful
voice of God's thunder, which oftentimes was exceedingly
entertaining, leading me to sweet contemplations of my
great and glorious God." [1]

If the supreme and positive love of God pervaded and
gave color to our love of his creatures, the creation would
be a source of more heartfelt pleasure than it now is. We

---

[1] Life of Edwards. Works, I. p. 20.

should then cherish a subordinate and proper affection for earth, and while it brought us the enjoyment that pertains to the lower sphere of the created and the finite, it would be still more valuable as the means of introducing our souls into the presence and enjoyment of God. Worldly pleasure if experienced too keenly and too long renders the heart intensely selfish. Beware of long-continued and uninterrupted earthly happiness. There is no heart so callous, so flinty, so utterly impenetrable to holy impressions, as that of a man of pleasure. Said Burns, who knew:

> " I waive the quantum of the sin,
> The hazard of concealing ;
> But O, it hardens all within,
> And petrifies the feeling."

Merely earthly enjoyment, moreover, sates and disgusts the rational mind of man. For this, notwithstanding its apostasy, has at times a dim intimation that there is, somewhere and somehow, a higher enjoyment and a genuine joy that never cloys, but which, as it runs through the fibres of the soul, carries with it an invigorating and appetizing virtue that produces a hunger and thirst after still more enrapturing influxes. Man enters with too much hilarity, and too absorbing a passion, into the enjoyment of this life, unless he is tempered and tranquillized by a superior affection for an Infinite Being. If without strength and hope in God as his ultimate and highest good, he is often filled with a happiness that is too tumultuous and stormy to be enduring. A storm cannot continue long, either in the world of matter or of mind. Hence, in these hours of excited fermenting revelry, there is often a faint intimation given to the soul, like the premonitory tremor before the earthquake, that its enjoyment is short-lived. The deeper part of the man, the solemn conscience, sends off tidings that it has no participation in this pleasure ; that, on the contrary, moral indignation and moral fear are the emotions down below, whatever may be the hilarity on the surface. But if, while that part of our nature which was made to take pleasure in temporal things is experiencing it, that other portion of our nature whose appropriate object is God is also having its wants met in Him, there is a tranquil and rational enjoyment diffused through the whole man. If the celestial world sends down its radiance into the terrestrial, there is everywhere a serene and pleasant light. Writers upon physical geography tell us that the presence of a mountain renders the atmosphere cooler in summer, and warmer in winter. A large mass of matter equalizes the temperature. In like manner, if in the horizon and atmosphere of our souls there is the presence of the Infinite God, there will be serenity, and no violent changes. In the summer of prosperity, the soul will be soberly joyful; in the winter of adversity, the soul will be serenely content. For the presence of the Eternal will be the main element of happiness in each instance; and He is always present and always the same. Though, therefore, in the lower region of earthly objects and relations there be darkness, and storm, and tempest, in the higher region of spiritual objects and heavenly affections there is a still air, and the light of the heaven of heavens is shining in its strong effulgence. And even when the clouds gather thick and black in the horizon of our mortal life, and there is mourning because its objects are passing away, this lucid light of heaven will steal into the black mass, and drive out the blackness, and drench these clouds with its radiance, and suffuse all along the horizon with the colors of the skies.

II. We have thus considered man as belonging to time, and found that he is miserable if his strength and hope are in the creature, and that he is blessed if his strength and hope are in God. Let us now, in the second place, contemplate man as belonging to *eternity* and sustaining relations to the invisible world, and see that the same assertion holds true, and commends itself with a yet deeper emphasis to our reflections.

Although the hour of death is, strictly speaking, a part of time, yet it is so closely joined to eternity that it may practically be considered as belonging to it. Observation proves that there are few conversions at the eleventh hour; and we may assume, as a general fact, that as a man is when lying upon his death-bed, so will he be forever and ever. For although it is possible, even at this late hour, to have the relation of the soul towards God changed from that of the rebel to that of the child, the possibility rarely becomes a reality. In that solemn hour, even if there be not the stupor of disease, but the soul is stung with remorse, and the awful idea of eternity throws a horror of great darkness over the whole inner man, it is extremely difficult to collect the mental powers, and with a clear eye look at sin, and with a sincere heart repent of it, and with an energetic faith trust in Christ's blood. If the man has gone through life, in spite of all the obstacles which a merciful God throws in his path to perdition, and in opposition to the repeated monitions of conscience and convictions by the Holy Spirit, without experiencing that change which alone fits him for an entrance into the kingdom of God, there is small hope that this great change will be wrought amidst the weakness and languor of disease, or the perturbation and despair of the drowzed soul which has only half awaked to know its real condition and the brink where it stands. We may therefore affirm, generally, that as a man is when overtaken by his last sickness, so will he be forevermore. We may therefore affirm, that practically the hour of death is for man a part of the eternal state. Time and eternity here blend in the experience and destiny of the soul.

How unblest, then, is a man, if in this last hour of time which is also the first hour of eternity, his strength is not in God. How wretched is he, if in these first moments of his final state, the farm, or the merchandise, or the book, or the father, or the child, or the wife, or the pleasures of social life, or the interests of civil life, are his only portion and support. He has enjoyed, it may be, much that springs from these temporal relations, and life in the main has gone well with him. Yet, as from the vantage-ground of this death-bed he looks back upon life, he sees as he could not while amidst its excitement and fascination, that after all it has been a "fitful fever," and that he is not to "sleep well" after it. He perceives with a vividness and certainty that he never felt before, that he has been a sinful man because in relation to God he has been a supremely selfish and idolatrous man. And now he feels that he is a lost man, because his strength is not in God, in the slightest degree. He finds that he has no filial love for his Maker. In the Scripture phrase, he is "alienated" from God, and "without" God, both in this world and in the next. He finds that the account between himself and his Maker is closed, and that God is entering into judgment with him, and bidding him look for his portion and his strength where he has sought it all the days of his sinful life. He hears those solemn and righteous words which are addressed only to those who have despised and rejected the offer of mercy: "Because I have called and ye refused; I have stretched out my hand, and no man regarded; but ye have set at nought all my counsel, and would none of my reproof; I also will laugh at your calamity; I will mock when your fear cometh. Then shall they call upon me, but I will not answer; they shall seek me early, but they shall not find me."[1] O my fellow man, if in your dying hour you cannot look up to God, and say : "Thou art the strength of my heart, and my portion forever," you are an unblest creature, and there is nothing but misery for you in eternity. Your spirit when it leaves the body will begin an everlasting wandering away from God. It will want to wander, and hide from his sight. It does not love him here and now, and therefore cannot abide his presence there and then. How full of wretchedness must such a spirit be when it enters the other world, where there is but one Object for any creature to lean upon, and yet that Object in relation to it is one of dislike, distaste, antipathy, and hostility. It must, therefore, turn in upon its own emptiness and guilt, because it has not made Christ its refuge, and God its strength.

The impenitent death-bed is a dark scene, and the impenitent eternity is the blackness of darkness. Let us turn from it to the believer's death-bed, which is a bright scene, and to the believer's eternity which is light inacessible and full of glory. When the soul which has really made God its strength is summoned to leave the body, and enter into the endless life, it is strong—stronger than ever; and happy—happier than ever. It is strong ; for it does not rest upon anything that perishes, and the everlasting arms are beneath. Though the fainting flesh and heart fail, yet God is the strength of the heart. The soul knows that it is departing from the objects amidst which it has had its existence, but not from the one great Being in whom it has lived somewhat holily and tranquilly on earth, and will now continue to live forever. Earthly relationships are disappearing, and earthly bands are breaking away from it, but the relationship of a child of God will ever belong to it, and the hopes and aspirations of this relation which it has been feebly but faithfully cherishing in an imperfect state are to gather force and intensity forever. Such a soul does not feel that its strength is waning, but that it is waxing stronger and mightier; and so with tranquillity, perhaps with triumph—"a mortal paleness on the brow, a glory in the soul"—it goes into the presence of God. As in the hour of death, we have seen that the kindling flashes of hell appear in the soul of the unpardoned, so the first streaks and rays of celestial glory stream through the penitent soul while it is leaving the body. It has a keener sense of holy enjoyment, calmer peace pervades it, and the endless heaven is begun. It feels, in the phrase of Leighton, that "the Eternal is now the internal," that the glorious God is its strength and portion, and that the infinite heart of God is its home. It has discovered "the beauty and excellency of forgiveness—as it is with God, as it is in his gracious heart, in his eternal purpose, in the blood of Christ, and in the promise of the gospel." It has no fear, and no wants unsupplied. With calmness, or with rapture, it commends itself into the hands of its God and Redeemer, and "flights of angels sing it to its rest" in the bosom of the Father.

To Christian believers, this subject is full of salutary instruction. If God really is our strength, we should not look with fear and anxiety into eternity, and we should not be unhappy here in time. It urges us, therefore, to a careful examination that we may know where our strength actually lies. And we need not seek long for this knowledge. The current of our thoughts and affections, if God is our portion, will become daily a stronger flood. We shall live as strangers and pilgrims, looking for a better country. Our hearts will not rest in houses, or lands, or honor, or friends, as their firmest resting-place, but in the living God. We shall die daily to the power of earthly things, and live unto Christ. We shall be gradually weaned from earth, and with more earnest desires look for heaven. We shall enjoy this life with chastened and sober pleasure, but our transport and exultation will be awakened by the "power of an endless life," by the love, and glory of God.

SERMON VII.

THE GLORIFICATION OF GOD.

ISAIAH xlii. 8.—" I am the LORD; that is my name: and my glory
will I not give to another, neither my praise to graven images."

THE name of a thing, provided it is a true and adequate
one, denotes the essential nature of that thing. When a
chemist has discovered a new substance, he is, of course,
compelled to invent a new name for it; and he seeks a
term that will indicate its distinctive properties. When,
for instance, that gas which illuminates our streets and
dwellings was first discovered, it was supposed to be the
constituent matter of heat, and the name phlogiston was
given to it—a name that signifies inflammability. But
when Cavendish afterwards more carefully analyzed its
nature and properties, and discovered that it enters very
largely into the production of water, it received the name
of hydrogen. In each of these instances the term was intended to denote the intrinsic nature and properties of the
thing. We are informed, in the second chapter of Genesis,
that when the Lord God had formed every beast of the
field, and every fowl of the air, " He brought them unto
Adam to see what he would call them; and whatsoever
Adam called every living creature, that was the name
thereof. And Adam gave names to all cattle, and to the
fowl of the air, and to every beast of the field." This was

before the apostasy of man, when the human mind possessed an intuition of both human and divine things that was superior to its subsequent knowledge; and hence those original denominations which Adam gave to the objects of nature were expressive of their interior and essential characteristics. Aristotle began the investigation of natural history, and his successors, for two thousand years, have diligently followed up the line of investigation; but that ethereal vision of the unfallen and sinless creature who had just come from the plastic hand of the Creator, and who possessed the unmutilated and perfect image of the Deity, penetrated further into the arcana of nature than have the toilsome investigations of his dim-eyed posterity. That nomenclature which Adam originated at the express command of God, and which the pen of inspiration has recorded as a fact, though it has not specified it in detail, must have been pertinent and exhaustive. The names were the things, the natures, themselves.[1]

God also has a name—not given to him by Adam, or any finite creature, but self-uttered, and self-imposed. When Moses, in Mount Horeb, after the vision of the flaming bush, said unto God : "Behold, when I come unto the children of Israel, and shall say unto them, the God of your fathers hath sent me unto you; and they shall say unto me, What is his name ? what shall I say unto them ?" the reply of God was : "I AM THAT I AM: and thus shalt thou say unto the children of Israel, I AM hath sent me unto you." The denomination which God prefers for himself, the name which he chooses before all others as indicative of his nature, is I AM, or its equivalent, Jehovah. Whenever the word Jehovah is employed in the Old Tes-

---

[1] Plato (Cratylus, 390) represents Socrates as saying that "the right imposition of names is no easy matter, and belongs not to any and everybody, but only to him who has an insight into the nature of things."

tament as the proper name of God, it announces the same doctrine of his necessary existence that was taught to Moses when he was commanded to say to his people that I AM had sent him unto them. The English name for the Deity, our word God, indicates that he is *good*—making prominent a moral quality. The Greek and Latin world employed a term (θεòς, deus) that lays emphasis upon that characteristic of the Deity whereby he *orders* and *governs* the universe.[1] According to the Greek and Roman conception, God is the imperial Being who arranges and rules. But the Hebrew, divinely instructed upon this subject, chose a term which refers not to any particular attribute or quality, but to the very being and essence of God, and teaches the world that God *must* be—that he not only exists, but cannot logically be conceived of as non-existent.[2]

This idea comes up in the text. " I am Jehovah "—for so it stands in the original Hebrew—" that is my name : and my glory will I not give to another, neither my praise to graven images." Here the Divine Being challenges glory to himself upon the ground of his very nature and being. He presents an exclusive claim to be supremely honored, because of his independent, and underived, and necessary existence. If, like creatures, he had once begun to exist, or if, like creatures, he could be conceived of as going out of existence, the foundation of such a claim would fall away, and he would have no more reason to arrogate supreme honor to himself than the angel Gabriel, or than the weakest man upon earth. But before the mountains were brought forth, or ever he had formed the earth and the world, even from everlasting to everlasting,

---

[1] This etymology is given by Herodotus, II. 52.
[2] A being respecting whom there would be no absurdity in saying that once he did not exist, or that he will cease to exist, is not infinite, but finite. And the finite is not God.

he is Jehovah—the I AM—and therefore he of right summons the whole universe into his temple, and demands from them the ascription of blessing, and glory, and wisdom, and thanksgiving, and honor, and power, and might, forever and ever.

The text, then, leads us to raise the question : What is it to glorify God? And the answer to it should certainly have interest for us, not only upon those general grounds which concern all men, but because we hold a creed which opens with the affirmation, that it "is man's chief end to glorify God, and enjoy him forever."

I. In the first place, it is implied in glorifying God, that we *think* of him, and *recognize* his existence. "The duty required in the first commandment," says the Larger Catechism (104), "is to worship and glorify God, by thinking, meditating upon, and remembering him."

No higher dishonor can be done to any being, than to forget and ignore him. In common life, if a man wishes to express the highest degree of contempt for a fellow-creature, he says : "I never think of him ; I do not recognize his existence." But this is the habitual and common attitude of man's mind toward the Everlasting God. This Great Being who exists of necessity, and who is the Creator and Preserver of all other beings, is ignored[1] by the world at large. God is not in their thoughts, and practically he is reduced to nonentity. For so long as we do not think of an object or a being, so long as we do not recognize its existence, it possesses none for our minds. Before Columbus discovered America, it could

---

[1] This word does not denote absolute ignorance, but the neglect to use knowledge. "If there be any nations that worship not God, they consist of brute and irrational barbarians who may be supposed rather to *ignore* the being of God, than to deny it." Boyle, quoted by Richardson *in voce*.

not be an object of reflection for the people of Europe and Asia, and therefore, in relation to the Old World, America had no existence. It had existence for God, and for higher intelligences. The sons of God knew of it, and shouted for joy over it as a part of that glorious world which rounded to their view upon the morning of creation. But until the bold Genoese navigator revealed it to the ken, to the thought, of Europe, it was a nonentity for Europe. The whole continent, with its vast mountain-ranges, and great rivers, and boundless plains, had scarcely the substance of a dream for the people of the Eastern world.

And just so is it in respect to the existence of God. He verily is, and fills immensity with his presence ; but how few of the children of men are constantly and habitually aware of it. How few of them are busied with thinking about him. How few of them make him real to their minds by meditating upon his being and attributes. Can you not recall some day in which you did not once think of your Creator and Judge ; in which, therefore, you wholly ignored his existence ; in which, to all intents and purposes, he was a nonentity ? So far as you could do it, you, on that day, annihilated the Deity. The same spirit, if united with the adequate power, would not only have dethroned God, but would have exterminated him.

And it does not relieve the matter to say that this is mere passive forgetfulness, and that there is no deliberate effort to do dishonor to God. This passive forgetfulness itself is the highest kind of indignity ; and is so represented in the Scriptures. " The wicked shall be turned into hell, and all the nations that *forget* God. Now consider this, ye that *forget* God, lest I tear you in pieces, and there be none to deliver." This is fearful language, and therefore the sin against which it is levelled must be great. And when we come to examine it we perceive that it is. For this unthinking forgetfulness of the greatest and most glorious Being in the universe betokens an utter unconcern towards him. It implies an apathy so deep, and so uniform, that the being and attributes of God make no kind of impression. When a proud nobleman passes by a peasant without bestowing a thought upon him, without noticing his presence in the least, we do not attribute this to any deliberate intention, any direct effort, to put an indignity upon an inferior. It is the unconscious dishonor, the passive forgetfulness, the silent contempt, which arises from an utter indifference and apathy towards the person. And such is the kind of indignity of which man is guilty in not thinking of God ; in forgetting that there is any such being.

Now, whoever would glorify God must begin by reversing all this. God must be in all his thoughts. He must recognize, habitually and spontaneously, the existence of his Creator and Judge. God must become as real to him as the sun in the heavens. The idea of the Deity must swallow up all other ideas, and dominate over them. Wherever he goes, the thought must be ever present to his mind : " Thou God seest me." Instead of this spontaneous forgetfulness, there must be a spontaneous remembrance of him. God must constantly impress himself upon the mind. Some of the early Christian fathers were fond of speaking of the Deity as " impinging " himself upon the human soul—as if he were some great body or mass that loomed up, and forced himself down upon the attention and notice of men. And such must be the relation between man and God, before God can be glorified. The first step towards the greatest of human duties, the first step towards the chief end of man, cannot be taken, until the creature begins to think habitually of God, and to recognize his eternal power and godhead. No man has made even a beginning in religion, until he has said, reverently, and feeling the truth of what he says : "Thou art Jehovah, the Great I AM ; that is thy name and thy nature ; and thy glory thou wilt not give to another, neither thy praise to graven images."

II. In the second place, it is implied in glorifying God, that we think of him as the *first cause* and *last end* of all things.

Here again, as in the preceding instance, we can arrive at the truth by the way of contrast ; by considering what is the common course of man's thought and feeling. Man naturally thinks of himself as the chief cause, and the final end. The charge which the apostle Paul makes against the apostate world is, that they worship and serve the creature more than the Creator. And the particular creature which every sinful man worships and serves more than the Creator, is *himself*. It is true that men pay regard to their fellow-men, and in a certain degree worship and serve them. But in every such instance it will be found, upon examination, that the worship and the service is only a means to an end. It is never an end. A man, for example, flatters, and perhaps even fawns upon a fellow-creature who is high in station, or in power, or in wealth. But it is only in order to derive some personal advantage thereby. The worship and service do not ultimately terminate upon the king or the millionaire, but upon the worshipper ; upon the devotee himself. It is not for anything that intrinsically belongs to the man of power, or the man of wealth, that the honor is accorded to him. Could the same personal advantage be secured by showing dishonor, as by showing honor, the selfish sinful heart of man would " whistle " both nobles and kings "down the wind." The ultimate idol is in every instance the important ego, the dear self.

It is surprising to see, and no man sees it until he endeavors to get rid of the evil, how intensely the soul of man revolves upon itself, and how difficult it is to desert itself and revolve around another. You, for example, give a sum of money to a poor and suffering family. The external act—what the schoolman would denominate the "matter" of the act—is good. And your fellow-men, who can see only the outward appearance, praise you as an excellent person. But let us look into the heart, and see if there really be the moral excellence, the true holiness before God, that is supposed. When the gift had been bestowed, did you not begin to congratulate yourself upon what you had done? Did not the left hand begin to know what the right hand had been doing? In other words, did not pride and self-worship begin to fill the heart, and was not the act, so far as the inward nature of it—what the same schoolman would call the "form" of it—is concerned, an egotistical one? Did you not worship and serve the creature more than the Creator, in this act—which yet was one of the best that you ever performed? Was there not a "sin" in this "holy thing?" Did not the "dead fly" spoil the "apothecaries' ointment?" For if the inward disposition had corresponded entirely to the outward act, in this transaction; if the act were a really holy one; it would have been done to the glory of God, and there would not have been a particle of self-worship in your experience. You would not have had the least proud thought of self in the affair, but would have humbly thought only of God. After giving the gift, you would have said as David did in reference to the gift which he and the people of Israel had made to God in the building of the temple: "But who am I, and what is my people, that we should be able to offer so willingly, after this sort? for all things come of thee, and of thine own have we given thee." You would have acknowledged that it is God who gives both the willingness to give, and the means of giving ; that He is both the first cause and the last end of all things. But, by the supposition, you did neither. You gave the sum of money as something which your intellect and hands had originated, and you took the merit of the gift to yourself. You worshipped and served the creature more than the Creator.

This, we affirm, is the natural, spontaneous bent of the human heart. The Christian confesses it, and mourns over the relics of it in himself, and longs for the time when his mixed experience shall end, and all these lingering remnants of idolatry shall be cleansed away, and he shall lose himself in the glory of God. And we are not afraid to submit the matter to the testimony and judgment of the natural man himself. No candid person will say that he naturally and spontaneously worships and serves his Creator more than he does the creature—more than he does himself. No truthful man will deny that his first thought is for himself, and his after-thought is for his neighbor and his Maker. And it is the very spontaneousness and unconsciousness of the selfishness that proves its depth and inveteracy. If a man were obliged to summon up his reflections and resolutions, every time that he worshipped and served the creature more than the Creator; if it were such a difficult matter for him to be selfish and proud, that he must be continually thinking about it, and contriving how he could compass it; if it cost him as much thought and effort to glorify himself as it does to glorify God, this would prove that the egotism is not so deep-rooted and total. But what a man is spontaneously and unconsciously, that he is in the very roots of his being; that he is intensely and entirely. This very naturalness and uniformity with which every unregenerate man makes himself his own centre, and terminates everything there, proves that this disposition is not on the surface, but is " the hidden man of the heart."

Now, whoever would glorify God must reverse all this. In the first place, he must think of and recognize God as the first cause of all things. If he possess a strong intellect, or a cultivated taste, instead of attributing them to his own diligence in self-discipline and self-cultivation, he must trace them back to the Author of his intellectual constitution, who not only gave him all his original endowments, but has enabled him to be diligent in the use and discipline of them. If he possess great wealth, instead of saying in his heart: " My hand and brain have gotten me this," he should acknowledge the Providence that has favored his plans and enterprises, and without which his enterprises, like those of many men around him, would have gone awry, and utterly failed. In brief, whatever be the earthly good which any one holds in his possession, its ultimate origin and authorship must be carried back to the First Cause of all things. Every man upon earth should continually say to himself, in the language of St. Paul, "What hast thou that thou didst not receive? Now if thou didst receive it, why dost thou glory as if thou hadst not received it?"

And this, too, must become the natural and easy action of the mind and heart, in order perfectly to glorify God. It is a poor and lame service that we render to the Most High, when we do it by an after-thought. If, for instance, when I have performed some action, or made some acquisition that is creditable, my first thought is a proud one, and my first feeling is that of self-gratulation; no second thought, no after-feeling, that has reference to God can be a high and perfect homage. The very first thought, the very first emotion, should have terminated upon Him; and only the second thought, the secondary feeling, should have referred to myself—if, indeed, there should have been any such reference at all. If man were as holy as he was by creation; if he stood in his original unfallen relation; the very firstlings of his mind and heart would be offered to his Maker. But as matters now stand, his first instinctive reference is always to his own power, and his own agency. And even when, as in the instance of the Christian, there is an endeavor to remedy the evil, to correct the error; when after the proud feeling of self has arisen, the believer treads it down, and mourns over it, and endeavors to acknowledge God as the first cause and author; how imperfect and unworthy is the homage that is rendered. It is true that our merciful and condescending God does not spurn such a service away, but sprinkles it with the blood of Christ, and accepts it as a sweet-smelling savor in Him; but this does not alter the fact that this is not the absolute and perfect homage and honor which is due from a creature. Suppose that the seraphim and cherubim should be compelled to rectify their service; suppose that for an instant they should lose sight of the transcending glory and excellence of the Creator, and their regards should drop down and terminate upon themselves as the authors and causes of their own excellences and endowments; what a " coming short " of the glory of God this would be! No, it is the directness and immediateness of the heavenly service that makes it a perfect one. Not even the thought of worshipping and serving themselves enters into the mind of those pure and holy spirits who live in the blaze, the unutterable light of God.

Again, it is implied in glorifying God, that we recognize him as the last end of all things. Every being and thing must have a final end—a terminus. The mineral kingdom is made for the vegetable kingdom; the vegetable kingdom is made for the animal kingdom; the animal kingdom is made for man; and all of them together are made for God. Go through all the ranges of creation, from the molecule of matter to the seraphim, and if you ask for the final purpose of its creation, the reply is, the glory of the Maker. And this is reasonable. For God is the greatest and most important, if we may use the word in such a connection, of all beings. That which justifies man in putting the dumb animals to his own uses, is the fact that he is a grander creature than they are. That which makes the inanimate world subservient to the animate— that which subsidizes the elements of earth, air, and water, and makes them tributary to the nourishment and growth of the beast and the bird—is the fact that the beast and the bird are of a higher order of existence than earth, air, and water. It was because man was the noblest, the most important, of all the creatures that God placed upon this planet, that he subordinated them all to him, and said to him in the original patent by which he deeded the globe to him: "Behold I have given you every herb bearing seed; have dominion over the fish of the sea, and over the fowl of the air, and over every living thing that moveth upon the earth."

Now, this principle holds good of the relation between the whole creation and its Creator. He is a higher and greater being than the whole created universe. The mass of his being, so to speak, outweighs all other masses. He never has created, he never can create, anything equal to himself in infinity and in glory. And therefore it is that he is the final end, the cause of causes, the absolute terminus where all the sweep and movement of creation must come to a rest. It is an objection of the skeptic, that this perpetual assertion in the Scriptures that God is the chief end of creation, and this perpetual demand that the creature glorify him, is only a species of infinite egotism; that in making the whole unlimited universe subservient to him and his purposes, the Deity is only exhibiting selfishness upon an immense scale. But this objection overlooks the fact that God is an infinitely greater and higher Being than any or all of his creatures; and that from the very nature of the case the less must be subordinated to the greater. Is it egotism, when man employs in his service his ox or his ass? Is it selfishness, when the rose or the lily takes up into its own fabric and tissue the inanimate qualities of matter, and converts the dull and colorless elements of the clod into hues and odors, into beauty and bloom? There would be egotism in the procedure, if man were of no higher grade of existence than the ox or the ass. There would be selfishness, if the rose and the lily were upon the same level with the inanimate elements of matter. But the greater dignity in each instance justifies the use and the subordination. And so it is, only in an infinitely greater degree, in the case when the whole creation is subordinated and made to serve and glorify the Creator. The distance between man and his ox, between the lily and the particle of moisture which it imbibes, is appreciable. It is not infinite. But the distance between God and the highest of his archangels is beyond computation. He chargeth his angels with folly. And therefore upon the principle that the less must serve the greater, the lower must be subordinate to the higher, it is right and rational that " every creature which is in heaven, and on the earth, and under the earth, and such as are in the sea, and all that are in them, should say, Blessing, and honor, and glory, and power, be unto Him that sitteth upon the throne, and unto the Lamb, forever and ever."

All this a man is to think of and to acknowledge, if he would glorify God. This must be his spontaneous habit of mind, as natural and easy to him as his present selfishness and pride, before he can mingle in that celestial company who stand on the sea of glass, and have the harps of God, and sing the song saying, "Great and marvellous are thy works, Lord God Almighty: just and true are thy ways, thou King of Saints."

1. In the light of this doctrine, as thus far expounded, we see, in the first place, the need of the *regeneration* of the human soul. It is difficult to convince the natural man of the necessity of such a radical change as the Biblical theory of the new birth, and the constant reiterations of the pulpit imply. Testing himself by the statutes of common morality, he does not see the need of such an entire revolution within him. But how stands the case, in the light of the truth which we have been discussing? Is it true that every human creature ought to sustain such an adoring attitude towards God as has been described? that he ought habitually to think of him, and acknowledge him as the first cause and last end of all things, and honor him as such? Is it true that it is man's chief end to glorify God, and that no man can be released from the obligation to attain the chief end of his existence? If so, then is there not absolute need of being "born of water and the Spirit?" Look into the existing character and disposition and see how strongly and totally everything terminates upon self; how even religion is tinged with subtle and selfish references, and how destitute the human heart is of all spontaneous and outgushing desires to exalt and honor the Creator; and say if there is not perishing need of a new heart and a right spirit. All spiritual excellence resolves itself, ultimately, into a desire to render unto God the glory due unto his name—into a desire to worship.

Religion is worship; and no creature, be he man or angel, who is destitute of a worshipping disposition, is religious. Morality, or the practice of virtue, is only the shell of religion. Religion itself, in its pure, simple nature, is adoration—the revering praise of God. The shell is good and needful in its own place; but it can never be a substitute for the living kernel and germ. It may protect it, and shield it, and adorn it; but it can never take its place. Try yourself, then, by this test; search and see what is the inclination and tendency of your heart in this particular, and we will leave it for you to say whether the human heart does or does not need the great change of the new birth; whether any man can see the kingdom of God without it; whether any man is fit to enter the upper temple with no outgushing homage, adoration, and worship in his soul.

2. In the second place, we see in the light of this subject why the individual Christian is *imperfectly blest* of God. His service is imperfect. There is much worship of self in connection with his worship of God. How many of our prayers are vitiated by unbelief; but unbelief is a species of dishonor to God. It is a distrust of his power and his promise. How many of our feelings, even our religious feelings, are tinctured with selfishness; but just so far as self enters, God is expelled. The Christian experience is a mixed one. It lacks the purity, and simplicity, and godly sincerity which admit but one object, and that is the Blessed God; but one absorbing desire and purpose, and that is to glorify him. It is impossible, therefore, in this condition of the soul, that we should experience the perfection of religious joy. "I am Jehovah," saith God; "that is my name, and my glory will I not give to another." God will not share homage and honor with any creature; and therefore it is, that when he sees

one of his children still lingering about self, like Lot's wife about Sodom—still anxious about his own worldly interests and his own worldly honor—he does not communicate the entire fulness of his blessing upon him. He hides his countenance from him; he keeps back many of the joys of his salvation; nay, he afflicts him and disciplines him, until he learns more thoroughly to make God the sole strength and portion of his heart, and to give unto him the glory due unto his name.

3. And thirdly, this subject discloses the reason of *languid vitality* in the Church, and its slow growth in numbers and influence. The Christian life is in low tone, because the Church gives glory to another than God. We do not say, and we do not believe, that the Church is destitute of a desire to acknowledge God as the first cause and last end of all things, and to render him homage and honor. The Church of the living God, with all its faults, is "the pillar and ground of the truth," and is dear to him as the apple of the eye. Nevertheless, every child of God will confess that there is much ambition, and vain glory, and creature-worship, mingled with the spirituality. Grace is hindered and hampered by indwelling sin. The plans and purposes of God's people are corrupted and damaged by a mixture of the lust of the flesh, and the lust of the eye, and the pride of life. In connection with their dependence upon God, they depend somewhat upon the arm of flesh. They rely in part upon their zeal, upon their excellences real or reputed, upon their position in the eyes of men. But God says unto his Church in every age and place: "Not by might nor by power, but by my Spirit," are believers to live and grow, and sinners to be converted. "Neither he that planteth, nor he that watereth, is anything, but God that giveth the increase. The wisdom of this world is foolishness with God; therefore

let no flesh glory in his sight." The particular point to
be noticed is, that this mixture of self-love and self-worship with the love of God, and the worship of God, must
be reduced down to a minimum, before the Church will
see great manifestations of the Divine presence. In the
ordinary state of the Church, there is too much of it to admit of such a blessing. When the people of God become
uncommonly humble and self-abased; when they feel
very profoundly that their covenant God is the Great I
AM, and that he will neither give his glory to another nor
share it with another, and that he alone will be exalted in
the earth ; then they lie low in the dust before Him, and
cry with Daniel : "O our God, hear the prayer of thy
servants, and their supplications, and cause thy face to
shine upon thy sanctuary that is desolate, for the Lord's
sake. O our God, incline thine ear and hear ; open thine
eyes and behold our desolations, and the city which is called
by thy name : for we do not present our supplications before thee for our righteousness, but for thy great mercies."
This is a prayer in which the creature retreats entirely,
and the Creator comes solely into view. Here is no self-
worship and vain glory ; but a pure outgushing recognition of God as Jehovah, the Being of whom, through
whom, and to whom, are all things. And hence the immediateness of the answer which that prayer received. "For,"
says the prophet himself, " whiles I was speaking, and
praying, and confessing my sin and the sin of my people
Israel, and presenting my supplication before the Lord my
God for the holy mountain of my God ; yea, *whiles I was
speaking* in prayer, even the man Gabriel, whom I had
seen in the vision at the beginning, being caused to fly
swiftly, touched me about the time of the evening oblation."

SERMON VIII.

THE DUTY OF REFERENCE TO THE DIVINE WILL.

JAMES iv. 13–15.—"Go to now, ye that say, To-day, or to-morrow, we will go into such a city, and continue there a year, and buy and sell and get gain : Whereas, ye know not what shall be on the morrow : For what is your life ? It is even a vapor, that appeareth for a little time, and then vanisheth away. For that ye ought to say : If the Lord will, we shall live, and do this, or that."

THE movements of human society are like those of the ocean ; calm and storm, light and darkness, level surfaces and mountain billows, succeed each other in swift and sudden contrast. Human life like a wave of the sea is driven of the wind and tossed. Men are constantly forming new plans, beginning new enterprises, and entering upon new and uncertain experiences. Hence it behooves them reverently to acknowledge their relation to the Almighty Being who inhabits eternity—their Maker, their Sovereign Ruler, their Judge, and their God. From amid the vicissitudes and uncertainties of this mortal life, it is their duty and privilege to look up to Him " with whom is no variableness or shadow of turning," that He may be the strength of their heart in their frailty and impotence. As the years of time lapse one after another, dying men should be reminded of the eternal years of God, and of their own destination to another world and an endless life. That we may be thus impressed, let us

attend to some reflections suggested by the text, relative
to the duty of *dependence upon God*, and *reference to Him*,
in all the undertakings and experiences of life.

I. The first remark suggested by the words of St.
James is, that mankind naturally do *not* feel and acknowledge their dependence upon their Maker. The language
of the natural heart is that which is rebuked by the Apostle :
"To-day, or to-morrow, I will go into such a city, and continue there a year, and buy and sell, and get gain." God
is not spontaneously in the thoughts and plans of men, and
human enterprises have little reference to the sustaining
and controlling power of the Almighty. Schleiermacher
defined the essence of religion to be the sense of dependence upon the Infinite Being. Tried by this test, multi-
tudes of men are destitute of religion.

We shall find this practical atheism, whether we scrutinize the narrow life of the individual, or the broader
life of the nation or the race. How rare it is to meet a
man imbued with the Old Testament spirit, saying, with
Moses, in the outset of every undertaking, "If thy presence go not with me, carry me not up hence." How few
possess the spirit of the patriarchs, who were bold as lions
provided that God led the way, but timid as lambs when
they could not see his footsteps. Many men rely upon
second causes, and never fall back upon the great First
Cause. They calculate upon a long life, because they inherit a good constitution ; they fear an early death, because their frame is slender ; they expect a successful issue
of their plans, because they are regarded by others as
shrewd and far-reaching men. In each of these instances,
the dependence is placed upon something this side of God.
The mind does not penetrate beyond all secondary causes
and agencies, and say, when " *He* taketh away our breath
we die," and " Except the *Lord* build the house they labor

in vain that build it: Except the *Lord* keep the city the watchman waketh but in vain." How few are in the habit of looking to God that they may be assisted and guided. Many men live as if there were no presiding mind in the universe; as if all the actions of mankind, and all the events of earth, were but the chance movements of an endless series controlled by no overruling power. If we should translate human conduct into words, would it not say: "All things are moving on aimless and without a guide; I will cast myself upon the current and trust to fortune for success. I am not a steward, and there is no account to be given hereafter. I will follow the inclination of my heart. Time is all and everything. Earth is the sum and substance. Man is his own centre, and ultimate end. I will look only to myself for resources of action, and will depend upon my own right arm for the accomplishment of my purposes. I will go into that great and prosperous city, and continue there twenty years, and buy, and sell, and get gain."

Though he might start back at the thought of deliberately uttering such language as this, yet does not every *prayerless* man utter the substance of it in his daily and hourly conduct? And there are millions of prayerless men in the world. Actions are louder and deeper-voiced than words, and does not a self-seeking, self-reliant, and prayerless life continually say to Almighty God, "I have no need of thee?" As we look back over the past years of our lives, do we not see that some of them have gone into eternity with no proper sense of dependence upon our Creator? Have we not planned and executed, toiled and studied, bought and sold, without any filial reference to our Maker and our Maker's will?

And what is true of the individual is true of mankind at large. We are not an humble, submissive, and trustful race of beings. Though created in the image of God, and living, moving, and having being in him, mankind have not acknowledged their relationship, and have not looked up to the Infinite Ruler of the universe for guidance and support. There is no fact taught by the history of the world more plain, and more sad to a right mind, than this. The nations of the earth, when left to themselves and uninfluenced by the truth and Spirit of God, have uniformly forgotten the Supreme Governor, and national life, like that of the individual, has not been marked by a humble confidence in Him before whom " the nations are as a drop of a bucket, and are counted as the small dust of the balance." Had this been an unfallen world, and had righteousness been its stability and harmony, it would in all ages, with one heart and mind, have acknowledged its entire dependence upon the King of kings. The universal human species, like the angelic host, would have looked upwards with a reverential eye, and sought the illumination that radiates from the Father of lights, and the counsel of Him who cannot err, and the strength of the Lord God Omnipotent. Such, however, has not been the attitude which man has taken before his Maker. He has founded and destroyed empires without a single glance of his eye upwards; he has enacted laws and abrogated them without taking counsel of the Supreme Law-Giver; he has gone to battle without reference to the will of the God of Battles, and has concluded peace with no offering of thanks to the Prince of Peace.

The thoughtful and Christian reader is struck with the atheism that pervades the secular history of man. Look, for example, at those great ancient empires: the Assyrian, the Macedonian, and the Roman. These immense bodies rose slowly, reached their culminating point, and declined gradually below the horizon, without any refer-

ence to the living and true God, so far as the aims and
purposes of their founders, and heroes, and monarchs, were
concerned. It is true that God controlled them, and employed them for his own wise purposes, and so he does
the vast masses of inanimate and unconscious matter that
crowd the material heavens. But what cared Ninus,
Romulus, and Alexander for that Being who sat upon the
circle of the earth while they were prosecuting their
ambitious designs, and who has since judged them, these
thousands of years, according to the deeds done in the
body? The conduct of Nebuchadnezzar is a specimen of
the conduct of the kings and kingdoms of the earth.
" The king walked in the palace of the kingdom of
Babylon, and spake and said, Is not this great Babylon
that I have built for the house of the kingdom, by the
might of my power, and for the honor of my majesty?"

II. The second reflection suggested by the text is, that
the *ignorance* and *frailty* of man is a strong reason why
he should feel his dependence upon his Maker. " Ye
know not what shall be on the morrow : for what is your
life? It is even a vapor that appeareth for a little time,
and then vanisheth away."

Man is a very ignorant being. Philosophers are disputing whether the human mind can have a " positive "
knowledge of the Infinite as well as of the Finite. In
the discussion, a positive perception is sometimes con-
founded with an exhaustive and perfect one. It is assumed that man's knowledge of the Finite is exhaustive
and perfect, and the conclusion follows that his knowledge
of the Infinite must be different. But man has no exhaustive and perfect understanding of any finite thing.
His knowledge in this direction, too, has limits as much as
in the other. The blade of grass which he picks up in his
fingers, and subjects to the microscope and chemical anal-

ysis, contains an ultimate mystery which he can no more completely clear up, than he can the mystery of the Divine eternity, or trinality. For the constitution of the smallest atom of matter involves such baffling questions as, What is matter? and, How is it created from nothing? In reference, then, to a perfect comprehension that excludes all mystery, the Finite is as really beyond the reach of the human mind as the Infinite. In relation to both of them alike, we may concede a positive and valid apprehension, but not an exhaustive and perfect one. In respect to all beings and things alike, be they finite or be they infinite, men must say, "We see through a glass darkly, and we know in part."

Again, man's knowledge is limited by time, as well as by the nature of objects. His knowledge of the present is imperfect, and he has no knowledge at all of the future. The past and present are the only provinces into which he can enter. The future is an inaccessible region, and he can know nothing of it until the providence of God guides him slowly into its secret and dark recesses. The morrow is separated from us by only a few hours, and yet we cannot predict with absolute certainty what the morrow will bring forth, any more than what eternity will bring forth. If by knowledge we do not mean mere probability, but absolute certainty, we are as ignorant of what will be on the morrow, as we are of what will be a million of years from now. Living in the sphere of change and experience, we are of necessity ignorant of all that time has not brought to our view. We wait in order to know, and we live to learn.

But God is in eternity, and the terms past and future do not apply to his existence. There is no succession of events in his omniscient consciousness. All that has been, is now, and ever shall be—the whole mass and amount of all history, so to speak—is constantly before his eye. Hence his omniscience is a fixed quantity. It is a cognition that is the same yesterday, to-day, and for-ever. It undergoes no increase, and no diminution. There is no future that is to disclose any new thing to him; and there is no past out of which his memory can bring anything forgotten by him. That part of our existence which we have not yet lived, is now as well known to his mind, as what we are thinking and doing this very moment.

It is not so with our knowledge. We have forgotten much that we once knew. It is probable, that in some instances more has been lost out of the memory than the faculty contains at any one time. An excursive student ranging from his youth over the whole field of knowledge, yet having an unretentive memory, at the close of life is not in conscious possession of one-half of the sum-total of all his acquisitions. The past is thus very inadequately known by us. The present glides by with so noiseless and insensible a motion, and we are so unreflecting, that we have but a partial knowledge of that. It is before our very eyes; yet seeing, we see not. And the future we do not know at all. Verily, man is of yesterday, and knows nothing.

Is not this ignorance of ours a strong reason why we should rely upon the all-knowing God? Though we know nothing in an exhaustive and perfect manner; though mystery enwraps us like a cloud; though the future is all uncertain, and we cannot even conjecture what it has in store for us; yet we are not shut up to the unhappiness that would result from such a sense of ignorance if unrelieved by other considerations. For a profound consciousness of human ignorance, taken by itself, has a direct tendency to render man desponding and despairing. This is the cause of the misanthropy and atheism which too often meet us in the world of letters. The enterprising and self-confident thinker believed that he could speculate his way through all the mystery, and attain a perfectly clear understanding and mastery of the problems of human life. Baffled and repulsed at a hundred points, he became the subject of an awful reaction, and sank into the belief that there is no such thing as truth, and no such being as God. But there is no need of this. Trust in God's wisdom, power, and goodness, cheers up the mind in these hours when the immensity and complexity of the universe is weighing upon it. Every man may say : " It is true that I am a being of limited powers. The ultimate essence of everything is beyond my ken, and I know not what will be on the morrow. But I am the creature of the great and wise God, and he graciously permits me to take hold of his strength, and to ask for his wisdom. He is the Father of lights, and giveth to all men liberally, and up-braideth not." By thus resting upon God, amidst all the ignorance and mutability of this existence, man derives to himself some of the calm wisdom and immutability of the Eternal One. If we were possessed of a simple and constant trust in Jehovah, our little life would repose upon his unchangeable existence, and would be embosomed in it. And although it would still have its changes, its ignorance, and its motion, yet these would occur in a region where there is no change, and in which there is perfect security. Our globe has its complex and swift motions, but the serene and ancient heavens contain it and all its orbit. Go where it may, it is still within a sphere of order and safety. It can never get beyond the reign of law. That immensity in which it moves is the dwelling-place of God, and " He who stretcheth out the heavens like a curtain, who layeth the beams of his chambers in the waters, and maketh the clouds his chariots," will impart harmony and regularity to all its movements. In like manner, if man would consciously live, move, and have his being in God, he would be filled with a glad and cheerful sense of security, firmness, and power, amidst the violent and rapid changes incident to this life, and the dark mystery that overhangs it. "He that trusteth in the Lord shall be as Mount Zion, that cannot be moved."

Again, the brevity and uncertainty of human life is another strong reason why man should feel his dependence upon God. "For what is your life? It is even a vapor that appeareth for a little time, and then vanisheth away." To employ the language of the Psalmist: "Men are as a sleep: in the morning they are like grass which groweth up. In the morning it flourisheth and groweth up: in the evening it is cut down and withereth." The longest life here in time seems short, and there is no one, however his years may have been lengthened out, who will not say with the aged Jacob in the one hundred and thirtieth year of his age, "*Few* and evil have the days of the years of my life been." Any length of life upon earth must appear brief to beings who like man were made to live in eternity. If our years were prolonged to the longevity of those who lived before the flood, the same sense of their brevity would possess us upon our death-beds, that will soon fill our souls as we come individually to lie down and die. Nothing but a fixed and unalterable existence can be free from the sensation of shortness and transitoriness.

But not only does human life seem short: it is so in reality. It has the transiency of the morning vapor, which hangs upon the edge of the horizon for a few moments, and then is dissipated by the wind and the sun. In thinking of human life, we are apt to think of the whole life of the entire race of man. The millions that have walked the earth for six thousand years become a single individual for us, and thus we are not so vividly impressed with the transiency of man's existence as we are when a friend or neighbor is struck down by our side, or when we are ourselves summoned to die. Yet every individual of the human family lived only his brief hour, was occupied with only his few personal interests, and then dropped a solitary unit into the abyss of eternity. One after one, for six thousand years, men have been living short lives, and the aggregate of them all is not a second of time, when compared with that endless duration which is the residence and the fixed state of each. "The whole time of the world's endurance," says Leighton, "is as but one instant or twinkling of an eye, betwixt eternity before and eternity after." What then is man, and what is man's life? "He dwelleth in houses of clay; his foundation is in the dust; he is crushed before the moth; he is destroyed from morning to evening; he perisheth for ever, without any regarding it."

III. The third remark suggested by the text is, that the proper way for men to acknowledge their dependence upon God is to *refer* to his will, in all their plans and undertakings. "Ye ought to say: If the Lord will, we shall live, and do this or that."

It is right and reasonable that the will of God should prevail everywhere, and in all time. The will of some being or other must be supreme and ultimate; otherwise the universe would be a theatre of contending factions. The old doctrine of dualism has always been regarded as uncommonly irrational, and never has had much currency. That there should be two eternal wills in everlasting conflict has appeared so very absurd, that errorists have been much more ready to adopt pantheism than dualism, and to absorb all wills into one. The chief work consequently for a creature is, to subject his purposes to those of the one Supreme Will. He must not for a moment suppose that he is at liberty to proceed without any reference to any one but himself. No such license as this is granted to him. It may be wickedly taken, but it is not granted. Man may have his own will only as it harmonizes with that of God. An arbitrary choice is not conceded to any subject of the Divine government. By the law, he is shut to one course, and one only. "Thou shalt love the Lord thy God with all thy heart. I have set before you life and death: choose *life*." That creature, therefore, be he angel or man, who claims the right to do as he pleases; to choose *either* life or death; to have his own way without reference to the law and will of the Creator, sets up an unlawful claim. It is like the claim which a tyrant sets up to arbitrary power. "He have arbitrary power!"—said Edmund Burke, in reference to Warren Hastings—"my lords, the East India company have not arbitrary power to give him; the king has not arbitrary power to give him; your lordships have not; nor the commons; nor the whole legislature. We have no arbitrary power to give, because arbitrary power is a thing which neither any man can hold nor any man can give. No man can lawfully govern himself according to his own will. We are all born in subjection to one great immutable pre-existent law, prior to all our devices, and prior to all our contrivances, paramount to all our ideas, and all our sensations, antecedent to our very existence, by which we are knit and connected in the eternal frame of the universe, out of which we cannot stir." Subjection to God's will is not the destruction of man's voluntariness; but if it were, he would be obligated to come under it. For God's supremacy is of more consequence than any attribute of a creature, however noble and precious it may be in itself. "Let

God be true, and every man a liar!" cries the apostle in his inspired zeal for God. "Let God be supreme, though all finite wills should be annihilated."

But there is no necessity that all men should be liars, in order to save the veracity of God; and there is no necessity that they should be forced to obedience, in order to save his supremacy. Obedience is free agency. The self-subjection of ourselves to the claims and plans of God is one of the freest, most genial, most joyful acts of which we are conscious. Most of our misery, nay, all of it, arises from our asserting our own wills. The instant we yield the point, and submit to our Maker, we are at rest. And this is proof that we are free; for wherever there is any compulsion, there is dissatisfaction and rest-lessness.

Man must, therefore, in his plans and purposes, refer first of all to the Divine Will. His prayer, and the real desire of his heart, must be: "Thy will be done on earth, as it is in heaven." This is the way in which he best shows his dependence upon his Maker. If he does not take a step without consulting God, and would not for the world form a purpose in opposition to Him, he is un-questionably a submissive and reliant creature. He is also a happy one. For God's will is the only firm ground to stand upon. All events occur in conformity with it, and whoever falls in with it is truly blessed. It is a remark of Lord Bacon, that if man would rule over nature he must first obey nature; that if he would be benefited by the great laws and forces of the material world, he must live and work in conformity with these laws; that if he attempts to resist or force nature, he brings failure and ruin upon himself. It is equally true, that if man would obtain happiness and peace from the Divine Government, he must conform to it. If he opposes and resists the will of God, he will in the end be ground to powder as it moves on in its eternal, irresistible, and wise course.[1]

Let us, then, learn to say in all the circumstances of life: "If the Lord will we shall live, and do this, or that." It is a lesson slowly learned by proud and selfish man. Oftentimes it must be beaten into him by repeated blows from a severe yet kind Providence. If such blows fall upon us, we must be dumb with silence because it is God that does it, and because we need it for our soul's good. But by a wise and thoughtful course, we may preclude the necessity of such a severe process. If we start with the doctrine that "no man liveth to himself, and no man dieth to himself;" if we fix it in our habits of thought that we are *creatures* of God, and not sovereigns in our own right; if we work upon this theory of human life; we shall be likely to keep ourselves in such a docile and dependent attitude that stern methods will not be needed. But even if severe trials should come upon us, we shall be the better prepared to bear them, and we shall find it easier to kiss the rod, and say, "Thy will O God, and not mine, be done."

---

[1] "The Christian mind hath still one eye to this, above the hand of man and all inferior causes: it looks on the sovereign will of God, and sweetly complies with that in all things. Neither is there anything that doth more powerfully compose and quiet the mind than this. It feels itself invincibly firm and content, when it hath attained this self-resignation to the *will of God:* to agree to that in every thing. This is the very thing wherein tranquillity of spirit lies. It is no riddle nor hard to be understood, yet few attain it. And what is gained by our reluctances and repinings, but pain to ourselves? God *doth what he will*, whether we consent or not ; our disagreeing doth not prevent his purposes, but our own peace. If we will not be led, we are drawn. We must suffer, if he will ; but if we will what he wills, even in suffering, that makes it sweet and easy : when our mind goes along with his, and we willingly move with the stream of his providence."—Leighton: On 1 Pet. iii. 17.

SERMON IX.

THE CREATURE HAS NO ABSOLUTE MERIT.

LUKE xvii. 10.—"When ye shall have done all those things which are commanded you, say, We are unprofitable servants : we have done that which it was our duty to do."

In this direction which our Lord gave his apostles, he announced a truth that is exceedingly comprehensive and far-reaching. It involves the whole subject of human agency as related to the Divine. It throws a flood of light upon the question whether a creature can perform good works in his own strength, and thereby bring God under obligation to him. Though a simple and unmetaphysical proposition, though so plain that a little child can understand it, this instruction of Christ to his disciples contains the key to the whole subject of human merit. It is the passage of Scripture which, perhaps more than any other, settles the dispute between the Protestant and the Papist; between the advocate of grace and the advocate of works.

Our Lord takes the ground that there can be no merit, in the absolute meaning of the word, in the creature before the Creator. No man can perform a service in such an independent, unassisted style and manner, as to make God his debtor. "Which of you," he says, "having a servant ploughing, or feeding cattle, will say unto him

immediately, when he is come from the field, Go and sit
down to meat? and will not rather say unto him, Make
ready wherewith I may sup, and gird thyself, and serve
me, till I have eaten and drunken: and afterward thou
shalt eat and drink. Doth he thank that servant because
he did the things that were commanded him? I think
not. So likewise ye, when ye shall have done all those
things which are commanded you, say, We are unprofitable
servants: we have done [only] that which was our duty
to do." The force of this illustration will not be completely felt, unless we call to mind the relation which an
Oriental servant sustained to an Oriental master. In this
Western world, where democratic ideas prevail, and the
extremes of human society are brought upon a level, it
would not be regarded as singular, if a servant, in return
for his service, should be addressed with the courteous
phrase: "I thank you." But in that despotic Oriental
world, where distinctions were carefully kept up, and the
relation of the servant to the master had been established
from time immemorial, and no one thought of disputing
it or of overleaping it, it would have seemed singular had
the master expressed his thanks for services which, according to the whole theory and structure of Eastern society,
were rigorously due from the inferior to the superior; and
still more, if he had proposed to exchange places with his
servant, girding himself in servile apparel, and waiting
upon him at table. Our Lord spoke to Orientals, and
all his illustrations, nay, even his cast of thought and
modes of speech, issued from the Oriental intuition; and
in order, therefore, to receive their full impression, we
must divest ourselves of many of our Occidental ideas,
and merge our individuality in that of the morning-
land.

The servant is an absolute debtor to his master, and his

master owes him nothing for his service. This is the theory of Oriental society and civilization. The creature is an absolute debtor to his Creator, and his Creator comes under no obligations to him by anything that he can do. This is the theory of morals and of merit, for the Orient and the Occident; for the angels in heaven and the devils in hell; for the whole rational universe of God. We find it woven into the whole warp and woof of Revelation. In the very twilight of the Patriarchal Church, we hear Eliphaz the Temanite asking: " Can a man be profitable unto God, as he that is wise may be profitable unto himself? Is it any pleasure to the Almighty [any addition to his infinite blessedness], that thou art righteous? or is it gain to him that thou makest thy ways perfect?" (Job xxii. 2, 3). Elihu repeats the thought in the inquiry: " If thou be righteous, what givest thou him? or what receiveth he of thine hand? Thy wickedness may hurt a man as thou art; and thy righteousness may profit the son of man" (Job xxxv. 7, 8). The Psalmist, bringing to mind the independence and infinitude of God, feelingly says in reference to his own graces and virtues: "My goodness extendeth not to thee, but to the saints that are in the earth, and to the excellent in whom is all my delight" (Ps. xvi. 2, 3). St. Paul flings out his voice in that confident and challenging tone which accompanies the perception of indisputable truth, and asks: " Who hath first given to God, that it should be recompensed unto him again? For of him, and through him, and to him, are all things" (Rom. xi. 35, 36). And with reference to the preaching of the gospel itself, and the long train of trials, and sorrows, and sufferings which it brought with it—even with reference to that wonderful self-dedication which St. Paul made of all that he had and all that he was, that whole burnt-offering of body, soul, and spirit, which he offered upon the altar of God—he says: "For though I preach the gospel, I have nothing to glory of: for necessity is laid upon me; yea, woe is unto me if I preach not the gospel" (1 Cor. ix. 16). From beginning to end, the teaching of Revelation is, that when the creature has done his whole duty perfectly and without a single slip or failure, if he boast, it must not be in the presence of God. Before creatures, and in reference to creatures, such a perfection might challenge admiration and lay under bonds; but not before the Great God and in reference to the Supreme Being. "If Abraham were justified by works, he hath whereof to glory; but not before God" (Rom. iv. 2).

We propose to mention the grounds and reasons of this. Why must every man, when he has done all those things which are commanded him, say, in reference to God, " I am an unprofitable servant; I have only done that which it was my duty to do ?"

I. In the first place, he must so say, and so feel, because he is a *created* being.

If a man originated himself, sustained himself in existence, arranged and controlled all his circumstances, and then by his own independent power should perfectly obey the moral law, he would perform a service for which he could demand from God a suitable compensation. Having out of his own resources, and without any assistance from the Supreme Being, rendered unto him a perfect character and a perfect life, he would bring the Supreme Being under obligations corresponding to the worth and worthiness of such a character and such a life. In this case, man and God would stand in the same relation to each other that any two creatures do; and whatever one of the parties should do in accordance with the wish or will of the other, would be a " profitable " service, and would bring the other under bonds to him. If one man, for example, complies with the desire of another man, and performs the service which he requests, the latter is a "profitable" servant to the former, and the former must "thank" the latter for it, and must render him an equivalent, unless he is willing to be under continual obligation to him. And this for the reason that men in relation to one another are independent agents. If I perform a service for a fellow creature, he is not upholding me in existence, ordering and controlling all my circumstances, and rendering me a continual assistance at the very time that I am at work for him. He had nothing to do with my origin, my continued existence, and the conditions under which I live and act. In relation to him, I am an independent agent ; and therefore what I do for him I do of myself, and what I give to him I give out of my own resources; and therefore I am a "profitable" servant to him, and he must "thank" me for what I have done, and for what I have given.

But this is not the state of the case between man and God. He made us, and not we ourselves. We do not sufficiently consider what is implied in the stupendous fact of creation from nothing ; and how utterly dependent a creature must be from the nature of the case. When an artisan manufactures a product of skill, say a watch or a plough, we call it his, because he fashioned the materials and put them together. A watch is very dependent upon its maker; and we cannot conceive of its bringing the watchmaker under obligations, or in any manner becoming a "profitable" servant to him deserving of thanks. But God does not merely fashion materials and put them together, in the act of creation. He calls the very elements themselves into being from nonentity. He originates the creature from nothing, by a miracle of omnipotence. How then can a creature bring the Creator under obligations? How can he from an absolutely independent position reach out to God a product, or a service, that merits the thanks of the Almighty? The very hand by which he reaches out the gift is the creation of the Being to whom the gift is offered. The very soul and body that stands up before God and proposes to bestow upon him a gift, is itself the pure make of God's sheer fiat. Its very being is due to his omnipotent power. The prophet Isaiah asks: "Shall the axe boast itself against him that heweth therewith? or shall the saw magnify itself against him that shaketh it? as if the rod should shake itself against them that lift it up, or as if the staff should lift itself, as if it were no wood" (Is. x. 15). Mere dead matter cannot exert any living functions. The saw cannot saw the sawyer. The axe cannot chop the chopper. They are lifeless instruments in a living hand, and must move as they are moved. It is impossible that by any independent agency of their own they should act upon man, and make him the passive subject of their operations. But it is yet more impossible for a creature to establish himself upon an independent position in reference to the Creator. Every atom and element in his body and soul is originated, and kept in being, by the steady exertion of his Maker's power. If this were relaxed for an instant, he would cease to be. Nothing, therefore, can be more helpless and dependent than a creature; and no relation so throws a man upon the bare power and support of God as the creaturely relation. A miracle might endow the saw with a power to saw the sawyer; and the axe with a power to cut the cutter. But no miracle could render the creature self-existent and self-sustaining, so that he could give to God something strictly from and of himself; something which he had not received; something whereby he could be " profitable " to God and merit his thanks.

II. In the second place, man cannot make himself " profitable " unto God, and lay him under obligation, because he is constantly *sustained* and *upheld* by God. " O Lord," says the Psalmist, " how manifold are thy works! in wisdom hast thou made them all: the earth is full of thy glory. So is this great and wide sea wherein are things creeping innumerable, both small and great beasts. These wait all upon thee, that thou mayest give them their meat in due season. That thou givest them, they gather; thou openest thine hand, they are filled with good. Thou hidest thy face, they are troubled; thou takest away their breath, they die and return to their dust. Thou sendest forth thy spirit, they are created; and thou renewest the face of the earth " (Ps. civ. 24–30). This is an accurate and beautiful description of the great process that is continually going on in the universe of God. Creation, preservation, and, when it pleases Him, destruction— these are the functions which the Supreme Ruler is unceasingly exerting in his boundless kingdom. The same power that calls the creature into existence from nothing is employed in keeping him in existence. It requires omnipotence to preserve the creature and provide for his constant wants, as much as it requires omnipotence to speak it into being in the outset; and some theologians have therefore defined preservation to be a constant creation. The divine energy that produced that leviathan which swims the ocean stream must be perpetually exerted, in order that he may not fall back into the abyss of nonentity from which he came. Wherever that sea-monster goes; whether he rushes league after league through the waters of the Atlantic or Pacific; whether he is skimming the seas in pursuit of his food, or whether like Milton's

Satan he lies "prone on the flood, extended long and large, floating many a rood"—in every inch of space, and at every point of time, he is upheld by creative power. And so it is with the billions of billions of creatures of all ranks and sizes, that crowd the material universe. Each and every one of them is just as truly supported as if a material hand were placed beneath it, and we could see the exertion of the upholding force. "The young lions roar after their prey, and seek their meat from God."

This is true of man. He goeth forth unto his work, and to his labor until the evening. But wherever he goes, and whatever he does, he stands, in Banquo's phrase, in the great hand of God. He draws every breath by a Divine volition; he takes every step by a Divine permission; he lives, moves, and has his being in his Creator. What an impression would this truth make upon us, did we but comprehend its significance and realize it. Should we see a superhuman hand suddenly reach down from the sky, and pick up a sinking sailor in the middle of the ocean from the engulfing billows, or snatch a little infant from the sea of flame in a great conflagration, we should believe that neither of them saved himself, but that God saved him. We should understand what is meant by preservation by the hand and power of the Almighty. We could not refer it to a law of nature, nor to the operation of chance. By the supposition, we saw the very hand that grasped the sinking sailor, or the burning infant, and no reasoning whatever could deaden the impression which that miraculous occurrence would make upon our minds.

Now, similar ought to be the impression made by the whole daily course of Divine Providence. Though constant and unceasing; though new every morning, fresh every evening, and repeated every moment; noiseless as the light, and ever-present as the atmosphere; yet if man were what he should be, he would be unceasingly conscious of God's supporting presence and power. He would not, as he now does, place something between God and his works so that God cannot be seen. He would not refer his own health, strength, wealth, poverty, sickness, weakness, happiness, sorrow, to the operation of merely natural causes, but ultimately to the direct will and power of his Maker. He would say and feel that when God sends forth his spirit, creatures are created ; and that when he taketh away their breath, they die and return to their dust. This is the Biblical view of Divine Providence. In the Bible everything is very close to God. Not only the miracle, but the ordinary occurrences and operations of nature are referred immediately to him. God thunders in the heavens. God lightens along the sky. "The voice of the Lord is upon the waters: the God of glory thundereth ; the Lord is upon many waters. The voice of the Lord is powerful; the voice of the Lord is full of majesty. The voice of the Lord breaketh the cedars" (Ps. xxix. 3–5). This is the inspired description of an ordinary thunderstorm. And it is the truest statement that can be made. For if the man of science tells me that the lightning and the thunder are the result of electricty, I must complete his statement by telling him that electricty itself is a creation of God. If he tells me that two clouds, each charged with its own positive or negative electricity, when meeting together produce the detonation that shakes the heavens and the earth, I must add to his explanation the still further statement, that these two clouds, and everything in or about them, are formed, and are made to sail together, by God's will. By everything in this thunderstorm, we are causally and ultimately carried back to the Divine decision. For why should the two clouds meet together just at this particular moment, and not a half hour later? Because of the will of Him who "maketh a decree for the rain, and a way for the lightning of the thunder" (Job. xxviii. 26). Why at any spot in the greensward do just so many spires of grass shoot up—no more and no fewer? Because of the will of Him who numbers the hairs of the human head, and makes one hair black and another white.[1]

This, we say, is the doctrine of the Bible concerning the preserving and sustaining providence of God. According to the Scriptures, no being is so close to man, and so close to nature, as the Author of man, and the Author of nature. One man may come very near to his fellow man. He may hear his words, feel his breath, touch his hand. But God is nearer to him than this. Every man is very close to himself. There are thoughts and emotions which no creature knows but himself. But the Searcher of the heart is closer to him than this. The forces of nature are very near to the objects of the natural world. The principle of vegetable life is inside of the tree and the flower; the principle of gravitation operates within the mass of rock or the planetary orb. Nothing, it would seem, could be nearer to nature than the life of nature. But God is nearer than this; because he is the maker and upholder of these very invisible principles, and this very indwelling life itself.

Returning now to the course of our argument, we say that the fact that man is so utterly and wholly dependent upon the immediate presence and unceasing support of God, renders it impossible that he should ever bring God under bonds to him, and merit his thanks, by anything that he can do. He is a receiver at every point, and at

---

[1] Matter is destitute of self-motion, and therefore cannot be either a prime mover, or a first cause.

every instant. He cannot give out a thing that has not first come in to him. "What hast thou," says St. Paul, "that thou hast not received?" There is therefore no starting-point in the attempt of man to be a "profitable" servant unto God, and to merit his thanks. He cannot take the first step. Before he can make a beginning, he must get outside of the providence of God; he must take his stand upon some position where he is no longer preserved and upheld by his Creator. So long as he occupies his present position, and all his powers and faculties are maintained in existence and operation by the power of God, so long he owes to God all that he is, and all that he can do; and, therefore, when he has done all things that are commanded him, there must not be the faintest rising of pride in his heart, and he must say, "I am an unprofitable servant, I have done [only] that which it was my duty to do."

III. In the third place, man cannot be "profitable" to God, and merit his thanks, because all his *good works depend upon the operation and assistance of the Holy Spirit.* Our Lord's doctrine of human merit is cognate with the doctrine of Divine grace.

Says the prophet Isaiah: "Lord, thou wilt ordain peace for us: for thou also hast wrought all our works in us" (Isaiah xxvi. 12). The original Hebrew here does not permit us to affirm that the prophet spake these words primarily with reference to spiritual exercises. He had in view providential dispensations; the protection which God had granted his people in the days that were past, and which was a pledge of favor in the future.[1] At the same time, however, these words are applicable to the inward agency of God in the human soul, and they have been so

---

[1] Alexander: On Isaiah xxvi. 12.

generally applied to this agency, that probably this is the reference that comes first into the mind of the mass of readers. This text is understood to teach the same that St. Paul teaches, when he says that it is "God that worketh in us to will and to do."

Now, we find in the fact that all good works are the product of the Holy Spirit in the human heart, a strong reason why the renewed man, though a faithful servant, is not a "profitable" one. It is because God works all our good works in us, that after we have done all things which are commanded us, we must say: "We are unprofitable servants; we have by God's grace done that which it was our duty to do."

When a man does wrong, he receives no assistance from God. A wicked person cannot say, "By the grace of God I am what I am." A sinful man cannot adopt Paul's words and affirm, "I live, yet not I, but Christ liveth in me." Sin in all its forms, be it original or actual, be it the inclination of the heart or the single act, is not the product of God "working" in the creature "to will and to do." On the contrary, it is a self-willed and hostile action on the part of man. When you think an evil thought, you may be certain that your Maker did not inspire it in your mind. When your heart swells with pride, malice or envy, you may know infallibly that God did not infuse it into your heart. When your will is determined to selfish and disobedient purposes, it is impossible that the Holy Ghost should have impulsed such a purpose. No sinful creature can look into the face of his Creator and say with Isaiah, "O Lord, thou hast wrought all our works in us." Sin is differentiated from holiness by this, among other modes, that it is purely the work of man. God is not the author of sin. It is true that the sinner is created and upheld by God, as entirely

as is the saint. In respect to the great functions of
creation and providence, all mankind, the good and the
bad, stand upon the same level, and there is no difference
among them. But when we pass to the use and operation
of these created powers and faculties, we discover a heaven-
wide difference. Some men lean upon God, ask for his
inward presence and assistance, and in reliance upon his
grace, think their thoughts, form their purposes, and perform their actions. They work good works, because their
deeds, in our Savior's phrase, "are wrought in God."
But other men, and at present they are the majority, think
their own thoughts, form their own selfish and independent
purposes, and perform corresponding outward actions,
with no reliance upon God's assistance, and no prayer for
his indwelling presence. And all such thoughts, purposes,
and actions are evil. You cannot define sin any better than
to say that it is the creature's sole work; the creature's
self-will. It is a species of moral agency that is not exercised in humble dependence upon God, but in opposition
to him. It is an attempt to be wholly independent of the
Almighty. The sinner works his own wicked works without any influence, impulse, or assistance from his holy
Maker. It is true, that in the very act of sinning, God
sustains in existence the faculties themselves—the very
mind, the very heart, the very will by which the sinner
sins—but he does not prompt the wicked thought in the
mind; he does not produce the wicked feeling in the
heart; he does not inspire the wicked purpose in the will.
The faculty by which a man sins is created and every
instant upheld by the Creator, but the sinning itself is the
work of the faculty itself. Hence, sin cannot be charged
upon God. We cannot impute our transgressions to him.

But it is not so with holiness. When we pass over to
this side, and consider the relation which God sustains to

righteousness, we find that he is not only the creator and preserver of our powers and faculties, but he also influences, prompts, inspires, and actuates them. He does not merely create a human will and maintain it in existence, and then leave it to itself to work out righteousness. He does not dismiss his people to their own independent and unassisted efforts. He well knows how weak and mutable the strongest human will is in reference to holiness; how liable it is to fall, even under the most favorable circumstances, as Adam fell in paradise; and how constantly it needs his almighty power, his eternal and self-subsistent goodness, to rest upon. And therefore it is, that while the shame and guilt of sin must be referred to the creature always and alone, the glory and honor of holiness must be referred to the Creator always and alone. When I have done wrong, I must say: "I am the guilty author of this sin; to me, and to me only, does the guilt and condemnation attach." But when I have done right, I spontaneously cry: "O Lord, thou hast wrought all my good works in me; the glory and the honor of this righteousness belongeth unto thee. Not unto man, not unto the creature, do I give the glory."

Now, is it not plain that if these representations are correct; if this is the relation which all holiness in the creature sustains to the Creator; if God really does work in every good man or good angel to will and to do; that man or that angel cannot bring God under obligations to him by any or all of his righteousness? The same principle of reasoning applies here that applies in the case of creation and providence. Create yourself and sustain yourself, and then do something which God requires, and you become a "profitable" servant. Perform a single good act without any assistance from God; think a single holy thought, feel a single holy emotion, without any influence or impulse from the Holy Comforter; and then you may demand a reward from your Sovereign upon the principle of abstract right. But so long as you are what you are, by the grace of God; so long as he enables you to keep his commandments; say unto him from the depths of a humble and a filial heart: "I am an unprofitable servant. I have done that which it was my duty to do; but I have done it in thy strength, and by thy gracious assistance."

The subject is fertile in inferences and practical conclusions, and to some of these we now devote the remainder of the discourse.

1. In the first place, we see in the light of our Lord's theory of human merit, why it is impossible for a creature to make *atonement* for sin.

There are only two classes of actions possible to man. He must either do right or do wrong. That the performance of sinful works will atone for sin, has never entered the head of the wildest visionary that ever rejected the evangelical method of forgiveness, and invented a theory for himself. No, men propose to satisfy Divine justice for the sins that are past, by good works. They have done wrong, and they would set themselves right with their reproaching consciences, and their holy Sovereign, by henceforth doing right. In this very attempt, so natural and spontaneous to man, we find an evidence of the rationality of the doctrine of atonement. The fact that a transgressor feels himself bound to do something to make amends for having heretofore done nothing, or for having done wrong, is proof that the idea of satisfying for sin is not so foreign and alien to the human reason as some theorists assert.

But the good works of a creature cannot be an atonement, because they are not his own independent and self-sustained agency. If God works these holy works in my soul, how can I offer them to him as a satisfaction to his justice for my sin in the past? How can I take money out of the purse of my creditor, to pay my debt to him? An atonement, from the nature of the case, must be an original and self-sufficient performance. Whoever makes one, must be able to furnish entirely from himself, and wholly out of his own resources, a full equivalent for the penalty that is due to sin. He must be a "profitable" servant, in reference to the great Divine attribute of justice. Little does that man understand the nature of an atonement, who supposes that he himself can make it. None but a Divine Being—a Being of creative energy, and self-subsistent position—can reach out to the eternal nemesis of God, a good work that is purely his own, because performed by an independent and self-sustaining power.

But, returning to the good works of the creature, let us see beyond all dispute that they cannot discharge the office of a satisfaction, and make him "perfect in things pertaining to conscience." We have observed that every good work in man or angel, is the effect of a Divine influence and impulse. Take the instance of an imperfectly-sanctified man, and see what you find. He puts up to God a prayer that is earnest and sincere, though mixed with sin—sinful unbelief, and sinful references to self. What of good there is in this "good work," as it is denominated, is due to the influence of the Holy Spirit. The warmth, the fervor, the importunity, and the spirituality in this exercise, are all owing—and the praying person is the first to say so—to the gracious impulses and promptings of God in the soul. Now, supposing that there were the inclination to do so, how could this prayer be employed as an offset for any past imperfection or sin of the soul? It is God's work in the Christian heart; how, then, can the creature arrogate it as his own, and claim to be a "profitable" servant thereby, and bring the everlasting justice of God under bonds to him by it? And so it is with every service or work of man, that is worthy of the epithet "good." All this portion of human agency is rooted and grounded in the Divine agency, in the most thorough manner conceivable. It is dependent not only by reason of creation and preservation, but of direct and immediate influence. The powers and faculties of a Christian are not only originated and upheld by their Creator, but they are directed, actuated, and assisted by Him, at every instant, and in every experience and action. Never, therefore, was there a greater contradiction and absurdity than that involved in the theory of justification by good works. If the good works were absolutely perfect works, and were performed by the creature by his own independent and unassisted agency, there might be some color of reason for the theory.[1] But the good works are not perfect. The best of men confess that their best experiences are mixed with remaining corruption; that they never did a single deed which they dare to say was absolutely sinless; and that, more than all, what of goodness there is in these imperfectly sanctified souls and lives is due wholly to the energy and grace of God. And therefore it is, that they never adopt the theory of justification by works. They are, indeed, liable to this legality and self-righteousness; and they hate it,

---

[1] Yet no adequate ground for it; since even an independent and sinless obedience of the law for the future by one who has broken it in the past, would not be a complete fulfilment of the law. Because the whole of this obedience is due in the present and future, and there is no overplus left for the past failure. Ready money for new purchases, says Owen, cannot pay old debts.

and struggle against it. But they never make it a dogma, and insert it in their theological system.

Now, surely, the natural man is not better than they. The sinful secular world, to say the very least, is no better qualified to furnish its own atonement than is the Christian Church. The doctrine of justification by good works will no more prove a solid foundation, in the day of adjudication, for the worldling or the moralist, than for the self-denying and struggling Christian. If the disciple of Christ did not create and sustain himself, and cannot perform good works in his own strength, neither did the man of the world create himself, or sustain himself; and neither can he perform good works without the same inward grace and assistance. All men, without exception, are shut up to the atonement of the God-man, if any atonement for sin is to be made and accepted. There is no other being but the Eternal Son of God who can stand up, having life in himself, having power to lay down his life and power to take it again, and from this self-existent and self-sustaining position can reach out to the triune Godhead an oblation for human guilt that is really and truly meritorious and cancelling. No being except one of the three Divine Persons can be "profitable" unto God. And He can. When the Son of God in human nature suffers for sin, then he *strictly* earns remission of sins for those who believe in him; he *absolutely* merits the acquittal at the bar of justice of all guilty sinners who trust in his sacrifice. When the elders of the Jews came to Jesus beseeching him that he would come and heal the servant of a certain centurion, they added "that he was worthy for whose sake he should do this, for he loveth our nation, and hath built us a synagogue." This Roman officer had brought the Jewish people under obligations to him, by the favor which he had extended to them from his

purely independent position as a Roman citizen, and an
agent of the Roman emperor. As a Roman, he was
under no obligation to build a Jewish synagogue. Thus
is it in respect to the Lord Jesus Christ, and his relations
to God and man. He is an independent Being. He owes
nothing to eternal justice, and sinful man, certainly, has
no claims upon him. When, therefore, such a Being
voluntarily takes man's place, and suffers in his stead, and
endures the full penalty which eternal justice demands,
he becomes meritorious for man's salvation ; he becomes
a "profitable" servant, because he has done *more* than it
was his duty to do ; he gives to the Eternal Godhead
something out of his own resources which he was not
obliged to give, and which is, therefore, cancelling ; and
every guilty and lost sinner, as he comes before the bar
of justice, may ask for the forgiveness of his sins and
plead as a sufficient and all-prevalent reason, the argument
employed by the Jewish elders : " For He is *worthy* for
whose sake this should be done."

2. In the second place, we see in the light of this subject why the creature, even though he be sinlessly perfect, must be *humble*.

Our Lord said to his disciples, "When ye shall have
done *all* those things which are commanded you, say, we
are unprofitable servants." Even supposing that there
has been an absolute conformity to the Divine command,
there must not be egotism and pride in a creature's heart.
For there has been no independent and self-supporting
agency. Everything that the pure and perfect archangel
does, is done in reliance and dependence upon the infinite and adorable Jehovah. And there is no humility in
the universe of God deeper than that which dwells in the
heart of the seraph before the throne. He possesses a
virtue which, if compared with that of the holiest man

that ever lived, is ethereal, sky-tempered, and able to resist the severest assaults of temptation and of Satan.
Milton represents the ruined archangel as starting back
abashed, at the sight of the pure and stainless cherubs
whom God had placed to guard our first parents from the
wiles of their adversary. "Abashed the devil stood, and
felt how awful goodness is." These cherubim before a
fellow-creature, and in relation to a fellow-creature, were
indeed strong and mighty. But in relation to the infinite
and eternal God, they were nothing. Their ethereal and
wondrous virtue, in comparison with the ineffable and transcendent excellence of the Supreme, was vanity. "He
chargeth his angels with folly." This, these holy and
blessed spirits feel; and they too, like the weakest man
upon earth struggling with temptation and faint with
fatigue, humbly adore that God only wise, and only good,
and only mighty, "of whom, and through whom, and to
whom are all things."

But how slight is our humility, in comparison with that
of these high and blessed spirits before the throne of God!
Pride is continually rising in our hearts over a holiness
that is exceedingly imperfect, being mixed with sin; over
a holiness that from beginning to end is the product of
God's grace within our souls. How elated we sometimes
are over one meagre, shrivelled excellence! If we perfectly obeyed the mandate of our Lord in the text, such
an emotion as vain-glory would never be experienced by
us. Let us then ponder our Savior's theory of creature-
merit more than ever. We are "unprofitable," servants,
even if we should render a perfect obedience. If our
faith in Christ's atonement were so perfect that it should
consume us with zeal for him and his cause, we should be
unprofitable servants, and bring him under no obligations
to us. If our dependence upon the grace of his Holy

Spirit were so implicit and entire, that it should enable us to keep perfectly all his statutes and commandments, we should still be unprofitable servants. We should still be under an infinite obligation to him for his life-blood poured out for the expiation of our guilt, and for the gracious influence of the Holy Spirit by which our sanctification is effected.

But we have not done all that is commanded us. Our faith in our Redeemer is very weak and imperfect. We know comparatively little, of the virtue there is in his blood to cleanse the guilty soul, and to impart to it the calm confidence of justification before God. We know little, comparatively, of the power of the Divine Comforter to strengthen the will, to sanctify the heart, and to bring the whole soul into captivity to the obedience of Christ. Our experience of the gospel is very stinted and meagre, in comparison with the fulness, richness, and freeness of its provisions. Such servants as we, so far from being " profitable," can with difficulty be called " faithful." Suppose that the Master should address us with the words, " Well done, good and faithful servant," should we not feel like saying to him, " Lord, when have we been faithful ; what hast thou seen in us that renders us worthy of such an address ? "

3. And this leads to a third and final inference from the subject, namely, that God does not require man to be a " profitable" servant, but to be a *faithful* servant.

In the last great day, Christ will say to his true disciples, " Well done, good and faithful servant, enter thou into the joy of thy Lord." God does not demand from his creatures a service that must be rendered from an independent position, that must be performed by a self-subsistent power, and that will bring him under obligation to the person so rendering it. Everywhere his command to the

creature is: "Be strong in the Lord, and the power of his
might. Trust in the Lord, and do good. Work out your
salvation with fear and trembling, for it is God that worketh in you both to will and to do. He that trusteth in
his own heart is a fool. Cursed is the man that trusteth
in man, and maketh flesh his arm." Such injunctions
and declarations as these imply that man must serve God
by leaning upon him; and that he must give back to God
that which God has first given to him. The servants, in
the parable, did not first create the five talents, or the ten
talents, independently of their lord, and then make them
over to him. He gave them the talents, and required
simply a right use and improvement of them. Thus is it,
in a still higher sense, in reference to man and his Maker.
Not only are the talents created and bestowed, but, as we
have seen, the very inclination and ability to make a right
employment of them issues from the same boundless source.
"We are not sufficient of ourselves to think any thing as
of ourselves; all our sufficiency is of God."

It is, therefore, a true and proper supplication that
Augustine puts up, when he says to God: "Give what
thou commandest, and command what thou wilt." This
corresponds with the Psalmist's promise: "I will run in
the way of thy commandments when thou shalt enlarge
my heart." The "faithful" servant is one who, feeling
his entire dependence and helplessness, does not propose
to labor in his own strength, and to proudly offer to God
something from his own independent resources, but simply
desires to lean upon God continually, to take hold of his
strength, and thereby keep all his commandments, and
glorify him in his body and spirit which are His.

And what an easy task is this. The yoke is easy, and
the burden is light. Our Maker does not command us to
be strong in ourselves; but to be strong in Him. He does

not require us to originate our own existence, to maintain ourselves in being, to labor upon an isolated and independent position, and to give unto him something that shall add to his essential happiness and essential glory. He furnishes everything, and only requires that we be faithful in employing his gifts. We are stewards of the manifold gifts of God; and it is required of a steward, simply and only, that he be found faithful.

Are we "faithful" servants? Since we cannot be "profitable" servants, the only thing that remains for us is to employ the innumerable gifts and bounties of God with fidelity. Our time, faculties of mind and body, wealth, opportunities of influence—everything that goes to make up our personality, and everything that is connected with our existence here upon earth—the whole man, body, soul, spirit, possessions, and influence in every direction, must be conscientiously used to honor God and benefit man. This, too, in reliance upon God.

Whoever is thus faithful, will be rewarded with as great a reward as if he were an independent and self-sustaining agent. Nay, even if man could be a "profitable" servant, and could bring God under obligation to him, his happiness in receiving a recompense under such circumstances would not compare with that under the present arrangement. It would be a purely mercantile transaction between the parties. There would be no love in the service, or in the recompense. The creature would calmly, proudly, do his work, and the Creator would calmly pay him his wages. And the transaction would end there, like any other bargain. But now, there is affection between the parties—filial love on one side, and paternal love on the other; dependence, and weakness, and clinging trust, on one side, and grace, and almighty power, and infinite fulness on the other. God rewards by *promise* and by *covenant*, and not because of an absolute and original indebtedness to the creature of his power. And the creature feels that he is what he is, because of the grace of God. There is no pride or boasting of heart, on his side. And the infinite Creator, who needs nothing, and cannot be brought under bonds by any of the works of his hands, pours out, the infinite fulness of his being and his blessedness upon a creature who rejoices in the thought that all that he is, is the work of Divine providence and grace, and all that he has accomplished, is the effect of God "working in him to will and to do of his good pleasure."

SERMON X.

FAITH WITH AND WITHOUT SIGHT.

John xx. 29.—"Jesus saith unto him, Thomas, because thou hast seen me, thou hast believed : blessed are they that have not seen, and yet have believed."

This is one of the most comforting and encouraging passages in the whole Scripture, to a doubting and anxious Christian. There is one instance upon record, in which it proved a strong support and consolation in an hour of great need. The late Dr. Arnold of Rugby, one of the most serious-minded and earnest men which England has produced in this century, was suddenly summoned to meet death and judgment. In the midst of perfect health he was attacked with spasm of the heart, and learned that in a moment he would be called into the infinitely holy presence of his Maker. He knew what this meant ; for the immaculate purity of God was a subject that had profoundly impressed his spiritual and ethical mind. He felt the need of mercy at the prospect of seeing God face to face ; and as he lay upon his death-bed, still, thoughtful, and absorbed in silent prayer, all at once he repeated, firmly and earnestly : " And Jesus said unto him, Thomas, because thou hast seen me thou hast believed : blessed are they who have not seen, and yet have believed." [1]   Here is

---

[1] Stanley : Life of Arnold, II. 283.

an actual case in which a single text operated like a cordial ; and a case, too, in which there was no fanaticism or self-delusion. For Arnold's mind was highly intellectual, and its natural tendency apart from the influences of Christianity was to criticism and skepticism. He was an Aristotelian in his mental type, and in all his scholarship and culture. But after an earnest Christian life, in the hour of sudden death, from which the litany of the Church which he honored and loved prays, " Good Lord, deliver us," he pillowed his head upon this blessed declaration of the Redeemer, and went to his rest. Let us, therefore, approach this text and this subject as no mere abstraction, but as one that has actually been efficacious and consoling in the supreme hour of a celebrated man.

This passage of Scripture suggests a comparison between faith aided by sight, and faith independent of sight. How does the faith of the Church in an age of miracles differ from its faith when miracles have ceased ? In answering this question, we propose, in the first place, to notice some of the advantages that were enjoyed by those who dwelt under the miraculous dispensation ; and in the second place, to consider the advantages experienced since the days of miracles.

I. In the first place, then, what were some of the advantages enjoyed by those who lived and served God in the times of *miracle ?*

They may all be summed up in the remark, that to a considerable extent the pious patriarch, and the pious Jew, and the first Christians, walked by sight. They believed because they saw. By this we do not mean that the ancient believer walked *wholly* by sight. Noah was " warned of God of things not seen as yet." Abraham went out of his old home "not knowing whither he went." And that long list of worthies mentioned in the

eleventh chapter of Hebrews, is represented as acting
without assistance from the objects of time and sense,
in the particular instances that are specified. But we
mean to say that, comparing these forerunners of ours
with ourselves, and taking into the account the whole
course of their lives, they were much *more* aided by sight
than we are.

For it was an age and dispensation of supernaturalism.
God was frequently breaking in upon the ordinary course
of events, and proving his existence by his visible presence. Who could doubt the doctrine of the Divine existence, who could be an atheist, as he stood under Mount
Sinai and heard a voice that shook the earth and heavens
saying: "Thou shalt have no other gods before me?"
Who could query respecting the possibility of miracles,
when he saw the waters of the Red Sea rising up like a
wall upon each side of him ; when he saw a dead man revived to life upon touching the bones of Elisha; when he
saw, as Hezekiah did, the shadow go back ten degrees
upon the sun-dial ; when he heard Christ call up Lazarus
from the tomb, and when he looked down into the vacant
sepulchre of the crucified Son of God ?

Now there was something in this, unquestionably, that
rendered faith in God's existence and God's power comparatively easy to the ancient believer. The senses, when
appealed to in this striking manner, by the exhibition of
supernatural energy, are a very great aid to faith. Seeing.
is believing. Jacob, for example, must have found it no
difficult thing to believe and trust in a Being who was
every now and then speaking to him, directing him into
new paths and places, watching over him, and delivering
him from difficulties and dangers. Such a communication as that which he received from the mouth of God in
the wonderful dream at Bethel, must have filled him with

an unwavering belief in both the existence and the kindness of God.

How differently the believer of the present time is situated, in this respect, it is needless to say. If we suppose miracles to have ceased with the age of the Apostles, then for eighteen hundred years there has been no exertion of miraculous power upon the part of God in the affairs of his Church. Generation after generation of Christians has come and gone, but no celestial sign has been given to them. They have believed that God is, and is the rewarder of those that diligently seek him, but they have never seen his shape nor heard his voice. They have had strong faith in the immortality of the soul, and the reality of a future life, but no soul has ever returned from the invisible world to give them ocular demonstration, and make their assurance doubly sure. In some instances, this reticence upon the part of God, this silence century after century, has produced an almost painful uncertainty, and wakened the craving for some palpable evidence of unseen realities. That interesting man, John Foster, is an example of this. "They never come back to tell us; they never come back to tell us," was his passionate ejaculation upon thinking of the impenetrable cloud which envelops those who have departed this life. And all these spasmodic and baffled attempts of the false spiritualism of this day, and of former days, are another testimony to the craving natural to man for some miraculous tokens and signs. Skeptics contend that the miracle is irrational. But, certainly, nothing is irrational for which there is a steady and constant demand upon the part of human nature. The hankering which man, in all ages and in all varieties of civilization, has shown for the supernatural, proves the supernatural—as the universal hunger for bread proves that there is bread, and as the steady and continual thirst for water proves that there is water. Otherwise, there is mockery in creation. Man as a religious being expects and must have some sensible signs from another world; and therefore there has never been a religion of any general prevalence which has not had its miracles, pretended or real. The ancient Paganism, and the modern Mohammedanism, equally with the Jewish and Christian religions, claim authority upon the ground of celestial credentials.

Our brethren, then, of the Patriarchal, the Jewish, and the Early Christian times, enjoyed this advantage over us. The aids of the senses were granted to them in the exercise of faith. They were not shut up as we are to a purely mental and spiritual act. "Because thou hast seen me, thou hast believed," might have been said to them all, as Christ said it to Thomas.

II. But our Lord said to his doubting disciple: "Blessed are they who have not seen, and yet have believed." In this remark, he evidently implies that those who believe in him and his word without the aid of those sensible manifestations which were enjoyed by Thomas and his fellow-disciples, receive a greater blessing than they did. Let us then consider, in the second place, some of the advantages which the Church of God experiences in these latter days, when there is *no miracle* to assist their faith.

1. In the first place, believing without seeing is a *stronger* faith than believing because of sight; and the stronger the faith, the greater the blessedness. If Thomas had put credit in the affirmation of the other disciples that they had seen the Lord, and had not insisted upon seeing for himself the print of the nails, and putting his finger into the print of the nails, it is evident that his faith in the Divine person and power of Christ would have been greater than it actually was. For Christ had foretold him, in common with his fellow disciples, that he was to

be crucified, and on the third day after his crucifixion would rise from the dead. Thomas had already witnessed the crucifixion, and knew that this part of his Lord's prophecy was fulfilled. If, now, he had exercised an implicit confidence in the remainder of Christ's prophecy, the instant that the other disciples informed him that they had seen the Lord, he would have believed them. But his doubt, and his demand to see and touch the risen Lord, evinced that his faith in the power of Christ to rise from the dead, and make his promise good, was weak and wavering. It needed to be helped out by sight, and therefore was not of so high and fine a type as it might have been. If we examine the Scriptures, we shall find that that faith is most pleasing to God, and is regarded by him as of the best quality, which leans least upon the creature, and most upon the Creator. Whenever man rests his whole weight upon God; whenever the Christian trusts the bare word of his Lord and Master without any aid from other sources; God is most honored. Take the case of Abraham. We have already noticed that in some respects he was not called to exercise so simple and entire a trust in the Divine word as we are. He lived in a period of miracle, and was the subject of miraculous impressions. But there were some *emergencies*, or critical points, in his life, when his faith was put to a very severe trial—times when, in the Scripture phrase, God "tempted" him. These were the instances in which his experience resembled more that of the modern than that of the ancient believer, and it is with reference to them that he is styled the "father of the faithful." Consider the trial of his faith when commanded to sacrifice Isaac. This child had been given to him by a miracle; for Isaac was born as truly against the ordinary course of nature as Christ himself. Abraham did indeed manifest doubt when God

promised him this son—showing that his faith at that
point was infirm. But when the promise had been fulfilled, and Isaac was growing up before him in beauty and
in strength, then he certainly knew that God is almighty,
and faithful to his word. Here, up to this point, the faith
of the patriarch was resting very much upon sight and sensible things. But when he is suddenly commanded to
take this very child who had been given to him by a
miracle, and whose death would apparently nullify the
Divine promise that in his seed all the kindreds of the
earth should be blessed—when he is commanded, without
a word of explanation, to sacrifice the son of promise, to
obey was the highest conceivable act of pure faith. It
did not rest at all upon any thing that could be seen. It
was mere and simple confidence in the authority and
power of God. He only knew that it was the Eternal
Jehovah who had given him the awful order to put the
sacrificial knife to the heart of his child, and the Eternal
Jehovah must be obeyed at all hazards. This was the
crowning act of faith upon the part of Abraham, and God
put great honor upon him for it, because Abraham had
put great honor upon God in hoping against hope, and
following in the path of the Divine command without a
ray of earthly light.

Now, it is to this uncommon species, this high degree
of faith, that the modern believer is invited. We have
never seen a miracle. We have never witnessed the manifestations of God's supernatural power. We have only
read the record of what He did, in this way, thousands of
years ago. It is indeed an authentic record, yet it cannot,
from the nature of the case, make such a startling impression upon us as would the very miracles themselves—as
would the very plagues of Egypt, the passage of the Red
Sea, the thunders of Sinai, the resurrection of Lazarus,

the darkness, the quaking of the earth, the rending of the
rocks and opening of the graves, that accompanied the
Crucifixion. As Horace long ago said: "That which
comes in by the ear does not affect us like that which
comes in by the eye." Our faith must therefore rest more,
comparatively, upon the simple authority of God. As an
act, it must be more purely mental and spiritual. Inasmuch as we see less with our outward vision, we must believe more with the very mind and heart. And here is
the greater strength and superiority of the modern faith.
The inward powers of the soul are nobler than the five
senses; and their acts have more worth and dignity than
the operations of the senses. Reason is a higher faculty
than sense. If I believe in the power and goodness of
God only because, and only when, I *see* their operation in
a given instance, I do not give him any very high honor.
There is no very great merit in following the notices of
the five senses. An animal does this continually. But
when I believe that God is great and good, not only when
I have no special evidence from material phenomena, but
when these phenomena seemingly teach the contrary;
when my faith runs back to the *nature* and *attributes* of
God himself, and is not staggered in the least by anything that I see, then I give God great honor. I follow
higher dictates than those of the five senses. I believe
with the mind and heart; and with the mind and heart I
make confession unto salvation. My faith is not sensuous,
but spiritual. I rectify the teachings of mere time and
sense, by the higher teachings of revelation and the spiritual mind.

That bold and eloquent North-African father, Tertullian, speaking of miracles, remarks: "I believe the miracle because it is impossible."[1] This remark has been a

---

[1] Credo quia impossibile est.

theme for the wit of the unbeliever, because he understood Tertullian to say that he believed an *absolute* impossibility. This is not the meaning of the celebrated dictum.
Tertullian means that he believes that a thing which is
relatively impossible—which is impossible with man—is
for this very reason possible with God. The Creator must
have the power to work a miracle, from the very fact that
the creature has no such power. For if God can never rise
above the plane upon which a creature acts, then it is a
natural inference that he is nothing but a creature himself.
If a thing that is impossible for man is impossible for God
also, what is the difference between God and man? "I
believe, therefore," says Tertullian, "that the Creator is
able to work a miracle, for the very reason that the creature cannot. Its impossibility in respect to finite power,
makes it all the more certain in respect to infinite. I believe the thing in reference to God, because in reference
to man and man's agency it is an utter impossibility."

This is sound reasoning for any one who concedes the
existence of God, and believes that he differs in kind from
his creatures. Tertullian only utters in a striking paradox
the thought of St. Paul, when he says to King Agrippa:
"Why should it be thought a thing incredible with you
that *God* should raise the dead?" and the affirmation
of our Lord: "The things which are impossible with men
are possible with God."

Now, this is the kind of faith that does not lean upon
the five senses, but goes back to the *rational idea* and *intrinsic nature* of God. The Supreme Being can do anything; and whatever he does is wise and good. This is
faith in its higher and stronger actings. The mind reposes upon God simply and alone. It does not ask for
the ways and means. All that it requires is, to be certain
that the Divine promise has been given; that God has

pledged his word in a given instance; and then it leaves all to Him. Whether the laws of nature work for or against the promised result is a matter of not the slightest consequence, provided that the Author of nature, who taketh up the isles as a very little thing, and holds the waters in the hollow of his hand, has said that it shall verily, come to pass. This is the simplest and strongest form of faith. "Blessed are they who have not seen, and yet have believed." And this is the form of faith to which we are invited.[1]

2. In the second place, faith without sight *honors God* more than faith that is assisted by sight. We cannot show greater respect for any one than to take his bare word. In human circles it is the highest praise that can be accorded, when it is said of a person: "I have his word for it, and that is enough." If we are compelled in a given instance to go back of the man's word or promise, and scrutinize his integrity or his pecuniary ability; if we must doubt the person and look into his character or circumstances, our faith in him is not of the strongest kind, and we do not put the highest honor upon him. There are comparatively few men of this first class and standing; comparatively few of whom the whole community with one voice will say: "We want no examinations and no guarantees; we trust the *man;* we have his word and promise, and this is sufficient." But when such men do stand forth year after year, strong and trustworthy because they fear God and love their neighbor as themselves, what an honor is put upon them by the implicit, unquestioning

---

[1] "To bottom ourselves upon the all-sufficiency of God, for the accomplishment of such things as are altogether impossible to anything but that all-sufficiency, is faith indeed, and worthy of our imitation."— Owen's Sermon, on the Steadfastness of God's Promises.

confidence which is felt in them—by the faith in the mere person, without the sight of his ways and means.

Precisely so is it with faith in God. Just so far as we withhold our confidence in him until we can see the wisdom of his ways, just so far do we dishonor him ; and just in proportion as we trust in him because he is God, whether we can perceive the reasons of his actions or not, do we give glory to him. Suppose a sudden sorrow is sent from his hand, that appears wholly dark and inexplicable—that a missionary is cut down in the bloom of life, and in the midst of great usefulness among an unevangelized and degraded population ; that a wise and kind father is taken away from a family that leans entirely upon him. If in these instances no questions are asked, and no doubts are felt or expressed ; if the Church and the children of God say with David : "I am dumb with silence because *Thou* didst it," what an honor do they render to God by such absolute confidence. And he so regards it, and accepts it, and rewards it.

For the faith in such cases terminates upon the very *personality* and *nature* of God. It passes by all secondary causes and agencies, and reposes upon the First Cause. Oftentimes our faith is of such a mixed character, that it honors the creature as much as the Creator. We exercise confidence, partly because God has promised, and partly because we see, or think we see, some earthly and human grounds for faith. For example, if we expect that the whole world will be Christianized, partly because of the Divine promises and prophecies, and partly because the wealth and civilization and military power of the earth are in the possession of Christian nations, we honor the creature in conjunction with the Creator ; and this is to dishonor him, for he says : " My glory will I not give to another." The faith of the Church is of the purest, highest kind, only when she trusts solely and simply in the promise and power of her covenant God, and looks upon all the favoring earthly circumstances as results, not as supports, of this promise. The fact that Christian missions are being aided very materially by the wealth, and civilization, and military power of the Protestant world, is not an independent ground of confidence that Christian missions will ultimately evangelize the earth. We must not put any earthly and human agency into equality and co-ordination with the Divine. The creature in itself is nothing; and it derives all its efficiency from God, who is the first cause and last end of all things. Take away the promises, and purposes, and controlling agency of God, and where would be the wealth, the civilization, and military power of Protestant Europe and America? If we rest our faith in a glorious future for our wretched world, upon what these can accomplish by an independent agency; if we rest upon *two* arms, the arm of God, and the arm of flesh, our faith is infirm, and it does no real honor to our Maker. " Sufficient is *Thine* arm alone, and our defence is sure." And it will be one of the signs of that mightier faith which will herald the dawn of the millennium, when the Church, leaving its mixed confidence in the Creator *and* creature; leaving its partial trust in wealth, civilization, arts, sciences, commerce, armies, and navies, shall settle down once more upon the one immutable ground of confidence—the word, and the power, and the pity of the Everlasting God. This was the mighty faith of the Early Church. The civilization of the Greek and Roman world was arrayed against them, and they could not lean upon it in conjunction with God, if they would. They were shut up to the mere power and promise of the Most High. They leaned upon God's *bare arm*. And what honor did they give Him in this; and how did he honor them in return!

We see, then, as the result of this discussion, that while our brethren of the Patriarchal, Jewish, and Early-Christian eras found it easier, in some respects, to believe in God and unseen realities, by reason of the supernatural manifestations that were granted to them, we of these last times enjoy the privilege of exercising a faith that is more robust and firm because more purely spiritual, and a faith that puts more honor upon God. Provided we do rise above the clogs of the body and of sense; provided we do exercise a simple unwavering confidence in God as God, in spite of all the outward infidelity of the day, and the more dangerous inward infidelity of our imperfect hearts; we shall hear him saying to us : " Others have believed because they have seen : blessed are ye, because ye have not seen, and yet have believed."

From this subject, it is evident that God is the *sole object* of faith. There is a difference between belief and faith ; between believing, and believing *in*, and *on*, and *upon*. We may believe a man ; we may believe an angel ; but we may believe in and on God alone. Faith is the recumbence, and resting, of the mind ; and the mind can find no rest in a creature. All creatures stand upon a level, so far as self-sufficiency is concerned ; and if we cannot find rest in ourselves, how can we in a fellow-worm. As we look into our own natures, and discover that they are ignorant, weak, and sinful, and then look around for what we lack, we shall never find it in a creature. All creatures are ignorant, weak, and finite. Only God is wise, mighty, and infinite. " Put not your trust in princes, nor in the son of man in whom there is no help. Happy is he that hath the God of Jacob for his help, whose hope is in the Lord his God."

Furthermore, if God is the sole object of faith, then we must beware of a *mixed* or *partial* faith. We must not trust partly in God, and partly in his creatures. He will receive no divided honors. As in our justification by the atonement, we cannot trust partly in the blood of Christ, and partly in our own good works, so in our more general relation to God, our confidence must not rest upon any combination or union between Him and the works of his hands. We are told by St. Paul, and we well know, that Christ must be our sole atonement, and that we must not attempt to add to his finished oblation by our own sufferings, or deeds. Our absolution at the bar of justice must be no composite affair; depending partly upon what our Substitute has done, and partly upon what we have done. The whole, or none, is the rule here. And so must be our faith in God. We must repose our whole weight upon Him alone. Anything short of this, dishonors that exalted and infinite Being who never enters into partnership with his creatures; that All-sufficient Being, of whom, and through whom, and to whom are all things.

We know these things, happy are we if we do them. It is the highest accomplishment of the Christian life, actually and perfectly to believe in God in Christ. We are continually pulled back from this blessed and this mighty act of faith, by our detestable pride and creature-worship. It is a great art to desert the creature in all its forms, and live and move in our Creator and Redeemer. Especially is it a great, a divine art, to do this in reference to our sin and guilt. Who shall teach us, when remorse bites, and anxiety respecting the last account weighs us down—who shall teach us how to believe in Christ, the Lamb of God, without a scintilla of doubt, with an absolute and undivided confidence? He Himself must do this. He is the author and the finisher of faith.

SERMON XI.

THE REALITY OF HEAVEN.

JOHN xiv. 2.—"In my Father's house are many mansions: if it were not so, I would have told you."

ALL Scripture is profitable, and conduces to the growth of the Christian. But some portions of it seem to be more particularly adapted than others to certain stages of his growth in the divine life, and certain experiences in his history. In the season of affliction, the heart loves to give itself utterance in the mourning and plaints of the afflicted Psalmist. In the hour of joy, it pours forth the flood of its thanksgiving and praise in the songs and anthems of the joyful Psalmist. If the believer feels the need of instruction and exhortation, he turns to the fulness and earnestness of the apostolic Epistles. If he needs encouragement and hopefulness in view of the sin and misery of the human race, he listens to the voice of the Prophets saying: "As the earth bringeth forth her bud, and as the garden causeth the things that are sown in it to spring forth: so the Lord God will cause righteousness and peace to spring forth before all nations."

If, however, a singular interest attaches to any one portion of the Bible more than to others, it is found in the Gospels. These parts breathe a peculiar spirit, and exert an uncommon influence upon the soul. The Christian often resorts to them, for they bring him into the personal presence of his Lord, and his spirit burns within him as Christ talks with him on the way to heaven. He enters into the house with his Master, and walks with him by the sea shore, and hears words that come directly from the mouth of God incarnate. He is thus brought near to the Infinite Being without trembling or terror, because the infinitude and glory are enshrouded in the garments of meekness and condescension. That awful fear of God as the Dread Unknown, which throws such a sombre color over the religions of the pagan world, is banished; for Christ is the only begotten of the Father, and full of grace and truth. By means of the Gospels, the believer converses with the Eternal One, as a man converses with his friend.

And of the Gospels, that of John is the most full of this kind of influence. He was the beloved disciple, and his is the beloved Gospel. He seems to have had granted to him a more direct and clear vision of the heart of the Redeemer, than was allowed to the other disciples. He leaned upon his breast at supper, and appears to have attained a fuller knowledge than did the others, of the mysterious and fathomless nature of the God-man.

Not only does this Gospel present to the contemplation of the believer themes of love and grace, but it everywhere offers to the human intellect the highest themes of truth and unsearchable wisdom. Its exordium is mysterious; revealing, in a way that no other part of Scripture does, the doctrine of the Triune God, and giving the fullest unfolding of the mystery that has yet been granted to the finite mind. And, running through the whole narrative, there is a series of high and deep disclosures concerning the being of God, and the problems of human destiny, that

renders this Gospel the most profound of all books.[1] At
the same time, while it is unsearchably mysterious, it is
wonderfully soothing in its influence upon the soul. Like
the Holy Ghost, it may well be called the " Comforter."
Full of deep wisdom, and full of deep love; full of mystery, and full of quickening instruction ; full of the awfulness and infinitude of Deity, and full of the beauty and
winning grace of a perfect humanity ; the Gospel of John
will ever be the solace and joy of the Christian in his loftiest and lowliest moods. He will always feel the truthfulness of the language in which the childlike Claudius describes his emotions while perusing this Gospel : " I have
from my youth up delighted to read the Bible, but
especially the Gospel of John. There is something in it
exceedingly wonderful ; twilight and night, and through
them the quick flash of lightning; soft evening-clouds,
and behind the clouds, the full-orbed moon. There is
something, also, so high, and mysterious, and solemn, that
one cannot become weary. It seems to me in reading the
Gospel of John, as if I saw him at the last supper leaning
upon the breast of his Master, and as if an angel were
holding my lamp, and at certain passages wished to whisper something in my ear. I am far from understanding
all that I read ; yet it seems as if the meaning were hover-
ing in the distance before my mind's eye. And even when
I look into an entirely dark passage, I have an intimation
of a great and glorious meaning within it which I shall
one day understand." [2]

Among the varied moods that are addressed and
comforted by the teaching of the Gospel of John, is that

---

[1] Bengel remarks of John xvii. ; " This chapter, of all the chapters in
Scripture, is the easiest in regard to the words, the most profound in regard to the ideas meant."

[2] Claudius; Werke, Bd. I. 9.

timorous and desponding temper which is produced by the fear of an exchange of worlds. Nothing contributes more directly to calm and assure the mind, than meditation upon those last discourses of our Lord which speak in such a majestic and sublime tone, and yet breathe a gracious, benign, and tranquillizing spirit. In them, the Eternal and Divine is strangely blended with the Finite and Human; so that the soul which receives their warm impression is both inspired with confidence in the Almighty Teacher, and love for the human friend. It is related that a strong and mighty mind on drawing near to the confines of eternity, and feeling the need of some unearthly and celestial support when flesh and heart were failing, was reminded by a friend of the beauty of the Scriptures, and of those general characteristics of revelation which so often blind the eye to the more special and peculiar truths of Christianity. He made answer—hastily interrupting his friend—"Tell me not of the beauties of the Bible. I would give more for the seventeenth chapter of John's Gospel than for all of them."

In meditating upon the utterance of our Lord recorded by St. John in the text, let us notice, in the first place, the familiar acquaintance with the heavenly world which is indicated by the words : " My Father's house ; " secondly, the definiteness of this world denoted by the words: " Many mansions ; " and, thirdly, its reality taught in the assertion : "If it were not so, I would have told you."

I. In the first place, the words, " My Father's house," betoken the most intimate *familiarity* with heaven. It is the home of Christ. Nothing more conclusively evinces the difference between Jesus Christ and other men who have lived and died upon the earth, than the confidence and certainty with which he spoke of the invisible world. Not only is there no doubt or hesitation in his views as expressed in his language, but there is no ignorance. He never says: " Now I know in part." On the contrary, we feel that he knew much more than he has disclosed ; and that if he had chosen to do so, he could have made yet more specific revelations concerning the solemn world be· yond the tomb. For all other men, there are two worlds —the one here and the other beyond. Their utterances respecting this visible and tangible sphere are positive and certain ; but respecting the invisible realm they guess, and they hope, or they doubt altogether. But for our Lord, there was, practically, only one world. He is as certain in respect to the invisible as to the visible ; and knows as fully concerning the one as the other. No mind unassisted by revelation ever reached the pitch of faith in the unseen and eternal that was attained by Socrates. But he was assailed by doubts ; and he confesses his ignorance of the region beyond the tomb. After that lofty and solemn description in the Phædo (113, 114) of the different places assigned after death, to the good, the incorrigibly bad, and those who have led a middle life between the two, he adds : " To affirm positively, indeed, that these things are exactly as I have described them, does not become a man of discernment. But that either this or something of the kind takes place in regard to our souls and their habitation —seeing that the soul is evidently immortal [1]—appears to me most fitting to be believed, and worthy of hazard for one who trusts in the reality. For the hazard is noble, and it is right to charm ourselves with such views as with enchantments." How different is the impression made upon us by these noble but hesitating words, from that which was made upon John the Baptist by our Lord's

---

[1] Φαίνεται οὖσα ἀθάνατόν. Says Vigerus, in loco, φαίνομαι often has a signification of certainty.

manner and teaching upon such points, as indicated in his
testimony: "He that cometh from above, is above all: he
that is of the earth is earthly, and speaketh of the earth:
he that cometh from heaven is above all: and what he
hath seen and heard, that he testifieth." How different is
Plato's dimness of perception, and only hopeful conjecture
respecting another life, from the calm and authoritative
utterance of Him who said to Nicodemus: "We speak
that we do know, and testify that we have seen. And no
man hath ascended up to heaven but he that came down
from heaven, even the Son of man who is in heaven." How
different is the utterance of the human philosopher from
that of Him who said to the cavilling Jews: "I am from
above, ye are from beneath; I go my way, and whither
I go ye cannot come; I proceeded forth, and came from
God; Doth this offend you? What and if ye shall see the
Son of man ascend up where he was before?" How different are the words of Socrates from the language of Him
who in a solemn prayer to the Eternal God spake the
words, blasphemous if falling from the lips of any merely
finite being: "O Father, glorify thou me with thine own
self, with the glory which I had with thee before the
world was." Christ, then, speaks of heaven and immortal
life as an eye-witness. The eternal world was no "dim,
undiscovered country" for him; and therefore his words
and tones are those of one who was "native, and to the
manner born."

There are periods in the believer's life when he needs
to cling hold of this fact, that his perturbation may be
calmed. The viewless world of spirit has never been entered by any mortal who has been permitted to return
and divulge its secrets. So long as man is in the flesh,
and accustomed only to objects of sense, it is a most baffling and mysterious world for him, and a shadowy solem-

nity invests it.   He is not familiar with its scenes and
objects.   Nay, he is so habituated to that which can be
seen and handled, that the very terms "spirit" and "spiritual" have come to denote the vague, the unknown, the
unfamiliar, and the fearful.   Without Revelation, the
world beyond is eminently a "dim, undiscovered country."
The Ancients, it is true, peopled it with the shades of the
departed, and divided it into the regions of the blest and
the regions of the unblest; but they still felt it to be an
unknown land, and a dark, mysterious air veiled it from
their vision.   The dying heathen, notwithstanding the
popular faith and the popular teachings respecting the
future life, dreaded to go over into it, not merely because
of the guilt in his conscience which caused him to fear a
righteous retribution, but also because of his uncertainty
and ignorance.   He turned his glazing, dying eye back to
the visible world, and longed for the continuance of a life
which, though it was full of unsatisfaction and wretchedness, was yet invested with clearness and familiarity.[1]   He
recoiled at the prospect of being hurried away from the
bright sunlight, and the green earth, into the obscurity
and darkness of the world of shades.   The pagan or instinctive view of death, and the future world, is vividly
delineated by the great dramatic poet in the feeling utterance of Claudio :

> " Ay, but to die, and go we know not where;
> To lie in cold obstruction, and to rot ;
> This sensible warm motion to become
> A kneaded clod ; and the delighted spirit

---

[1] Says Achilles to Ulysses in the lower regions : "Speak not another
word of comfort concerning death, O noble Ulysses ! I would far rather
till the field as a day laborer, a needy man without inheritance or prop-
erty, than rule over the whole realm of the departed."—Odyssey XI.
488.

> To bathe in fiery floods, or to reside
> In thrilling regions of thick-ribbed ice ;
> To be imprisoned in the viewless winds,
> And blown with restless violence round about
> The pendent world ; or to be worse than worst
> Of those, that lawless and uncertain thoughts
> Imagine howling ! 'tis too horrible !
> The weariest and most loathed worldly life
> That age, ache, penury, and imprisonment
> Can lay on nature is a paradise
> To what we fear of death."

Although man enlightened by Revelation has a much more definite knowledge respecting the future life, he is not entirely divested of this sense of uncertainty about his future existence. Though the gospel has brought life and immortality to light; has shot some rays into the gloom of eternity; man still feels that it is an unfamiliar world. How and what he shall be when his spirit is disembodied, he knows not. He is ignorant of the mode of existence upon the other side of the tomb. Living in the light of Christianity, knowing certainly that there is another world than this, and that Christ came out from it and dwelt for a time in this world, and then "ascended up where he was before," man is still filled with some of the dread that overshadows the heathen, and like him clings with earnestness and nervousness to this visible and diurnal sphere. And for many men dwelling in Christendom, the other reason for dread that exists in the case of the pagan is also existing. The merely nominal Christian, like the pagan, knows that there is unpardoned sin upon the soul, and the pale realms of eternity are therefore, as were the gates of paradise for the departing Adam and Eve,

"With dreadful faces thronged, and fiery arms."

Though the believer ought to be raised by his faith

above all these fears, and the future life should be familiar as his own home to him, yet he is often conscious of uncertainty and misgiving when he thinks of an exchange of worlds. He cannot at all times confidently say: "It is my Father's house." He has little positive hope and desire to enter it. He does not steadily and habitually seek a better country, even a heavenly. He, too often, clings to life with anxiety, and the summons to depart sends perturbation and trembling through his soul. It is a mysterious world, and although he professes to have a God and Redeemer within it, yet he fears to enter.

Now the words of our Savior: "My Father's house," should calm and encourage us. We should believe with a simple and unquestioning faith, that they really indicate the nature of the spiritual world for the Christian—that eternity for the disciple of Christ is *home*. They should also invest the future world with clearness and familiarity. It should not be for us a vague and mystical realm, but our most cheerful home-thoughts should gather around it; we should cherish the home-feeling regarding it; and to our inward eye, it should present the distinctness and attractions of a father's house. That this may be the case with us, it is not in the least necessary to know the exact mode of our future existence. It is enough to know that the "Lord Jesus Christ shall change our vile body, that it may be fashioned like unto his glorious body, according to the energy whereby he is able even to subdue all things unto himself." It is enough to know that "when he shall appear, we shall be like him: for we shall see him as he is." We need only to believe the words of our Savior: "In my Father's house are many mansions." We need nothing but that unquestioning spirit which rests upon the word and power of an omniscient God and Redeemer, and which commends itself to the guardianship of Him who has promised to be with his Church, and with every member of it, "always, even unto the end of the world."

II. In the second place, we are to notice the *definiteness* of the spiritual world, indicated by the words: "Many mansions." This language does not denote a dim, airy immensity; an unlimited ether in which the disembodied spirits shall wander; a shadowy realm in which ghosts pale and silent shall flit to and fro, like bats in twilight. Our spirits are finite and individual, and we start back at the thought of a dreamy existence diffused through a vague and indefinite infinitude. We recoil at the thought of a fluctuating and unfixed mode of being. Though flesh and blood cannot enter the kingdom of God, and we ought not to look for the material objects of this planet in a spiritual world, yet both Scripture and the profound instincts of our minds affirm a body for the clothing of our spirits, and a definite residence adapted to it. There is that within us which dreads a slumbering and uncertain mode of being. We are persons, and we instinctively desire the existence of a person, and a dwelling-place amidst personal relationships and circumstances.

The phrase "many mansions" denotes that there is a definite and appropriate residence beyond the tomb, for our finite and distinctly personal spirits; a residence in which they can unfold their powers in a well-defined and self-conscious manner; in which they can think, and know, and feel as vividly as they do here; in which as happy individualities they can look upon the face of a personal God and worship him; in which as blessed intelligences they can apprehend his excellence, and glorify him forevermore.

With all the spirituality with which the Word of God describes the abodes of the blest, there is united a remarkable clearness. In all other books, the great hereafter looks dim, strange, and forbidding; but in the Bible it appears real, natural, and life-like. In representing the kingdom of God as spiritual, Revelation keeps in view the wants of a finite creature, and therefore heaven is where the face of God shines with a more effulgent brightness than elsewhere, and where there is the most marked and impressive consciousness of his presence. There are times, even in the Christian life upon earth, when the veil is partially withdrawn, and that august Being whom man is prone to picture to himself as like the all-pervading air, or the mystic principle of life in nature, reveals speaking lineaments, and a living eye that meets his eye; moments when the finite spirit meets the Infinite face to face, and glances of Divine love and approbation send ineffable peace through it. And such, only in a perfect degree, will be the relation which the believer will sustain to God in the future life. He will see Him as He is. He will be a child, and God will be a Father. His existence will be that of distinct and blessed self-consciousness. He will dwell in " mansions."

III. In the third place, we are to note the *reality* of the heavenly world, denoted by the remark of our Lord: "If it were not so, I would have told you."

Man, here below, lives so entirely among sensible things, and meditates so little upon spiritual objects, that he comes to look upon that which is spiritual as unreal, and upon material things as the only realities. For most men, houses, and lands, and gold are more real than God and the soul. The former address the five senses, whereas " no man hath seen God at any time," and the soul is not apprehensible by any sensuous organ. Yet the invisible God is more real than any other being, for he is the cause and ground of all other existence. It was an invisible Mind that made the material chaos from nothing, and brooded over it, and formed it into an orderly and beautiful cosmos. The invisible is more firmly substantial than the visible. "The things which are seen were not made of things which are seen; the things which are seen are temporal, but the things which are not seen are eternal." Still, it cannot be denied that mankind reverse all this, and look upon spiritual things and the invisible world as very unreal and phantom-like. They do not have sufficient faith in an unseen future life, to live for it; and they do not regard it as so real and important, that their whole earthly existence should be devoted to a preparation for it.

Now, it is from such a mass of earthly and sensuous men, holding such views of the invisible, that the Christian is taken. He is born into the new spiritual kingdom, and professes to believe that God is, and that the soul verily is, and that heaven and hell are everlasting realities; but still the views and mental habits of the old carnal nature cling to him. He finds it difficult to live habitually with reference to eternity, to be continually conscious of the presence of God, and to act with an unwavering certainty of heaven. He is still much possessed by the spirit of this world, too frequently he finds his home among its vanities, and he attaches too much value to its objects. Hence, when the prospect of an entrance into eternity opens before him, he feels unprepared. He needs time that he may fix his thoughts upon God and invisible things, in order to realize that God is, and feel that he is going into a world more solid and satisfying than the one he is leaving. He has lived too carnal a life; he is not so spiritually minded as he should be, and his conversation has not habitually been in heaven; and therefore it seems to him as if he were entering a cheerless and ghostly realm. Thus the unfaithful Christian is surprised by death, and perturbation comes over him as he lies down to die. He is not so much at home in eternity as he is in time ; and hence he is in bondage to the fear of death, and shrinks from the exchange of worlds.

One remedy for such a state of mind, for such a practical unbelief in God and heaven, is to be found in meditation upon the words of Him who came down from heaven, and who is in heaven. "If it were not so," says our Lord, "if there were not many mansions in heaven ; if it were not my home, and the home of my Father, and of the holy angels, and of the spirits of just men made perfect; I would have told you, I would have undeceived you." This is the language of the Redeemer to his disciples, spoken that they might not be troubled or afraid at the prospect of his departure from them to God, or at the thought of their own departure out of this world. This voice of his sounds encouragement, through all ages, to the body of believers. It issues from the "mansions" of heaven, and for all who hear it, it is a voice that cheers and animates. It comes forth from the invisible world, and bids the Christian prepare to enter it ; to expect the entrance with a hopeful and cheerful temper ; nay, to be longing for the time when he shall go into the presence of God unclothed of the mortal and sinful, and clothed upon with the immortal and the holy.

It is evident from this unfolding of the subject, that the Christian needs an *increase* of faith. If he profoundly believed that God is his Father, and loves him ; that Christ is his Saviour, and intercedes for him ; that the Holy Spirit is his Sanctifier, and dwells in his heart—if he profoundly believed what the Word of God commands him to believe, that all the mercy and power of the triune Godhead is working out the eternal salvation of his soul, and that the Godhead dwells in a real and blessed world, and is preparing him for an entrance into it that he may be a priest and a king there forever—if he believed this with an undoubting and abiding faith, he would go through this life "tasting the powers of the world to come." And when the hour came to depart hence, he would leap for joy because his salvation draws nigh ; because he is soon to experience the truth of that glowing declaration : " Eye hath not seen, nor ear heard, neither hath it entered into the heart of man to conceive the things that God hath prepared for them that love him."

We should therefore pray, as did the disciples of our Lord, for an increase of faith ; and we should cultivate this particular habit and grace. Let us fix these particular truths and facts in our minds, and habitually ponder them : That heaven is a reality, if it were not, Christ would have told his followers so ; that the dwelling-place of God must be an actual and happy abode ; that our Father's house is adapted to the wants and capacities of our finite personal spirits ; and that its " mansions " are open to receive them when they leave the body. Let us believe and doubt not, that for all who are in Christ there is an ineffable blessedness in reserve, and that it will never end ; that all who sleep in Jesus shall " with open eye behold the glory of the Lord, and be changed into the same image from glory to glory by the Spirit of the Lord."

SERMON XII.

PURE MOTIVES THE LIGHT OF THE SOUL.

MATTHEW vi. 22.—" The light of the body is the eye; if therefore thine eye be single, thy whole body shall be full of light."

THE human eye is the most striking and expressive feature in the human constitution. Of all the physical organs, it is the one that is closest to the soul. Though composed of flesh and blood, of muscles and tissues—the toughest of muscles, and the most reticulated of tissues—it nevertheless seems to be half spiritual and immaterial. A man's hand, a man's foot, is hard matter, is solid stupid flesh and blood; but a man's eye gleams with ethereal fire, and his very soul radiates from it. The science of phrenology seeks the mind in the skull; but it would have been more successful in deducing human character from the physical structure, if it had studied that organ of vision which is always instinct with the soul and the soul's life. The skull of some animals approximates in its form to that of man; as the many attempts to trace a connection between man and the brute prove. But no brute's eye approximates in its expression to that of the human being. The eye of the ox is large, liquid, and soft; and the old Greek called the queen of the Olympian heavens the " ox-eyed Juno." But there is no morality, no human intelligence, and no human affection, in it. The ideas of God, and law, and conscience, are not written in the eye-ball of the ox as they are in that of every living man. Look into the eye of the faithful dog, or the patient ox, and you perceive a blank in reference to all that higher range of being, and that higher class of ideas, which lies at the basis of accountability and religion. But look into the eye of the African or the Esquimaux, and through all the dulness and torpor there gleams out upon you an expression, a glance, that betokens that this creature is not a mere animal, but is moral, is rational, is human.

"The light of the body," says our Lord in the text, "is the eye." This is a strong statement. Our Lord does not say that the eye is the instrument by which light is perceived, but that it is the light itself. And there certainly is a striking resemblance between the nature of the eye and that of light. The eye is adapted and preconformed to the solar ray. The crystalline lens, the watery humor, the tense silvery coating—everything that enters into the structure of this wonderful instrument of vision—has resemblances and affinities with that lucid shining element, the light of the sun. Plotinus long ago remarked that the eye could not see the sun, unless it had something solar, or sun-like, in its own composition. Mere opaque flesh and blood has no power of vision. We cannot see with the hand or the foot. In this sense, then, the eye is the light of the body. The original Greek word (λυχνός) in the text, which is translated light, literally signifies a lamp. The human eye is a burning lamp placed inside of the human body, like a candle behind a transparency, by which this "muddy vesture of decay," this dark opaque materialism of the human frame is lighted up. "The lamp of the body is the eye; therefore when thine eye is single, thy whole body also is full of light; but when thine eye is evil, thy body also is full of darkness. If thy whole body, therefore, be full of light, having no part dark, the whole shall be full of light, as when the bright shining of a candle doth give thee light." (Luke xi. 34, 36.)

But in employing this illustration it was not the purpose of our Lord to teach optics. It is true that his words agree incidentally with optical investigation; even as all the incidental teachings of Revelation concerning the material universe will be found to harmonize with the facts, when they shall finally be discovered by the groping and disputing naturalist. But the Son of God became incarnate for a higher object than to teach the natural sciences. Our Lord's casual allusions to the structure of earth, and of man, are made only for the purpose of throwing light upon a more mysterious organization than that of the human eye, and of solving problems infinitely more important than any that relate to the laws and processes of the perishing material universe.

The great Teacher, in his Sermon on the Mount from which the text is taken, had been enjoining it upon his disciples to live not for time but for eternity. "Lay not up for yourselves treasures upon earth, where moth and rust doth corrupt, and where thieves break through and steal. But lay up for yourselves treasures in heaven, where neither moth nor rust doth corrupt, and where thieves do not break through nor steal. For where your treasure is, there will your heart be also." (Matt. vi. 19-21.) This devotion to the concerns and realities of another and better world than this, Christ also tells his disciples, must be single-minded and absorbing. "No man can serve two masters; for either he will hate the one, and love the other, or else he will hold to the one, and despise the other. Ye cannot serve God and Mammon." (Matt. vi. 24.) The illustration borrowed from the human eye comes between these two thoughts, in St. Matthew's report of our Lord's instructions to his disciples; showing that by it, he intended to illustrate and enforce the necessity of singleness of purpose in the Christian life and profession. As the eye must not see double, but must be "single," in order that the body may be full of light; so there must be no double-mind, no wavering purpose, no impure motive, if the Christian would not walk in darkness.

We are, therefore, led by the connection of thought in our Lord's discourse, to consider the clear, luminous, and crystalline eye as a symbol of a pure, sincere, and single motive. And we propose in two particulars, to show that as the eye is the light of the body, so *pure motives are the light of the soul.*

By a pure motive is meant one that is founded in a sincere desire to honor God. Christian men are sometimes troubled to know whether their purposes and intentions are upright. They fear that they are sinister, and mixed with corruption. But the test is easy and sure. Let the person ask himself the question : "Do I in this thing honestly seek to exalt my Maker, and advance his cause in the world ? " If this can be answered in the affirmative, it precludes both pride and sensuality—the love of human applause, and the love of worldly enjoyment—which are the two principal lusts that vitiate human motives. By a pure motive, then, is meant one that is founded in the sole desire to glorify God ; and of such an one we confidently affirm that it is the light of the soul.

I. In the first place, it is the light of the soul, because it relieves the mind of doubts concerning the path of *duty.*

The single-eyed desire to please and honor God is a sure guide to a Christian, when he is perplexed in regard to the course of action that he ought to pursue. There are many instances in which it is difficult to decide what is the path of duty. There is nothing in the nature of the thing, or of the case, that settles the question; and, therefore, the only mode in which it can be settled is to raise the question respecting the personal intention.

Suppose, for illustration, that a Christian man, by that course of events which is the leading of Providence, is called to consider the proposition to change his place of residence, or to engage in another occupation or line of business. There is nothing intrinsically right or wrong in either of these measures. There is no moral quality in them; and therefore he cannot determine in respect to them from their intrinsic character, as he can when the proposition to lie, or to steal, or to do an act that is evil in itself, is presented to him. He must, therefore, if he would carry his Christianity into his whole life, and have it penetrate all his plans and movements—he must, therefore, in deciding what is duty in such instances as these, raise the question: How shall I most exalt God in the promotion of his cause in the world?

Suppose, again, that a young Christian is called upon to decide what his course in life shall be; whether he shall devote it to secular or sacred pursuits; whether he shall go into the market-place and buy and sell and get gain, or whether he shall go into the pulpit and preach the gospel to sinful men. Now, there is nothing in the mere prosecution of trade or commerce that is intrinsically right or intrinsically wrong; and neither is there anything holy, *per se*, in the calling of a clergyman. Everything depends upon the motive with which each is pursued. And the question by which this young Christian shall decide whether he shall be a layman or a clergyman, is the question: In which calling can I most glorify God?

These are specimens of an unlimited·number of cases in which the Christian is called to decide respecting the path of duty, when the cases themselves do not furnish the clue. This whole wide field is full of perplexity, unless we carry into it that clear, crystalline eye which fills the body full of light; that pure motive which is a sure guide through the tangled pathway. The Romish casuist has dug over this whole field, but it has yielded him very little good fruit, and very much that is evil. Instead of putting the conscience upon its good behavior; instead of telling his pupil to settle all such perplexity by the simple, evangelical maxim: "Whether therefore ye eat, or drink, or whatsoever ye do, do all to the glory of God;" instead of insisting first and chiefly upon the possession and the maintenance of a pure motive and a godly intention; the Romish casuist has attempted to discover an intrinsic morality in thousands of acts that have none, and to furnish a long catalogue of them all, in which the scrupulous and anxious soul shall find a rule ready made, and which he shall follow mechanically and servilely.

Perhaps there is no part of this field of human duty and responsibility, that more needs the clear shining light of a pure motive and intention, than that which includes the intercourse between religious men and the men of the world. The Church of Christ is planted in the midst of an earthly and an irreligious generation. It cannot escape this. St. Paul told the Christians of his day, that they could not avoid the temptations of pagan society except by going out of the world; and it is still as true as ever, that the Church must be exposed to the lust of the flesh, and the lust of the eye, and the pride of life, so long as it dwells here in space and time. And this fact renders it necessary for the Christian to decide many difficult and perplexing questions in morals and religion. They arose in the days of the apostles. Sincere and scrupulous believers were in doubt whether they should eat of meat that had constituted a part of a sacrificial victim offered in an idol's temple; and whether they should observe, or should not observe, the sacred days of the old Jewish dispensation. These things had in them no intrinsic morality; while yet the questions that were involved in them affected the purity and whole future growth of the Church. St. Paul laid down the rule by which they were to be settled. "Meat commendeth us not to God: for neither if we eat are we the better; neither, if we eat not, are we the worse. But take heed lest by any means this liberty of yours become a stumbling-block to them that are weak." The Christian must beware lest, by insisting upon his own personal rights, he hinder the progress of the gospel. There was nothing good or bad, in itself considered, in this partaking of food that had come into external connection with the abominations of idolatry and paganism. But if a Christian, by asserting and using his unquestionable right and liberty in a matter like this, should either directly or indirectly injure the cause of Christ, he must forego his personal right and yield his personal liberty. Says the noble and holy apostle Paul: "If my eating of meat—which is both my right and my liberty, so far as my own conscience is concerned—if my eating of meat interferes in any way with the spirituality and growth in grace of any professing Christian, I will eat no meat while the world stands." He decides the right and the wrong in such instances, not by the intrinsic quality of the act, nor by his own right and liberty as a private person to perform it, but by the moral and religious influence upon others, and thus, ultimately, by his own personal motives in the case. He desires and intends in every action to glorify God, and promote his cause in the world;

and this pure intention guides him unerringly through that field of casuistry which, without this clue, is so perplexing and bewildering.

Now, how beautifully does all this apply to the intercourse which the Church must hold with the world, and to that class of questions that arise out of this intercourse. A Christian man must mingle more or less in unchristian society. He is brought in contact with the manners and customs, the usages and habits, the pleasures and amusements of a generation that is worldly, that fears not God, and is destitute of the meekness and spirituality of Christ. A thousand perplexing inquiries respecting the path of duty necessarily arise; and they must be answered. Let him now look at them with that clear, honest, open eye, which is the light of the body. Let him decide upon the course which he shall pursue, in any given instance, by the illumination of a simple, single purpose to honor the Lord Christ and promote the Christian religion in the world. If this be in him and abound, he cannot go astray. To him it may be said, as the prophet Nathan said to David: "Do all that is in thy heart"—act as you please—"for the Lord is with thee."

It is easy to perceive that the application of such a maxim as that of the apostle: "Whether therefore ye eat, or drink, or whatsoever ye do, do all to the glory of God," would pour a light upon any possible question of duty that could not lead astray. No man will run much hazard of taking a wrong step in morals, or religion, whose eye is single, and steadily directed toward the honor of his Maker. It is possible, indeed, for him to err in judgment, for he is human and uninspired, but it is not very probable. And even if, owing to human infirmity, he should be mistaken in a perplexing and difficult case, it will be an error of the head and not of the heart. If it was really his desire and intention to please God and promote his cause in the world; if the Searcher of the heart saw that he meant well; then the will will be accepted for the deed. " For where there is a willing mind, it is accepted according to what a man hath, and not according to what he hath not." But errors of judgment will be very rare on the part of one who is actuated by a pure motive. He will walk in the light, and be one of the children of light. "He that loveth his brother," says St. John, "abideth in the light, and there is none occasion of stumbling in him." It is the effect of a genuinely benevolent and fraternal feeling toward a fellow-man, to prevent all misunderstandings, or to remove them if they exist. There can be no double-dealing where there is brotherly love. In like manner, if the soul is full of pure affection for God, and of a simple desire to honor him, there can be no occasion of stumbling in the path of duty. Such a soul walks under the broad, bright light of noon-day.

II. In the second place, a pure motive is the light of the soul, because it relieves the mind of doubts concerning religious *doctrine*.

In every age of the world, there is more or less perplexity in men's minds respecting religious truth. Pilate's question: "What is truth?" is asked by many a soul in every generation. Although Christianity has been a dominant religion in the world for eighteen centuries; although it has left its record and stamp upon all the best civilization and progress of mankind; although it has conducted millions of souls, through the gloom and sorrow of earth and time, to a peaceful death and a hope full of immortality; and although there is confessedly nothing else to take its place, in case it be an imposture and a lie; yet some men still doubt, and are in perplexity to know if it really be the way, and the truth, and the life. This is skepticism in its extreme form. But it may assume a milder type. There may be no doubt in regard to the truthfulness of Christianity so far as its principles agree with those of natural religion, and there may still be a strong doubt in regard to the evangelical doctrines. A man may believe that there is a God; that right and wrong are eternal contraries; that the soul is immortal; that virtue will be rewarded, and vice will be punished in another world; and yet doubt whether there is a triune God; whether man is apostate and totally depraved; whether the Son of God became man, and died on the cross to make atonement for human guilt; whether a man must be born again in order to a happy eternity. Many are perplexed with doubts upon these evangelical doctrines, as they are called, and at times would give much to know if they are in very deed the absolute and eternal verities of God.

Now we say that a pure motive, a single sincere purpose to exalt God, will do much toward clearing away these doubts. "If any man," says our Lord, "will do his will, he shall know of the doctrine." It is impossible in a single discourse to take up these truths of revealed religion one by one, and show how a pure motive will flare light upon each and every one of them, and teach a man what he ought to believe and hold. We will, therefore, select only one of them, and make it the crucial test by which to try them all.

There is no doctrine about which the doubts and skepticism, nay, the sincere perplexity of men, hovers more continually, than about the doctrine that man is by nature depraved and deserving of eternal punishment. Probably, if the world of unbelievers could be convinced of the truth of this particular tenet, their doubt and unbelief upon all the other doctrines would yield. This is the citadel in the fortress of unbelief.

Now let a man look at this doctrine of the guilt and corruption of man, as it is stated in the Christian Scriptures, and as it is presupposed by the whole economy of Redemption, and ask himself the question, whether he will most honor God by adopting it, or by combating and rejecting it. Let him remember that if he denies the doctrine of human guilt and corruption, he nullifies the whole Christian system, because he who nullifies the sin of man nullifies the redemption of the Son of God. St. Paul told the Corinthians, that if there were no resurrection of the dead, then Christ had not risen ; and if Christ had not risen, the faith of every one who had believed in him was vain. In like manner, if man is not a lost sinner, then there is no Divine Saviour and no eternal salvation, for none is needed. There are no superfluities in the universe of God. Whoever, therefore, denies the reality of a sin in the human race which necessitated the incarnation and atoning death of the Son of God, puts upon God that great dishonor of disputing his veracity which is spoken of by St. John : "If we say that we have not sinned, we make him a liar, and his word is not in us. He that believeth not God, hath made him a liar, because he believeth not the record that God gave of his Son." (1 John i. 10 ; v. 10.) But the "record" spoken of is the doctrine that man is a lost sinner—so utterly lost that no one but the eternal Son of God can save him ; and even He can do this only by pouring out his atoning life-blood. Now can any man desire and purpose to glorify God, while disputing Divine Revelation and denying the apostasy and sin of mankind, respecting which God has left such a clear record in his Word, and which constitutes the only rational ground for the death of the Lord Jesus Christ ?

No, it is the confession and not the denial of human depravity that glorifies God. Two men went up into the temple to pray, one of whom acknowledged the guilt and corruption of man, and the other denied it; and we are informed by the highest authority that the prayer of the former was well-pleasing to the Most High, and that of the latter was an abomination to Him. The men who glorify God are possessed of the publican's spirit. They do not adopt the pharisee's theory of human nature. They cry, "God be merciful to me a sinner." And the declaration concerning them from the lips of the Eternal is: "To this man will I look, even to him that is poor, and of a contrite spirit, and trembleth at my word." (Is. lxvi. 2.)

In settling the question, therefore, respecting the unwelcome doctrine of human depravity and its endless punishment, a pure motive will pour a flood of light. If this one thing alone could but be introduced into the heart of the doubter himself, we have small fear that the most humbling, and in some respects the most difficult, truth in the Christian system, would be accepted. If the mind of the skeptic, or of the groping and really perplexed inquirer, could but be filled with an absorbing concern for the Divine honor; if every such one could but be brought to sympathize with St. Paul when he cried: "Let God be true, and every man a liar;" we would leave it with him to say which is the absolute and indisputable truth—the doctrine of human virtue, or the doctrine of human sin.

Employ, then, this test and criterion of religious doctrine. Ask yourself the question, in reference to any and every tenet that challenges your attention, or solicits your credence, "Does its adoption glorify God?" The arguments for the Christian system—and by the Christian system we mean evangelical Christianity—are strong, and grow stronger as the ages wear away. But there is one argument too often overlooked, or underestimated.

It is the fact that this system exalts God, and properly abases man. We find an evidence of its divinity in this very thing. All the natural religions, all the wild religions of the globe, reverse this. They exalt the creature, and abase, yea debase, the Creator. Like the old Ptolemaic astronomy, like their own absurd theories of the material world, they place the little world of man at the centre of the boundless universe. Christianity, like the Copernican system, restores everything to its right relations, and arranges everything about its real and true centre. God is first, last, and midst. Of him, through him, and to him, are all things. The first question, therefore, to be asked concerning every doctrine, and every system, is the question: "Does it promote the Divine glory?" The great and first maxim for human action, and human speculation, is the maxim: "Whether, therefore, ye eat, or drink, or whatsoever ye do, do all to the glory of God."

This then is the eye with which we are to pierce through all the doubts and darkness of earth and time. This pure motive is the light of the soul. How simple, and how beautiful it is—simple as the light of heaven; beautiful as the crystalline eye itself. Only carry with you this desire and longing to exalt the great and wise Creator, and you cannot go astray. You cannot go astray in the actions of your daily life. You cannot go astray in the thoughts and opinions of your own mind. The very motive will envelop you, always and everywhere, like an atmosphere. Your whole soul "shall be full of light, having no part dark; as full of light as when the bright shining of a candle doth give thee light."

SERMON XIII.

THE LAW IS LIGHT.

PROVERBS vi. 23.—"The law is light."

THE fitness and beauty of this comparison of the law of God with light are seen immediately. If we consider the nature of law, we find that it is like the nature of sunlight. There is nothing so pure and clean as light, and there is nothing so pure and stainless as the divine law. We cannot conceive of a mixture of light and darkness, and neither can we conceive of a mixture of holiness and sin. The one may expel the other, but they can never so mingle with each other as to form one compound substance, or quality. Light is always a bright and shining element; the law of God is always a perfectly pure thing.

Again, there is nothing so ubiquitous as the light. It is everywhere. Our earth and all the heavenly bodies swim in it. Its universal presence is necessary, in order that there may be order and beauty in the material universe. When God would change the void and formless chaos into a world, he first created, not life, as we should have anticipated, but light, and shot it through the gloom. How penetrating an element it is, and how wonderfully does it search out all the secret places in nature, and take up its dwelling in them. It enters with a gentle yet a powerful entrance into the hard diamond, and gives it its gleam and sparkle. It tenderly feels its way into the delicate pupil of the human eye, and lights it up with a bright and radiant glow. It melts with a serene and mellowing effect into the firmament above us, and makes it a fit canopy and pavilion for the globe. Its going forth is from the end of the heaven, and its circuit unto the end of it, and there is nothing hid from the radiance thereof.

How very like this light in the material universe is the law of God in the rational. How naturally does the one suggest and symbolize the other. Hence the Psalmist, after alluding to the sun, the great bearer of light, and to his running like a strong giant through the heavens, abruptly, yet by a very natural transition, begins to speak of "the law of the Lord" as perfect; of the "statutes of the Lord" as right; of the "commandment of the Lord" as pure; of "the judgments of the Lord" as true and righteous altogether.

Again, to follow the resemblance, the moral law is the ordinance which establishes and governs the moral universe. The command, "Let there be light," founded and sustains the material world; and the command, "Let there be supreme love of God," founds and sustains the rational and responsible world. And as the proclamation of the physical law was requisite in order to the existence of the physical world, so was the proclamation of the spiritual law requisite in order to the existence of the spiritual world. Both commands are universal and all-pervading. The law of God, therefore, like the light, is ubiquitous. Within the rational and responsible sphere, law is everywhere. Not, indeed, in the same degree, but in the same species. For there are different degrees of moral light, as there are different degrees of natural light. As there is the twilight of the morning, and the brightness of the noonday, and the many degrees of light between these all running into each other by insensible gradations, so there is the dim light of finite reason in the imbruted pagan, and the light of supreme reason in the infinite God shining in its strength and intolerable brightness, and the infinite number of degrees between these extremes. Everywhere in this rational world does this legal light, in a fainter or a brighter manner, shine ; for a being without a spark of moral intelligence, without a particle of conscience, is a brute. Everywhere in this responsible world, does this law, with greater or less power, manifest its presence. It may be a law written only upon the fleshy tablet of the heart, as in the instance of the heathen. It may be written on the heart, and in the revealed word of God, as the dweller in a Christian land has it. It may be written on the heart, and read again in the countenance of that God who " is light, and in whom is no darkness at all," as spirits in eternity have it. But everywhere its presence in some degree is presupposed in a responsible world—" for where no law is, there is no transgression." Its presence, moreover, is a penetrating one, like that of light. It pierces where we should not expect to find it. It is witnessed in the remorse which it awakens when it has pierced through the thick and dark degradation of paganism. It is seen in the blood of the victims by which the pagan attempts to expiate the guilt of having violated law, and resisted light. It is revealed in the uneasy consciences of men living in a Christian land, which can be pacified only by the blood of Him who was " made a curse for man." It is found in hell, and creatures dread it and feel its terrible power, because it is light divorced from life ; mere law without love. It is found in heaven, and the saints enjoy it, because for them it is light, and life, and love, all in one. Wherever the omnipresent God is, there is his law. Wherever there is a creature possessing the sense of responsibility to God, there is also a knowledge, in greater or less degree, of that commandment by which its conduct toward him should be regulated. Issuing from God, then, moral law flows out into all places of his dominion, as light radiates from the sun, and constitutes a clear, crystal element in which all accountable beings live, either as light or lightning; either as the light that rejoices them if they obey, or the lightning that blasts them if they disobey—even as the natural light is the dwelling-place of all material things; though sometimes it is the benign light of an autumnal noon, or the soft light of a summer evening, and sometimes it is that chemical incandescence which, in the old geological eras, burned up the primeval forests, of which the coal-beds are the cinders. How truly, then, " the law is light," if we consider the purity of its nature, or the universality and penetration of its presence.

But our main object is to show the similarity between the moral law and the material light, by looking at its influences and effects in the soul, rather than by analyzing its intrinsic nature. And the subject naturally divides into two parts, when we remember that there are two classes of beings, the evil and the good, who sustain relations to this law.

We shall, in this discourse, direct attention to some effects produced by the Divine law in the *Christian believer*, that are like the effects of light in the world of nature.

I. In the first place, the moral law *reveals* like sunlight. It makes the sin which still remains in the Christian a visible thing. The apostle Paul notices this point of similarity, when he remarks: " All things that are reproved are made manifest by the light, for whatsoever doth make manifest is light." And our Lord implies the same resemblance, when he says: "This is the condemnation, that light is come into the world, and men loved darkness rather than light, because their deeds were evil. For every one that doeth evil hateth the light, neither cometh to the light, lest his deeds should be reproved. But he that doeth truth cometh to the light, that his deeds may be made manifest that they are wrought in God."

Believers are continually urged in the Scriptures to bring their hearts into the light of God's law, that they may see the sin that is in them. It is as necessary, in order to know our characters, that we should scrutinize them by this illumination, as it is that the naturalist should bring the plant, or the insect, whose structure he would comprehend, into the bright daylight. And if we would thoroughly understand our intricate and hidden corruption, we must by prayer and reflection intensify the light of the moral law, that it may penetrate more deeply into the dark mass, even as the naturalist must concentrate the light of the sun through the lens, if he would thoroughly know the plant or the insect.

How wonderfully does the holy searching law of God reveal our character! In the silent hour of meditation, when we are alone with it, and carefully compare our conduct with its requirements, how unworthy and guilty do we find and feel ourselves to be, and how earnestly do we look unto Him "who is the end of the law for righteousness, unto every one that believeth." Truly the law is "the candle of the Lord, searching all the inward parts." It discloses, when its light is thus brightened by meditation, much sin which in the carelessness of daily life escapes our notice. The light, in the hour of self-examination, goes down to a lower plane, and reveals a lower and more hidden sin. It makes its way in among the motives, the propensities, the desires and affections of the heart, and brings into clear view the plague-spot itself—the evil nature and disposition. Sin is a sallow plant of darkness, and grows best in the night, like the nightshade and other poisonous plants. Hence it avoids the light, and will not come to the light, lest it be reproved. But when we resolutely throw open the soul, and permit the light of God's truth to shine in, then we come to know the deadly growth which has been springing up rankly and luxuriantly within us—a growth of which we had not been distinctly aware, and which is difficult to root up. Every Christian who is at all faithful to himself, and to God, has experienced these illuminating and revelatory influences of the law. It has frequently dazzled him by its pure white light, and he has felt himself to be exceedingly depraved. He has been astonished at his corruption, as the dying saint was when he sighed: "Infinite upon infinite is the wickedness of the heart." With the Psalmist, he has cried out to God: "The entrance of thy words giveth light; I have seen an end of all perfection, thy commandment is exceeding broad."

We cannot leave this head of the discourse without directing particular attention to the fact, that for the believer the law makes these disclosures of character in a *hopeful* and *salutary* manner. In their own nature they are terrible. The unbeliever cannot endure them, and hence he avoids them as the criminal avoids the officer of justice. But the believer, by virtue of his union with Christ, and appropriation of his vicarious atonement, has been delivered from the *condemning* power of the law. The "curse" of the law, Christ his Surety has borne for him. The demands of justice have been completely satisfied by the Son of God, his High Priest. This fact places him in a new and secure position in respect to the Divine law and government. His legal status, or standing, is safe. There is no condemnation to him as in Christ Jesus. Hence, whenever he searches his heart, and compares his character and conduct with the requirements of the Divine law, and finds that he has incurred its condemnation, he does not fall into servile terror and despair, like the impenitent unbeliever. By reason of his faith in Christ's oblation, he is prepared for these revelations. From his high evangelic position, he cries out : " Let the disclosure of character come : let me know the full depth and extent of my guilt and corruption. Christ is my atonement, and his blood cancels everything. Let the righteous law smite me; it shall be a kindness, in that it leads me to my Redeemer." Hence this light of the Divine law is of a cleansing and illuminating, and not of a burning and blasting nature for the believer. He makes use of the law only for preceptive purposes, in order to know his moral state and condition. And he has no further use for it. He does not expect, or look, to be *justified* by it. When it demands penalty for the sins that are past, as it righteously does, and he most cordially concedes the righteousness of the claim, he points it to the satisfying death of Christ. And when it demands a perfect performance of its commands, as it justly does, he looks to Christ for grace, inclination, and power, to render such an obedience. In this way, the believer stands upon a high vantage-ground in reference to law. He enjoys all the beneficent and educating influences of the law, without any of those dreadful judicial and retributive impressions which are experienced by the legalist, the moralist, the unbeliever, upon whom the entire law, both as precept and penalty, weighs down as an intolerable burden, because he has not cast himself and his burden upon Christ. For the legalist has appealed to Cæsar, and to Cæsar he must go ; the unbelieving, unevangelic man has referred his case to justice, and to justice it must go.

Thus is the moral law like the material light, in reveal-ing, in bringing to light. And for the believer it is a mild and radiant light which he does not fear, and which his soul loves more and more. Like the cup of a flower, his heart opens itself to the pure ether and element, and drinks it in with eagerness and joy. And as the flower by thus turning towards the light becomes like the light itself in some degree, and acquires an airy and almost im-material texture in the process, so does the Christian's heart come to be a pure and holy thing like the law. The law is in his heart, and appears more and more in his ac-tions, until at length, when that which is perfect is come, his whole nature and entire being is transmuted into a living spontaneous law of righteousness.

II. In the second place, the law, for the believer in Christ, *attracts* like the light. Light in the material world universally attracts. If the smallest pencil of light, through the smallest possible aperture, fall upon the plant in a dark place, it immediately shoots towards it. And when the sun rises up and bathes the world in light, how all nature rises up to meet it. The very leaves of the trees look up, and the flowers spread out with a richer bloom, to welcome its coming. A more vigorous and spirited life circulates throughout nature, and the whole landscape seems as if it were ascending like incense to the God of light. Just so does the moral law attract the world of holy beings. They love the law for its intrinsic excellence, and seek it with the whole heart. They cannot live without it, and would not live without it if they could. They see in it a tran-script of the character of God whom they adore, and therefore they gaze at it, and study it. "O how I love thy law, it is my meditation all the day," is the utterance of their hearts. And yet more than this. Their very natures are pure like the law ; and like always attracts like.

If there be in any soul even the least degree of real holiness, there is a point of attraction upon which the law of
God will seize and draw. Holiness is never an isolated
thing in any creature. It came from God, and it goes
back to God, and returns again increased and strengthened.
Hence there is a continual tendency and drift of a holy
soul towards the holy One. As the power of gravitation
draws with a steady stress all things to the centre, so do
truth and righteousness, inhering in the Divine nature,
like a vast central force attract all pure and holy creatures
towards their seat. Have you not, in the more favored
hours of your religious life, experienced what the Scripture denominates the "drawing"—the attraction—"of the
Father," when by the illumination of his Spirit he disclosed to you the excellence of his statutes and commandments, and you panted after conformity with them as the
hart panteth after the water-brooks? Did not the beauty
of holiness attract your ardent gaze, and prompt the prayer
that it might be realized and seen in your own personal
character? As angelic purity dawned more and clearer
upon your vision, and you saw how desirable and blessed
it is to be spotless and saintly, how glorious the law that
disciplines, and regulates, and purifies, appeared to you.
You wished that your soul might cast off its old garments
of sin and earth, and might go up and bathe forever in the
pure, limpid waters of heaven—that your heart might become a perfectly clean heart, ever gently yet powerfully
drawn by the commandment toward the Sovereign. You
said with the Psalmist: "Thy word is very pure, therefore thy servant loveth it. The law of the Lord is perfect; more to be desired is it than gold, yea than much fine
gold: sweeter also than honey and the honey-comb."

This view of the Divine law as an attractive energy is
an encouraging one to the believer. It affords good

grounds for the perseverance of the saints. For this operation of the law of God in a renewed heart is ceaseless and constantly augmenting. As well might we suppose the power of attraction in the material world to be an intermittent one, and subject to interruption and cessation, as to suppose it in the spiritual. The great force of gravitation never becomes tired and weary in the planets and molecules of matter ; and neither do the truth and Spirit of God within the believer's soul. As the Christian is drawn nearer to God, the influence of the Divine law is greater and greater. It obtains a more complete mastery over his appetites and passions ; it dwells with a more constant residence in his affections ; it actuates his conduct with a more delightful and easy power. What a cheering view of the future career of a redeemed spirit does this way of contemplating the moral law present. Forever increasing in its influence, as it is forever drawing the creature nearer its Father and God. The goal is an infinitely distant one, and yet as he is passing along this limitless line he feels an allurement at each and every one of the innumerable points, as powerful and as entirely master of his soul as if he were at the end of the infinite career.

III. In the third place, the law, for the believer in Christ, *invigorates* like light. This point of resemblance between the moral law and the light of the sun is plain, though somewhat less obvious at the first glance. For although we more commonly think of the air as the invigorating element in nature, yet it is true of the light, that its presence is necessary in order that the spirits of a man may be lively and in vigorous action. That plant which grows up in the darkness is a pale and weak thing. The season of repose and inactivity is the night time. In the hours of darkness, the living powers of the body go to rest, and their instruments, the limbs, are as still and motionless as when death itself has set its seal upon them. But when the world again "covers itself with light as with a garment," man feels its awakening and stimulating power. The living currents of his frame circulate more quickly, spring and buoyancy are imparted, and he "goeth forth unto his work and to his labor until the evening." And not only does man feel the invigoration of light, but nature does also. Mere air is not all that is necessary in order to growth; the clear shining effulgence of heaven must be poured abroad, that there may be freshness and bloom in the natural world.

Similar to this is the effect of the moral law upon one who is resting upon Christ, both in respect to the law's condemnation and the law's fulfilment. For we cannot but again remind you, that the believer sustains a totally different relation to the Divine law from that which the unbeliever sustains, and it casts a very different light upon him from that which it darts and flashes into the impenitent soul. The steady, cheerful light of a summer's day is very different from the wrathful, fitful lightning of the black thunder-cloud. The power of law to condemn, to terrify, and to slay, as we have before remarked, is departed, because Christ has received the stroke of justice upon himself. For the disciple of Christ, the law is no longer a judge, but only an instructor. The terrors of the law have lost their power, and he is relieved from that weakening, benumbing fear of judgment which utterly prevents a cheerful obedience. Fear hath torment; and no creature can love and serve God while he is in torment. The disciple of Christ is a free and vigorous man spiritually, because his Redeemer has released him from the bondage and anxiety which the law, as a condemning judge, and an inexorable, unhelping exactor, causes in every unbeliever. Take away fear, and take away bondage, and you impart energy and courage at once. As soon as a criminal is released from the sentence of death, and his chains are knocked off, his old vigor and life return again; his frame dilates once more, his eye kindles, and his heart swells and beats again, because he is no longer under sentence of death, and no longer a bond slave.

Not only does the law impart spiritual vigor to the believer because it has ceased to be his condemning judge, and has become a wise and good schoolmaster to lead him to Christ, but it invigorates him because by virtue of his union with Christ it has become an inward and actuating principle. It is no longer a mere external statute, with which he has no sympathy, and which merely terrifies him with its threat. His heart has been so changed by grace that he now really loves the law of God. The apostle Paul, speaking of the sinner and of the sinner's relation to the law, affirms that for such an one " the law is the strength of sin." In case the heart is at enmity with God's commandment, the commandment merely provokes, elicits, and stimulates the inward depravity, but does nothing towards removing it. The commandment which was ordained to life—which, in a right state of things, was adapted to fill the human soul with peace and joy—is found to be unto death, and actually fills it with despair and woe. But for the believer, this very same law is the strength of holiness. The Psalmist remarks of the righteous man : " The law of God is in his heart; none of his steps shall slide." When the human soul is regenerated, the Divine law is written not merely on but in the tablet of the heart. It becomes a feeling, an affection, an inclination, a disposition within it. Have you ever seen a Christian in whose active and emotional powers the law of God had come to be a second nature ? Have you ever seen one whose actions were easily and sweetly controlled by the Divine commandment, and whose central and inmost experiences were but expressions and manifestations of it? And was not that Christian a strong and vigorous one? Did he not run the race, and fight the fight, with a firm and determined bearing; calm in adversity, equable and serenely joyful in prosperity; wending his way faithful and fearless into eternity? Never is the spirit of a man in such a vigorous condition, and its energies in such a healthful and active play, as when it is impelled and actuated by law; and who but the renewed man is thus actuated? Never is man such a free and spirited creature, as when he spontaneously listens to the voice of truth and duty. As the apostle says: He is "filled with the spirit of *power*." The poet Wordsworth,[1] personifying the law of order which prevails in the natural world, and which prevails inwardly as all the laws of nature do, addresses it thus:

> Flowers laugh before thee on their beds;
> And fragrance in thy footing treads;
> Thou dost preserve the stars from wrong;
> And the most ancient heavens through thee are fresh and strong.

So is it, in a far higher sense, with the law of God in the spiritual world. Wherever it prevails inwardly as a principle, and not outwardly as a threat, there is order, vigor, beauty, and strength. Creatures who listen to it in this spontaneous style are strong in the highest of strength —in the strength of holiness, in the " confidence of reason " and righteousness.

IV. In the fourth place, the law, for the believer in Christ, *rejoices* like the light. This feature of resemblance is evident at the very first glance. "Truly the light is sweet, and a pleasant thing it is for the eyes to behold the

---

[1] Ode to Duty.

sun." In nature, the hour of joy is the morning hour.
All creatures and things are filled with gladness at the up-
rising of the light.[1] It is related in ancient story that the
statue of Memnon, when the first rays of the morning
gilded it, began to tremble, and thrill—the hard por-
phyritic rock began to tremble, and thrill, and send forth
music like a swept harp. Thus does nature thrill under
the first touch of light, and warble forth its harmonies.
And such, too, is the joy-giving influence of righteous law
in the heavenly world, and such is its effect in the individual believer. What rapture the contemplation of the
Divine commands imparted to the heart of the royal
harper. How his soul accompanied his harp, in singing
with jubilance the praises of its Author. Hear him:
"Thy testimonies have I taken as an heritage forever;
for they are the rejoicing of my heart. I rejoice at thy
word as one that findeth great spoil." Joy in the law of
the Lord—positive, blood-felt delight in having it rule
over and in the soul—is the sure sign of a right state.
Miserable is that creature of God for whom obedience to
law is a task and a disgust. There are no hirelings in
heaven. Service there is its own reward. The law of
God is to be our companion forever, either as a joy or a
sorrow, either as bliss or bale ; and we must, therefore,
come into such an inward and affectionate relation to it, as
to make it bliss and not woe. We must rejoice in its holy
presence, when with a severe and just eye it rebukes our
sin, and leads us to the Cross for pardon. We must be
gladdened with its benign and enrapturing presence, when
with a calm peace in the conscience it rewards us for obedience. We must find our heaven in our conformity to

---

[1] Compare Schiller's Wilhelm Tell, Act I., Scene iv. ; and Milton's
Samson Agonistes, 90-93.

God. It must be our meat and drink to do the Divine will. For eternity is not lighted by the light of the sun, nor by the light of the moon; but the Lord God himself is the light thereof. The happiness of our spirits, if they are saved, will not be found in material things. It will not issue from the streets of gold, from the gates of pearl, from the jewelry and adornments of a material city. These are but emblems and faint foreshadowings. The bliss of the blest will be righteousness, peace, and joy in the Holy Ghost—the consciousness of perfectly loving God, and of being beloved by Him. The creature can have no higher joy than to dwell in God's holy presence, a holy being for-ever. There is no emotion so ecstatic as that which swells the heart that can sincerely say with St. Paul: "I am Christ's, and Christ is God's." Truly the law will be light in that perfect world; the great sun of the system. It will send out its invigorating and gladdening rays, which will penetrate, like the tremulous undulations of the solar beam, into the inmost spirit. It will warm and quicken the whole heavenly world into life—into holy life, into pure activity, into serene enjoyment.

It follows from this unfolding of the subject, that the great act of the Christian is the act of *faith;* and the great work of the Christian is to *cultivate* and *strengthen* his faith. "This is the work of God, that ye believe on Him whom he hath sent." We have seen that the moral law, like the material light, reveals, attracts, invigorates, and rejoices, only because the soul sustains a certain special relation to it—only because it is trusting in Christ for deliverance from its condemnation, and for grace to fulfil it in future. What then should we do, but with still more energy obey the great command, and believe on the Lord Jesus Christ with a more childlike and entire trust. If the holy law of God has ever cast any cheering and pleasant light upon us, it has been by virtue of this faith. If the law shall ever become all-controlling within us, it will be through this faith. Faith in the Redeemer is the alpha and omega, the first and the last, the beginning, middle, and end, in the religious experience. This alone renders the moral law an operative and actuating principle within us. By no other method can we ever fulfil the law.

We have compared the law to the sun of our system. It is a disputed opinion of some astronomers, that far beyond our sun, and all other suns, there is a point in immensity around which, as the ultimate centre of centres, these myriad suns of myriad systems all circle. That point one has asserted to be the throne of God. So, too—if it be allowable to borrow an illustration from a doubtful physics—if the Divine law, and whatever else there may be in the great immensity of truth, is ever to become an efficient force and centre of motion for the lost soul, it must all of it revolve around the final centre and power, namely, simple and hearty faith in the Son of God. Faith in Christ sets up the throne of God in the soul, and when this is done, all things come into right relation to it, and move in proper order round it. Let us then pray: "Lord, increase our weak faith." Let us then toil—by reading and meditating upon God's Word, and by constant supplication for the teaching of the Holy Spirit—after a bolder, firmer, and more operative faith.

SERMON XIV.

THE LAW IS THE STRENGTH OF SIN.

1 CORINTHIANS xv. 56.—"The strength of sin is the law."

ANY man who thinks or feels at all about the sin that is in him, knows that it is strong; and, also, that it is the strongest principle within him. His will is adequate for all the other undertakings that come up before him in life, but it fails the moment it attempts to conquer and subdue itself. He rules other men, but he does not rule himself; and, in more senses than one, "he that is slow to anger is better than the mighty, and he that ruleth his spirit than he that taketh a city."

The experience of the Christian, likewise, demonstrates that sin is the most powerful antagonist that man has to contend with. That great struggle through which the believer passes, in order to be freed from the bondage of corruption, summons the strongest energies of the soul, and stretches the cords of the inner man to their utmost tension. Nay, more, this heat and stress of the Christian race and fight evinces that man must be "strong in the Lord," in order to overcome sin. "The power of God's might" must descend and dwell in the human soul, or else it will sink in the struggle. And when the finite spirit is endued with this power from on high; when it is laden, as it were, with the omnipotence of God; how does it tremble and reel under the burden. When the human soul is pervaded by the presence of its Maker, in the hour of searching convictions, and especially of severe struggle with long-indulged habits of sin, how does it stagger to and fro like a drunken man. Were it not that the influences of the Divine Spirit, while they press the soul down, at the same time hold it up, and prevent it from being utterly cast down, the frail creature would not be able to endure such a strain. If the man were all permeated by a power that convicts but does not renovate; that wakens a sense of guilt, but does not apply the atoning blood; that sets the whole inward being into commotion, but does not tranquillize it with the sense and assurance of forgiveness and love; like the person in the Gospel possessed with a dumb spirit, he would be "torn, and be as one dead." Nay, he would be dead with that death of the spirit which is a vitality of anguish. These pangs and throes, attending that process which our Lord denominates a "birth" of the soul, show how stubborn and inveterate is the sin which it subdues and eradicates.

What is the cause of this mighty strength of sin? The apostle in the text asserts, somewhat remarkably, that it is the *law of God*. "The strength of sin is the law."

By the law is meant the sum of all that a rational being ought to do, under all circumstances, and at all times. It is equivalent to duty—using this term to denote the collective body or mass, if we may so say, of all the requirements of conscience upon a man. It includes all that is implied in the word right, and excludes all that we mean by wrong. At first sight, it appears passing strange that a law of this description should, in any sense, be said to be the strength of sin. Yet such is the explicit assertion of an inspired apostle. And elsewhere the same apostle seems to vilify the ten commandments. He tells us that "when the commandment came, sin revived;" and that "sin, taking occasion by the commandment, deceived him, and wrought in him all manner of concupiscence." (Rom. vii. 8, 9, 11.)

We cannot understand these statements, unless we take into view the difference in the relation which a holy and a sinful being, respectively, sustains to the moral law. The assertion in the text is only a relative one. St. Paul does not lay down an absolute and universal proposition. He means that the pure and holy law of God is the strength of sin for a *sinner*. For the saint, on the contrary, it is the strength of holiness; and had the apostle been speaking of the holy, he would have said this. The law is identically the same thing in both cases, and therefore the difference in its effects must be attributed to the different attitude which the natural and the spiritual man, respectively, holds toward it. In the instance of the holy being, the law of righteousness is an *inward and actuating principle*. It is his own loved and chosen law, and he obeys it because it is one with his inclination, and he would not do otherwise. But for a sinful being, the law of God is only an *outward rule*, and not an inward principle. Law does not work sweetly and pleasantly within the sinner, but stands stern and severe outside of, and over him, commanding and threatening. The moral law is not internal and spontaneous to the natural man. If he attempts to obey it, he does so from fear, or self-interest, and not from the love of it. It is not his own chosen law in which he delights, but a hated statute, to which his heart and inclination are in deadly opposition. The "law of sin" is the sole inward principle that rules him, and his service of sin is spontaneous and willing. In short, the law of righteousness is the strength of sin for the sinner, because it is *extraneous*, and *hostile*, to his will and affections. It is written upon his conscience, but not written into his heart. God's law and the human conscience are one and harmonious; but God's law and the human will are diverse and antagonistic. Hence the Scriptures describe regeneration as the *inwardizing* of the moral law. "This shall be the covenant that I will make with the house of Israel: After those days, saith the Lord, I will put my law in their inward parts, and write it in their hearts; and I will be their God, and they shall be my people." (Jer. xxxi. 33.) According to this description, to regenerate a man is to make the law of God internal, impulsive, and spontaneous, where before it has been external, compulsory, and threatening; it is to convert duty into inclination, so that the man shall know no difference between the commands of God and the desires of his own heart.

Before proceeding to unfold and illustrate the truth taught in the text, let us notice the fact, that the two principles, or in St. Paul's phrase "laws," of holiness and sin, which operate in the moral world, in order to have efficiency must be within the heart and will. If the law of righteousness, for example, does not abide and work in the inclination and affections of a man, the mere fact that it is inlaid in his conscience will not secure obedience. The ten commandments may be cut into the hard, unyielding stone of the moral sense, but unless they are also written in the soft, fleshy tablet of the heart, they will be inoperative, except in the form of conviction and condemnation. The moral law must be "in the members," in St. Paul's phrase—that is, it must be wrought into the feelings and disposition of the person—before it can be effectual and productive.

The laws or principles of holiness and sin may fitly be compared with the great fruitful laws that work and

weave in the world of nature. All these laws are *internal.*
They start from within, and work outward. They per-
meate and pervade, and not merely affix and attach themselves to, the products of nature. The principle of life in
the tree is not dropped down upon the tree like dew from
without, but rises up from within it like an exhalation.
How wonderfully productive and mighty, because internal,
are the movements of the law of vegetable life, which car-
pets with bright flowers the meadows of half a continent,
and sends the sap through every twig of every tree in its
vast forests. This law lives, and develops itself, within
these productions.

All this holds true of the mental world, equally with
the physical. In the upper blessed realm of heaven, the
law of holiness works as an inward and spontaneous force
in every one of its inhabitants. Issuing from the infinite
and glorious Fountain of purity, it takes its course through
all the happy spirits, producing the fruits of holiness
throughout its bright track, and building up a beautiful
world of order, light, and purity. And it is equally true,
that throughout the realm of hell, the law of sin as an inward principle of life and action—self-chosen, it is true,
and not forced upon any one, yet internal to the will, and
thoroughly inwrought into the affections — is working
within every individual member of that world. And the
fact that there is such a realm, where the principle of evil in
antagonism to the principle of good is unfolding itself, and
multiplying its unsightly and deadly products, should make
every man thoughtful, and lead him to inquire most earnestly: "Am I in and of this realm? am I, in Christ's
phrase, 'from beneath'? is the law of sin the inward and
actuating principle of my will?"

In the light of this illustration, let us now look more
closely at the attitude which the unrenewed will maintains

toward the Divine law. The law of righteousness, confessedly, is not the inward, actuating force in a sinner's will. It is the law of sin which is "in his members"—which is internal to him—and which, consequently, is the only one that can bear fruits. And how rank and luxuriant they are; with what ease are they produced; how willingly and spontaneously does he sin. There is nothing artificial or mechanical in man's iniquity. There are no spurious and "dead" works on the side of transgression. Sin is always alive and genuine. Man is never a formalist, or a hypocrite, in his disobedience. This work is hearty, and springs from an inward principle. Yet the law of holiness is the one that ought to bear the fruit. But it cannot, until it ceases to be external and threatening, and becomes internal and complacent. So long as the existing inimical relation continues between the moral law and the voluntary faculty; so long as the law of God is a letter on the statute-book of the conscience, but not a letter written in the fleshy tablet of the heart; so long must it be inoperative, except in the way of death and misery. The law of holiness must cease to be outwardly comminatory and dreadful, and become inwardly attractive and beloved, before any fruits of righteousness can spring up. Is not this righteous law "the strength of sin" in us, so long as it merely weighs down with a mountain's weight upon our enslaved wills? so long as it merely holds a whip of scorpions over our opposing inclination, and lashes it into anger and resistance? so long as it merely presents the sharp goads of duty that stab our unwillingness? How can there be any moral growth, in the midst of such a hatred and hostility between the human heart and the moral law? Cicero tells us that the laws are ineffectual in war-time—"*silent leges inter arma.*" And neither can flowers and fruits grow on a battle-field. As well might we suppose that the vegetation which now constitutes the coal-beds grew up in that geological era when fire and water were contending for possession of the planet, as to suppose that the fruits of holiness can spring up when the human will is in obstinate and deadly conflict with the human conscience. So long as the heart of man sustains this outside and hostile relation to holiness, and righteousness comes before it as the hated quality and the stern command of another's will, and is not in the least its own sweet inclination, obedience is impossible. The law of righteousness can produce no effects in character and conduct until it is obeyed from an inward impulse and spontaneity, as the law of sin now is.

We have thus, in a general way, noticed that the Divine law is "the strength of sin," whenever it is an external commandment coupled with a threatening, and not an internal principle coupled with an affection. Let us now consider some particulars which illustrate and explain more fully this doctrine of the text.

I. In the first place, so long as the law sustains this extraneous relation to the heart and will, there is no *genuine obedience*. For genuine obedience is voluntary, cheerful, and spontaneous. The child does not truly obey its parent, when it performs an outward act, outwardly insisted upon by its superior, from no inward genial impulse, but solely from the force of fear. So also the moralist, in whom the law has not become a hearty principle of willing action, does not truly comply with it. He may perform some outwardly moral acts, but he does them mechanically and insincerely; and neither mechanism nor insincerity is of the nature of obedience.

It is here that we see the difference between a moral man and a religious man. The moralist attempts, from considerations of prudence, fear, and self-interest, to ex-

ternally obey the external and comminatory law of God.
It is not a law that he loves, but one which he would keep
because of the penalty attached to it. And yet, after all
his attempts at obedience, he is conscious of utter failure.
In his moments of reflection, he sees that it is no genuine
compliance and submission which he renders, and that it
is not valid before Him who looketh not on the outward
appearance, but upon the heart. And at times, perhaps,
he would wish that this selfish attempt to square accounts
with his Maker might be supplanted by a free, filial impulse of the soul—that his conscience might be converted
into his will. But the renewed and sanctified man, so far
as he is such, "obeys from the heart the form of doctrine
that is delivered" unto him. The holy law, though imperfectly, yet predominantly, has become his inclination,
and overflows in holy feelings and acts. "The law," in
the phrase of the Psalmist, "is within his heart, and none
of his steps shall slide." The Holy Spirit has inwardized
it. The law has become his natural disposition, and when
he acts naturally he acts holily, and when he sins he is
uneasy, because sin is unnatural to a renewed heart.

Again, we may perceive that the obedience rendered to
the law by one who does not feel it to be his own law, is
not real and genuine, by noticing the appearance which it
exhibits. Everything that is genuine, spontaneous, and
voluntary, wears the garb of grace and beauty; while that
which is false, pretended, and constrained, has the look of
deformity. That alone which is alive, and the product of
an inward principle, is beautiful. The growing plant,
with the dew fresh upon it, immediately attracts our gaze;
but we turn away from the splendid artificial flower. So
is it with the appearance which the moralist and the believer, respectively, presents. The one is rigid, hard, and
formal. We feel instinctively that he is a precise and un-

happy person; that he rather endures his religion than enjoys it. The other is a free, cheerful, pliant creature. The Son hath made him free, and he is free indeed. His is the obedience of love and of nature; not of fear and compulsion. The principle of spiritual life—the moral law now made internal, and one with his heart and will—is warm and plastic within him, and carries warmth, vigor, and robustness through the whole system. All his acts of obedience to the Divine commands are what we expect from him. They suit him, and wear no forced look. In fine, the difference between the fruits of the law of holiness when it is in the heart, and those of the same law when it is merely in the conscience, is like that between those fruits into which the vegetative principle has infused cooling juices, rich flavors, and pleasant odors, and those imitations of fruit which are lifeless and tasteless.

Another criterion of genuine obedience is love. But so long as the law sustains this extraneous and hostile relation to the heart and will, there is no love of it, or its Author. Examine the feeling of the unrenewed though perhaps moral man, and do you find that calm, settled affection for the statutes and commandments of God which evinces that they are wrought into the very fibre and texture of the soul? Have they not been expelled from the affections, and does not the man sometimes wish that he could expel them also from his conscience? And even if he sometimes attempts to obey them because he fears to transgress them, yet does he not, in the depths of his soul, wish that he could free himself from their everlasting restraint? And although, from the same motives of fear or selfish prudence, he may repress violent outbreaks of passion and rebellion, yet is all within him calm and serene? Is there not a noiseless friction and wearing within? Is he not at schism with himself? Are not conscience and will con-

tinually at war? Even if the surface be placid, and there
is not a ripple upon it, yet far down in the fountains of
his soul ; in those depths where the feelings, and propensities, and all the main and primal agency of the man has
its source.; in those lowest recesses, where the real character of the man is to be sought for ; is there not a restless
eddying and whirl? No man can love God's law in this
state of things. No man can have a cordial affection for
it, until it becomes the inward and actuating principle, the
real inclination of his will ; until his will is renewed, and
he obeys the law because he would not do otherwise. Yet
the law overhangs him all this while, and since it cannot
produce the fruits of peace and holiness, it betakes itself
to its other function, and elicits his corruption, and exas-
perates his depravity. And thus the law, for the sinner,
is the stimulus and strength of sin.

II. In the second place, so long as the extraneous relation
spoken of continues between law and will, there not only is
no true obedience, but *obedience is impossible.* For the law
is entirely outside of the executive faculty. It is in the
conscience, but not in the heart. It consequently gives no
impulse and aid to right action, but only passes a penal,
damning sentence, the effect of which is paralyzing. The
law sternly tells the man that by his own determination and
fault he is " dead in trespasses and sins," and condemns
him therefor ; but so long as it is merely didactic and
comminatory, and not impulsive and indwelling, he derives
from it none of that strength which empowers to righteousness. The man in chains is not animated and assisted
to freedom, by being merely informed that he is chained,
or by being sternly commanded to tear off his chains.
Until the law has become the loved and chosen law of the
will, as well as the organic law of the conscience, it cannot
be obeyed. God's law follows man like God's omnipres-

ence, and if he ascend into heaven it has authority there, and if he descend into hell even there conscience affirms that it must be obeyed; but wheresoever it follows him, if he does not love it he cannot obey it, if it is not in his will it can produce no fruits of holiness. The tree cannot bear fruit, if the principle of life is outside of it. The tree is dead.

But in the Christian, the law of holiness, by virtue of his regeneration and union with Christ, has become inward, spontaneous, and voluntary. It is no longer a mere fiery letter in his conscience, giving him knowledge of his sinfulness, and distressing him therefor; but it is a glowing and genial impulse in his heart. His duty is now his inclination, and his now holy inclination is his duty. The two are one, and undivided in his consciousness. The schism in the soul is healed. Through the renewing influences of the Spirit of God, the commandment has again become a vital force in the soul, as it was before the fall. As the apostle calls it, it is "the law of the Spirit of life in Christ Jesus"—the living spirit of law. And this is the reason why the Christian, in proportion to the closeness of his union to Christ, and the simplicity of his faith in Him, finds it easy, pleasant, and natural to keep the Divine law. The law in a Christian is spontaneous and self-executing. Says an old divine: "The law of the Spirit of life within the renewed will is as if the soul of music should incorporate itself with the instrument, and live in the strings, and make them, of their own accord, and without any touch or impulse from without, dance up and down and warble out their harmonies." [1]

1. This subject as thus unfolded shows, in the first place, that it is an *immense work* to make such an entire

---

[1] Cudworth : Sermon before the House of Commons.

change and reversal in the relations that now exist between man's will and the Divine law. The problem is, to transmute the law of God into the very inclination of a man, so that the two shall be one and the same thing in the personal experience, and the man shall know no difference between the dictates of his conscience and the desires of his heart. The investigation has demonstrated that there is now, not only no such unity and unison between will and conscience in man, but that the former is deadly hostile to the latter, and wholly extraneous to it. It shows, moreover, that until the right harmonious relation is established again between these two fundamental parts of man ; until the constitutional and the voluntary are once more in unison ; all other adjustment is useless, so far as the eternal world is concerned ; that it is in reality no adjustment at all; that the man must, in our Lord's phrase, "make the tree good, and so the fruit good, or else let it remain corrupt, and its fruit corrupt."

We appeal to the daily experience of every thinking person, whether this is not the truth. Are we not aware, that if our will and affections do not undergo such a change in their central determination and inmost bent, that the law of holiness becomes spontaneous to them, and vital within them, all of our desultory attempts under the goadings of conscience to keep it are in vain ? Do we not know that unless our heart is in the work of obedience, we do not and cannot obey ? When the law of God, reaching to every thought, and to every word, merely stands *over* us, and *above* us, commanding and threatening, and our wills and affections are hostile and resistant, instead of being sweetly blended and accordant, do we not see that nothing holy and spiritual can be done in this state of things ? So long as our executive and affectionate powers stand in this alien and outside relation to the law, can there be any geniality or complacency toward it? Until we can say with the Psalmist: "I *delight* to do thy will, O my God; yea, thy law is *within* my heart," can we render the Psalmist's obedience?

The change in the human soul which establishes this inward relation and accordancy between will and conscience; is denominated in Scripture a "birth," a "new creation," and is the most marked change which a rational spirit can undergo, with the exception of that great catastrophe by which it falls from the heavens to the hells. Without such a change, the being is in continual antagonism and war with himself, and with God. "There are times," says Tholuck, "in the life of the natural man, when he seems to be possessed with a demon that tears and weakens him. When, with the swelling power of passion circling in his veins, and the whole world with its enjoyments opens itself wide for his gratification, he hears the solemn voice of law saying: 'Deny thyself, deny thyself,' what commotion rises within him! What wonder is it, if, when excited to madness by this holy commandment which he hates but fears, he cries out: 'Let me tear off these bands; let me cast away these cords'?" [1] Such a commotion and ferment, which more or less violent arises in the soul of man in some periods of his life here on earth, and will last forever if it is not stilled by a work of grace within, evinces that in our natural state we are not in right relations; for where right relation exists there is harmony and peace. This fact must be acknowledged to ourselves, and receive our earnest attention. This renovation of the affections and the will—this production of new character—must occur here in this world, or it will never occur. And after its occurrence, it will still be a slow and

---

[1] Tholuck: Predigten, II. 54.

toilsome process to root out the remainders of sin, and re-move the last elements of discord and dissension from the soul.

2. The second inference from this subject must have been already anticipated—that this inwardizing of the Divine law; this "putting the law in the inward parts, and writing it in the heart" (Jer. xxxi. 33); is *the work and office of the Holy Ghost.* It is the result of God's "working in man to will and to do." Sinful man is spir-itually impotent, and feels himself to be so, particularly when he undertakes to become the very contrary of what he is ; when he tries to make himself as totally holy as he is totally sinful. Let a man look into his own soul, and see how spontaneously he now does wrong, and how delicious it now is to indulge himself in that which is forbidden ; and then let him remember, that in order to heavenly perfec-tion and blessedness he must come into such an exactly contrary moral state, that it will be just as spontaneous for him to do right, and just as delicious for him to keep the commandments of God—let him, we repeat, look into his heart and see what the character now is, and what it must become in order to heaven, and then say if he does not need the operation and aids of Divine grace. Nothing so throws a man upon his knees, and prompts the utterance : "I am the clay, be thou the potter; turn thou me and I shall be turned ; purge me with hyssop and I shall be clean ; create within me a clean heart, O God"—nothing so drives man away from himself to his Maker and Sa-viour, as a clear understanding of the immensity of the work that must be done within his own soul before it is fit for the heavenly state.

The subject clearly demonstrates the necessity of the new birth, and of the sanctification of body, soul, and spirit, that follows it. "Except a man be born again, he cannot see the kingdom of God." We have seen from the unfolding of the text, and human experience will corroborate it, that so long as the Divine law is not an inward principle of willing and cheerful action for us, and we do not love it from the heart, it can only be "the strength of sin" for us. It only accuses of sin; it only revives and stimulates the inward corruption; it only detects and brings sin to light. This is all the law can do for us as sinners. The Word of God informs us of a method by which this state of things can be changed, and we can stand in the same relation to the law of righteousness that God himself does, and the holy angels. It is by the washing of regeneration, and the renewing of the Holy Ghost. If we ask for this we shall receive it. If we seek it, we shall find it. "For if ye being evil know how to give good gifts unto your children, how much more shall your heavenly Father give the Holy Spirit to them that ask him." We must pray importunately and incessantly for renewing and sanctifying grace. When God answers that prayer—and, in the parable of the widow and the unjust judge, Christ commands every man to pray until he gets an answer—when God answers that prayer, the law of holiness shall be made the strength of holiness in our heart and in our will. It shall become a living principle within us forever, gathering strength and acquiring settled firmness as we pass on through the ages of a blessed eternity, and producing in richer and richer bloom the fruits of holiness and love.

SERMON XV.

THE SENSE OF SIN LEADS TO HOLINESS, AND THE CONCEIT OF HOLINESS LEADS TO SIN.

JOHN ix. 41.—"Jesus said unto them, If ye were blind, ye should have no sin: but now ye say, We see; therefore your sin remaineth."

SOME of the most striking and significant teachings of Christ are put into the form of a verbal contradiction. Taking them literally, they not only contain no sense, but are not even self-consistent. Such, for example, is the declaration that "he that findeth his life shall lose it, and he that loseth his life shall find it." If we read this text in its connection, so as to understand the intent of our Lord's teaching, we not only comprehend it, but we perceive that he could not have adopted a more terse and effective mode of conveying his meaning. The apparent and verbal contradiction: "He that finds his life shall lose his life, and he that loses his life shall find his life," only serves to impress the lesson all the more vividly upon the mind. The same remark holds true of such sayings as these: "Whosoever hath not, from him shall be taken away even that he hath. Therefore speak I to them in parables; because they seeing, see not; and hearing, they hear not." In these instances the impressiveness of the truth taught is all the greater, from its being couched in terms that would nonplus a mere verbal critic. For such a critic would begin his analysis and ask: "How can anything be taken away from one who has nothing? How can a man see and not see; how can he hear and not hear; at one and the same time?"

The passage of Scripture which we have chosen for a text is another striking example of the same sort. "Jesus said unto them, If ye were blind, ye should have no sin: but now ye say, We see; therefore your sin remaineth." This startling statement had been preceded, and called out, by another equally startling and apparently self-contradictory. For Christ had said to the Pharisees: "For judgment I am come into this world, that they which see might be made blind." Here, if we interpret the language in a bald and literal manner, the Son of God represents his mission to be one of darkness and not of light. He who calls himself the light of the world, here speaks of himself as coming into it, not for the purpose of illuminating the human soul, but of darkening it. The Pharisees were perplexed by such a statement, and asked: "Are we blind also?" To whom our Lord made the reply: "If ye were blind, ye should have no sin: but now ye say, We see; therefore your sin remaineth." That is to say: "If ye Pharisees felt yourselves to be blind; if ye were conscious of your mental darkness; ye would open your hearts to me, the light of the world, and the sin of unbelief, which is the greatest of sins, would no longer be chargeable upon you. But ye are self-satisfied; ye feel no need of my teachings; ye say in the pride of your minds, We see; therefore the sin of unbelief remains and rests upon you."

We condense the teaching of this passage of Scripture in the proposition, that *the sense of sin leads to holiness, and the conceit of holiness leads to sin.*

I. In the first place, the sense of sin conducts to holiness, upon the general principle of *demand and supply*. We are in the habit of saying, in respect to earthly affairs, that the demand will always create a supply. If one nation requires grain from abroad, another nation will plant, and sow, and reap, to meet the requisition. If America needs certain manufactured fabrics which it cannot well produce, the artisans of Paris and Lyons will toil to furnish them. From year to year, in the world of trade and commerce, the wants of mankind are met by the operation of this principle. Though there may be a temporary dearth, and the demand may go unsupplied for a time, yet this does not continue long. The rise in value stimulates production, and the empty markets are filled again, perhaps to repletion.

The same fact meets us in the operations of Divine Providence. The goodness of God is over all his works. He opens his hand, and satisfies the desire of every living thing. He gives to the beast his food, and to the young ravens when they cry. The supply equals the demand. This is the ordinary and common course in the physical world, under the government and providence of God. Famines are the exception, and not the rule. Seed-time and harvest fail not from century to century. The demand for food is supplied. And there is no surplus to be wasted. There is a wonderful adjustment between the physical wants of man and the physical objects that meet them. Though harvests of grain wave over the whole globe, and millions of mouths are to be fed, the corn and wheat of the world never falls alarmingly short, and, what is equally remarkable, never rots in large amounts in the granaries. How wonderful is that eye which sees the end from the beginning, and though there is an infinitude of elements that enter into the problem—millions of hungry mortals, and billions of bushels of grain—yet, as in the instance of the manna, "he that had gathered much had nothing over; and he that had gathered little had no lack." Under the ordinary care of Providence, every man, in the phrase of Malthus, finds a cover laid for him at the table of nature; and those are the exceptions in which the craving creature is sent empty away; in which the demand is not met by the supply.

Much more is this true within the kingdom of religion and grace. If God is ready and desirous to meet a demand within the physical sphere; if his benevolence leads him to feed the ravens, and "providently cater for the sparrow;" his mercy and compassion render him still more ready and willing to supply the spiritual wants of his sinful creatures. We do not realize it, and perhaps we do not believe it, but it is a blessed and actual fact that God takes greater pleasure in filling the hungry soul, than the hungry mouth; in feeding the immortal spirit, than in feeding the mortal body. His declaration is explicit, that he is more willing to give the Holy Spirit to them that ask him, than an earthly parent is to give bread to his children. If there were only a *demand* upon the part of man for the heavenly food, as urgent and importunate as there is for the earthly food, the supply would be immediately forthcoming, and in infinite abundance. If man craved grace as much as he craves wealth, or honor, the heavens would drop down and dissolve in a rain of righteousness. Were mankind as hungry for holiness and purity as they are for bread; did the human soul pant for God as it does for pleasure and fame; the consequences would astonish men and angels. For no sinful creature, so long as he is under an economy of grace, can come to know his religious necessities without crying out for a supply. Can a man hunger, without begging for food? Can he thirst, without pleading for water? Neither can a sinner become conscious of his corruption, without praying : " Create within me a clean heart O God, and renew within me a right spirit." And whenever this is done, it is absolutely certain that the necessities of the soul will be supplied from God, their appropriate source ; that the supply will equal the demand.

The promises of God are more explicit and unconditional in respect to heavenly blessings, than in reference to earthly. We are permitted, for example, to pray for our earthly bread, for physical health and strength, for the divine blessing upon our worldly affairs. And there is no doubt that such requests are often granted. But it is not so surely certain that God will answer the prayer for daily bread, as it is that he will answer the prayer for the forgiveness of sin. You may beg God to restore you to health from sickness ; to give you competence instead of poverty ; and he may see fit not to grant your prayer. But if you put up the publican's petition : " God be merciful to me a sinner ; " if you entreat with David : " Deliver me from blood-guiltiness O God, thou God of my salvation ; " you will certainly obtain an answer. For the forgiveness of sin is a spiritual blessing, and it can never do you any injury to grant it. Your prayer for health or earthly prosperity, if answered, might harm your soul for time and eternity. But there is no danger to your soul in pardoning its sins ; and now that Christ has made an atonement for sin, there is no danger to the Divine government in such a remission. You may be uncertain, therefore, whether in the instance of a supplication for temporal blessings you will obtain them ; and whenever you put up such a petition, you must couple it with the proviso ; " If it seem good unto thee, O God ; and if not, then thy will and not mine be done." But when you ask God to be merciful unto you, and sprinkle your conscience with the blood of Christ ; when you beseech him to change

your earthly and corrupt nature into his own pure and
holy likeness; you need not put in this proviso. For God
has expressly informed you that it is *always* his will that
a sinner repent of his sin, and seek the Divine mercy in
the blood of Christ; that it is *always* his desire that the
"wicked forsake his way and the unrighteous man his
thoughts;" and that he is *always* inclined to have mercy
upon a penitent man, and to abundantly pardon him. Hear
the declaration upon this point, precisely as it stands
in the fifty-fifth chapter of Isaiah. "Seek ye the Lord
while he may be found, call ye upon him while he is near.
Let the wicked forsake his way, and the unrighteous man
his thoughts: and let him return unto the Lord, and he
will have mercy upon him; and to our God, for he will abundantly pardon. For my thoughts are not your thoughts,
neither are your ways my ways, saith the Lord. For as the
heavens are higher than the earth, so are my ways higher
than your ways, and my 'thoughts than your thoughts."
In all this cordial invitation and generous promise, there
are no limitations specified. Our merciful God and Saviour does not tell us that he will forgive sin, and sanctify
the sinful soul, *provided* he sees it to be compatible with
the attributes of his own nature, with the administration
of his government, and with the best interests of the creature so to do. All this is provided for. The death
of Christ has already made the pardon of sin compatible with the Divine attributes, and the Divine government; and the pardon of sin never had anything in it
that conflicts with the best interests of the sinner. The
invitation is: "Come, for all things are ready." Having
given his Son, God can now with him give all spiritual
blessings. The greater includes the less. There are now
no limitations, or obstructions, in the way of granting these
spiritual gifts to any sinner who wants them; and we may

approach the throne of the heavenly grace, and ask for them "without an if or an and." Whoever goes to God asking, in the name of Christ, such gifts as the remission of sin and the sanctification of his heart, needs put in no proviso. To bestow such gifts as these always promotes the glory of God, and always promotes the eternal welfare of the creature. Therefore this prayer is always heard, if it be presented through the Mediator. "This is the confidence that we have in him, that if we ask anything according to his will [*i.e.*, in accordance with his method of salvation in Christ], he heareth us : and if we know that he hear us, whatsoever we ask [*i.e.*, if we know that our petition belongs to the class that is invariably granted], we know that we have the petitions that we desired of him." 1 John v. 14, 15.

But all this abundant supply supposes a demand. All this free grace postulates a sense of sin. No man can pray this prayer for a spiritual blessing; this prayer which is always answered; this prayer which is not hampered by provisos; unless he hungers for mercy, and hungers for holiness. And he cannot hunger for mercy and holiness unless he feels his destitution. The penitent consciousness of sin is always attended with a spiritual craving; and the spiritual craving always finds the spiritual supply in the gospel ; and thus we see the truth of the first part of our proposition, that a sense of sin leads indirectly and ultimately to holiness.

II. We are now ready to show, in the second place, that the conceit of holiness leads to sin. And here we are met in the very outset with the fact, that *a conceit is in its own nature sin*. It is self-deception ; an imaginary opinion, founded upon no real basis. A conceited man is, in so far, a bad man. His self-flattering opinion may relate to a matter of minor importance, or of major importance

—to the features of his face, or the qualities of his character—but just so far as in either instance his judgment is
warped and false, there is moral obliquity in him. There
is pride ; and pride in all its forms is sin.

A conceit of holiness, then, is sin and leads to more sin.
The disposition of the Pharisee—the disposition to say,
"We *see*"—is an insuperable obstacle to every good and
gracious affection in the heart. Christianity is eminently
a religion for the poor in spirit; for those who have no
self-flattering confidence. Conceit, therefore, in all its
modes and degrees, utterly prevents the rise and progress
of holiness within the soul. But more than this, the conceit of holiness exerts a positively corrupting influence upon
the heart. Its effect is not merely negative. It not only
prevents a man from becoming meek and lowly, but it
puffs him up with pride, and fills him with sin. Let us
examine this point somewhat in detail.

Religion is both a matter of the understanding, and of
the heart. It consists in a true knowledge of Divine
things, and a proper feeling in view of them. Spiritual
perception in combination with spiritual emotion constitutes the sum and substance of practical holiness. If
either is lacking, or deficient, the character is lacking, or
deficient. What now is the effect of a conceit of holiness
upon a man's knowledge of God and himself? The apostle Paul answers this question very flatly, when he says:
"If any man think that he knoweth anything, he knoweth
nothing yet, as he ought to know." Self-flattery is fatal
to all spiritual discernment. In the first place, it prevents
a true knowledge of one's own heart. The Pharisee who
said in his self-complacency: "God I thank thee that I
am not as other men are," was utterly ignorant of his own
character. He imagined that he knew everything in respect to himself, but he knew absolutely nothing as he

ought to have known. Wrapped up in a false opinion and estimate of his own righteousness, he was not only blind, but utterly impervious to the light. And in the second place, self-conceit precludes all true knowledge of God. The apostle John tells us, that " he that loveth not knoweth not God, for God is love." There must be some holy affinity between the heart of man and the Divine nature, in order that the former may apprehend the latter. And there must be humility also, in order to a spiritual discernment. God repulses a proud intellect. He will not permit it to enter the secret penetralia of his being. He shuts himself up from all haughty scrutiny on the part of his creatures; and the history of human speculation is the record of the baffled attempts of man's pride of understanding to comprehend the Infinite and Eternal. "To this man will I look, saith the Lord, even to him that is poor, and of a contrite spirit, and trembleth at my word." Whether, therefore, we have reference to the knowledge of self, or to the knowledge of God, we see that a conceit of holiness conducts to sin. That spiritual discernment which is one whole side and phase of holiness is utterly vitiated by it. So long as it exists, a man can know neither himself nor his Maker. And without knowledge religion is impossible.

The other side of holiness consists in the affections of the heart. "Thou shalt love the Lord thy God with all thy heart, and thy neighbor as thyself." The injurious influence of a conceit of holiness upon the emotions is even more apparent than upon the perceptions. Our feelings are shy and retiring, and hence it is more difficult to feel than it is to understand. How often does a man say : " I perceive the truth, but I do not realize it." And nothing is more deadening to emotion than pride. In everyday life, we observe the hardening effect of this vice. Let man or woman be carried, by prosperity, out of the circles in which pure tastes and moderate desires rule, into the circles of frivolous and ambitious life, and how rapidly do the feelings die out of the soul. The ingenuous and beautiful emotiveness which marked the early life disappears, and a cold, unemotional self-collectedness takes its place. The flush and bloom of the soul is dried up by the arid breath of artificial society; by the "pride of life;" and all that is substituted in the place of it is a thin, hard varnish, or a still harder enamel. But bad as this is in the social sphere, it is yet worse and more fatal in the province of religion. If you would extinguish all religious sensibility within yourself, become a pharisee. "The leaven," says our Lord—the characteristic quality—"of the pharisee, is hypocrisy." Not necessarily deliberate and intentional hypocrisy, but any self-deception, any false conceit or opinion. A man may be hypocritical without deliberately putting on the cloak of false appearances. It is not necessary that he should take a trumpet, and go out into the street and sound the trumpet, and make a long prayer. This is only the extreme of the sin. Any degree of self-complacency, any degree of false estimate of our own character, belongs to the species. So long as I do not smite upon my breast and cry, "God be merciful to me a sinner;" so long as I cherish any grade of self-righteousness, any false conceit of myself; I am pharisaical. Our Lord undoubtedly intended to make but two general classes, by relating that story of the publican and pharisee; and his searching eye sees in every individual man, either the spirit of the self-righteous, or the spirit of the self-condemned. The leaven of the pharisee is the leaven of human nature—the disposition to think more highly of ourselves than we ought to think, and the indisposition to think soberly, humbly, and truthfully. And this leaven of the pharisee accounts for the absence of religious sensibility which everywhere meets us. So long as this false estimate is characteristic of men, it is impossible for them to feel seriously and tenderly the claims of God, and the plague of the heart. Here, too, as in every other province, pride hardens and deadens the emotions. Here, too, the conceit of holiness, the false self-estimate, leads to sin.

The practical lesson derivable from this text, as thus unfolded, is a plain and serious one. We learn from it, *the necessity of obtaining the sense of sin.* Our Lord said to the Pharisees: " For judgment I am come into the world, that they which see not might see, and that they which see might be made blind." One great purpose of his mission was to make a discrimination of character, by the searching tests which he should apply. If, therefore, we would obtain any eternal benefit from his mission, we must enter into the spirit of it, and work in accordance with it. And the only mode in which we can do this, is to acquire the consciousness of sin. It is our first duty, to become " blind." So long as we think that we " see," or say that we " see," we are out of all saving relations to the gospel, and cannot become Christians.

It was the remark of a thoughtful philosopher, that the beginning and foundation of true science is a willingness to be ignorant. By this he meant, that if the human mind proudly insists upon a perfect comprehension of everything, it will comprehend nothing. He advocated, therefore, a moderate and modest estimate of the powers of the human understanding, an acknowledgment and recognition of the mysteries of religion and of nature, and, generally, a reverent and humble attitude of the mind toward all truth. But with how much more truth can it be said, that the beginning and foundation of religion is a willingness to be ignorant, and poor, and blind, and naked. Though, therefore, the teaching is old and oft-repeated, let us urge it once more upon you, to seek a sense of poverty, of ignorance, and of sin, that you may be prepared for the riches, the knowledge, and the holiness of the gospel. The instant a vacuum is produced, the atmospheric air will rush into it. And the instant any human soul becomes emptied of its conceit of holiness, and of its self-righteousness; the instant it becomes an aching void, and reaches out after something purer and better; it is filled with what it wants.

The sense of sin operates very much like an instinct in the physical world. An instinct is an uneasy feeling of want, that leads to some action or movement. The young bird, for example, that has never yet left the nest, when its wings and feathers have reached the proper point of maturity, begins to be restless. It wants to fly. Instinct, that most mysterious characteristic which the Creator has impressed upon the entire animal world, is drawing the little creature away from the narrow house in which it was hatched, into the wide and boundless firmament of heaven. And it will never be freed from this restlessness, until it actually spreads its wings, and soars away never to come back. Now, a sense of sin—a true and penitent sense of sin—operates in the same manner. It is a restless and uneasy feeling in the human soul, that leads to some action or movement. It is true that it differs from a healthy physical instinct, in that it is a token of disease, and not of health. The instinct of the little bird, leading it to fly, is a part of its original created nature; a part of that primal creation which God pronounced "good;" while the sense of sin in apostate man results from moral disease, and is indicative of a perversion of man's original constitution. Still the result is the same, in each instance.

The penitent sense of sin fills man with a dissatisfaction with his present condition, and an aspiration after a better one. He becomes weary of the narrow nest of time, and earth, and sense, and sin. He longs to soar out of it, and beyond it, into the firmament of God.

Can you wonder, therefore, that the preacher, in all ages of the Church, has said so much concerning the sense of sin? that he is so constantly urging upon his hearers, the importance and necessity of becoming conscious of the plague of the heart? He knows that when this point is reached, the principal part of the work, so far as his agency is concerned, is accomplished; and that so long as his hearers are destitute of this experience, nothing has been done, and nothing can be done, toward their spiritual welfare. There must be awakened within them a spiritual instinct, an internal uneasiness, a restless craving for something different, and something better. They must cease saying, "We see," and begin to confess and cry out, "We are blind, and poor, and miserable, and naked, and in want of all things."

Get, then, a conviction and sense of personal unworthiness before God. Dismiss all other aims and enterprises, and direct your thoughts, and efforts, and prayers, to this one thing. It would be worth the toil of many years, if you could thereby induce into your hearts such a sense of sin as that to which David gives utterance in the fifty-first psalm; to which the publican gave expression when he smote upon his breast, and cried, "God be merciful to me a sinner;" to which the prodigal son gave expression when he said, "Father, I have sinned against heaven and before thee." The devotee of mammon will toil for years to acquire a fortune; the devotee of art will "scorn delights, and live laborious days," to become a great painter, or a great sculptor. Each of these men can say: "This one thing I do." Each of them is a man of one idea. But there is something more important than wealth and art. The everlasting peace and purity of the soul is of infinitely greater moment than any painting or statue, than mountains of gold and silver. And the way to this peace and purity is through the consciousness of corruption. We get the beatific vision, by first becoming "blind." It is the sense of sin that leads to holiness. We urge you to become a devotee to this subject, a man of this one idea. Determine to know yourself, whether you know anything else or not. Dare to be ignorant of many things, if thereby you can acquaint yourself with God and be at peace. Toil for a knowledge of your own heart, as you would toil to understand chemistry, if your aspiration were to become a chemist; to understand the Greek language, if it were your ambition to become a Grecian. With what cheering emotions would the people of God, and the angels of God, view such an earnestness upon the part of the unregenerate. How hopeful would the Christian Church become, if it should suddenly discover that men were betaking themselves to the study of their own corrupt natures, and were determined to find out how sinful they actually are in the sight of God.

As an encouragement to this endeavor, we remind you, in conclusion, that in it you may confidently rely upon the aid and influence of the Holy Spirit; upon the teaching and illumination of the Third Person in the Godhead. Should you propose to yourself to become merely a chemist, or a Greek scholar, or a sculptor, or a millionaire, you would not necessarily rely upon any such aid or influence. You might work with the ordinary powers and faculties of the human soul, sustained by the ordinary power of Divine Providence. A man does not need the supernatural influences of the Holy Ghost, in order to become either learned or wealthy. And too generally scholars and millionaires toil on in their own strength, without even knowing whether there be any Holy Ghost.

But in everything pertaining to religion, and the welfare of the soul, we are entirely dependent upon gracious influences and impressions. And in urging you to this toil and effort to obtain a humble sense of personal unworthiness before God, we say unto you in the language of the apostle : " Work, for it is God that worketh in you." We remind you of the great and cheering motive which you have to commence the study of your own heart, in the fact that the Holy Spirit is the Searcher of the heart, and his enlightening influences are promised and proffered. Were you to be isolated from God, and to be compelled to acquire this salutary self-knowledge by your own unaided scrutiny, we should have no hope of your succeeding. The human heart is deceitful above all things, and its innumerable devices and self-flatteries would be too much for you. The very heart which is to be searched, and whose corruption is to be discovered, would persuade you that all is well, and that your anxiety is needless, or greatly exaggerated. But God is greater than our heart, and knoweth all things. He understands the devices and deceits of the human soul, and will conduct every man safely through them who submits to his guidance.

From this time forth, then, scrutinize your personal character, in reliance upon the inward illumination of the truth and Spirit of God. Your first and indispensable work and duty is, in our Lord's phrase, to become " blind "—to become conscious of mental darkness and ignorance. Christ has " come into the world, that they which see not might see, and that they which see might be made blind." One would think it to be an easy and a simple matter, to comply with such a requisition.

We are not commanded or expected to furnish the light; but merely to become sensible of our darkness. God does not oblige us to create the food by which our souls live, but simply to hunger after it. We have only to open our mouths, and he will fill them. By his prophet he says: "Open thy mouth wide, and I will fill it. Come, buy wine and milk, without money and without price."

All spiritual blessings, from first to last, are gifts of God, without any equivalent being expected from us. This knowlege of our hearts, of which we have been speaking, is one of these gratuities. Any man can have it for the asking. If, therefore, any man neglects it, and does not come into possession of it, it is because he dislikes it. He does not want to know his own heart. He prefers to continue in ignorance. And for a soul that desires to remain in the ignorance of sin; that prefers the darkened understanding of the state of nature, to the enlightened mind of the state of grace; there is no hope. If there is no demand, there is no supply. To such a soul must be addressed those solemn words of our Lord: "Light has come into the world; but thou lovest darkness rather than light, because thy deeds are evil."

SERMON XVI.

THE IMPRESSION MADE BY CHRIST'S HOLINESS.

LUKE v. 8.—"When Simon Peter saw it, he fell down at Jesus' knees, saying: Depart from me; for I am a sinful man, O Lord."

THE occurrence which called forth this at first sight singular request from Peter, is one of the many interesting incidents which throw such a charm over the narratives of the Evangelists. Christ had entered into the fishing-boat of his newly called disciple, that, free from the pressure of the people who thronged to hear him, he might teach them those truths which are spirit and life to all who receive them into good and honest hearts. Having ended his discourse, he requested Peter to move his boat into deeper water, farther from the shore, and to "let down his net for a draught." The disciple complied with the request, more, it would seem, from respect to his Master, than from any expectation of a successful result, for he says: "Master, we have toiled all the night and have taken nothing; nevertheless at thy word I will let down the net." But that word was the word of "Him by whom all things were made, and without whom was not anything made that was made." Though the disciple did not at that moment realize it, yet God Almighty was standing beside him in the little fishing-boat—that infinite Being who possesses a mysterious power over all the world of natural as well as spiritual life. Hence the miraculous draught of fishes which followed the obedience of Peter. This wonderful event came unexpectedly upon him. The certainty that he was in the presence of a higher Being than man, then flashed upon him. With this knowledge, a sense of his own sinfulness arose within him, and the spontaneous utterance of his heart was : " Depart from me, O Lord, for I am a sinful man."

This is the natural effect of all immediate and startling manifestations of the Deity to fallen man. The flash of lightning produces a twinge of conscience; the roll of thunder makes the guilty tremble.[1] Should God instantaneously rend the heavens and come down, as he will in the day of doom, every eye would see him, and every soul would be conscious of sin. When the same dread Being, by a series of searching and significant questions respecting the wonderful movements and processes in the world of nature, had brought into clear light his own greatness and majesty, Job, the sinful man, answered the Lord and said : " Behold, I am vile; what shall I answer Thee ? I will lay my hand upon my mouth." Those questions which God put out of the whirlwind : " Where wast thou when I laid the foundations of the earth ? Hast thou commanded the day-spring to know its place ? Hast thou entered into the springs of the sea, or hast thou walked in the search of the depth ? Doth the hawk fly by thy wisdom, and stretch her wings towards the south ? Doth the eagle mount up at thy command, and make her nest on high ? "—these significant questions were, for the patriarch, what this miraculous draught of fishes was for the apostle. And hence the like result in each instance—an abasing sense of sin in the more immediate presence of God. In that hour when the fingers of a man's hand came forth

---

[1] Compare Horace, Odes, I. xxxiv.

and wrote incandescent letters upon the wall of the palace, the countenance of Belshazzar, the guilty Babylonian monarch, was changed, and his thoughts troubled him, so that the joints of his loins were loosed, and his knees smote one against another. (Dan. v. 6.) When Daniel, the man greatly beloved of God, yet not freed from the taint of mortal corruption, saw the vision of the contending empires, and heard the explanatory words of the archangel Gabriel, "he fainted and was sick certain days." And when he afterwards saw, upon the banks of Hiddekel, One clothed in linen, whose loins were girded with fine gold of Uphaz, his body like the beryl, his face as the appearance of lightning, his eyes as lamps of fire, his arms and his feet like in color to polished brass, and the voice of his words like the voice of a multitude, "there remained no strength in him: for his comeliness was turned into corruption, and he retained no strength." (Dan. viii. 27; x. 8.)

There are various modes in which the Divine character is brought vividly before the mind, and thus the feeling of sinfulness educed. There are many objects which are the occasion of directing attention to the holiness and immaculateness of God, and thus, by contrast, of disclosing the imperfection and pollution of man. Material nature is full of symbols, which are a kind of language by which the soul is told of spiritual truths. "The heavens declare the glory of God." The clear cerulean sky speaks of God's purity to the soul that desires and strives to be pure, and sorrowfully feels its corruption. The crimson of the clouds that gather round the rising sun reminded the guilt-smitten and lowly Cowper, of the blood which cleanses and atones:

> " Light appears with early dawn
> While the sun makes haste to rise ;
> See *His* bleeding beauties drawn
> On the blushes of the skies."

But while the manifestation of God in the works of his hands has power to display the Divine excellence, and by contrast, human corruption, the manifestation of God in the flesh, the *incarnation* of the Deity, has a far greater power. Many a man has had fleeting emotions called up by the former that have produced no abiding effect.[1] Many a man, amidst the glorious or terrible scenes of the material world, has had transient feelings of awe, and perhaps an evanescent sense of ill-desert. But these influences from nature, though when made effective by higher ones they may form a part of the current which bears the spirit back to God, are not the primary and most efficacious influences. It is the view of God manifest in the flesh, alone, which produces a salutary sense of sinfulness. Christ assures his disciples in his farewell discourse to them, that he will send them the Holy Ghost who will glorify Him ; for he should receive of His, and should show Him unto them. (John xvi. 14.) The Divine Spirit, in this promise, is represented as tributary to Jesus Christ. Through this heavenly teaching, they should obtain a view of the Son of God and the Son of man that would be as palpable for the mind and heart, as his bodily form had been for their senses. This knowledge of Christ's person and work is impossible to the natural man. " The world," that is, the worldly mind, says Christ, " cannot see me, nor know me ; but ye see me, for I am in you, and will be

---

[1] Whether nature teaches any religious truth, depends altogether upon the moral condition of the pupil. Justus Möser, in his "Letter to the Savoyard Vicar," in which he refutes Rousseau's theory that natural religion, or the religious sentiment, is sufficient for mankind, and that there is no need of doctrines and creeds, remarks that "the preaching of the works of God which we have daily before our eyes is like the chattering song of a canary bird, which the owner at length ceases entirely to hear or notice, while every one who comes into the room is deafened by it."—Hagenbach : Vorlesungen, I. 217.

with you." (John xiv. 17–19.) Let us, then, turn our reflections to some features in this portraiture of the Redeemer by the Holy Ghost, which are fitted to cause the
imperfectly sanctified Christian to cry out with the apostle Peter: "Depart from me, for I am a sinful man, O
Lord."

I. In the first place, a view of the *character* of Jesus
Christ awakens the feeling of sinfulness. It is absolutely
perfect. Sanctity both in mind and heart is found at its
height in it. Even he who has contemplated it long, and
carefully, feels that but little of its fulness and richness
has been seen. For Christ is the brightness of the Father's
glory, and the exact image of his person; and therefore
cannot be found out to perfection. The character of Jesus
is fathomless; and what has been remarked of Christianity
by one of the early Roman bishops, may with equal truth
be said of the character of its Author: "It is like the
firmament; the more diligently you search it, the more
stars will you discover. It is like the ocean; the longer
you regard it, the more immeasurable will it appear to
you." When the characteristic qualities of Christ are
distinctly beheld in their holy and spotless beauty by a
sinful man, the contrast is felt immediately. The instant
that his eye rests upon the sinlessness of Jesus, it turns
involuntarily to the sinfulness of himself. He realizes that
he is a different man from "the man Christ Jesus;" and
that except so far as he is changed by Divine grace, there
can be no sympathy and union with him. In this clear
light, he is conscious that his is a defiled and polluted nature, and that it is not fit to come in contact with the purity
of the Son of God. His own forebodings and fears of judgment have nothing in common with the innocence and
serenity of Jesus. He feels that he is not worthy of companionship with so spotless a Being, or to enter that pure

world where Christ sitteth at the right hand of the Holy Father, and where all the spirits that surround him are immaculate. Though he knows that unless he is ultimately a constant companion of the Redeemer, he must be shut out from him, and be " filthy still," yet the sense of unworthiness thus awakened by contrasting himself with the Saviour prompts him instinctively to say : " Depart from me, O Lord, for I am a sinful man." Seeing no spot or wrinkle upon the soul of Christ, and comparing his own spotted and wrinkled soul with it, a sense of amazement rises within him that he should become the temple of the Holy Ghost, and that his unclean spirit should be selected by the Eternal Father and the Eternal Son to make their abode in.

This is a proper and blessed mood for an imperfectly sanctified Christian. It corresponds with the facts of the case. When he obtains this clear view of Christ's perfections, he becomes truly meek—the most difficult of the graces—and is filled with that penitential lowliness of heart which keeps him at the foot of the cross. How can pride, the essence of sin, dwell in such a spirit ? It is excluded. For the believer is absorbed in this view of his immaculate Redeemer, which shames him, yet rouses him to action and imitation. He has " the ornament of a meek and quiet spirit," because the holy eye of the Master is upon him, and he knows himself to be an unworthy disciple—yet a disciple, and not an enemy of the Lord.

II. Intimately connected, in the second place, with a view of Christ's character, is that of Christ's *daily life*. When this with its train of holy actions passes before the mind of the believer, it produces a deep sense of indwelling sin. For the every-day life is the unfolding and accent of the character ; and the same elements of power that are found in the one appear yet more clearly in the other.

That celestial spotlessness in the inmost nature and disposition of Christ, which awakens the consciousness of sin,
when reappearing in the daily conduct of Christ produces
the same effect. Or rather its effective power is enhanced,
inasmuch as it comes into our notice active and working
amidst the ordinary relations and circumstances of human
life. It was only an internal principle before ; it is now
an external product, bright and beaming with energy, and
displaying itself in the very midst of men and things.
The dark root has become a brilliant flower. Every observer knows the additional force which a moral principle,
or attribute, acquires as soon as it takes up its residence
in a man, and is shown out in a man's conduct. What
wonderful energy, for example, did the abstract doctrine
of justification by faith gain to itself, when it became incarnate in Martin Luther ; incorporated into the substantial mass of his feelings and moral wants. The moment
that it ceased to be a mere letter upon the page of Scripture, where it had been through all the papal centuries,
and became a vivid principle of belief and action in the
heart of the reformer, that moment it acquired a power
under God to make the falling Church stand up in the
pristine vigor of its youth. It became a possessing spirit,
as it were, dwelling in Luther's mighty and passionate
nature, and sending though his instrumentality a reforming
influence through the Church, and through the world. Or,
to take another instance, let the principle of avarice, the
abstract vice, twine itself into the moral nature of a man,
and become a concrete working force within him, and how
it turns all that he touches into gold ; how it transforms
the very man himself, so that it issues from him like black
rays, and throws an air of miserliness and hard-hearted-
ness over him in all the relations of life.

Now, the attribute of Divine holiness appears in this

vivid biographical way, in the daily conduct of Christ. Our Saviour was God with all his attributes manifested in the flesh—a perfect and blameless man, therefore, in all the varied relations of human life; knowing both the weakness and the strength of humanity, yet in all cases without sin. And what a holy phenomenon is his life in the flesh! The human nature which he assumed is transfigured and glorified by this indwelling of Divinity, and becomes its white and glistening raiment.

If, now, we obtain a clear view of Christ's daily life, and let our own worthless life be seen in its light, we shall feel deeply that we are fallen creatures. When we witness his constant holiness and love, appearing wherever he appears, be it before a friend or an enemy;[1] when we never for an instant see the placid surface of his soul ruffled by passion, but always find spiritual objects mirrored in quiet beauty there; when we notice the absolute control which he possessed over all the energies and impulses of his spirit; how even his most fleeting thoughts were all pure, and even his most evanescent feelings were suffused with the righteous and holy love which was his nature—when we behold all this exhibited in a life among wicked men, and virulent enemies, and amidst strong temptations, are we not painfully reminded of our passionate, impetuous, ungoverned, and sinful life? If we would but study with humble earnestness the biography of Christ, as detailed in the Gospels, we could not fail of becoming convinced of sin; and as in this way we carried ourselves back to the time when he was upon earth, and placed ourselves within the circle of his influence along with his first disciples, we should, through grace helping us, acquire that constant

---

[1] It is a tradition of the Church, that "Peter wept whenever he remembered the sweet mildness of Christ which he showed in his daily conversation."—Luther on Galatians v. 21.

sense of unworthiness, in comparison with Him, which runs through their narratives. His whole pure life would disclose our corruption ; and we should receive a healthful influence from many a slight incident in the Gospel narratives which now escapes our careless eye, even as a healing virtue was once experienced by touching the mere hem of his garment.

In what has thus far been said, it has been assumed that there is remaining sin even in the most spiritual and excellent of Christ's disciples, and that if fitting objects are presented, the feeling of unworthiness will rise up as naturally as the power of a magnet will exhibit itself when its appropriate eliciting object is brought near it. But the consciousness of sin takes on two forms, which may be distinguished but not divided from each other. Only one form—that of a sense of corruption, and of unconformity with the law of God—has been principally in view, in what has thus far been said respecting the character and life of Christ. The other form which the consciousness of sin assumes, is that of a sense of guilt, and of merited exposure to punishment. The feeling which prompts a transgressor to say: "I have disobeyed the law of God, and deserve to suffer for it," is plainly distinct from the feeling which leads him to say : " I am carnal and corrupt in my propensities, and desire to be made pure and spiritual." The reference in the first instance is an external and objective one—namely, to the majesty of God, and the claims of his law. In the last instance, the reference is an internal and subjective one—namely, to the condition and wants of the human heart. The feeling of guilt goes away from self, and terminates upon another Being, even God, the Holy, and the Just. It is, therefore, less liable to be mingled with selfish elements than is the feeling of inward corruption. This latter is blended with a sense of personal unrest and unhappiness, and hence needs to be watched lest it degenerate into a refined selfishness. The two feelings are clearly distinguishable, although they exist side by side in the soul; and both are equally necessary in order to a complete evangelical experience. The consciousness of culpability, or of *crime*, is one of the most radical and profound phases of human consciousness; and it can be removed only by the most strange and wonderful of agencies. It is easier to provide for man's corruption, than for man's guilt. The Holy Ghost, by a sanctifying agency, can remove the soul's pollution; but only the substituted passion and agony of incarnate Deity can remove the soul's guilt. Spiritual influences can purify, but they cannot expiate. Had there not been this crimson tincture of criminality in human depravity, the incarnation and passion of the Second Person in the Godhead would not have been necessary. Had there been no guilt to atone for, the Triune God could have sat in the heavens, and by an inward influence have turned the human heart to righteousness, even as the rivers of water are turned.

It is this guilt-consciousness which gives itself vent in the sacrifices of Heathenism, as well as those of Judaism. It is this emotion, working, it is true, in an obscure, yet in a powerful manner, and filling him with that anxious foreboding of a coming retribution of which St. Paul speaks, that causes the pagan to yearn after a sacrifice of "richer blood" than that of bulls and goats, and makes the blood of Christ so grateful to his anguished spirit, when the missionary says: "Behold the Lamb of God—behold the real and true atonement for sin." Much as man fears punishment, his moral nature is so constituted that it demands it, in order to its own satisfaction. Man's heart hates the penalty of sin; but man's conscience insists upon it. And it opens to us a very solemn view of the final state of a lost soul, when we consider that that very judicial infliction which is the cause of its distress, is felt by itself to be just and necessary under the government of God. So deeply has the Creator implanted the judicial principle in man, that wherever he may be, it demands, by an instinctive action that is altogether independent of the wishes of the heart, that law and justice take their course, even if he be miserable to all eternity. And it is to provide for this dispassionate and impartial sense of ill-desert, which is so distinct from the sense of corruption and misery, that Christ's atoning death on the cross is so distinct from the Holy Spirit's work within the heart. One thing is set over against another, in the plan of Redemption. Christ's blood expiates my guilt. Christ's Spirit purifies my corruption.

This sense of sin as related to justice should hold a prominent place in the Christian experience; and in proportion as it is first vividly elicited by the operation of the law, and then is completely pacified by a view of Christ as suffering "the just for the unjust," will be the depth of our love towards him, and the simplicity and entireness of our trust in him. Those who, like Paul and Luther, have had the clearest perception of the iniquity of sin, and of their own criminality before God, have had the most luminous and constraining view of Christ as the "Lamb of God;" while, at the same time, the life of Christ in the soul, the process of sanctification, has reached its highest degree, and matured the fruits of holiness in their richest bloom. The experience was not one-sided, and thus neither side suffered.

III. Having thus directed attention to the fact that there is such a distinct feeling as guilt, we remark, in the third place, that the contemplation of the *sufferings* and *death* of Christ both elicits and pacifies it, in the believer. Christ's whole life upon earth was a continuous state of humiliation and suffering, but his last anguish and death are represented as eminently the atoning sacrifice for the sin of the world ; inasmuch as at this point the flood of his sorrows reached its height, and gathered and settled upon Calvary, like a tarn of deep and black water in a volcanic crater. Hence a clear view of those scenes in the Garden, and on the Cross, will arrest the believer's attention, and fix his thoughts upon that particular quality in himself, that specific element in sin, which rendered the agony and death of such a Being necessary. As he becomes a witness of that mysterious distress under the olive trees—that inward shrinking of One who never shrank before, and who never shrank afterwards—which wrung from him the earnest yet submissive prayer : " O my Father, if it be possible let this cup pass from me ; " as he follows him through his trial of mockings and scourgings, and sees the consummation of his Passion upon the cross, and hears the words : " My God, why hast thou forsaken me ? " betokening greater anguish in the soul than the body was undergoing—as the believer obtains a clear understanding of all these events, he is instinctively prompted by the feeling of personal ill-desert which now rises within him, to say : " The punishment which I deserve was assumed by that innocent God-man. He, then and there, was wounded for my transgression, was bruised for my iniquity." He sees in the death of Christ a manifestation of God's righteous displeasure against sin, and says to himself : " If it was not possible to let that cup pass, and if Eternal Justice could throw no lenitive into the bitter potion which the sinner's Substitute voluntarily put to his own lips, does not the real criminal himself deserve to 'drink of the wine of the wrath of God, which is poured out without mixture into the cup of his indignation?' " Absorbed in the con-

templation of this great Divine sacrifice for the sin of the
world, the feeling that retribution is what a sinner deserves
swallows up for the time all others; and the believer
stands before the bar of justice taking sides with the law
against himself, and heartily confessing that his condemnation is righteous. Whoever beholds human transgression in the light of the Cross, has no doubts as to the
nature and character of the Being nailed to it; and he has
no doubts as to his own nature and character. The distinct and intelligent feeling of culpability forbids that he
should omit to look at sin in its penal relations, and enables him to understand these relations. The vicarious
atonement of Christ is well comprehended because it is precisely what the guilt-smitten conscience craves, in its restlessness and anguish. The believer now has wants which
are met in this sacrifice. His moral feelings are all awake,
and the fundamental feeling of guilt pervades and tinges
them all; until, in genuine contrition, he holds up the Lamb
of God in his prayer for mercy, and cries out to the Just
One: " This oblation which Thou Thyself hast provided is
my propitiation; this atones for my sin." Then the expiating blood is applied by the Holy Ghost, and the conscience
is filled with the peace of God that passeth all understanding. "Then," to use the language of Leighton,[1] "the
conscience makes answer to God: 'Lord, I have found
that there is no standing in the judgment before thee, for
the soul in itself is overwhelmed with a world of guilti-
ness; but I find a blood sprinkled upon it that hath, I am
sure, virtue enough to purge it all away, and to present it
pure unto thee. And I know that wheresoever thou find-
est that blood sprinkled, thine anger is quenched and
appeased immediately upon the sight of it. Thine hand
cannot smite when that blood is before thine eye.'"

---

[1] Commentary on 1 Peter iii. 21.

We have thus considered the effect, in awakening a sense of sin, produced by a clear view of the character, life, and death of Christ. But how dim and indistinct is our vision of all this! It should be one of our most distinct and earnest aims, to set a *crucified* Redeemer visibly before our eyes. "I determined," said St. Paul, "to know nothing among you, save Jesus Christ, and him crucified." There are other aspects of the God-man which we may contemplate in their own time and place; but he is not upon a high and firm evangelic position, who finds it difficult to account for the *death* of the God-man; who detects in himself the secret query whether there really is anything in the nature of sin, and the character of God, that renders it rational and necessary. For, such doubt and querying originate in a defective knowledge of sin. Only bring out into vividness the consciousness of guilt; only fill the soul with a sense of utter ill-desert, and there will be the uplifting of the despairing eye to that central Cross, and the simple looking will be the explanation of the mystery, as it stills the throbbing conscience. This accounts for the immediateness with which Christ on the Cross is beheld, if beheld at all; and the reason why he cannot be seen by indirection, and roundabout. Like a flash of light; like an explosion of sound; the peace of God takes the place of remorse, when guilt and atonement come together in the personal experience.

It is our duty, and our wisdom, to cultivate a purer and more spiritual conviction of sin, that we may feel that spiritual hunger, and that spiritual thirst, which makes Christ's atonement vital to the soul. His own words are: "Except ye eat my flesh and drink my blood, ye have no life in you." But how can the full-fed and self-satiated be famine-struck? How can the self-indulgent and luxurious know anything of burning thirst? How can torpid sin feel guilt? We need to experience the keen incisive force of God's truth, and God's law, cutting into our proud flesh, and by its probing preparing us for the balsam and the balm.

Let us, then, lift up our hearts, and seek this preparation for the sprinkling of the blood of expiation. Let us by every means in our power—by prayer, by self-examination, and by absorbing meditation upon Christ's character, daily life, and last sufferings—awaken a pure and poignant sense of unworthiness and ill-desert, so that when we give utterance to it in the words of Peter: "Depart from me, for I am a sinful man, O Lord," the Lord himself shall say to us: "Be of good cheer, thy sins are forgiven thee."

SERMON XVII.

CHRISTIAN HUMILITY.

1 Peter v. 5.—"Be clothed with humility:"

Humility is a grace that pertains exclusively to the Christian religion. The better codes of pagan morality recommend some of the virtues of our religion—such as benevolence, justice, truthfulness, and the like—but this quality of meekness, which is so prominent in the Scriptures, and with which we are commanded to be "clothed" as with a garment, escaped the notice of the heathen sages. They do not appear to have distinguished between a reverential and proper prostration of soul, and a cringing, cowardly meanness of temper. Hence the Greek word (ταπεινοφροσύνη) employed by the New Testament writers to denote this grace, which is one of the fairest fruits and distinctive marks of the religion of the gospel, in its original classical meaning signified a servile pusillanimity. The man who possessed this quality, in the opinion of the proud Greek, was a man of small soul.[1] So that in this instance, as in many others, a single word, by being brought into the service of Christian doctrine, and

---

[1] Trench (Synonyms of the New Testament) shows, however, that Plato, and particularly Aristotle, sometimes approached the borders of the truth in respect to this moral trait.

employed as the vehicle of Christian truth, is thereby ennobled, and becomes the exponent of a higher and better idea; a specimen of what Christianity does for everything that comes to be in any way connected with it. Man, when he has become a Christian, is a higher style of man than he was before. Nature, when viewed by a Christian eye, and mused upon with a Christian contemplation, is transfigured, and sounds forth a deeper music, and shows a richer bloom than meet the ear and eye of the worldling. So true is it, that "godliness is profitable for all things."

In looking for a moment into the *nature* of humility, we discover, as has been remarked, that it does not involve meanness or servility. It is not pusillanimity. It contains no element that degrades human nature, or exposes it to legitimate contempt. It is not the quality of a slave, but of kings and priests unto God. It is a necessary trait in all *finite* character, and therefore it is perfectly consistent with an inviolable dignity and self-respect. Look at it as it appears in living beauty in the pattern-man, the model of humanity—in Him who was "meek and lowly of heart." Christ was the ideal of man. Our nature reached its acme of perfection in him. But throughout his entire human life upon earth, he was a lowly and condescending being. Not a scintilla of pride or arrogance ever flashed in his actions. The sweetest and most gentle meekness pervades the whole appearance which he presents in the Gospels. It casts its silver, softening light over all his life ; it is the serene element in which he lived, moved, and had his being. And yet, how dignified was the Son of man. The potentates of the world are fond of arrogating to themselves the title of "serene highness." By it, they would indicate that their exaltation is so lofty, that it is unaffected by the contests and turmoil of the lower region in which the common mass of men live. Their position is wholly inaccessible, and therefore their temper is perfectly calm. But what a "serene highness" envelops the character of Christ, like a halo. What greatness accompanies the gentleness. Even Rousseau, who had no meekness, and no love for the trait, acknowledged that the character of Christ is the most lofty one in history. He thought it so sublime as to say, that if it had been the mere idealizing and invention of the unlettered evangelists, they would have performed a greater miracle than even the character itself was.

And do we, in contemplating the character of Jesus, find that the humility which he exhibited lowers it in the least in our estimation? Look at that scene in which this trait appears in a very striking manner—the washing of his disciples' feet. "Jesus [though] knowing that the Father had given all things into his hands, and that he was come from God, and went to God"—this Divine Being, while holding all things in his power, and issuing from Eternity, and returning to it when he chose— [yet] "riseth from supper and laid aside his garments, and took a towel, and girded himself. After that, he poureth water into a bason, and began to wash the disciples' feet, and to wipe them with the towel wherewith he was girded." Connected with this in itself menial act, is there even the slightest thought of self-degradation? We may be astonished at the condescension, as Peter was when he cried: "Lord, dost thou wash my feet?" But the idea that Christ forfeited his personal dignity; that he forgot his human position, and did an improper act, out of keeping with it; never for an instant enters our minds, as we read this narrative and ponder upon it. Does not this menial office, which would excite pity if performed by a slave from fear or compulsion, cause us involuntarily to bow in reverence? When the Roman pontiff, surrounded by his cardinals and announced by a salvo of artillery, with great pomp and external show apes this beautiful and dignified condescension of the Son of man, and washes the feet of a Roman beggar, the spectator looks on with scorn, or turns away in pity. But not so with the original, of which this is the poor and blasphemous mimicry. The blending, in the God-man, of a divine dignity and majesty, with a human and affectionate condescension towards his disciples and his brethren, will ever waken admiration in him who is possessed merely of a cultivated taste, like Rousseau; much more must it waken revering love, and a desire really to imitate it, in the believer who feels his own unworthiness, and beholds in Christ the "brightness of the Father's glory, and the express image of his person."

These considerations are sufficient to indicate the true nature of humility, in contradiction to the pagan conception of it. We are certain that there is nothing in it kindred to servility, or pusillanimity, when we see it lending a charm to the most perfect and symmetrical life that was ever lived upon earth. We can form a very safe estimate of any quality or trait, by looking at it in actual daily life; by seeing it as it weaves itself into the web of human actions and relations. If it look lovely and admirable there; if we find it, in Wordsworth's phrase,

> "not too good
> For human nature's daily food,
> And yet a spirit still and bright,
> With something of an angel light,"

then it must be so in its abstract, intrinsic nature. Humility, therefore, must be a worthy and noble trait; for it was an attribute of the noblest of beings; it runs like a bright silken thread through the holiest and most beautiful life.

We are commanded, in the text, to be "clothed" with this grace; to wear it as a garment that wraps the wearer all over like a cloak; to appear in it as a habit or dress wherever we go. Let us notice some of the reasons for this command. And inasmuch as the light of the gospel first disclosed this grace, which had escaped the notice of the wisdom of this world, let us view it in this light. Let us take our stand upon Christianity, and from what it teaches concerning the nature of God and the nature of man, and their mutual relations, let us see that there are conclusive reasons why every man, without exception, should be humble.

I. In the first place, humility is becoming to man, because he is a *creature*. There is no difference so great as that between the Creator and the creature. The distance between man and the house which he builds, or the cloth which he manufactures, is very great, but it is not equal to that between God and man. The house and the cloth are made out of existing materials; but God made man out of the dust of the earth, and the dust of the earth he made out of nothing. In this creaturely relation, therefore, there is not the slightest opportunity or ground for pride. Shall a being who was originated from nonentity by almighty power, and who can be reduced again to nonentity by that same power—shall a being who a little while ago had no existence, and in an instant might vanish into non-existence, swell with haughtiness? Surely, humility is the fitting emotion for a created being. "Talk no more so exceeding proudly: let not arrogancy come out of your mouth; for the Lord is a God of knowledge, and by him actions are weighed" (1 Sam. ii. 3).

The distance between man and his Maker is so great,

that the instinctive feeling which is elicited is that of
dread. If we examine the pagan religions, we discover
that a vague and oppressing terror before the Deity is the
predominating emotion in them all. They denominate
him the " Unknown God," and Paul found even the cultivated Greek bowing down in abject fear. But such an
emotion as this is destructive of true humility. It is too
tumultuous and terrifying, to allow of such a gentle, such
a quiet, and such an affectionate feeling as the gospel lowliness and meekness. If the human soul be filled with a
shadowy and anxious dread before an agnostic God, and it
ignorantly worships him under the suffocating influence of
this feeling, there can be none of that intelligent and calm
self-prostration which the text enjoins. We must have
some truthful and definite apprehension of God; he must
be something more for us than a dark abyss of being into
whose vortex the little atom is swallowed up and lost; in
order to bow down before him with filial reverence, and
entire submission. Revelation gives man this clear and
intelligent view. It darts a bright beam of light through
the infinite distance which separates the creature from the
Creator. It reveals him as " the high and lofty One that
inhabits eternity; " and *also* as " dwelling with him that
is of an humble and contrite heart, to revive and to bless."
It describes him as the august Being whose name is " I am,"
the " Holy Lord God Almighty which was, and is, and is
to come ; " and *also* as " the God and Father of our Lord
Jesus Christ," through whom we have the forgiveness of
sins, and the hope of everlasting life. In combining the
infinite majesty with the infinite condescension, the Bible
lays the foundation for a genuine humility that is heaven-
wide from the servile terror of the pagan devotee. It is a
tender and gentle emotion. Well does our Lord say, that
he who carries it as a yoke, finds it an " easy " one ; that

he who bears it as a burden, feels that it is a "light" one. Well does he say, that that soul which learns of him, and becomes meek and lowly of heart, "finds rest."

Humility, again, is an ennobling emotion, because it brings man into his right position before God. That being belittles himself who gets out of his place, and occupies one that does not belong to him. In our Lord's parable, the man who took the highest seat in the synagogue disgraced himself in the very act. He went where he was not entitled to go, and he was put back where he properly belonged. But he who took the lowest room, he who did not claim the highest place as his proper position, was rewarded for his humble and just estimate of himself by the invitation to "go up higher." Precisely so is it with the creature's relations to God. He who is conscious of his insignificance before his Maker, and in comparison with his Maker, is thereby exalted to a height that can be reached in no other way. We see this in the act of worship. When we adore the Infinite Jehovah, and give him the glory that is due unto his name, our whole mood and temper is lowly. And we are in our right place. We ought to lie low at the footstool of the Eternal. And having done this; having worshipped the King eternal, immortal, and invisible; we are exalted in the very act. Our feeble, finite, created nature is never clothed with such dignity, as when we are showing reverence to our Sovereign. Why is it that the very posture of worship, the posture of humility, elicits respect from all beholders? No one can look upon the devotions of even an ignorant papist before a crucifix at the corner of the street, or of an ignorant Mohammedan with his face towards Mecca, without a degree of consideration. There is a fellow-creature who, in attitude at least, is bending before the infinite majesty of heaven; and though we know that his worship is blind and superstitious, it would shock our sensibilities should he be insulted, or interrupted in his prayer. There is dignity in worship. "Those thoughts," says Lichtenberg, "elevate the soul which throw the body upon the knee." The act of adoration, in which the spirit of humility reaches its height, is the sublimest one of which the creature is capable. And this, because it is that act in which he confesses and feels himself to be a *creature*—a being who was originated from nothing by the fiat of the Creator, and who possesses nothing that he has not received.

II. In the second place, humility is becoming to man because he is a *dependent* being. He who is independent, and does not owe his existence, or the continuance of it, to any other than himself, is not called upon to be humble. Humility would be unbefitting in the Great God. He must of necessity possess the calm consciousness of independence, and self-subsistence. And yet this is not pride. God cannot be proud, any more than he can be humble. For pride supposes a comparison with another being of the same species, and a degree of rivalry with him. But with whom can God compare himself; and towards what other being can he feel the least emotion of emulation? He dwells in the solitude of his own unapproachable excellence, and therefore he can neither be lifted up with haughtiness, nor bowed down in lowliness. But man is not such a being. All his springs are in God. He is dependent for life, health, and all temporal things. He is dependent, above all, for spiritual life and health, and all the blessed things of eternity. In the strong Scripture phraseology, he "lives, moves, and has his being" in God. He is kept in existence, and watched over by the minute, the microscopic providence of God, with more kindness than the mother guards her infant, and therefore the least that he can do, is to look up with an adoring eye and meekly acknowledge his dependence. Certainly, that creature ought to be very lowly who is finite and helpless, and yet has an eternity depending upon the life he leads here. Standing as man does on the shore of an illimitable sea, upon which he is to embark, with no power in himself to support and guide over its dark expanse, he should be very humble and very trusting. The sound of those "waters rolling evermore" should send far into his heart a feeling of weakness, and dependency. His whole life upon the raging billows of time ought to be one continued act of lowly trust, one continued state of meek reliance.

But this does not exhaust the subject under this head. Man is dependent not only upon his Creator, but also upon his fellow-creature. He is part of a great whole, and is therefore in a state of connection and interdependency. No man can stand up alone, and sustain himself without any assistance from his fellow-men. Even he who practically denies his dependence upon God, acknowledges either directly or indirectly his dependence upon man. How many men are humble, nay, are abject, before a fellow-worm, because they are in some way dependent upon him, but are proud in the sight of God, by whom both they and their fellow-creatures are sustained. Thus does man, even in his sin, confess his own weakness. In a life and world of sin, he clings to his frail fellow-sinner for support. The thought of being cut off from all connection with others alarms him. Were the whole human family to be removed from the planet by death, with the exception of a single individual, and this single person were to be reprobated by God, and thus cut off from all connection and intercourse with any being human or divine, he would be a terror to himself. What fear would settle like a cloud upon him, if having no trust in the Almighty he found no fellow-creature to run to, though only for a temporary solace and stay. Standing in such absolute loneliness in the middle of the universe, with neither God nor man to lean upon, methinks he would desire annihilation. So firmly and profoundly implanted in human nature is the instinctive longing for social intercourse with a fellow-being, and the desire to rest upon some other than self. And ought not this species of dependence, also, though it be a minor one when compared with the creature's dependence upon God, to minister to a lowly heart? Should not every man esteem others better than himself, be thankful for the benefits which he is constantly receiving either directly or indirectly from others, and, in the end, looking up to the great First Cause, humbly adore him as the Being who sits above all these minor agencies, upholding and controlling as they work and interweave among themselves far beneath him? Since men are all walking together in this state of existence as it were in a starless night, and their feet stumble among the dark mountains, they should mutually recognize their obligations to each other, and there should be no boasting. The sense of their dependence would render them meek and lowly ; and this meekness and gentleness would naturally beget that *love* of their neighbor as themselves, which is the sum of the second table of the law.

III. In the third place, man should be humble because he is a *sinful* being. What has been remarked of man as created and dependent will apply to all beings but God. The first two reasons which we have assigned for humility are valid for the angels and the archangels. They are creatures, and they are dependent. And if we would find the deepest humility in the universe, the most profound lowliness of heart, we must seek it in the shining ranks of heaven ; in the wing-veiled faces of the seraphim. But there is another special reason why man should be humble which has no application to the holy angel. Man is a sinner. When Jehovah appeared "sitting upon a throne high and lifted up," the seraph cried and said, "Holy, holy, holy is the Lord of hosts; the whole earth is full of his glory." But the prophet Isaiah upon seeing the very same vision said, "Woe is me! for I am undone; because I am a man of unclean lips, and I dwell in the midst of a people of unclean lips; for mine eyes have seen the King, the Lord of hosts." The seraph was humble as a creature merely. The man was humble as a sinner as well as a creature.

The fact that we are transgressors before God should abase us in the dust before him. The heart of a criminal is no place for pride, and he ought to stand afar off, and cry, "God be merciful." Considering the peculiar attitude in which guilty man stands before God, self-abasement ought to be the main feeling in his heart. For in addition to the infinite difference there is originally between himself and his Maker, he has rendered himself yet more different by apostasy. The first was only a difference in respect to essence; but the last is a difference in respect to character. How strange it is that he should forget this difference, and entering into a comparison of himself with his fellow-men should plume himself upon a supposed superiority. The culprits are disputing which shall be the greatest, at the very instant when their sentence of condemnation is issuing from the lips of their Judge! How poor a thing it is, to see a little creature over-estimating himself for qualities, the possession of which he owes to the very Being against whom he is in rebellion. How vain and futile a thing it is, for a little atom to attempt to isolate itself from everything else and float alone in immensity, endeavoring, contrary to great laws, to lead a separate existence by itself and for itself, and, in this attitude of rebellion against the Creator and Ruler of all, boasting with exultation and self-complacency. It is absurd, on the very face of it.

> "Proud man,
> Drest in a little brief authority,
> Plays such *fantastic* tricks before high heaven
> As make angels weep."

There is still another consideration under this head which strengthens the motive for humility. We have seen that the fact of sin furnishes an additional reason for self-abasement, because it increases the distance between man and God; it has also made him still more *dependent* upon God. There is no helplessness like that of a convicted and imprisoned criminal. He cannot stir hand or foot. He cannot say a word in his own defence, for he has been tried, and proved guilty. He cannot employ force to deliver himself, for he is shut up behind solid walls and iron grates. He is utterly dependent upon the sovereign power which has sentenced and imprisoned him. Such is sinful man in relation to the Divine government. He is the most helpless of the helpless. Nothing but pure and mere mercy can deliver him. But nothing interferes with the exercise of mercy like pride in the criminal. A proud man cannot be forgiven. It involves a self-contradiction. If there be self-asserting haughtiness in the heart, God can neither bestow grace nor man receive it. There can be no forgiveness, unless there be confession of sin, and godly sorrow. Mere remorse furnishes no opportunity for the exercise of clemency. The devils are full of this feeling, and yet are as antagonistic to the Divine mercy as fire is to water. It is not the "sorrow of the world," the sorrow of hell, but the "godly sorrow," which prepares the soul to receive the sweet and blessed absolution of heavenly pity. But this feeling is a *humble* one. Penitence is very lowly. In fact, the difference between the two sorrows— the sorrow of the world, and the godly sorrow—is due to the presence or the absence of humility. The sense of sin takes its character from the temper of the soul. When it wakes up in a proud and hard heart, it wears and tears it. It becomes remorse—that "sorrow of the world which worketh death," the main element in eternal death, the "worm" and the "fire." But when the sense of sin is wakened in a humble and broken heart, there is no laceration. It becomes that "godly sorrow which worketh repentance unto life." It produces that subdued, tender, chastened tone of feeling which leads man in lowly faith to the foot of the Cross.

> "Remorse is as the heart in which it grows:
> If that be *humble*, it drops balmy dews
> Of true repentance; but if proud and gloomy,
> It is a poison-tree that, pierced to the inmost,
> Weeps only tears of poison."[1]

If, therefore, we would have the sense of sin produce any salutary and blessed results within us, we must obtain a meek and lowly spirit—one that does not proudly fight against the convictions of conscience, and thus rouse that faculty to vengeance and despair, but which acknowledges and confesses the justice of its charges, and humbly waits for the mercy of God, who pours the oil of joy into such a heart. If, then, you ever have your attention directed to your transgressions, and the conviction of sin and the feeling of ill-desert is roused, do not proudly try to smother and quench it, for it will prove to be a fire shut up in your bones that will ultimately burn to the lowest hell. On the

---

[1] Coleridge: Remorse, Act I., Scene i.

contrary, be humble ; confess the sin with meekness, and look to the blood of Christ for its pardon. Then you will understand how it is that when you are humble then you are exalted, and when you are weak then you are strong. When the sinner's stout and self-righteous heart yields, and he meekly acknowledges his sin, by this very act he takes hold of the justifying righteousness of the Redeemer, and then he is exalted, and then he is safe.

IV. A fourth, and most powerful reason, why man should be clothed with humility, is found in the *vicarious suffering* and *atonement* of Christ in his behalf. The apostle Paul, directing Titus to enjoin upon his hearers " to speak evil of no man, to be no brawlers, but gentle, showing all meekness unto all men," assigns as a special reason the fact, that the " kindness and love of God our Saviour has appeared toward man, in the washing of regeneration and renewing of the Holy Ghost through Jesus Christ our Saviour." The Cross of Christ is the great motive to a meek and lowly temper. He who has a vivid view of those dark scenes in the innocent life of the Blessed Redeemer, and considers the purpose for which he was in an agony and sweat great drops of blood, cannot cherish pride in his heart, unless his heart is the heart of Judas. Feeling himself to be a condemned sinner, and beholding the Lamb of God " made a curse for him," and bearing his sins in His own body on the tree, all self-confidence and self-righteousness will die out of his soul. Coming down from Calvary, he cannot straightway forget what he has seen, and return as did the malignant Jews to the pomp and vanity of the earthly Jerusalem, and live a proud and sensual life. On the contrary, he finds in the sufferings and death of Christ a motive both for self-abasement, and for hope—a motive for self-abasement, because in the bright light around the Cross he sees his sins to be scarlet and crimson; a motive for hope, because of the free and full forgiveness that is offered. Nothing subdues a haughty spirit like the passion and agony of the Saviour for the sin of the world. There is a strangely softening power in the blood of Christ. The fabled Medusa's head was said to turn every one who looked upon it into stone; but the Cross and the Holy Sufferer upon it is a sight that converts the beholder from stone into flesh.

Such, then, are the conclusive reasons and motives for Christian humility. We are creatures; we are dependent creatures; we are guilty creatures; and we are creatures for whom the Son of God has suffered and died. It is a grace much insisted upon by our Lord, and very difficult for our proud natures to acquire and cultivate. But it must be acquired. Pride is the inmost substance of sin. Adam desired to be "as gods, knowing good and evil." Lucifer, the Son of the Morning, aspired to the throne of the Eternal. Both the angel and the man fell by pride. Humility is the opposite grace and virtue. It is the slowest and latest of any to take root again in our apostate nature. Even when we have bowed down in true lowliness of heart, the very first emotion, oftentimes, that springs up after the act, is the emotion of pride. We are proud because we have been humble! So subtle and inveterate in our souls is that "old serpent," that primitive sin whereby the angels fell, and whereby man transgressed.

We must, therefore, cultivate this particular grace as we would cultivate a choice exotic flower in an unkindly soil and clime. We must toil to "be clothed with humility." We must habitually feel our entire dependence upon God, and also our secondary dependence upon man. We must cherish a deeper sense of personal unworthiness. And above all, we must behold the suffering Lamb of God, and remember the deserved damnation from which he has saved us. "Put on, therefore, as the elect of God, holy and beloved, bowels of mercies, kindness, humbleness of mind, meekness, long-suffering, forbearing one another, and forgiving one another, if any man have a quarrel against any; even as Christ forgave you, so also do ye."

SERMON XVIII.

1 CORINTHIANS viii. 2.—"If any man think that he knoweth anything, he knoweth nothing yet as he ought to know."

In reading this text, we must lay a strong emphasis
upon the word "think," if we would feel the force of it.
St. Paul would teach certain members of the Corinthian
Church, who were inclined to place a high estimate upon
a philosophical comprehension of religious truth, and who
therefore were liable to a spurious kind of knowledge,
that if any one of them conceitedly supposed or imagined
himself to comprehend the gospel mysteries, he was in reality utterly ignorant concerning them. This party in the
Church claimed to possess a more profound apprehension
of Christian truth than the rest of the brotherhood. They
were filled with an intellectual pride and ambition that
blinded them to the real and sanctifying meaning of the
Gospel. They thought they knew. The apostle tells them
that such knowledge as this puffs up, but that real Christian love builds up; and adds, that "if any man *think*
that he knoweth anything, he knoweth nothing yet as he
ought to know." The doctrine of the text, therefore, is,
that *pride vitiates religious knowledge.* We proceed to
mention some particulars in respect to which this appears.

I. In the first place, pride injures our religious knowledge in respect to its *quantity* or *extent*. If this feeling be
in the heart, we shall not see so much, nor so far. The
apostle refers to that disposition which leads a man, when
he has made some addition to his stock of knowledge, to
stop and review it, and boast of it. He has in mind that
self-complacent spirit which is not content with the apprehension of truth, but which must sally forth and tell the
world how much it knows. These Corinthian disciples
were anxious to make an impression by their supposed superior insight into Christian doctrine. They gloried in
their attainments, real or reputed ; and hence St. Paul
says to them : "If any man among you seemeth to be wise
in this world, let him become a fool, that he may be wise.
For the wisdom of this world is foolishness with God.
Therefore let no man glory in men." Let no man plume
himself upon his own personal acquisitions, or upon the
knowledge of that particular human teacher—that Paul,
or Apollos, or Cephas—whom he calls his master.

Such a self-complacent spirit as this tends to diminish
the quantity or extent of a man's knowledge, because it
prevents him from surveying and travelling over the *whole*
field. Having obtained a partial view, he stops to congratulate himself upon his discovery, and to inform others
how much he has seen. His self-gratulation blinds his
eye to the vast spaces that still stretch away in every direction, and that still remain to be explored. He is like a
traveller among the Alps, who, having ascended the first
range of hills, and seeing the lower valleys, should imagine,
or "think," that he had exhausted Switzerland—had taken
up into his senses and soul that whole vast expanse of
mountains, valleys, lakes, streams, chasms, verdure, and
eternal snow, which constitutes the physical heart of Europe. That tarrying upon the heights already reached,

and that self-congratulation upon the scanty view that first broke upon the eye, was fatal to a comprehensive vision. This man who "thinks" that he knows Switzerland, knows nothing yet as he ought to know.

This is especially true of the apprehension of divine things. The instant a Christian begins to dwell upon his knowledge of God, or of himself, with any degree of self-complacency, he begins to stop his growth in knowledge. Take, for illustration, the knowledge of his own heart—of its corruption and its plague. So long as the Christian perceives indwelling sin with a simple and enlightened perception of its turpitude, and humbly mourns over it and confesses it, so long he makes advance in this species of knowledge. One shade or aspect of sin conducts him to the next, and so on in indefinite progression, until he becomes widely learned in the human heart, and profoundly abased before God. But the instant he begins to think of the extent to which he has gone in self-inspection, and to glory in his self-knowledge, that instant he brings the whole process to a stand-still. He creates an eddy in the flowing stream of his self-reflection, and whirls round and round, instead of moving onward and onward. And unless the volume of water starts once more, and gets out of this whirlpool; unless the Christian ceases to think of how much he knows, and to boast of it; unless he returns to that simple perception that is accompanied with humility and sorrow; he will never know any more of his own heart than he now knows. And even this degree of knowledge will not stay by him. "To him that hath shall be given, and he shall have more abundance; but from him that hath not, shall be taken even that he hath." These slight measures of self-knowledge, over which he has boasted, will themselves be absorbed in the pride of the heart, and disappear entirely from the experience.

We might select other features in the Christian experience, and apply the same reasoning to them, with the same result. He who contemplates the character of God, with no side glances at himself in the way of pride at his fancied wisdom; he who simply beholds the glory of the Holy One, and bows down before it in reverence and awe; is carried forward from one vision to another. But the instant he begins to admire the results of his contemplation and study in this direction, the charm is dissolved. The face of God is veiled, and he sees it no longer. He, again, who, having perceived the adaptation of the atonement of the Lord Jesus Christ to the guilty conscience, begins to be proud of his perception, destroys the perception. If having seen the Lamb of God, he begins to feel meretorious because he has seen Him, and to glory in his spiritual discernment, his soul fills up with darkness, instead of a clearer and purer light. The knowledge of these divine things cannot be chased after, and boasted over in this style. If you would see your shadow distinctly, stand still and look at it. The instant you begin to run after it, or grasp at it, you set it to wavering; you destroy its sharp outlines, and its exact parts and proportions. So, too, the instant you snatch at, and try to seize hold of your religious experiences and perceptions, that you may hold them up triumphantly before the eyes of men, and flaunt them before the world to your own praise —the instant you begin to review your knowledge for self-gratulation, you damage and vitiate it. You injure it in its quantity. You do not see so far, or so comprehensively, as you would had you the meekness of wisdom.

II. In the second place, pride vitiates our religious knowledge in respect to its *quality*, or *depth*. Knowledge seems to have two properties that correspond with two of the geometrical dimensions. It extends out in every direction like a plane surface; and it runs downward, and reaches upward, like a right line. How natural it is to speak of a superficial knowledge—a knowledge that runs to the superficies or surface of things. And it is equally natural to speak of high thinking, and deep thinking—of a species of reflection that penetrates above and below the surface. In the first head of the discourse, we were engaged with knowledge as spreading out sidewise in all directions, and we saw that it was circumscribed and limited by the disposition to be conceited and boastful. Pride vitiated it, by reducing its compass and extent. We have now to notice how the same sin renders it less profound; preventing it from reaching up into the heights, and sinking down into the depths of divine truth.

The moment the mind begins to compute the distance it has gone, it stops going. It cannot do two things together at the same instant. If, therefore, under the influence of pride, it pauses to see how profound it has become, to congratulate itself upon its profundity, and to tell the world its success, it adopts a suicidal course. It damages its knowledge in respect to quality. It ceases to be as pure and deep as it was while the mind was wholly absorbed in the contemplation of truth. Take an example, for illustration. Suppose that a sinful man directs his thoughts to his own sinfulness. Suppose that he fixes his attention upon some one sinful habit, say covetousness, to which he is inclined, and begins to see plainly its odiousness in its own nature, and in the eye of God. The longer this process continues, the more intent and absorbing the application of his mind to this one subject, the deeper is his view. He goes down lower and lower into his own heart, and his knowledge becomes purer and more profound in its quality. Now suppose that his attention is diverted from his sin itself, to the consideration of the fact that he has been exploring and probing his sin ; suppose that he begins, as it were, to look over his own shoulder, and see what he has been doing; is it not evident that his sense of the iniquity of his sin will begin to grow more shallow, and that he will come up to the surface of his heart again, instead of penetrating its recesses? The sin of covetousness will not appear so odious to him, because he begins to " think " that he understands all about it ; and in the end the assertion of the apostle is verified in his case : " If any man think that he knoweth anything, he knoweth nothing yet as he ought to know."

III. In the third place, pride vitiates our religious knowledge, in respect to its *practicality*. This is perhaps the greatest injury that is done to our apprehension of divine things, by our self-conceit and egotism. It is a great evil to have our knowledge diminished in its quantity and quality, in its extent and depth, but it is an even greater evil, to have its practical character and influence injured. The only purpose for which we ought to wish to understand religious truth is, that we may be made better by it. We ought not to desire to know God, except that we may become like him. We ought not to make any scrutiny into our own sin, except for the purpose of getting rid of sin. There is no species of truth or knowledge that is so purely practical, as religious truth and knowledge. The very instant, therefore, it loses this practicality, by any fault or wrong method of our own, it loses its most important element for us. It degenerates into mere speculation, and hardens the heart, instead of melting it into sorrow and love.

The first duty incumbent upon a man when he has obtained some new view of divine truth is, to *apply* it. But there is nothing that so interferes with such a personal application as pride, or self-gratulation. He who seeks to understand the doctrines of Scripture only that he may admire himself, or be admired by others because of his knowledge of Scripture, will never bring them home to himself; will never employ them for purposes of self-improvement. A French rhetorician relates the following anecdote, to show how impenetrable the vainglorious mind is to the sharp arrows of truth, and how exceedingly difficult it is to induce such a mind to allow any practical turn or application of a moral idea. " One day," he says, " the Abbé de St. Cyran happened to touch, in the presence of Balzac, upon certain religious truths which he developed with great force. Balzac, intent upon gaining from this some beautiful thought to enshrine at some future time in a page of his own, could not help exclaiming, ' That is admirable;' contenting himself with admiring, without applying anything to himself. ' Balzac,' said the Abbé, ' is like a man who, standing before a superb mirror which shows him a stain on his face, should content himself with admiring the beauty of the mirror, without removing the stain.' Balzac was delighted more than ever with this, and still forgetting the practical lesson altogether, in his attention to the pertinence of the illustration, cried in a yet louder tone, ' Ah, this is more admirable than all the rest.' " [1]

"Seest thou a man wise in his own conceit," says Solomon, "there is more hope of a fool than of him." When a man is destitute of knowledge, and feels himself to be so, he can be approached by a teacher, and instruction can be imparted. But when it is the thought of his heart that he comprehends the whole subject, and that no one can teach him, the prospect of his becoming enlightened is hopeless. Precisely so is it in regard to the practical ap-

---

[1] Bungener: Preacher and King, 38, 39.

plication of divine truth. He who listens to the teaching of the sanctuary, with the notion or imagination that he has completed the work of applying it to himself, and therefore hears merely for others, or for merely intellectual improvement, is in a most unfavorable position to receive salutary impressions. This is the hazard that accompanies a steady attendance upon public worship, without faith, repentance, and a Christian profession. The mind of such a person becomes filled with the doctrines of the gospel, and they command his unhesitating assent. They are so true for his intellect, that he never thinks of disputing them. And, at the same time, he never thinks of applying them to himself practically. There is a species of mental pride, a pride of knowledge, perhaps a pride of orthodoxy, that hinders him from listening with a tender conscience, and a meek and lowly heart. Perhaps it would be better, if such a hearer might, for a time, be brought into skeptical conflict with the truth. Perhaps there might be more hope of his conversion, if, instead of this cold and undisturbed assent to the Christian system which is accompanied with so much self-complacency, and so little self-application, there might rush in upon him some of those obstinate questionings that would destroy his ease of mind, and bring him into serious collision with the law and truth of God. He might then, perhaps, realize that the Word of God is the most practical, because it is the most truthful and searching, of all books; that there is not a teaching in it that does not have a bearing upon the most momentous interests of the human soul; and that the question which every man should put to himself, whenever he reads it, and whenever he listens to it, is the question : " What is it to *me ?* What shall *I* do in reference to it ?"

Thus have we seen, that "If any man think that he knoweth anything, he knoweth nothing yet as he ought to know "—that pride vitiates our knowledge of religious truth, in respect to its quantity, its quality, and its practicality.

That is a very instructive chapter in the Old Testament history which records the punishment that came upon David, because he numbered the people. We are not informed, by the sacred historian, what was the particular wickedness of which the king of Israel was guilty, in this instance. It was not the mere taking of a census. Moses had twice numbered the people, without any rebuke from God; and upon the face of the transaction, there does not seem to lie any harm. It was well, that the ruler of a kingdom should know the number of his army; it was well, that the shepherd of Israel should count up his flock. The most probable explanation is, that the monarch took this census of his kingdom from pride, as Hezekiah showed the treasures of his palace to the ambassadors of the king of Babylon. Therefore God punished him. It is the same spirit that numbers up spiritual attainments, and the same disapprobation of God attends it. What is the moral difference between showing the heathen king the silver, and the gold, and the spices, and the precious ointment, in order to make an impression upon him for purposes of self-aggrandizement, and showing to one's own self, or to others, the mental treasures, for purposes of pride and vanity? What is the difference in the motive, between David's boastful counting up of his men of war, and the Christian's boastful counting up of his knowledge, his graces, and his good deeds?

1. In deducing, therefore, the lessons which this subject suggests, we remark, in the first place, that spiritual pride is the most *subtle* of sins. "Now the serpent was more subtle than any beast of the field which the Lord God had made." The species of sin which is rebuked in the text,

and which we have been considering, does not approach
the Christian from the outside. It does not issue from
flesh and sense, but from the intellect itself. It is the sin
of Lucifer, the Son of the Morning. That archangel was
not tempted to revolt against the authority and government of the Most High, by the low and flesh-born solicitations which are continually assailing the sons of men. His
substance was incorporeal, and his nature ethereal. The
five senses, which are the avenues through which many
enticements to sin approach the children of Adam, formed
no part of his constitution. He fell from a purely intellectual temptation, and his wickedness was what the apostle denominates "*spiritual* wickedness." The sin of pride,
to which the believer is liable, is a sin of the same species
whereby the angels fell. In wrestling against it, we
"wrestle not against flesh and blood, but against principalities, against powers, against the rulers of the darkness
of this world, against spiritual wickedness in high places."
(Eph. vi. 12.) There is every reason to believe, that when
the child of God becomes sinfully self-conscious, and ego-
tistic; when he ceases to be an actor, and converts himself
into a spectator; when he reviews his conduct with self-
complacency, and is puffed up with knowledge, instead of
built up with charity; when he thinks more highly of
himself than he ought to think; he is particularly the
victim of the wiles of Satan, that Old Serpent, that subt-
lest of the creatures of God. When other artifices fail;
when the believer proves to be on his guard against the
more common and outward temptations of earth; then
the Arch Deceiver plies him with one that is purely mental, and spiritual. He fills him with the conceit of holiness, and the conceit of knowledge. This puffs him up,
and leads him to commit that great sin which is condemned
in the declaration of God, through the prophet Isaiah: "I

am Jehovah, that is my name, and my glory I will not give to another." Under the impulse of this temptation, the creature defrauds the Creator of the glory which is his due, and comes short of the chief end of his own creation. Spiritual pride is thus the last resort of the Tempter, and whoever is enabled by divine grace to foil him at this point, will foil him at all points. "That which first overcomes man," says St. Augustine, "is the last thing man overcomes." The pride by which the angels fell, and which was the principal quality in the Adamic transgression, lingers longest and latest in the experience of the Christian. "Some sins," remarks an old divine, "may die before us, but this hath life in it as long as we. It is, as it were, the heart of all other sins; the first to live, and the last to die. And it hath this advantage, that whereas other sins are fomented by one another, this feeds even on virtues and graces, as a moth that breeds in them, and consumes them, even in the finest of them, if it be not carefully looked into. This hydra, as one head of it is cut off, another rises up; it will secretly cleave to the best actions, and prey upon them. And therefore is there so much need that we continually watch, and fight, and pray against it; and be restless in the pursuit of real and deep humiliation—to be nothing, and desire to be nothing; not only to bear, but to love our own abasement, and the things that procure and help it." [1]

---

[1] Leighton: On 1 Pet. v. 5. The same testimony respecting the nature of spiritual pride is borne by Richard Baxter. "For my part, when I consider the great measure of pride, self-conceitedness, self-esteem, that is in the greater part of Christians that ever I was acquainted with —we of the ministry not excepted—I wonder that God doth not afflict us more, and bring us down by foul means, that will not be brought down by fair. For my own part, I have had as great means to help me

2. And this carries us to the second lesson suggested by the subject, which is, that spiritual pride especially requires the aid and influence of the *Holy Ghost* to overcome it. Nó spirit is a match for the subtlety of Satan but the Eternal Spirit. When the mystery of iniquity worketh; when "that Wicked is revealed whose coming is after the working of Satan, with all power, and signs, and lying wonders, and with all deceivableness of unrighteousness;" St. Paul tells us that "the Lord shall consume him with the Spirit of his mouth, and shall destroy him with the brightness of his coming." (2 Thess. ii. 7–10.) The believer will fall a victim to these arts of the Deceiver, unless he is both enlightened and empowered. His very virtues and graces themselves are, oftentimes, the egg out of which spiritual pride is hatched. With Cowper he can say:

> " When I would speak what thou hast done
> To save me from my sin,
> I can not make thy mercies known,
> But self-applause creeps in."

---

against this sin as most men living ever had; first, in many years' trouble of mind, and then in near twenty years' languishing and bodily pains, having been almost twenty years at the grave's mouth, and living near it continually ; and lastly and above all, I have had as full a sight of it in others, even in the generality of the professors, and in the doleful state of the Church and State, and heinous, detestable abominations of this age, which one would think should have fully cured it. And yet, if I hear but either an applauding word from any of fame on one side, or a disparaging word on the other side, I am fain to watch my heart as narrowly as I would do the thatch of my house when fire is put to it, and presently to throw on it the water of detestation, resolution, and recourse to God. And though the acts through God's great mercy be thus restrained, yet the constancy of these inclinations assures me that there is still a strong and deep root." Baxter: The Right Method for Spiritual Peace and Comfort.

The believer, therefore, needs to have that singleness of eye which is never dazzled with any of the flatteries of either his own heart, or of Satan himself. He needs to have his whole body full of that heavenly light which will chase out every lingering remnant of darkness, and of egotism. And who but the unerring Spirit of God is the author of such a spiritual illumination as this? The discourses of our Lord are full of solemn injunctions to be single-eyed, single-minded, and not to let the left hand know what the right hand doeth. Simplicity and godly sincerity, he continually emphasizes; and these are the exact contraries of self-deception and pride. But who can attain to this, as a steady and spontaneous habit and frame of soul, without the teaching of the Holy Ghost? And by that teaching it can be attained. There is a power in God, the Creator of the human soul, and the Searcher of the human heart, to produce within it a guileless simplicity —that beautiful trait which Christ saw and praised in Nathanael, when he said: "Behold an Israelite indeed, in whom there is no guile." It is that holiness which is so simple, childlike, and ingenuous, that it is unconscious of itself. It is that divine knowledge which is so pure, and deep, that it never reviews itself, and never inflates in the least. It is that mental absorption in God and divine things, of which the Old Mystics say so much, whereby the will of the creature and the intellect of the creature are so completely subject to those of the Creator, that the difference between them cannot be distinguished in the religious experience. It is that union with Christ which is so intimate and central, that the instant the believer says with St. Paul, "I live," he is obliged with him to add immediately, "yet not I, but Christ liveth in me." Such a union as this, resulting in the extinction of self-assertion

and vainglory, is the product of the Holy Spirit working in us to will, to feel, to think, and to act. It results
from walking in the Spirit, and praying in the Spirit;
yea, praying that prayer of which the apostle remarks:
"The Spirit helpeth our infirmities; for we know not
what to pray for as we ought; but the Spirit itself maketh intercession for us, with groanings which cannot be
uttered."

SERMON XIX.

JAMES ii. 24.—"Ye see then how that by works a man is justified, and not by faith only."

THIS affirmation of the inspired apostle James seems to flatly contradict that famous assertion of the inspired apostle Paul which is so often quoted, as containing the pith and substance of the evangelical system. St. Paul, in his Epistle to the Romans, after proving that all mankind are guilty before the law, and consequently cannot be acquitted by it, draws the inference : " Therefore, we conclude that a man is justified by faith without the deeds of the law." (Rom. iii. 28.) This doctrine has come down from age to age, as the cardinal truth of Christianity. The Church has been pure or corrupt, according as it has adopted or rejected it. Protestant as distinguished from Papal Christianity rests upon it as its proof text. Men are evangelical or legal, according as they receive or reject it. And yet St. James, in the text, affirms distinctly and positively, that " by works a man is justified, and not by faith only."

There is certainly a verbal contradiction between these two apostles. Should these two isolated passages of Scripture be read to an inhabitant of Saturn ; should they be taken out of their connections, and be made known to any one who was utterly unacquainted with the Scriptures as a whole; should they be found, like some old Greek or Sanskrit inscription, cut into a marble tablet, with nothing going before them to explain, or following after to illustrate, their meaning, they must undoubtedly be set down as conflicting with each other. The words in the one statement contradict the words in the other.

But a verbal contradiction is not necessarily a real contradiction. Inconsistency in words is compatible with consistency in ideas. In order to charge a contradiction in the thought, or doctrine, we must evince something more than a contradiction in the language. The letter sometimes kills the sense, but the spirit makes it alive. It is the ulterior meaning, which must be gathered from the intention of the writer as seen in other parts of his discourse, and especially from the immediate context, that must interpret the phraseology. Human language is an imperfect instrument to express so subtle a thing as thought. Hence we shall find that, oftentimes, it labors under the idea or truth which is sought to be conveyed by it, and this laboring appears in a verbal contradiction. Some of the very highest truths, owing to the poverty of human language, can be expressed only in phraseology that involves an utter inconsistency if taken according to the mere letter. Consider, for example, the schoolman's definition of the Divine omnipresence. " God," he said, " is a circle whose circumference is everywhere, and its centre nowhere." This diction is utterly self-contradictory. Read it to a mere mathematician, who should have no inkling of the great truth that was sought to be conveyed by it ; who should look at it as a purely verbal and mathematical statement; and he would tell you that there is and can be no circle whose centre is nowhere, and its circumference everywhere, and that the terms of such a proposition are absurd. And yet it is one of the best definitions that have been given of the omnipresence of God. It impresses the inscrutable immensity of the Deity, the mysterious boundlessness of his being, upon the mind, in a very vivid and striking manner. And it is the impression made, which is the truth and fact in the case. Take, again, the famous statement, that "the soul is all in every part of the body." The purpose of this verbal contradiction is, to show that the immaterial spirit of man cannot be localized in a section of space. The soul of a man is not seated in the hand, or in the foot; in the heart, or in the head. It is not contained and confined in any one part of the human body, for it causes the movements of every part. It thinks through the brain; it feels through the nerves; and it lifts weights through the hand. It exists, therefore, in one part as much as in another; and therefore no one organ can be asserted to be its sole locality, and residence. And yet, on the other hand, it would not be correct to say that the soul is *diffused* through the whole body, and has exactly the same form and figure as the body. The soul has no extended form, or figure; as it would have if it were spread out through the whole material structure. It is not correct to say that a part of the soul is in the head, and another part is in the foot, and another part is in the hand. The soul cannot be subdivided and distributed in this manner. The *whole* soul is in the hand, when the hand is lifted up; and in the foot, when the foot is set down. The *whole* soul, the entire conscious ego, is in each nerve, and at every point of it, when it thrills; and in each muscle, and at every point of it, when it contracts. And to express these truths and facts, so mysterious and yet so real and true, the philosopher invented the verbal contradiction, that " the soul is all in every part of the body." And the same use of language meets us in everyday life, as well as in the speculations of the philosopher. When, for instance, you are mourning the loss of a beloved friend, and you wish to convey the truth, that his death was gain to him but loss to you, you say, in concise and pointed, yet verbally contradictory phrase: "It is the survivor that dies." When, again, you desire to express the truth, that indiscriminate praise is worthless; that a critic who pronounces everything presented for his judgment to be good and excellent, deserves no regard; you do it in the sententious, but verbally contradictory proverb: "He who praises everybody, praises nobody." Again, would you express the truth which Solomon conveys in his question: "Hast thou found honey? eat so much as is sufficient for thee, lest thou be filled therewith, and vomit it," you do it in the homely verbal contradiction: "Too much of a good thing, is good for nothing." These examples might be multiplied indefinitely. The proverbs of a nation—which are the condensed and pointed sense of the people, the truest of truths—are very often couched in phraseology that, if taken in a literal signification, is absurd.

Before we conclude, therefore, that two writers are in conflict with each other, we must first determine their general aim and purpose, and interpret particular individual statements accordingly. Two questions always arise, in this comparison of one author with another. First, are they looking at the same thing; and, secondly, if so, do they occupy the same point of view. The perspective point is everything, in judging of the correctness of a picture. And this is specially true of religious objects, and truths. The spiritual world is so comprehensive and vast, that no observer can see the whole of it at once, and from a single point of vision. He must pass from point to point, and obtain view after view. He must walk about Zion, before he can tell the towers thereof. It is because of the infinitude of divine truth, that there are so many apparent contradictions—so many "paradoxes," as Lord Bacon denominates them—in the Christian system. It is for this reason, that there are more verbal contradictions in the Bible than in any other book. In one place we read: "Answer a fool according to his folly"; and at another: "Answer not a fool according to his folly." Upon one page we are told that, "Whosoever is born of God doth not commit sin"; upon another that, "If we say we have no sin, we deceive ourselves, and the truth is not in us." These propositions are verbally contradictory, and yet when read in their connections, and explained in the light of the general drift of Scripture, they convey the highest truth in the most striking and impressive manner. The several authors of the inspired volume look at the great system of religious truth from many points of view, and each sees and depicts a different side of it. And he is the wise man who, instead of employing the microscopic vision of a fly crawling over a cornice, or some small ornament of the great temple of truth, is able to survey with the eye of an architect all their individual representations, and to combine them into one grand and all-comprehending scheme.

These remarks prepare us to consider the verbal contradiction between the apostles Paul and James, and to determine whether it is a real and irreconcilable one. The two writers are contemplating the same thing—the sinner's justification before God. Paul asserts that "a man is justified by faith, without the works of the law"—that is, by faith only. James affirms that "by works a man is justified, and not by faith only." Both are speaking of the sinner's justification; but *not to the same class of persons*, and, therefore, *not from the same point of view*. One is arguing against *sincere legalists*, and the other against *hypocritical believers*. This explains, and harmonizes, the difference between them.

I. St. Paul is addressing *legalists*—a class of errorists who maintained that man's works of morality are the ground of his justification; are a satisfaction of the law for past transgressions, and entitle him to the rewards of the future life. The religionist of this class makes the same use of his own virtues, acts, and merits, that the evangelical believer makes of the blood and righteousness of Christ. He rests in them for justification and acceptance before God. Now to this class of persons, the apostle Paul says: "By the works of the law, shall no flesh be justified; by the deeds of the law, there shall no flesh be justified; a man is justified by faith, without the deeds of the law." (Gal. ii. 16; Rom. iii. 20, 28.) It was with reference to their particular opinion, that a man's own works could atone for sin and merit heaven, that the apostle asserts that man's works are worthless and useless. Standing upon this position, and addressing moralists and legalists, he could say without any qualification, that a sinner is justified by mere and simple faith in Christ's vicarious sacrifice, without the addition to it, or combination with it, of any of his own works, good or bad. The expiatory work of Christ is in and of itself a complete satisfaction, and there is no need of completing the complete. There is no need of gilding refined gold, or painting the lily. There is no need, even if it could be done, of supplementing or perfecting the Divine provision for the forgiveness of sin, by a human agency. The oblation of Christ is sufficient, alone, and by itself, to satisfy the broken law; and he who trusts in it as the sole ground and reason of pardon, need not bring with him a single jot or tittle of his own work. And when any sinner begins to look around for something wherewith to appear before the awful Eternal Justice, and answer its demands, he discovers the worthlessness of even the best of human works. There is nothing *expiatory* in human virtue. There is no judicial suffering in it. Good works do not bleed; and "without the shedding of blood there is no remission." To attempt, therefore, to expiate sin by performing good works, is not an adaptation of means to ends. It is like attempting to quench thirst, by eating bread. Bread is necessary to human life considered as a whole, but it cannot slake thirst. So too, good works are necessary to human salvation taken as a whole, but they cannot accomplish that particular part of human salvation which consists in satisfying the law for past transgressions. Without personal holiness no man shall see the Lord, and yet no amount of personal holiness can wash out the stain of guilt. All this, which tallies exactly with St. Paul's declaration, is understood by the sinner, the instant he sees guilt and atonement in their mutual relations. While he perceives very clearly, that in reference to other points, and other purposes, Christian character is indispensable, and good works must be performed, yet having respect to the one single, momentous particular of deliverance from the penalty of the law, he very clearly perceives that good works are good for nothing. They cannot enter into the account, for purposes of justification, even in part. The atonement for sin is not partly the death of Christ, and partly the merits of the sinner. It is the death of Christ alone, without any works of the law. "I feel"—says Chalmers—"that the righteousness of Christ unmixed with baser materials, untempered with strange mortar, unvitiated by human pretensions of any sort, is the solid resting-place on which a man is to lay his acceptance before God, and that there is no other; that to attempt a composition between grace and works is to spoil both, and is to deal a blow both to the character of God, and to the cause of practical holiness." [1] Such is the doctrine of the apostle Paul respecting justification, as enunciated from his point of view, and having reference to the moralist and legalist.

II. We are now, in the second place, to examine the doctrine of the apostle James, upon the same subject, as stated from his point of view, and with reference to a wholly different class of persons. For, the errorists whom St. James was combating were *hypocritical believers*, and not sincere legalists. They did not deny the doctrine of justification by faith. They did not, like the moralist whom St. Paul opposed, affirm that man could be justified by the works of the law, either wholly or in part. On the contrary, they were orthodox in theory, evangelical in phraseology, and profuse in their declarations that works were useless, and that nothing but faith could save the soul. This is evident from the course of the apostle's reasoning with them. "What doth it profit, my brethren, though a man *say* [pretend] he hath faith, and have not works? Can [such] faith save him? If a brother or sister be naked, and destitute of daily food, and one of you *say* unto them, Depart in peace, be you warmed and filled : notwithstanding ye give them not those things which are needful to the body : What doth it profit? Even so faith, if it hath not works is dead, being alone." This reasoning implies, that the opponents of the apostle James were not in the least tinctured with the Judaistic theory of justification by works, but were using the evangelical doctrine of justification by faith in such a way as to abuse it. They were not zealous sticklers for the law, but hypocritical and false professors of the gospel.

---

[1] Chalmers' Memoirs, II. 190.

Accordingly, St. James combats, not St. Paul's true faith, but the spurious faith of these errorists. He attacks what he denominates "dead faith." Probably there is an allusion here to St. Paul's use of the word, when he speaks of " dead works," and of being " dead to the law." James tells these hypocrites, who are boasting of their faith, and making it the cloak of licentiousness, that as there is a dead work, spoken of by St. Paul, so there is a dead faith, such as they are professing ; and neither the dead work nor the dead faith can save the soul. The class of errorists whom he opposes " *said* " they had faith. They pretended to trust in the person and work of the Son of God ; but they had never been truly convicted of sin, had never felt godly sorrow, and had never exercised an evangelical peace-giving confidence in atoning blood. They were hypocrites. Their faith, in James's phraseology, was " alone." It had no connection with works. It was not an active and operative principle in the heart, but the mere breath on their lips. It was a counterfeit, and not the genuine thing of which St. Paul speaks. Now, in disparaging such a hypocritical non-working faith as this, and affirming that it could not justify a sinner, St. James is not disparaging sincere and true faith, and falls into no real contradiction with St. Paul. Standing upon the position of James, and called to address the same class of persons, Paul would have spoken in the same manner. He would have plainly told hypocritical men who were professing an inoperative and spurious faith, and making it an opiate for their conscience, and a cloak for licentiousness ; who were saying to the naked and destitute Christian brother, " Depart in peace, be thou warmed and filled," but were doing nothing for his relief—he would have plainly and solemnly told them that such faith could not save them. He would have asked the same question with James : " What doth it

profit, though a man say he hath faith, and have not
works; can faith [that has not works] save him?" There
would have been no danger of legalism, or of misconception;
for they would have understood that by "faith," he meant
their faith—their non-working and hypocritical profession.[1]
And standing upon the position of Paul, and called to address an altogether different class of errorists, who expected
to atone for sin by their own works and merit, the apostle
James, with his Old Testament conceptions of law and expiation, and his stern uncompromising view of sin as guilt,
would have spoken of a living and true faith in the sacrifice of the Lamb of God—" our Lord Jesus Christ, the
Lord of glory," as he affectionately and reverently calls
him—as the only act whereby a sinner can be delivered
from his guilt, and the curse of the violated law.

There are two proofs of this latter assertion, to which
we direct attention for a moment.   In the first place, the
apostles James and Paul both alike accepted that statement of the essential principles of the gospel which was
formulated in the Apostolic convention.   In the fifteenth
chapter of the Acts of the Apostles, there is an account of
an assembly of the apostles and elders, to discuss the question in dispute between the converted Jews and the converted Gentiles, whether obedience to the Mosaic law was
necessary in order to salvation, or whether a simple faith
in the person and work of Christ was sufficient.   The decision was unanimous, that faith in Christ was the only
essential requisite.   This decision was sent out in a letter
to all the churches, and has gone down from century to
century, as an inspired declaration of the real nature of

---

[1] In the original (James ii. 14), the hypocrisy of the faith is indicated
by the presence of the article in one instance, and its absence in the
other. The hypocrite says that he has faith—πίστιν anarthrous; the
apostle asks if ἡ πίστις—this *kind* of faith—can save him.

Christianity. James advocated, in the convention, the same views with Peter and the other apostles, and lent the weight of his authority and influence, in favor of the doctrine of justification by faith without the works of the law.

In the second place, there is proof in this very Epistle, which St. James addresses to " the twelve Jewish tribes which are scattered abroad," that he considered faith, and not works, to be the cardinal truth of Christianity. In the course of the discussion, the supposition is made, that faith and works can be separated, and exist the one without the other : " Yea, a man may say, Thou hast faith, and I have works." (James ii. 18.) The apostle, in his answer to this, so shapes his statement, as not only to deny the possibility of any such divorce between the two, but also to show that he considered faith to be the root and principle, and works only the fruit and evidence, of justification. For although he is laying a very strong emphasis upon works, yet he does not say, in reply to this supposition that faith and works can be separated : " Shew me thy faith without any works, and I will shew thee my works without any faith." But his answer is one that Paul himself would have given in a similar case : " Shew me thy faith without thy works "—a thing that is impossible—" and I will show thee my faith *by* my works." The implication of this answer is, not only that true and living faith cannot exist without showing itself in good works, but that good works are secondary to faith, as being its effect and evidence. Works are not the root, but the branches. And in dealing with a legalist, we can easily imagine St. James to accommodate the language of St. Paul, used in another connection : " Boast not of the branches. But if thou boast, remember that the branches bear not the root, but the root bears the branches. Boast

not of your works ; but if you boast, remember that works
do not produce faith, but faith produces works."

The doctrine of St. James, then, to say it in a word, is,
that a man is justified by a *working* faith. In some passages of his Epistle, " works " signifies " true faith." The
text is one of them ; and it might be read : " Ye see, then,
how that by a working faith a man is justified, and not by
a faith that has not works." In order to present, strongly
and impressively, the truth at which he was aiming, he
resorts to a well-known rhetorical figure, and puts the
effect for the cause—the works of faith, for faith itself.
" Works " stand for " working faith," when he asserts
that " Abraham was justified by works, when he had offered up Isaac his son ; " and that " Rahab was justified
by works, when she sent the messengers out another way."
In these instances, the term " works " denotes the *genuine*
faith that works, in contradistinction to the *spurious* faith
that does not work. Dead faith has no energy, and no
work in it. Living faith is full of energy, and full of
work ; and therefore, by the metonymy of effect for cause,
may be denominated " work "—as Christ so calls it, when
he says : " This is the work of God, that ye believe on
him whom he hath sent." (John vi. 29.) This also explains the meaning of St. James, when he says, that
" Abraham's faith wrought with his works, and by works
was faith made perfect." Abraham's act of obedience to
the Divine command to sacrifice his son, was a work that
proved beyond all doubt that his faith was sincere and
" perfect," and not spurious and hypocritical. This " work,"
therefore, might well stand for, and represent, the mighty
" faith " that produced it. In saying that Abraham and
Rahab were " justified by works," St. James is conceiving
of, and describing faith as an *active* and *working principle*,
like that which St. Paul has in mind, when he speaks of

"faith which worketh by love" (Gal. v. 6); when he thanks the Thessalonians for their "work of faith" (1 Thess. i. 3); and when he urges Titus to preach in such a manner, that "they which have believed in God might be careful to maintain good works" (Titus iii. 8). The contradiction between the two apostles is, therefore, verbal only, and not real. Both hold the same evangelical doctrine.[1]

This exhibition of the agreement between Paul and James leads us to notice, in closing, the importance of guarding the doctrine of gratuitous justification against abuse, by showing the natural and necessary connection between it and sanctification. St. James, in his day, found a class of persons in the church who made Christ a minister of sin, and who "sinned," knowingly and wantonly, "that grace might abound." Because the blood of Christ cleanseth from all sin, they inferred that they might indulge in sin. If they stained themselves, it was easy to wash the stain out. Because good works could not avail, either wholly or in part, to atone for transgression, therefore they need not perform them for any purpose whatever. The righteousness of Christ was sufficient for their justification, and therefore they need not follow after holiness, or seek inward sanctification. In this way, they abused the grace of God, and converted that truth which is a savor of life unto life, into a savor of death unto death. It is often remarked,

---

[1] The Westminster Confession, XI. ii., admirably sums up the whole truth, in the following proposition : "Faith is the alone instrument of justification ; yet it is not alone in the person justified, but is ever accompanied with other saving graces." The first half of this proposition contains St. Paul's statement, that "a man is justified by faith without the deeds of the law ; " and the second half of it contains St. James's statement, that "faith, if it hath not works is dead, being alone." To say that a man is justified by "faith alone," is not the same as to say that he is justified by "faith that is alone."

that the greatest of blessings when perverted becomes the greatest of evils. And so it is with the doctrine of gratuitous justification. If any man makes use of it as an opiate to his conscience, and a means of indulging himself in sin, or ease in Zion, he becomes fearfully selfish, and fearfully hardened. He treads the atoning blood under foot. There is evidence in the Epistle of James, that those who were thus maltreating the gospel, and abusing the doctrine of free grace in Christ, were very far gone in earthliness and sin. The kind of sins which the apostle rebukes, and the style in which he does it, evince this. He severely reproves them for their regard for human distinctions, in exalting the man with a gold ring and goodly apparel, and humbling the poor man in vile raiment; for their reckless use of the tongue, in slandering and boasting; for their grasping after office and authority, in endeavoring to be "many masters;" for their quarrelling, envying, and even "fightings"—moving the apostle to address them sternly: "Ye adulterers and adulteresses, know ye not that the friendship of the world is enmity with God?" for their inordinate avarice, which led them to "keep back the hire of the laborer by fraud, and to heap up treasure for the last days;" for their sensuality, in "living in pleasure and wantonness on the earth, and nourishing their hearts as in day of slaughter." (James ii. 1–9; iii. 1–v. 6.) These sins, thus specified and rebuked, seem to have crept into the Jewish-Christian churches to whom St. James addressed his Epistle; for there is no reason to suppose that he would have thus particularized them, had they not been in existence. And they are aggravated transgressions. It was no ordinary corruption that had come into these scattered churches, by the abuse of the doctrine of free grace.

Human nature is the same now that it was then; and it

becomes necessary, therefore, for the believer to guard against even the slightest tendency to live at ease in the Church, because the Church is not under law but under grace. If the blood of Christ is a complete atonement for our sin, this is a reason why we should resist unto blood striving against sin, and not a reason why we should supinely yield to sin. If there is no condemnation to them that are in Christ Jesus, this is a reason why we should dread to incur any new condemnation, and not a reason why we should add to the already immense debt which Christ has assumed for us.

The effectual preservative against such a tendency as this, is to remember the wholesome doctrine of St. James, that a man is not justified by a dead faith, but by a *working* faith. A dead faith has no justifying efficacy, because, as St. Paul remarks of a heathen idol, "it is nothing in the world." It is a nonentity. A dead faith—a faith that does nothing, and produces nothing—is nothing. It is a pretence. It is sheer hypocrisy. It can no more save the soul, than sin can save it.

Try yourself, then, by this test. Does your faith in Christ's atonement *work?* When you have trusted in the blood and righteousness of Christ for acceptance with the holy God, do you find that this reliance of your heart then goes out into acts? Does it go out in love, peace, joy, long-suffering, meekness, hope? These are internal acts of the mind and heart; and they are the fruit, and evidences of faith. Does it go out in external acts—in prayer, praise, labor for the good of souls, discharge of the various duties of a Christian profession? If this is your happy case, yours is a working faith, and a justifying faith. Notice that these works—this peace, joy, hope, prayer, praise, Christian benevolence, and discharge of duty—are not the ground and reason of your justification, but only the effect and fruits of it. You are accepted of God, and acquitted by him, solely and simply because you confide in Christ's death for sin. You are justified by this one act of faith in Christ's atonement, apart from any of these resulting works. And being thus justified, you then act out your faith in and by these works—internal and external. There is no legality in your experience, and yet you keep the law with great particularity. While you do not look to the law in the least for justification, you nevertheless magnify and honor the law by your obedience to its requirements. You do not obey the law in order to obtain the forgiveness of your sins. They are already forgiven for Christ's sake. That part of your salvation is secure. But you obey the law because you *are* forgiven ; because you love to obey ; and because it is the command of God to obey. You obey it because your faith in Christ's blood is living, and not dead ; is working faith, and not inoperative faith ; is sincere faith, and not hypocritical faith —the genuine principle which St. Paul praises and defends, and not the counterfeit which St. James condemns and attacks.

SERMON XX.

THE CHRISTIAN IMPERFECT, YET A SAINT.

COLOSSIANS iii. 12.—"Put on, therefore, as the elect of God, holy and beloved, bowels of mercies, kindness, humbleness of mind, meekness, long-suffering."

IT appears singular to the reader of St. Paul's Epistles, that the apostle in one passage speaks of Christians as perfect, and in another as imperfect. At one time, he describes them in terms that would lead us to infer that they are holy as God is holy ; and at another, he speaks of them as full of sin and corruption. In the text, he denominates them "the elect of God holy and beloved," and yet immediately proceeds to exhort them to the possession and practice of the most common Christian graces—such as humility and forgiveness. In a preceding paragraph, he tells the Colossians that they "are dead to sin, and their life is hid with Christ in God," and then goes on to urge them to overcome some of the most gross sins in the whole catalogue—" mortify, therefore, your members which are upon the earth ; fornication, uncleanness, inordinate affection, evil concupiscence, and covetousness which is idolatry." (Coloss. iii. 3–5.)

This characteristic is very strikingly exhibited in St. Paul's Epistles to the Corinthians. We know from both of the letters which he wrote to this church, that there was much corruption within it. Planted in the midst of one of the most vicious cities of the pagan world, the converts to Christianity had been drawn forth from a very unclean paganism, and after their conversion they were exposed to the strongest temptations. Some of their number yielded to them. The apostle calls upon the Corinthian church to discipline one of its members for incest ; he rebukes them for their shameful abuse of the Lord's Supper ; for their party spirit, and jealousies, that led them to take sides with men—with Paul, and Apollos, and Cephas ; and for the bickerings and litigations that arrayed Christian against Christian, even in the courts of the idolatrous pagan. And yet, in the opening of his first Epistle, St. Paul addresses such a church as this, in the following terms: "I thank my God always on your behalf, for the grace of God which is given you by Jesus Christ; that in everything ye are enriched by him, in all utterance, and in all knowledge ; even as the testimony of Christ was confirmed in you ; so that ye come behind in no gift; waiting for the coming of our Lord Jesus Christ; who shall also confirm you unto the end, that ye may be blameless in the day of our Lord Jesus Christ." (1 Cor. i. 4–8.)

How are we to explain such opposite representations ? Is the Christian "holy and beloved," and yet at the same time vile and polluted ? Is he "dead to sin and his life hid with Christ in God," and also a wretched man "tied to the body of this death," and crying out, "Who shall deliver me ?" Can he say with the Psalmist, "Preserve me, O my God, for I am holy," and with Isaiah, "I am undone, I am a man of unclean lips ?" Does St. Paul correctly describe the experience of a renewed, man, both when he utters himself in the confident phrase: "I live, yet not I, but Christ liveth in me ;" and when he expresses his anxieties in the affirmation, that he struggles daily

with indwelling corruption, and "keeps his body under,
lest he should be a cast-away from God?" It is even so.
This is one of the paradoxes of Christianity, as Lord Bacon
calls them. "A Christian," he says, "is one that believes
things his reason cannot comprehend, and hopes for things
which neither he nor any man alive ever saw; he believes
three to be one, and one to be three, a father not to be
older than his son, and a son to be equal with his father;
he believes himself to be precious in God's sight, and yet
loathes himself in his own; he dares not justify himself
even in those things wherein he can find no fault with himself, and yet believes that God accepts him in those services wherein he is able to find many faults; he is so
ashamed as that he dares not open his mouth before God,
and yet he comes with boldness to God, and asks him anything he needs; he hath within him both flesh and spirit,
yet he is not a double-minded man; he is often led captive
by the law of sin, yet, it never gets dominion over him;
he cannot sin, yet can do nothing without sin; he is so
humble as to acknowledge himself to deserve nothing but
evil; and yet he believes that God means him all good."
These are contradictions to the carnal mind. These things
are foolishness to the Greek. Richard Porson, one of the
most learned classical scholars that England ever saw, and a
profound admirer of Lord Bacon, tells his reader that he
knows not what to make of this list of paradoxes, and
actually raises the query, whether Lord Bacon might not
have been laboring under a momentary fit of skepticism,
at the time he penned them. This "specification of the
characteristics of a believing Christian," by the most sober and sagacious of English philosophers and statesmen,
which the believing Christian cannot peruse without profound admiration at the depth of its evangelical insight,
and tender emotion for the comfort it gives him—this de-

lineation of the inmost heart of the gospel, and of the Christian experience, actually raised doubts in the mind of a learned man of this world, whether Bacon of Verulam was not the subject of a lurking skepticism ! "We preach Christ crucified, unto the Jews a stumbling-block, and unto the Greeks foolishness." (1 Cor. i. 23.)

These paradoxes are not self-contradictions. The declaration : " When I am weak, then I am strong," does not affirm and deny the same thing. It affirms that when the sinful and helpless man feels and confesses his utter impotence, then the holy and almighty God comes to his rescue and salvation. The affirmation that the Christian " believes himself to be precious in God's sight, yet loathes himself in his own ; that he is often led captive by sin, yet it does not get dominion over him;" is self-consistent and true, because one side of the proposition does not conflict with the other side. Verbally contradictory it is logically harmonious.

In the light of these remarks, let us proceed to explain how it is, that the apostle Paul can address a very imperfect church like the Colossian, with the title of " holy and beloved ; " and why the Word of God calls an imperfectly sanctified believer a "saint ? "

The reason why a believer in the Lord Jesus Christ, although struggling with sin here on earth, is designated by the very same term employed to describe the pure and perfect spirits in heaven, lies in the fact that he is a *new creature.* " If any man be in Christ, he is a new creature ; old things have passed away, and all things have become new." If a man's moral nature has undergone a radical change, it is proper to speak of him with reference to such a transformation, and to employ language that in another connection and reference would be both strange and untrue. Suppose, for illustration, that the genius of John

Milton, by the miraculous power of God, should have been converted in the fourth year of his age into the genius of Isaac Newton. Suppose that the poetical nature of the author of the Paradise Lost, should have been transformed into the scientific nature of the author of the Principia, at an early period in life, before the maturity of the mental powers had arrived. In this case, would it not be correct and proper to employ concerning this " new man " within the man Milton, this new basis for thought and investigation, all the phraseology which we now apply to Sir Isaac Newton? Though only four years old, and though the relics of the old poetical nature might be still lingering in him, like fragments of rich crimson tapestry in an old royal palace, still we could say of this youthful convert from poetry to science, that he was a perfect mathematician; that the law of gravitation was within his ken; that the theorems of the Principia were all scored in his young brain. That which is inlaid in man by the power of God is destined to a development; and the unfolding cannot be thwarted. And therefore it is, that we may describe a morally renewed man, in the very opening of his career, by terms and phraseology derived from the close of it. We may call him a "perfect" man, because he is destined to become such. We may call him a " saint," because God has elected him to be one, and will carry out his purpose. We may call him a citizen of the kingdom of heaven on high, because a principle of holiness has been implanted within him that will bring him there.

Such application of language is spontaneous and natural to us, in daily life. Whenever we discover an inward basis for a particular result, we do not hesitate to speak of the result as if it had already occurred. You see, for illustration, a man lying upon a bed in a hospital, and are told that he is sick with pulmonary consumption. The

hollow cheek, the hectic flush, the emaciated flesh, the
gasping inspiration, all show that the man is in the last
stages of that terrible disease concerning which Machiavelli remarks, that " in the beginning it is easy to cure but
difficult to understand, but in the end, is easy to understand and difficult to cure." ¹ As you look upon him, you
say to yourself : " He is a dead man." You spontaneously
anticipate the natural result. The breath of life is still in
him. He looks into your eyes with the glance of human
intelligence. He is not cold and silent in death. He
speaks to you, and you to him. Yet you say : " He is a
dead man." There is a basis for death in him. The principle of mortality, the power of death, is within him, and
you merely ante-date, by a few days, weeks or months, its
inevitable consequences and results.

The Scriptures reason in the same manner, concerning
the state and condition of the unrenewed man. They call
him dead, long before his body actually dies, and long before his soul feels the pangs of the second death. Though
the sinner is apparently happy and well, engaged in the
business and pleasures of earth, the blood coursing vividly
in his veins, and his spirits bounding and free, yet the
solemn and truthful Word of God describes him in terms
that are borrowed from the dust and crumble of the tomb.
They never regard him, or call him, a living man. " Awake,
O sleeper, and Christ shall give thee life," is the startling
tone in which they speak to the impenitent man of business, and man of pleasure. Christ everywhere represents
it as his mission, to impart life. The Son of man is lifted
up upon the atoning cross, " that whosoever believeth in
him should not perish, but have eternal life. He that believeth not the Son shall not see life. Except ye eat the
flesh of the Son of man, and drink his blood, ye have no

---

¹ Machiavelli : The Prince, Ch. III.

life in you. If one died for all, then were all dead." This is the view which the Scriptures take of every unregenerate man, because they perceive in him a principle of sin, and spiritual disease, that will just as surely develop into the death and woe of hell, as the principle of physical disease will expand and unfold into the pangs and dissolution of the body. As in the instance of the renewed man, the Scriptures ante-date the natural and certain consequences of the new birth, and anticipate the natural and certain results of the new principle of spiritual life, and denominate the Christian a saint, holy and beloved, long before he reaches the heavenly world, and long before he attains to sinless perfection, so upon the same principle, they ante-date the sure and unfailing development of sin in the natural man, and, long before he actually enters the sad world of woe, speak of him as dead and lost. On the side of sin, as well as on the side of holiness, it is natural and proper to see the fruit in the seed, and to attribute to the little seed, all the properties and qualities of the ripe and perfected fruit. "Whatsoever a man soweth, that also shall he reap."

Let us now consider some of the lessons, that are taught by the fact that God denominates his imperfectly sanctified people, "holy and beloved," the "saints of the Most High God."

I. The first lesson to be derived from this subject is, that the child of God should not be *discouraged* because he discovers indwelling sin, and imperfection, within himself. A believer in the Lord Jesus Christ ought never to be discouraged. He ought to be humble, watchful, nay, sometimes fearful, but never despondent, or despairing. David, Paul, and the Colossian church were imperfect. But they were new men in Christ Jesus, and they are now perfectly holy and happy in heaven.

The duty of the Christian is, to assure himself upon scriptural grounds of his regeneration, and then to " work out his salvation with fear and trembling, because it is God that worketh in him to will and to do." The fact that he is a new creature, if established, is a proof that God is helping him in the struggle with indwelling sin; and when God helps, victory is sure in the end. Believers are commanded to " examine themselves," not for the purpose of seeing whether they are perfectly sanctified, but " whether they be in the faith." We may make our self-examination minister to our discouragement, and hindrance in the Christian race, if, instead of instituting it for the purpose of discovering whether we have a penitent spirit, and do cordially accept Christ as our righteousness, we enter upon it for the purpose of discovering if we are entirely free from corruption. Remainders of the old fallen nature may exist in connection with true faith in Christ, and a new heart. Paul bemoans himself, saying : " The good which I would I do not; but the evil which I would not that I do." But Paul was certain that he trusted in the blood of Christ for the remission of sin; that he was a new man in Christ Jesus, and influenced by totally different motives from those that actuated him when he persecuted the Church of Christ; that he loved Christ more than the whole universe, and " counted all things but dung that he might win Christ," and become a perfect creature in him.

The first and chief thing, therefore, which the Christian should have in his eye, in all his self-examination, is, to determine upon scriptural grounds whether he is a renewed man. The evidences of regeneration are plain, and plainly stated. We have already hinted at them. A sense of guilt and cordial acceptance of Christ's atonement, a desire to be justified by his precious blood, a peaceful confidence in God's righteousness and method of justifying a sinner—this is the first and infallible token of a new heart, and a right spirit. Then, secondly, a weariness of sin, "a groaning, being burdened" under its lingering presence and remaining power, a growing desire to be entirely delivered from it, and a purer simpler hungering after holiness—these are the other evidences of regeneration. Search yourselves to see whether these things be in you, and if you find them really, though it may be faintly and feebly, in your experience, do not be discouraged because along with them you discover remaining corruption. Remember that as a man struck with death is a dead man, so a soul that has been quickened into life is a living soul, even though the remnants of disease still hang about it and upon it. The "new man" in Christ Jesus will eventually slay stone-dead the "old man" of sin. The "strong man" has entered into the house, and bound the occupant hand and foot, and he will in time "spoil his house."

The truth that God will carry forward his work in the renewed soul, and that the principle of piety implanted by Divine grace will develop to perfection, may indeed be abused by the false Christian; but this is no reason why the genuine child of God should not use it for his encouragement, and progress in this divine life. One of the evidences of regeneration, however, if considered, will prevent all misuse of the doctrine of the saint's perseverance. A "groaning, being burdened" by the remaining presence of sin, is a sign of being a new creature. How can a man have this grief and sadness of heart at the sight of his indwelling corruption, and at the same time roll sin as a sweet morsel under the tongue? How shall one, whose great burden it is, that he is tied to the body of sin and death, proceed to make that burden heavier and heavier, by a life of ease, indifference and worldliness? "How

shall we that are dead to sin live any longer therein ? "
No, my brother, if you really groan, being burdened because you are still so worldly, so proud, so selfish, so sinful,
you are a new creature. You never did this in the days
of your impenitency. You were "alive without the law,"
then. You did not feel the heavy, weary, weight pressing
down upon you. You did not say with the Psalmist, as
you now do: "My sin is ever before me." This very imperfection which you now painfully feel, is the very evidence that you are on the way to perfection ; it is the sign
that there is a new principle of holiness implanted in your
soul, one of whose effects is this very consciousness of remaining corruption, and one of whose glorious results will
be the final and eternal eradication of it, when the soul
leaves the body and enters paradise.

II. The second lesson taught by the subject, is the duty
of the Christian to *cultivate* the new nature, and *develop*
the new principle of holiness.

"Put on," says St. Paul, " as the elect of God, holy and
beloved, bowels of mercies, kindness, humbleness of mind,
meekness, long-suffering." By this, it is not to be understood, that mercifulness, kindness, humility, meekness, and
patience, are graces that are to be originated by the Christian, and *added* to his character by his own agency. These
are traits that belong intrinsically to the " new man" in
Christ Jesus. These are qualities that issue from the
" new heart," and the " right spirit," which the regenerat-
ing power of God has originated. To "put them on,"
therefore, is to put them forth ; to elicit them ; to draw
them out from within, and exhibit them in daily life.
They are all contained germinally in the regenerate mind ;
and the particular duty which is devolved upon the believer
is that of training them.

Do you ask, How ? We answer : By taking every occasion to exercise them. One of the graces is "kindness" —a gentle, affectionate, benevolent feeling towards every fellow-creature. Every opportunity that you seize to give expression to such a sentiment, elicits what is within you; it draws upon the reserve and strength of your religious character in that particular direction, and trains it. Why is it that these "bowels of mercies," as St. Paul phrases it; this yearning compassion for the human soul; is so striking a characteristic of devoted teachers in church schools and mission schools, in home and foreign missionaries, and in all that class of Christians who are engaged in personal efforts for the salvation of men? It is because they "put on" this particular grace, by exerting it in daily life. Strain day after day upon a particular muscle, and it will begin to swell and rise above the flesh. You do not create the muscle by this effort, but you stimulate and strengthen it.

There is too much Christian character lying dormant, and latent, because there is so much neglect of self-culture in the Church. We have no confidence in the attempt to cultivate an unrenewed man into piety. He must be born again, in order that there may be something to cultivate —something to educate, to elicit, in St. Paul's phrase, to "put on." But we have great confidence in the endeavor to cultivate a really renewed man. When a new heart has been formed, a new character has been produced, a new principle of religious life has been implanted by the Holy Spirit, then no process is more successful and beautiful than the process of cultivation. It is like cultivating a garden full of living things. Every prudent use of the pruning-knife; every ministry of earth, air, water, and nourishment; contributes to elicit the vital powers and principles. Just so it is in the garden of the Lord. If Christians were only as diligent in self-cultivation as many an ambitious student is, nay, as many an ascetic papist or pagan devotee is, their growth would surprise even themselves. The secular scholar shuts himself from business and pleasure; he "scorns delights, and lives laborious days;" in order that he may gain renown, and "leave something so written to after-times as men will not willingly let die." Suppose that every professing Christian should devote himself with an equal assiduity, to the training of his own soul in divine knowledge and piety. Suppose that, like the scholar, he should make business and pleasure second and subservient to the one ruling principle of his mind and heart. Would not that principle—and he has professed before angels and men, that it is the principle of faith in Christ's blood—be as powerfully stimulated, and as vigorously elicited, as is the principle of literary ambition in the ardent and toiling student?

Suppose, again, that every member of the Christian Church should spend as many hours in prayer, as many a Papist or Mohammedan does in his daily devotions, would not the religious character of the Church be stronger, deeper, and purer than it now is? Suppose that all the myriads and millions in the visible Church were as self-sacrificing as the Hindoo ascetic who walks, perhaps creeps, hundreds of miles, to pay his devotions at a pagan shrine; who swings himself round and round upon the sharp hooks, or mortifies his body even to mutilation—suppose that there were the same readiness to make an effort to be *highly* religious, in the average of professing Christians, that there is in these select few of the Papal Church, or the Mohammedan world, would not the results and fruits be remarkable?

For you will bear in mind, that a given amount of power applied from a sanctified motive, and principle, will ac-

complish vastly more than when applied from an unsancti-
fied motive and principle.   If at heart you are a moralist,
or a worldling, your attempt to be holy and obedient to
God will accomplish nothing in the long run, because your
heart is not right with God.   All your effort to be good,
and to do good, from an unregenerate position, is a dead
lift.   But if you are renewed in the spirit of your mind,
then all your endeavors to cultivate yourself in holiness;
all your self-denial, mortification of the body, and devotion
to duty; is like the application of mechanical power at the
end of a long lever, and over a firm fulcrum.   The renewed man possesses what the mechanic terms a "purchase."   His lift is not a dead lift, like that of the Pagan
or Mohammedan devotee; like that of the Roman Catholic
ascetic; like that of the Protestant moralist.

"Put on, therefore, as the elect of God, holy and beloved, bowels of mercies, kindness, humbleness of mind,
meekness, long-suffering."   As those who have been renewed by Divine grace, and who possess a different spirit
and character from that which belonged to you in the days
of your impenitence, educate and elicit every Christian
grace.   Cultivate your Christianity.   It is worth cultivating.   It is worth protecting from the cold blasts, and rude
assaults of earth.   Fence in the vineyard of the Lord.
Put a hedge around it.   Then the wild-boar of the wood
shall not ravage it; then the soil shall not be trodden
down to hardness and barrenness, by the feet of the
passers-by.

SERMON XXI.

SANCTIFICATION COMPLETED AT DEATH.

1 CORINTHIANS ii. 9.—" Eye hath not seen, nor ear heard, neither have entered into the heart of man, the things which God hath prepared for them that love him."

THESE words primarily refer to the higher knowledge which is in reserve for the Christian in heaven. St. Paul is speaking to the Corinthian church of "the wisdom of God in a mystery, even the hidden wisdom which none of the princes of this world knew." He tells them that they know something of it here, but shall know far more of it hereafter. Upon earth, they see "through a glass darkly," but in heaven they shall see "face to face." In the next world, all doubts and perplexities shall be removed from the understanding, and the mind shall enjoy clear and satisfactory perceptions of divine things. All the previous views upon such subjects will seem so dim, in comparison with the final vision and disclosure, that it may be said that eye has never seen, nor ear ever heard, nor heart ever conceived of it before. Not that the spiritual man while here below has had no inkling of the eternal vision, and no glimpse of the eternal truth; but his knowledge is so inferior to what is poured into the mind when it enters heaven, that it seems nothing in comparison.

But although the primary reference of the text is to an

intellectual perception, rather than to an emotional enjoyment; though the apostle directs attention rather to the soul's knowledge, than to the soul's happiness; yet it is natural to refer these words, as we so generally do, to the blessedness of the redeemed in heaven. Probably the majority of readers suppose that "the things which God hath prepared for them that love him"—those particular things which the apostle had in mind, as not visible by the earthly eye, not audible by the mortal ear, and not cognizable in this mode of existence—are the same that are described under the glowing imagery of the sea of glass, the sapphire pavement, the jasper foundations, and the gates of pearl. It is the heavenly happiness, rather than the heavenly knowledge, which commonly comes into mind when this text is quoted. And this, we have said, is natural and proper. No violence is done to the apostle's teaching, when his words are followed in to their implication, and followed out to their full significance. For, heavenly knowledge produces heavenly happiness. To see, with a clear calm perception, the truths and the facts of eternity, is joy. Much of the dissatisfaction and unrest of the Christian life, upon earth, arises from indistinct and inadequate perceptions. The soul "sees through a glass darkly," or, as the original signifies, "looks, through a mirror, into an enigma." It gropes its way in twilight, and a thick atmosphere. Like the mariner in a fog, it peers into the distance, and strains the eye, but sees no distinct object. In such a condition, though there may not be positive unhappiness, because there is hope that the winds and the sun will dispel the mist, yet there is no full and complete satisfaction. Not until the sun actually shines, and the long line of the coast quivers in the liquid light, and the mountain ranges lift themselves into bold view, are the eye and the heart of the mariner at rest.

Spiritual knowledge, then, in its influence and effects, is spiritual enjoyment, and the words of the apostle may therefore be understood to teach, that the *happiness* which a believer will experience in heaven is so surpassingly great, in comparison with what he has experienced upon earth, that it may be said that his eye has not seen, nor his ear heard, nor his heart conceived of it.

In order to understand this truth, and feel its impression, we must remember that the Christian life upon earth is a *race* and a *fight*, and consequently cannot be a rest and a paradise. The Scriptures uniformly represent the course and career of a believer, this side the grave, as one of conflict, toil, and effort. " Except a man take his cross daily, he cannot be my disciple. In the world, ye shall have tribulation." These are the declarations of the Founder of Christianity, and they enunciate the real nature of his religion, as it must exist in a world that is sinful, full of temptation, and unfriendly to holiness. " We are troubled on every side; we are perplexed; we are persecuted; we are cast down. We continually bear about in the body, the dying of the Lord Jesus. We are always delivered unto death, for Jesus' sake." These are the assertions of one of the most eminent and successful of Christ's disciples; and although he was called to experience more of external opposition and persecution than the Church at large, it is probable that he had his compensation, in being freer than most Christians from internal conflict and trouble. Whether, then, we consider the direct declaration of Christ himself, or the complaints of his people, we find that the life of a believer, so long as he is upon earth, is one of effort and struggle.

For those who live in the peaceful times of the Church, this struggle and endeavor is chiefly of an inward kind. The life of a Christian, in more senses than one, is a hid-

den life. What a subterranean current of temptation, and
resistance, is silently running at this very instant in millions
of human hearts. The world sees none of it ; but the unseen combat with the invisible foe is every moment going
on. How unceasingly is the conflict between the new man
and the old man, the conscience and the will, the spirit
and the flesh, the grace of God and the indwelling corruption, waging in the soul of every child of God. In the
market-place, in the house of God, in the privacy of the
closet, in the intercourse of the household, how incessantly
is the temptation presenting itself, and how constantly by
the grace of God is it repulsed. Sometimes the wish
arises that the temptations of this earthly course might be
concentrated, and that the destiny of the soul might be decided by a single terrible conflict, instead of by this slow,
pertinacious, life-long warfare. The acquisition of holiness,
by a renewed man, resembles the ancient wars which were
prolonged sometimes for more than a generation. The
Dorians of Laconia fought seventy-six years with the Dorians of Messene, for the supremacy of that little patch of
earth, the Peloponnesus. The Roman contended thirty
years with the Samnite, for the possession of Italy, and
forty years with the Carthaginian, for the dominion of the
world. And the Christian fights his fight with the world,
the flesh, and the devil, not in a day or a year, but through
all his days, and all his years.

Now it is plain, that such a state of things cannot last
forever. "There remaineth a rest, for the people of God."
Man was not designed by creation, to be eternally running
a race, and eternally fighting a fight. He was intended
for harmony, for peace, for joy. Nothing but sin has introduced such a condition of affairs. This struggle, and
effort, results from the endeavor to get free from an unlawful and wrong state of the soul. Had man not fallen,

his career would have been the serene and unhindered one of the angels of God. It was his original destination, to be conformed to law without any struggle of opposing desires; without any collision between will and conscience. As created, and unfallen, there was in man not the slightest conflict between his duty and his inclination, and consequently there was no need, so far as the Divine intention was concerned, of any race, or any fight. When, therefore, the grace of God quickens the " spirit," and slays the "flesh," in any individual man, and thus initiates that conflict between the two which St. Paul describes in the seventh chapter of Romans, it is not for the purpose of continuing the conflict through all eternity. It is a struggle only for time, and is to cease when time is over. The intention is, to bring in that perfect and blessed condition of the soul, in which all the powers are in right relations; in which the higher shall firmly rule the lower, and the lower shall submissively obey the higher.

Accordingly, the text teaches that the Christian who has been patient and faithful in running the race, and fighting the fight, will finally be relieved from the necessity of strain and effort. " Eye hath not seen, nor ear heard, neither have entered into the heart of man, the things which God hath *prepared* for them that love him." The believer's experience here upon earth has been trying and painful, and must not be taken as a specimen of the heavenly life. God has provided a blessed calm, and rest, beyond the tomb. It is something far beyond what the eye has seen here, what the ear has heard, what the heart has conceived of.

The believer is sometimes disheartened, from imagining that his life in eternity will be much like his life in time. As he throws his glance forward, he seems to see stretching before him an endless series of temptations and resistances, of successes and failures. As it is here, so he thinks it will be there—a perpetual race, an everlasting fight. But he should remember that the great God his Saviour intends to "perfect that which concerneth him;" to complete the work of sanctification in his soul. And this, too, by a direct intervention, when the soul leaves the body. As, at the new birth of his soul, God the Holy Ghost regenerated him by an instantaneous efficiency that was supernatural, and not a mere link in the ordinary movements of nature and providence, so, at death, the remaining corruption which the race and the fight have not succeeded in purging away, shall be removed by a corresponding decisive energy on the part of the Great Sanctifier. This must be so. For our text tells us of a " preparation" —a personal and direct arrangement upon the part of God. And how is the sin which the holiest of men are conscious of in their very dying hour to be cleansed away, except by the finishing strokes of Divine grace? They have struggled with their inward corruption for many long years. They have not been idle in keeping the heart. They have not been unsuccessful; for they have grown more saintly, to the close of life. And yet, like St. Paul, although "having the first fruits of the Spirit they still groan within themselves, waiting for their adoption, to wit, their complete redemption." (Rom. viii. 23.) At the same rate of progress as in the past, it would require years; it might require one whole life-time after another; to extirpate entirely the remaining depravity. How shall it be cleansed away, and the soul stand a spotless soul in the presence of Him who cannot endure the least taint of depravity, except by that crowning and completing act of grace, by which the imperfectly sanctified believer, in a moment, in the twinkling of an eye, becomes a "justified man made perfect;" by which, when the believer beholds his Lord, "he shall be like him, for he shall see him as he is."

We live in a world of natural laws and operations, and for this reason find it difficult to get out of the circle of slow and gradual processes. Our Christian character, here below, forms and matures very much like the fruits of the earth—first the blade, then the ear, then the full corn in the ear. The oak builds up its fabric, by a slow assimilation of the nutritive elements, and compacts its fibre, by a long conflict with the winds and the storms ; and we, too, strengthen our moral force, and confirm our virtue, by a similar method. We are in the habit, consequently, of supposing that there is no other method than this gradual one, and limit the Divine efficiency by it. We forget that God is the sovereign of both realms—the natural and the supernatural—and that he is able and free to work in either of them. Even in our own personal history, he has so wrought. That act by which, when we were dead in trespasses and sins, he made us alive unto righteousness, is not explainable upon natural principles. It was not by the gradual method of growth and education, that we made the passage from nature to grace. We were " created anew " in Christ Jesus. After the passage was made, we did indeed find that a process was commenced within our hearts that bore all the marks of a gradual, a continuous, and, alas ! a very slow movement. Our inordinate and earthly affections declined very gradually. Our envy, our pride, our malice, waned away so slowly, that we sometimes queried whether it was a waning, or a waxing. On the other hand, our devout and spiritual affections—our love, joy, peace, faith, hope—grew so slightly and feebly, that we could be certain that they had grown, only by comparing ourselves with ourselves after long intervals. Our sanctification has been progressive, and not instantaneous ; and in these respects finds its parallel in the leaven that gradually pervades the whole mass, and in the mustard-seed which requires months and years for its expansion. But our regeneration was instantaneous. We have, therefore, within the sphere of our own experience, the proof that God works both instantaneously and progressively ; by a method that is startling, and a method that is uniform. He begins a work by a fiat, and then he carries it forward by a culture. He instantaneously creates us new men in Christ Jesus, and then he gradually educates us towards the stature of perfect men in Christ Jesus.

We are not, therefore, to limit the Divine efficiency either to a creating, or to an educating function, solely. We ought not to suppose that because our regeneration was instantaneous, the development and maturing of Christian character must be so likewise, and that therefore we may neglect the means of grace and of growth. And on the other hand, we ought not to think that because our sanctification proceeds so gradually, and is worked out by the trial, temptation, and discipline of a whole life-time, therefore all rapid changes are forever excluded from our future history, and God will never intervene with a more determined and decisive influence.

Our text helps us out of our proneness to err, by directing attention to what God is intending to do in the souls of his children, when in his providence they shall be summoned before him. No one can appear in his presence with remaining sin. "Without holiness no man shall see the Lord." But we know that so long as we are in the flesh, the "motions of sins in our members " do continue to molest, and sometimes to foil us. Between the last moments upon earth, and the first moments in heaven, there must, therefore, pass upon us that transformation by which the imperfect believer becomes the perfected saint. It is not a radical change, like that which introduced us into the kingdom of God. It is not the formation of a new heart, and a right spirit. But it is the completion, by a swift and mighty act of the Holy Spirit, of a process that was commenced it may be long years ago, and which has lingered and fluctuated with our feeble and hesitating efforts after holiness. He who upon earth has run the race, and fought the fight, will discover in that supreme moment when he first stands face to face with the Holy One, that Divine grace has been sufficient for him. He will find himself to be perfectly holy, and perfectly happy. All that he has heretofore experienced of peace and joy is as nothing, in comparison with the blessedness which now fills his soul. Eye hath not seen, nor ear heard, nor heart conceived of it before. In comparison with the past imperfection, the present spotlessness, and purity, and complete deliverance from all corruption, will appear almost incredible. Undoubtedly the feeling of surprise will mingle with the other emotions that will distend the redeemed soul, when it enters heaven. And this surprise will spring from the strange consciousness of being *sinless*. That moral corruption which was born with the soul; which grew with its growth, and strengthened with its strength; which received, indeed, its death wound by the sword of the Spirit, in regeneration, yet continued to show signs of lingering vitality down to the very hour of bodily dissolution—that sin which has been a steady element in the consciousness of the man, never leaving nor forsaking him so long as he was upon earth, is now gone forever. Well may " the redeemed of the Lord come to Mount Zion, with singing and everlasting joy." Well may they say: " Eye hath not seen, ear hath not heard, neither hath it entered into the heart of man to conceive of the wonderful transformation which the final act of sanctifying grace produces in the soul."

It was owing to the opinion that the complete sanctification of the Christian must be brought about by the ordinary influences of the Spirit, in the use of the common instrumentalities, that the doctrine of a cleansing in the intermediate state crept into the Church. Thoughtful and spiritual minds, like Augustine for example, perceived that indwelling corruption attends the Christian up to the very hour of death. They knew that no sin, however slight, can appear before God. Hence they supposed that the last stages of sanctification must occur beyond the tomb. They imagined that a certain period must be allotted in the future life to the imperfectly sanctified Christian, in which his remaining corruption should be removed by the ordinary method of trial and discipline, and he thus be made "without spot, or wrinkle, or any such thing," preparatory to going into the light of the Divine countenance. But upon their own principles, there was no need of such an intermediate cleansing. Their view of grace ought to have precluded it. Augustine and his followers held, with great decision, the doctrine of *irresistible* grace—the doctrine of an immediate and powerful energy of the Holy Spirit, by which the most marked changes can be wrought instantaneously in human character. Had they applied this theory of Divine influence to the completion of the work of sanctification, as they did to its inception, the notion of a gradual purgation beyond this life would not have arisen in their minds.

The text, then, has turned our attention to that final act of God's redeeming grace, spoken of in the Westminster Shorter Catechism (37), by which, "at death, the soul of a believer is made perfect in holiness, and immediately passes into glory." The eye hath not seen its operation, the ear hath not heard it, and the heart of man cannot comprehend it. Yet it is one of "the things which God hath prepared for them that love him." Having begun a work of grace in the fallen soul, he will carry it forward unto "the day when he makes up his jewels "— the day of the perfecting and final act of grace—and every child of God may say confidently with the apostle: "I am persuaded that he is able to keep that which I have committed to him against that day."

I. In view of this truth, we remark, in the first place, that Christians should encourage themselves in their continual race and warfare upon earth, by the recollection that they are *not destined to run, and to fight forever.* A time is coming when will and conscience, duty and inclination will be perfectly identical. This conflict between the flesh and the spirit is eventually to cease, and holiness will be the natural and irrepressible activity of the soul. We know, by bitter experience, how easy and effortless the process of sinning is to a sinner ; we shall one day know, how easy and effortless the process of obedience is to a saint. There is a time coming, when the sorrow and fear by which God is now educating us will end, and we shall never grieve or be anxious again. Affliction will have accomplished its work within us, and then God will wipe away all tears. There is a time coming, when the weak and struggling human will is to be no more solicited and staggered by temptation ; when there will be no remaining corruption to send up its appetites, and no unfriendly world of outward objects to seduce the soul from God. The race and the fight are not for eternity, but only for time.

II. In the second place, the Christian should drive off sluggishness, by recollecting that " *a man is not crowned, except he strive lawfully.*" (2 Tim. ii. 5.) He must not fold his arms, and neglect the keeping of his heart here upon earth, because there is such a power in God to perfectly sanctify the human soul. Sanctifying influences are granted to man, not absolutely and unconditionally. They come to him in connection with the covenant of grace. They are a part of an economy. He therefore who has not entered into that covenant, and is not living under the economy as a whole, cannot participate in the benefits of a part of it. The whole or none, is the rule in spiritual things. He, therefore, who does not daily take up his cross on earth, must not expect to be the recipient of that crowning grace of the Holy Spirit which perfects the soul in holiness. This is the fatal error in the Sacramentarian theory of grace. The Papist supposes that a person may live an earthly and unspiritual life, and yet that by virtue of the merely outward baptism of the Church, the cleansing influence will be imparted. He forgets the apostolic dictum: "That a man is not crowned, except he strive lawfully"—that only he who carefully observes the rules of the game, and of the arena, is entitled to the rewards of the victor. He who attempts surreptitiously to obtain the prize ; he who would *steal* the garland or the crown ; will be repulsed ignominiously, and with contempt. He who thinks to secure those great and lofty things which God has prepared for them that love him, without passing through the antecedent and preparatory steps and stages, will in the last day meet with a terrible rebuke for his presumption, and his selfishness, and his worthlessness.

This consideration is enough to drive off sluggishness, and urge the Christian to constant activity. The completing of any work implies that it has been commenced, and has passed through some stages of progress. If there be nothing begun, it is absurd to speak of a finishing stroke. Every sin, therefore, that is resisted, every temptation that is repulsed, and every grace that is strengthened in the daily struggle, brings the work so much the nearer to its conclusion. By these efforts we evince that we "love

God "—that we prefer his service, yearn after his holiness, and aspire after his blessedness. And "for those that love God," there "is prepared what the eye hath not seen, nor the heart conceived of."

III. In the third place, the Christian, in view of the fact that God will eventually complete the work of sanctification, ought *never to be discouraged, or despair of the result.* If the doctrine of the text be true, the believer is certain to succeed. Let him "not be weary in well-doing, for in due season he shall reap, if he faint not." That is a fine sentiment which Plutarch puts into the mouth of Coriolanus. In a battle with the Volscians, the Romans under Coriolanus had charged with fury, and broken the enemy's centre, and put them to a total rout. As they were starting upon the pursuit, they begged of their general, who was shattered and half-dead with wounds and fatigue, that he would retire to the camp. "It is not for the victor to tire of the battle," was the reply of Coriolanus, as he joined in the onward rush and sweep of his army. It is not for a believer in the Lord Jesus Christ; it is not for one who has been sprinkled with the expiating blood, and has been born of the Holy Ghost; to tire of the battle between the flesh and the spirit. Though the conflict may continue for many long years; though very often "the spirit is willing, but the flesh is weak;" though sometimes "the sorrows of death compass the soul, and the pangs of hell get hold of it;" still, the victory is sure in the end. Upon such terms we can well afford to fight. Who would hesitate to enlist in a war, if he knew infallibly that he should survive, that he should conquer, and that he should obtain everything that he fought for? Yet such is the state of the case, with those that "love God," and are "the called according to his purpose." Every soul of man which here upon earth daily takes up the cross, is rapidly nearing that point where it shall lay it down. Every disciple of Christ who here in time walks with him in tribulation, and temptation, is approaching that serene and sheltered spot where temptation and tribulation are absolutely unknown. One thing is as certain as the other. Does a man know that he is daily fighting the fight; he may know infallibly, then, that one day he shall as victor cease the conflict, and lay down his armor.

SERMON XXII.

WATCHFULNESS AND PRAYERFULNESS.

1 PETER iv. 7.—" Watch unto prayer."

In explaining this injunction of St. Peter, we shall show the importance of a watchful and prayerful spirit, by considering the *innate disposition* of the human heart. We shall find the argument derived from the fact that man is naturally inclined to sin; or, in the phrase of Scripture, is " born in sin and conceived in iniquity ; " is of the strongest kind for obeying the command : " Watch unto prayer."

The inborn disposition of any creature whatever is a fundamental and most important part of it. It lies at the centre, and is at once the fountain whence the whole external conduct flows, and the cause of its being what it is. The innate disposition of a tiger is the source of his fierce and ravenous actions; that of the lamb, of its gentle, harmless, and timid demeanor. The great difference in the outward behavior of these two creatures is due to the difference in the inward nature, or disposition.

Man also possesses an innate disposition ; and it is the fountain whence issue all his outward acts. His every-day life and conduct is as true an exhibition of the human disposition, as the brute's every-day life is of the brute's disposition. We can predict with as much certainty what the conduct of a man with a sinful disposition will be, if he is not deterred by fear, or shame, or some other selfish motive, from acting it out, as we can what the conduct of a tiger will be if he is struck. "Out of the heart," says our Lord, "proceed evil thoughts, murders, adulteries, fornications, thefts, false witness, blasphemies. A good man, out of the good treasure of the heart, bringeth forth good things; and an evil man, out of the evil treasure, bringeth forth evil things." (Matt. xii. 35; xv. 19.)

The connection between the outward conduct and the inward disposition is so invariable and certain, that the Scriptures do not hesitate to pass even below the range of animal life, for illustrations. Our Lord compares the relation which a bad life bears to a bad heart, to that which exists between the vegetable principle and its products. "Every good tree bringeth forth good fruit; but a corrupt tree bringeth forth evil fruit. A good tree cannot bring forth evil fruit; neither can a corrupt tree bring forth good fruit." (Matt. vii. 17, 18.) And hence he lays it down as a general principle that the only way in which mankind can be really improved is by a change of the heart, or natural disposition. "Either make the *tree* good, and his fruit good; or else make the tree corrupt, and his fruit corrupt." (Matt. xii. 33.) The conduct inevitably follows the character; and therefore there can be no total change of conduct, except by a radical change of character.

But the purpose for which the innate disposition of a man is compared with that of a brute, and even with the unconscious vital principle in a tree, is merely to illustrate the truth that the outward flows from the inward, all the world over. Go where we will; pass through all the ranges of matter and of mind; we shall find it to be a universal fact, that that which is without emanates from that which is within. But the comparison cannot be pressed any fur-

ther than this. While the inborn and natural disposition
of a man is analogous to that of an animal, and even to the
noxious principle in a plant or tree, in respect to the single
particular of its being the source of external products, the
analogy stops here. The sinful nature of man differs from
the ravenous nature of a lion, or the deadly virus of the
upas tree, in many respects ; and especially in regard to
the immensely important feature of *responsibility to law.*
The innate disposition of a fallen man is self-willed, and
culpable. Man is accountable at the bar of God, for his
wicked heart, as well as for his wicked actions. St. Peter
said to Simon the sorcerer : " Thy heart is not right in
the sight of God. Repent therefore of this thy wickedness, and pray God, if perhaps the thought (ἐπίνοια) of thy
heart may be forgiven thee." (Acts viii. 21, 22.) He
called him to repentance, not merely for the sin of propos-
ing to purchase the miraculous power of the Holy Ghost
with money, but for the avaricious, worldly, and ungodly
disposition that lay under it. But the brute is responsible
neither for his disposition, nor his actions. The lion's carnivorous nature is not a guilty one, because the lion had
nothing to do with its origin. It is not self-willed, but
created by God. It is as much a part of the original creation as the gem in the mine, or the poisonous life of the
deadly tree. The evil heart of man, on the contrary, out
of which proceed the evil thoughts, the murders, and the
adulteries, was no part of the six days' creative work upon
which God looked down, and pronounced it " good."
Man's sinful disposition, though innate because transmitted
from Adam, was not created by Almighty God. It is not
man's first and original disposition as he came from his
Maker's hand, but a second and subsequent disposition
originated by man himself. God made man upright, and
all the " treasure of the heart "—all the inward disposition

—was "good." The present "evil treasure of the heart"
—the existing sinful disposition of the will and affections—
began after the Creator's work was ended. It is the product of the creature. This carnal mind, this sinful heart,
this selfish inclination, this wicked disposition, from which
all wrong acts issue, is the consequence of human apostasy.
It came in with Adam's fall. It is both self-will, and ill-
will. It is unforced and spontaneous self-determination
in every man, deserving to be punished because "it is
enmity towards God, is not subject to the law of God,
neither indeed can be." St. Paul has it in view, when he
affirms that "we are by nature the children of wrath."
(Eph. ii. 3.) And the Westminster Creed repeats this inspired declaration, when it asserts that "every sin, both
original and actual, being a transgression of the righteous
law of God, and contrary thereunto, doth in its own nature
bring guilt upon the sinner, whereby he is bound over to
the wrath of God, and curse of the law, and so made subject
to death, with all miseries spiritual, temporal, and eternal."

It was a position of the English deists, that man is exactly
as God made him ; and that therefore he is as irresponsible
as the brute, for the evil inclination of his heart. They
denied the free fall of man in Adam, and contended that
he comes by his so-called sinful nature as the animal does
by his carnivorous propensity—namely, by the creative act
of the Deity—and that consequently he is no more blame-
worthy for being murderous, or envious, or selfish, in his
inclination, than is the tiger for being ravenous. Says
Lord Herbert of Cherbury, one of the most moral of this
school of thinkers : " Men are not hastily to be condemned
who are led to sin by bodily constitution. The indulgence
of lust and anger is no more to be blamed than the thirst
occasioned by dropsy, or the drowsiness produced by
lethargy."

But this theory is refuted by human consciousness. No man ever felt that it is true; and millions of men have felt that it is false. Millions have confessed the guilt of their hearts, and mourned over it. If this position were the real truth and fact, it must sooner or later have become a matter of conscious experience for some portion of the human family. An actual and stubborn fact cannot be perpetually hid under a bushel. But who of the sons of Adam was ever really and positively conscious of innocency, for his malignant and murderous inclination? for his envious and selfish spirit? for his sensual and cruel disposition? Who ever had the abiding and unassailable conviction, that human character is a wholly irresponsible matter? Furthermore, what does *remorse* signify and teach upon this point? A man may assert that he is not accountable to God for either his character, or his conduct; but there are certain moments, when an internal moral anguish makes him conscious that he is. Else why the anguish? Why this moral torture, as the man reads his own heart, and studies his own character? Is the brute, with whom the theorist compares himself, and puts himself on a level, ever distressed because he has a fierce and ravenous disposition? Remorse of conscience which appears at times in every man, and which has made the death-bed of some of these theorists a dreadful scene, is conclusive that man comes by his sinful disposition in a responsible manner—by free-will, and not by God's creative act. For, does the wise and good God torture his creatures wantonly, and for nothing? Does God put man upon the rack of conscience in this life, and punish him in the next life, knowing—as he must know, if it is a fact—that there is no just ground for it in the voluntary agency of man? There is, indeed, a mystery surrounding the free fall of all men in Adam, and the responsible origin of human depravity—as much mystery as there is in the origin of the soul itself, and no more—but something more than mystery is requisite to establish the position, that man is now exactly as God made him, and that he is not guilty for his selfish disposition and malignant inclination. Here is this remorse, which is a species of vital logic. Arguments against it are like arguments to prove that fire does not burn, when live coals are heaped upon a man's head, and the fire is eating into the flesh.

With this brief notice of the fundamental importance, and the culpability of man's sinful inclination, we proceed to notice the call that is made by it upon the Christian, for watchfulness and prayerfulness. For although the believer has the new heart, or holy inclination, produced by his union with Christ, he still has the remainders of the old evil inclination proceeding from his union and fall with Adam. These relics furnish a great and strong reason for the apostle's injunction: "Watch unto prayer;" and for the Saviour's urgency: "Watch and pray lest ye enter into temptation; the spirit truly is willing, but the flesh is weak.".

I. The first characteristic of man's sinful disposition, requiring watchfulness upon the part of a Christian, is its *spontaneity*. This is that quality in a thing which causes it to move of itself. The living spring, speaking metaphorically, spontaneously leaps up into the sunlight, while standing water must be pumped up. Living matter, in animate existence, moves spontaneously, of its own accord, while the corpse must be moved mechanically—must be lifted and carried out. The feelings of the heart, when it is full of life and hope, burst forth spontaneously, while the manifestation of feeling by a sad and hopeless heart is forced. Spontaneity, then, is the power of self-motion. The spring, in a figure, lifts itself up; living matter moves of itself; and warm buoyant feelings require nothing but their own force to set them in play.

Now, the sinful inclination, or disposition, or heart of man is spontaneous in its action. Sin in all its forms, original or actual, is unforced. Its motion is self-motion. But a thing that can move of itself is able to move at *any* moment, and is *liable* to move. Did the movement depend upon something other than self, and on the outside, there would not be so much liability. Were man reluctantly urged up to sin by some other agent than himself, there would be less call for watchfulness. But the perfect ease, and pleasure, and spontaneity with which he does his own sinning, calls for an incessant vigilance not to do it. The imperfectly sanctified Christian needs not to make a special effort, in order to transgress. If he simply remains careless and unwatchful, the self-moving inclination will do its own work without any struggle on his part. Hence, he is liable to sin at any instant. Within him, there are the relics of an evil disposition which by its very nature, and quality, as easily and readily sends up evil thoughts, feelings, and desires, as the fire of a furnace sends up smoke and sparks.

Let us look into our own breasts, and see if there are not remainders of our original depravity which, if not watched, will lead us into disobedience at any and every moment. Are there not propensities which are constantly able, and liable to start into action? How liable we are to be proud, angry, vain, impure. Or, to specify less evanescent feelings, how liable we are to worldliness, to languor and deadness respecting heavenly objects, to carnal-mindedness. And, except as we " watch unto prayer," have we any security that they will not spontaneously rise into exercise at any instant, and take possession of us altogether?

Our success in overcoming sin depends very much upon our suspiciousness, and apprehensiveness—upon our fearing that sin may get the mastery at any time. If we felt, as St. Paul did when he feared lest he should be a castaway, that underneath, in the depths of the heart, there are spontaneous inclinations constantly liable to come up to the surface and acquire power by having a free exercise, we should watch and pray as unceasingly as he did. For, these sinful propensities, if kept down in the regenerate soul, will finally die out. It is not so with the unregenerate. He who substitutes morality for religion, and attempts to regulate and repress his sinful inclination without crying importunately to God for a clean heart, and a right spirit—he who tries to make the fruit good, without first making the tree good—this man labors in vain. For though he bury his evil propensities for a time, they will live underground. Toiling hard, he may choke down his pride for this hour, but in the very next it comes up in ten-fold strength. By dint of great effort, he may wrestle down his envy and ill-will as he meets this fellow-man, but it rises before he thinks of it, on seeing the next man that he dislikes. There is nothing *within* the unrenewed man that can cope with, and subdue the evil inclination— no faith, hope, love, and peace; no new heart and right spirit, with which to wage war with the sinful nature. Hence, it is a fight without armor; a dead lift without any purchase. But the believer has been born of the Spirit. There is within him a positive principle of faith, and love, and holy life, implanted by the Holy Ghost in the depths of the soul, which will ultimately slay all sin, provided only that sin be kept down. If, by watching the remainders of our wrong disposition, we will prevent them from coming forth into thoughts, words, and acts; if we will confine them, and keep them side by side with the " new man," and compel them to stay down in the depths of the soul, the sword of the Spirit will eventually pierce them and kill them with a total and everlasting death. If, on the contrary, we are unwatchful and prayerless, and allow indwelling sin to have free play and exercise, we have no reason to expect that it will ever be slain. Can religion in the heart conquer sin in the heart, if we do not bring the two into close contact, and conflict ? How can godliness get the victory, if we allow sinfulness to flee away and rush out into life and action, and give it a fair field ? No, we must watch these remains of our sinful nature which are so liable to move, and which unless repressed move of themselves. We must compel them to stay down, until God the Spirit by constantly coming into contact with them has killed them stone dead, never to stir again. If we repress the outbursts of sin, we shall discover with joy and courage that the sinful inclination is really becoming weaker and weaker, and the new principle of divine love stronger and stronger. We shall find the dying spasms of sin becoming more and more feeble, until, O wonderful event ! sin is completely and forever dead in the soul.

II. A second characteristic of man's sinful disposition, requiring watchfulness and prayerfulness in the Christian, is the fact that it can be *tempted* and *solicited* to move, at any moment.

We have, thus far, spoken of the power which sin possesses of moving of itself, spontaneously ; of that quality, by virtue of which it does not need any particular solicitation, in order to its exercise. Our sinful inclination possesses this characteristic ; for do we need any particular urging, or tempting, to be worldly minded, and to live away from God? Is it not our natural disposition to do this ; and must we be specially provoked to it ? But we are now to speak of that additional characteristic of man's sinful disposition, by virtue of which it is capable of being stimulated and elicited by temptations; and if we should watch unto prayer because sin can move of itself, most certainly should we because it can be solicited to move, and we live in a world full of such solicitations. If gunpowder were liable to self-explosion by virtue of its own inherent properties, we should watch it most carefully even if we were to keep it like truth at the bottom of a well; but if we were compelled to store it in a forge continually full of sparks, there would be no limit to our vigilance lest it should be ignited by some one of them.

How easily is the remaining sin in us tempted and drawn out into exercise by tempting objects, and how full the world is of such objects. A hard word, an unkind look, a displeasing act on the part of another, will start sin into motion, instanter. Wealth, fame, pleasure, fashion, houses, lands, titles, husbands, wives, children, friends— in brief, all creation—has the power to educe the sinful nature of man. He is continually coming in contact with things that allure him to transgress God's law. He is surrounded by them. He is buried in them. He is touched at a million points by the temptations of earth. Look at our own situation, as we find it every day of our lives. See how we are encircled by objects, every one of which is competent to start the old carnality into vigorous action. See what temptations come from our business, and how many they are. See what solicitations come from our families, and how many and strong they are. Consider what inducements to forget God, and to transgress his commandments, come from the worldly or the gay society in which we move. Is not the powder in the midst of the sparks? If unwatchful and prayerless, it is certain and inevitable that we shall yield to these temptations.

How can we prevent sin from breaking forth, tempted and allured as it is at all points, if we do not " watch unto prayer ? " Why, but because we do not soberly watch like soldiers on guard, are we so much under the power of temptations ? Why, but because we do not importunately pray, have the lust of the flesh, and the lust of the eye, and the pride of life, such a disastrous influence at this very moment upon our professed piety ?

The fact, then, that temptations are liable to elicit the remaining corruption in the Christian's heart, is a strong reason why he should obey the apostle's injunction in the text. Says the saintly and " white-robed" Leighton : " The children of God often find to their grief, that corruptions which they thought had become cold dead, stir, and rise up again, and set upon them. A passion or lust that after some great stroke lay a long while as dead, stirred not, and therefore they thought to have heard no more of it, though it shall never recover fully again to be lively as before, yet will revive in such a manner as to molest and possibly to foil them yet again. Therefore it is continually necessary that they live in arms, and put them not off to their dying day." [1]

III. A third characteristic of man's innate disposition requiring watchfulness and prayer, is the fact that it acquires the *habit* of being moved by temptation.

It is more difficult to stop a thing that has the habit of motion, than one that has not, because habit is a second nature and imparts additional force to the first one. This is eminently true of sin, which by being allowed an habitual motion becomes so powerful that few overcome it. The great majority of wrong habits that have been formed in human hearts were never broken up—are everlasting things.

---

[1] Leighton : On 1 Peter iv. 1.

The drunkards who have left their cups, the gamblers who have reformed, the thieves who have become honest men, the liars who have ceased lying, the unchaste who have become pure, and the profane who have forsaken their oaths, are very greatly in the minority. Miserable indeed is that soul which allows sin to strengthen and fortify itself by constant exercise. Even if it is eventually overcome by the grace of God, it will only be by resisting unto blood. "Because," says an old divine, "the nature of habits is like that of crocodiles; they grow as long as they live; and if they come to obstinacy or confirmation, they are in hell already, and can never return back. For as Pannonian bears, when they have clasped a dart in the region of their liver, wheel themselves upon the wound, and with anger and malicious revenge strike the deadly barb deeper, and cannot be quit from that fatal steel, but in flying bear along that which themselves make the instrument of a more hasty death, so is every vicious person struck with a deadly wound, and his own hands force it into the entertainments of the heart, and because it is painful to draw it forth by a sharp and salutary repentance, he still rolls and turns upon his wound, and carries his death in his bowels, where it first entered by choice, and then dwelt by love, and at last shall finish the tragedy by Divine judgments and an unalterable decree." [1]

Inward sin, in an unwatchful and prayerless person, inevitably acquires the habit of being moved by temptation. He falls gradually into such a state, that whenever an object solicits his remaining corruption he yields uniformly, and with little or no resistance. He who is in such a case is on most dangerous ground. For says the apostle John, "Whosoever sinneth hath not seen God, neither known

---

[1] Jeremy Taylor's Sermon, on Growth in Sin.

him "—by which is meant, as the context shows, " Whosoever sinneth *habitually* hath not seen God, neither known him." We may be surprised once into sin as Peter was; we may fall once into sin as David did; and upon weeping bitterly as did the first, and crying for mercy out of a crushed heart as did the last, the atoning blood of Christ shall cleanse our conscience again. But we cannot self-indulgently sin on, and on, and commit the very same wicked thing day after day, and feel that we are forgiven, or hope to be forgiven.

The chances, if we may use such a word, are against the conquest of habitual sins, because of the strong power which they acquire over the voluntary faculty. The more usual a sin becomes in a man's experience, the weaker the will to resist it becomes; and hence in the drunkard, for example, habit, even in this life, has almost annihilated will to good. Just so fast as the habit of intoxication gains upon him, just so fast does he lose his power of self-control. The one force is antagonistic to the other, and one exists in inverse proportion to the other. The inebriate gradually ceases to be his own man, and comes to belong to the appetite for rum. This owns him, and uses him. It starves him with hunger, and pinches him with cold, and strips him of character, and deprives him of the common human feelings, and does with him just as it pleases.

For a thoughtful observer, there is something strictly awful in beholding the paralyzing and destructive power which sin, when habitually indulged, acquires over the human will. The self-gratifying propensity, by being allowed to develop itself unwatched and unhindered, slowly but surely eats out all virtuous moral force as rust eats out a steel spring, until the being in the terrible bitter end becomes all habit and all sin. " Sin when it is finished bringeth forth death." (James i. 15.) In the final stage of this process, the guilty self-determining agent reaches that dreadful state where resistance to evil ceases altogether, because he has at length entirely killed out the energetic and resolute power of resistance which God gave him, and meant that he should use, and which if he had used would have grown stronger and stronger, through Divine assistance, until it reached the state of confirmed and eternal holiness. The cravings and hankerings of unresisted sin at length become organic, as it were, and drag the man, and " he goeth after them as an ox goeth to the slaughter, or as a fool to the correction of the stocks, till a dart strike through his liver." For though the will to resist sin may die out of a man, the conscience to condemn it never can. This remains eternally. And when the process is complete, and the responsible creature in the abuse of free agency has perfected his own self-destruction, and his will to good is all gone, there remain these two in his immortal soul : sin and conscience, or, in the Scripture metaphor, " brimstone and fire."

The " ruin " of an immortal soul is no mere figure of speech. There is no ruin in the whole material universe to be compared with it, for transcendent awfulness. The decline and fall of the Roman Empire was a great catastrophe, and inspires a thoughtful and solemn feeling ; but the decline and eternal fall of a moral being, originally made in the image of God, is a stupendous event. When it happens ; when the Apocalyptic angel descends, and cries mightily with a strong voice saying, " Babylon the great is fallen, is fallen ; " the kings of the earth, and the merchants of the earth, " stand afar off to see the smoke of her burning, and tremble for the fear of her torment." This event, thus symbolically shadowed forth, is the final result of sin in a self-determining will—the finished consequence of permitting a sinful inclination to compact and confirm itself by habitual indulgence, until it destroys the power of resistance, and the being is hopelessly ruined and lost.

We have thus mentioned and illustrated three reasons derived from the intrinsic nature of sin, why Christians should " watch unto prayer." Sin is spontaneous, and therefore is able to move at any instant. Sin can be solicited by temptation, and therefore is liable to move at any instant. Sin can become habitual, and habit is a second nature destroying the power of resistance. Much that has been said applies to sin in its general aspects, as pertaining to man universally ; but so far as this point is concerned we must dismiss it with the single remark, that from the very nature of sin and of the soul, except a man get rid of sin, he must perish. Sin is the slow, and sure, and eternal suicide of a human will.

But let us make an application of this subject to ourselves, as imperfectly sanctified believers. We cannot think of entering heaven with a mixture of sin in our hearts. We must acknowledge that the relics of a very profound and powerful sinful nature are still within us, which interfere with our peace, keep us distant from God, and are hostile to spirituality and a heavenly mind. How do we expect that these remainders of corruption are to be destroyed ; and how do we expect to obtain that holiness without which no man shall see the Lord ? Do we frequently raise these important questions ; and are we properly anxious to become pure and saintly ?

Perhaps we are in a careless state, and are indulging in some particular sin with little or no compunction. If so, we do well to remind ourselves that anxiety, and even distressing doubts, would be a more hopeful condition than is this state of lethargic indulgence. For, " seest thou a man wise in his own conceit ? there is more hope of a fool than of him." And, seest thou a church member habitually committing and enjoying a particular sin, and carelessly deeming himself to be safe? the angels looked down upon him with more hope when he was an inquiring and self-despairing man, than they do now.

But perhaps we do feel our sinfulness, and yet do not make the effort that results in its conquest. Perhaps we indulge in known sin, and experience a certain kind and degree of sorrow regarding it, but do not cut off the right hand, and do not pluck out the right eye. This moral condition, also, is one of great danger. Christ, it is true, does not "break the bruised reed." "He knoweth our frame, he remembereth that we are dust, he is very pitiful and of tender mercy." But we must not suppose that the feeling of mere regret, with no active resistance, is all that he demands from us. We must not lay the flattering unction to our souls, that God commiserates our indolence and ineffectual efforts. These efforts are ineffectual, because we are not sufficiently in earnest, and are unfaithful in seeking Divine help. We restrain prayer. We let down our watch. We must not deceive ourselves into the belief that God indulgently pities our unfortunate condition, as we may call it in our hearts. Sin is *guilt*. All sin is guilt. Christ poured out his blood to atone for it—*all* of it—and we must resist unto blood in order to overcome it —*all* of it. The path of duty and safety is plain. All will be well, if we *watch* more than we have, lest we fall into temptation ; if we *pray* more than we have, for power over sin. Vigilance and supplication must pervade our whole life as believers. The Christian must stand constantly braced, and expecting to meet a foe at every step. Every nerve should be tense, and every muscle tight drawn. And this, with an eye ever looking "up to the hills from whence cometh his help," should be his attitude through

life. True, it will be a life of sweat, and toil, and sometimes of aching pain; but there will be some lulls in the
fight, and some elysiums in the pilgrimage, and the everlasting rest will be all the sweeter for the unceasing effort.
That is a blessed moment for the Christian, when after his
long watch, and weary conflict, and fatiguing strain, he is
suddenly called into that walled city, " at once a fortress,
and a temple," over whose safety God watches; where he
can lie down beside the peaceful river of the water of life
without any solicitude, and where the grapple and tug of
spiritual warfare are over for eternity.

" Watch and pray lest ye enter into temptation. Watch
therefore: for ye know neither the day nor the hour,
wherein the Son of man cometh. Blessed," says the
Saviour—and this word has a world of meaning coming
from his Divine lips—" blessed are those servants whom
the Lord when he cometh shall find watching."

SERMON XXIII.

UNCEASING PRAYER.

1 THESSALONIANS v. 17.—" Pray without ceasing."

THE apostle Paul, in enjoining the duty of unceasing prayer upon all Christians, does not bind upon them a heavy burden which he himself will not move with one of his fingers. He does not regard it as a burden but a privilege, and he presents them an actual example of continual supplication to a faithful and prayer-hearing God, in this world of temptation and this valley of tears. He tells the Roman brethren, that " God is his witness, whom he serves with his spirit, in the gospel of his Son, that without ceasing he makes mention of them always in his prayers." To the Thessalonian church he says : " We give thanks to God always for you all, making mention of you in our prayers, remembering without ceasing your work of faith, and labor of love, and patience of hope." And in another paragraph of this same Epistle, he assures them that he " thanks God without ceasing, because when they received the word of God, which they heard first from him, they received it not as the word of men but of God." To his dearly beloved pupil Timothy, he writes: " I thank God, whom I serve from my forefathers with pure conscience, that without ceasing I have remembrance of thee in my prayers day and night."

A man who could bear such testimony respecting himself, in the matter of prayer, surely can speak out in bold and stimulating tones to all Christians, as he does in the text: " Pray without ceasing." He has done so himself. He knows the preciousness of the privilege. He has " tasted and seen that the Lord is good. In the day when he cried, God answered him, and strengthened him with strength in his soul."

The subject of Prayer, which is suggested by the text, is a comprehensive one. The theme is fertile. Perhaps no topic has engrossed more of the thought of wise and good men, than the communion which the soul of man is permitted to hold with its Maker. We purpose to consider two aspects of the general subject: First, that prayer must be incessant from its very nature; and, secondly, that unceasing prayer is feasible.

I. Observe, in the first place, that prayer must be unceasing, from the *nature* of the act. Prayer is intercourse with God, and God is the being in whom the creature lives and moves. To stop praying, therefore, is to break the connection that is established between the feeble and dependent worm of the dust, and the almighty One. We perceive immediately that a man must breathe without ceasing, because by the function of breathing his lungs, and thereby his whole physical system, are kept in right relation and connection with the atmosphere. His body lives, moves, and has its being, in atmospheric air, and therefore the instant the process of inspiration and expiration is stopped, it is cut off from the source of physical vitality and dies. For this reason, if a man breathe at all, he must breathe all the while. From the very nature of breath, we infer the necessity of constant breathing.

We are too apt to forget that such comparisons as these, instead of losing their force when applied to religious and spiritual subjects, are truer than ever. When I say to you, that a man's body lives, moves, and has its existence in atmospheric air, and that it must swim in it as a fish swims in the sea, in order to live and breathe, you take me literally. You believe and are certain, that continual communication must be kept up between the human lungs and the outward air, in order to human life. But when the apostle Paul tells you, as he did the philosophers of Athens, that the human soul lives, moves, and has its being in God, why are you, and why are all men so much inclined to take him figuratively, and to put such an interpretation upon the language as shears it of its full and literal force? It is as strictly true that the religious being and the eternal wants of the soul depend upon communication with God, and will suffer and die without it, as that the physical nature and needs of the body depend upon communication with the vital air, and will suffocate without it. Each statement is literally true within its own sphere, and with reference to the specific things to which it refers.

But it may be objected that if such is the fact, why is it that mankind do not invariably and constantly suffer distress, when this communion with God ceases to take place? Why are not prayerless men in unceasing anguish of mind? If the human body is removed from the free open air of heaven, and shut up in the Black Hole of Calcutta, the report comes instantaneously from the entire physical organization, that the established relation between the fleshly nature and the material world has been interfered with. The lungs begin to heave and pant, the perspiration oozes out of every pore, the face is flushed with crimson, and the eyes glare and stare in their sockets. But the human soul exists from day to day without intercourse with its Creator, and yet we perceive no indications of mental distress. The worldling puts up no prayer, and is out of all communication with God ; but we do not see in his mental experience any signs or tokens of spiritual agony, corresponding to those which we have mentioned in the instance of physical suffocation. This worldling, in the Scripture phrase, is " without God in the world," and yet · for aught that appears he is enjoying existence, and would be willing to live on in this style indefinitely. Ask this carnally minded man, if he would take a lease of prayerless, godless life for one hundred years, and he answers, Yea. How does this tally with the doctrine that the human soul needs intercourse with God, with as pressing and indispensable a necessity as the lungs need air ?

To this we reply, that as man is composed of two natures, so he is capable of living two lives. By his body he is connected with earth and time ; by his soul he is connected with God and eternity. He is capable therefore, and it is his original destination, to be associated with both of these worlds at one and the same time, in a just and proper manner, cherishing a pure, and temperate, and happy life in the body, and a holy and blessed life in the soul. This would have been his condition had he not apostatized ; and in this case his double and complex being would have been thoroughly alive, in all its parts. There would have been no death of any kind in him, and no death could have assailed him.

But for the very reason that he possesses two natures, and can live two lives, it is possible for him to gratify the desires of only one nature, and to lead only one life, here upon earth. It is possible in this state of existence, for the flesh to live on and enjoy itself, while the spirit is dead in trespasses in sins. It is possible for three-score years and ten, for a man to put himself in absorbing communion with earth and time, and to cut himself loose from all intercourse with God and heaven, and yet not be in mental distress, for the reason that the lower nature is living on and enjoying itself. One life temporarily takes the place of the other, and thus it is that a human creature, here upon earth, can pamper his body while he starves his soul; can live in worldly pleasure, while the nobler part of him is out of all connection with its appropriate objects.

There is a class of animals that are amphibious. They are capable of living both in the sea and upon the land. They are related by their physical structure both to the air and the water. If therefore the beaver, for example, is for a season debarred from the river, he can exist upon the shore ; or if he is temporarily driven from the shore, he can live in the river. These amphibious creatures can dispense with communication with one of the worlds with which they are constitutionally connected, because they have communication with the other one. So is it with man here in time. If he can absorb his lower nature in the objects and pursuits of sense, he is able to dispense with intercourse between God and his higher nature, without distress. If the amphibious animal can breathe upon the land, he need not gasp and pant upon the land, like the fish when taken from his native element.

But while this is so, it is none the less true, that the soul of man is the principal part of him, and that therefore he cannot *permanently* escape distress, if out of communication with God and heaven. This half-way life, of which we have spoken, is not possible in *eternity*. No man can live happily in sense and sin forever and ever. These amphibious animals, to which we have alluded, cannot dwell year after year in only one element. This half-way life of theirs is possible only for a short time. The whale can exist for a while in the unfathomed depths to which the harpoon has driven him, but he must sooner or later come to the surface to blow. The beaver cannot, like the fish, remain permanently in the watery element to which he has fled from his pursuer. Each nature asserts its rights ultimately, and if its wants are not met ultimately, suffocation and agony are the consequence.

And so it is with man's double nature, and the two worlds to which they are related. For a few short years, man can live a half-way life without great inconvenience or distress. For three-score years and ten, he can restrain prayer and stifle the soul, and not feel misery, because the body is thriving and happy. But he cannot live in this way in only one of his natures, and that the lowest and meanest, forever and ever. He must at some time or other come to the surface for breath. The wants of the immortal spirit must ultimately make themselves felt, and no gratification of the bodily desires can then be a substitute.

It is in this manner, that we prove that the soul of man needs God in the same organic, and constitutional way, that his body needs air. It will not do to judge of the primitive and everlasting necessities of a rational being, by looking at his pleasures and pains in this brief and transitory mode of existence. We must take him into eternity, in order to know whether he can suffocate his soul and be happy, while he gives only his body light and air. We must look at him beyond the tomb, if we would know whether he can be blessed while he is alive to sin, and dead to righteousness. We must remove him altogether from earth, to see whether he can live in only one of his natures and that the lowest of them.

Returning now to the subject of prayer, we see, after this brief discussion of the true relation that exists between the soul of man and the Everlasting God, that prayer is its vital breath, and that therefore it must be unceasing from its very nature. We cannot appeal to the experience of a prayerless person upon the point, because he has none; but we appeal confidently to the consciousness of a Christian, and ask him whether a complete and final cessation of prayer, in his own case, would not work the same disastrous consequences in his mental condition, that the stoppage of breath would in his physical. Suppose that a cloud should overshadow you, and a voice should come out of the cloud, saying: "Pray no more; the ear of God is heavy and cannot hear;" suppose, in other words, that that calming, sustaining, strengthening, and comforting intercourse which your spirit has been permitted to enjoy with God, in the time that is past, were absolutely foreclosed and shut off. Would not your soul begin to gasp and struggle, precisely as your body does when the atmospheric air is expelled, or vitiated by a deadly gas? Blessed be the mercy of God, we have never been put to the trial, and therefore can only conjecture what our mental distress would be, if we were absolutely precluded from prayer and supplication. What a sinking sensation would fill the heart of a mourning believer, if, at the very moment when death had come into his household, and cut down a life to save which he would gladly have given up his own, he should find it impossible to pray; if he should discover that the heavens above him were brass, and the earth beneath him was iron, and that no cry from his wailing, sorrowing spirit could ever pierce the heavens again. What an agony would swell the soul of a convicted sinner, if, at the very instant when the moral law was coming in upon him, and the convictions of guilt and the fears of judgment were rising and surging within him like waves lashed by the storm, he could not cry out: "God be merciful to me a sinner," because there was no longer any intercourse between the creature and the Creator. Man has become so accustomed to this blessing and privilege, that he does not know the full meaning and richness of it. Like other gifts of God, nothing but the complete and absolute deprivation of it would enable him to apprehend the infinity of the good which is granted to a feeble, helpless creature, in permitting him to enjoy the society and intercourse of the great and glorious Creator.

A second and further proof that prayer is unceasing in its nature is found in the fact, that God is *continually* the *hearer* of prayer. An incessant appeal supposes an incessant reply. God does not hear his people to-day, and turn a deaf ear to them to-morrow. He who prays to God without ceasing, finds that God hears without ceasing. Such is the declaration of God himself, upon this point. When Solomon had erected the temple, and had dedicated it as a house of prayer, the Most High, so to speak, localized Himself in it, and promised to give continual audience to all sincere worshippers and suppliants there. "The Lord appeared to Solomon by night, and said unto him, I have chosen this place to myself for an house of sacrifice. Now mine eyes shall be open, and mine ears attent unto the prayer that is made in this place. For now have I chosen and sanctified this house, that my name may be there *forever;* and mine eyes and mine heart shall be there *perpetually.*" (2 Chron. viii. 12–16.) Had there been from that time to this an unceasing volume of sincere supplication ascending unto God within that temple, there would have been an unceasing audience upon the part of God within that temple from that time to this. Jehovah is faithful to his promise, and had the Jewish nation been faithful to the covenant which God made with Abraham; had they continued to observe the statutes and commandments of the Lord, and to worship in his temple in the beauty of holiness down to the present time; they would in that very temple, down to this very moment, have found that God is immutably the hearer of prayer. There is not, now, one stone left upon another, of that magnificent structure which Solomon built for the honor of Jehovah, and the Jewish nation are scattered to the four winds of heaven; but this does not disprove the Divine faithfulness in the least. If there is no prayer, there can of course be no answer to prayer. If the creature ceases to pray, God of necessity ceases to hear. If the worshipper ceases to go into the temple, God, of course, goes out of it. But so long as the Jew, or the Gentile, pours out his soul in supplication, he will find that God is the constant hearer of supplication, and that he changeth not. And had that chosen and highly favored people continued to pray like Moses, and Samuel, and David, and Nehemiah; had they remained true to the teachings of the Law and the Prophets; had they known the day of their visitation from the Most High, when the promised Messiah, the Incarnate God, came down among them; had they welcomed the Redeemer, and found in the gospel of the New Testament only the blossom and bright consummate flower of the religion of their fathers; their temple would be still standing, and prayer would still be offered in it as of old. They would have been preserved a chosen generation and a royal priesthood, down to the present time. Jehovah himself would have kept them as the apple of the eye, amidst all the mutations and downfall of empires. The stars in their courses would have fought for them. Persia, Macedon, Rome, and all other kingdoms, might have gone to ruin, but Israel would have stood, to show that the Lord is upright, that he is a rock, and that there is no unfaithfulness in him.

It is this truth that enables us to interpret rightly those positive and unqualified declarations in the Old Testament, concerning the everlasting continuance of the Jewish Church and State. Consider the following, which is a part of the message that Nathan the prophet was commissioned to deliver to David the King: "Thus shalt thou say unto my servant David, thus saith the Lord of Hosts, I took thee from the sheepcote, even from following the sheep, that thou shouldest be ruler over my people Israel; and I have been with thee whithersoever thou hast walked, and have cut off all thine enemies from before thee, and have made thee a name like the name of the great men that are in the earth. Also I will ordain a place for my people Israel, and will plant them, and they shall dwell in their place, and shall be moved no more: neither shall the children of wickedness waste them any more as at the beginning. And it shall come to pass when thy day shall be expired, that thou must go to be with thy fathers, that I will raise up thy seed after thee which shall be of thy sons; and I will establish his kingdom. He shall build me an house, and I will establish his throne *forever*. I will settle him in mine house, and in my kingdom *forever:* and his throne shall be established *forevermore.*" (1 Chron. xvii. 7-14.) The primary reference in all this is to the spiritual kingdom of the Messiah, who was to be born in the line of David and Solomon, and the prophecy in this particular is in the process of fulfilment, and will be fulfilled. But there is also a secondary promise of a temporal kingdom, and a continuance of the Jewish people in power and honor to the end of time. And had they been faithful to the covenant with their fathers, every jot and tittle of this positive and unqualified promise of perpetual earthly prosperity would have been performed. The spirit of prayer, had it inspired the heart of the Hebrew nation down to the present time, as it inspired Moses, Samuel, Daniel, and Nehemiah, would have met with a continual answer from Him who sitteth upon the circle of the earth, and who has revealed Himself as the hearer of prayer. That answer would have related to the temporal as well as the eternal welfare of the covenant-keeping people—for godliness has the promise of the life that now is, as well as of the life that is to come—and whatever changes might have occurred in other nations of the earth, Israel would have remained a standing monument of the Divine power and faithfulness, and Jerusalem would still have been the city of the Great King. Nay, in this case, the whole history of the world would have been altered. Jerusalem upon earth, like the Jerusalem which is above, would then have been the "mother of us all." The worship of the true God, and of Jesus Christ his Son, would have overcome the idolatry of the secular monarchies and emperors, and the world would have been evangelized many centuries since.

And what is true of a people is true of an individual. The believer who prays without ceasing finds that God hears without ceasing. In his own experience, he discovers that the Divine ear is constantly attent to the voice of his supplication. The faintest desire meets a response. The Being with whom he seeks intercourse stands perpetually waiting. The immutability of God is demonstrated to him in the fact, that go whenever he will to the throne of grace he finds a listening ear, and an outstretched hand. "The young lions do lack, and suffer hunger; but they that seek the Lord shall not want any good thing. The eyes of the Lord are upon the righteous, and his ears are open unto their cry." God as the Creator has established such a relation between the body of man and the vital air, that there must be a continual supply of air; and therefore he has encompassed him with a whole atmosphere which is surrounding him upon all sides, and pressing upon him at every point. The instant he inhales with his lungs, he finds the invigorating element ready for him. And God as the Saviour has established such a relation between the renewed soul and himself, that there must be an unceasing intercommunion; and therefore, in the gospel of his Son, he proffers himself to his redeemed creature, and whenever the heart pants out its desire, it finds its ever-present supply. The unceasing prayer is met by the unceasing answer.

II. We pass now, in the second place, to inquire into the *feasibility* of unceasing prayer. How is a man to pray without ceasing?

Before proceeding to the immediate answer to this inquiry, it is obvious to remark, that the fact that prayer is the only mode by which the creature here upon earth can hold intercourse with his Maker, goes to prove that such an intercourse must be practicable. It must be a possible thing for man to enter into communication with God. It cannot be, that the great and wise Creator has called a finite and dependent creature into existence, and cut him off from all access to Himself. So far as God is concerned; so far as the original arrangements in and by creation are concerned; it must not only be possible, but a duty for the human soul not only to converse with God, but to hold an uninterrupted converse with him. We can no more suppose that our Creator would have made a rational and immortal spirit in his own image and likeness, without any power and privilege of communing with his Maker, than that he would have created a pair of lungs without any atmosphere in which they could expand. One of the most profound and spiritual divines, of one of the most thoughtful and spiritual periods in the history of the Church—we mean John Howe—has written at length upon what he denominates the "conversableness" of God; namely, those characteristics in the Deity that incline him to hear prayer, to listen to praise and adoration, and to receive from the whole rational universe the homage which is due to his infinite and glorious nature and name.[1] He shows conclusively that the Creator, from his very constitutional qualities, delights to put himself in communication with his rational creation; that he does not shut himself up in the isolation of his trinity, and his eternity, and enjoy his own absolute self-sufficiency, but overflows, with the fulness of his being, into the craving and recipient natures of angels and men. This he does, not because he is dependent upon his creatures for his own enjoyment, but simply that he may make them holy and happy. St. Paul taught this to the philosophers of Athens. "God that made the world, and all things therein, seeing that he is Lord of heaven and earth, dwelleth not in temples made with hands; neither is worshipped with men's hands, as though he *needed* anything, seeing he giveth to all life, and breath, and all things. And hath made of our blood all nations of the earth, for to dwell on all the face of the earth; and hath determined the times before appointed, and the bounds of their habitation; that they should *seek* the Lord, if haply they might feel after him and find him, though he be not far from any one of us: for in him we live, and move, and have our being." (Acts xvii. 24-28.) This "conversableness;" this benevolent and condescending willingness to hold intercourse with a race of finite creatures who cannot by any possibility do anything to benefit God, and add either to his happiness or his power, and who can-

---

[1] Howe: Living Temple, Ch. VI.

not by any possibility make themselves profitable to the Most High ; this spontaneous and generous readiness to give to the creature everything beneficial, and receive from the creature nothing that is beneficial in return, is shown by this most excellent thinker to be the very nature and character of the Infinite and Eternal Godhead.

This being so, it follows of course, that so far as God is concerned, and so far as all his arrangements in the original constitution and character of man are concerned, prayer is not only feasible, but feasible in the highest degree. If the intercourse is broken off, it cannot be by any action upon the part of God. If man finds it difficult or impossible to pray, and to pray without ceasing, it must be owing to some change that has taken place in his own nature and inclination. God is the same yesterday, to-day, and forever. He is just as conversable, just as friendly, and just as ready to give out everything while he receives nothing in recompense, as he ever was. It is apostasy and sin, alone, that have stopped the intercourse between man and his Maker; and apostasy and sin are man's work and agency.

1. Taking up, then, the question, How is a man to pray without ceasing ? it is obvious, in the first place, that he must have an *inclination* to pray. Constant supplication implies a habit of the mind and heart, and this implies a steady disposition to hold intercourse with God. We do not suppose it to be possible to perform any act, and especially any religious act, continually and unceasingly, by the mere exercise of volitions without any inclination. A man does not follow even an earthly calling, day after day, and without interruption through his whole life, unless his heart is in the work. How long, think you, would the merchant continue to prosecute a line of business which he utterly disliked, and to which he must force himself by a voilent resolution every time that he engaged in it ? Nothing is

done in this world for any great length of time, that is not done spontaneously, easily, and from a settled inclination.

The distinction between a man's volitions and his inclination is very great and important, and many errors both in the theory and practice of religion arise from overlooking it. They differ from each other, as the stream differs from the fountain; as the rays of the sun differ from the solid orb itself; as the branches differ from the root of the tree. A man's volitions, or resolutions, spring out of his disposition, or inclination, and in the long run do not go counter to it. The stream cannot be sweet, if the fountain be bitter; and a man's resolutions cannot be holy, if his heart or inclination is sinful. The stream cannot change the character of the source from which it flows, and neither can a man's volitions alter the natural disposition from which they all issue, and of which they are the executive and index.

Our Lord directs attention to the difference between an inclination and a volition, when he says: "Out of the heart proceed evil thoughts, murders, adulteries, thefts, and such like; a good man out of the good treasure of his heart bringeth forth that which is good, and an evil man out of the evil treasure of his heart bringeth forth that which is evil." Here he represents the particular act of murder or theft, which is performed by a particular resolution or decision of the man's will, as issuing out of a deep central disposition of his will lying back of it. If there be no murderous inclination, then no single act of murder can be committed. So long as there is nothing but a "good treasure of the heart," full of love to God and man, no single wrong act can be done; and so long as there is nothing but an "evil treasure of the heart," full of selfishness, and enmity towards God and man, no single right act can be performed. "A good tree," says our Lord,

" cannot bring forth evil fruit ; neither can a corrupt tree bring forth good fruit." The inclination determines all the particular volitions and choices ; and hence Christ teaches his disciples, and all mankind, that the change from sin to holiness must begin at the centre and source of all individual transgressions—must begin, not by making a resolution, but by receiving a new inclination from God the Spirit. " Either make the *tree* good, and his fruit good ; or else make the tree corrupt, and his fruit corrupt." As if he had said : " It is vain and futile to attempt to produce a moral change, by altering the volitions of the will ; the inclination of the will, out which these all spring and by which they are all determined, must be entirely converted and reversed."

And among the many reasons that might be assigned for this, is the fact that there can be no *steady* and *unceasing* action in religion, unless there be an inclination. And here we are brought back again to our subject, and see the bearings upon it of this brief discussion of the difference between an inclination and a volition. We are asking how a man can pray without ceasing. We desire to know, in what method he can keep up a continual intercourse with God. It is plain that if there is no foundation for it in the tendency of his mind, and the disposition of his heart, such an incessant prayerfulness as we have been speaking of—a praying that is as uniform and unbroken as breathing itself—cannot be maintained. Suppose an entire destitution of the inclination to draw near to God, and then ask yourself the question : " Can I pray without ceasing, by lashing myself up to the unwelcome service ; by sternly forcing my will up to the disagreeable work, by dint of resolutions and volitions ? " Even supposing that the prayer, so far as its quality is concerned, could be made acceptable upon this method ; even supposing that God would listen to a prayer in which there was no spontaneous inclining of the heart and affections; could the prayer become an unceasing one by this method? Would not the man grow inexpressibly weary, and soon end the useless effort?

We lay it down, therefore, with all confidence, that nothing but a praying disposition of the heart can enable any one to obey the apostle's injunction to pray without ceasing. And if this do exist, supplication will be constant and uniform. If it be true that an evil tree cannot bring forth good fruit, it is equally true that a good tree cannot *but* bring forth good fruit. Can you prevent a living, thriving tree from putting forth its buds and blossoms in the spring? You may employ all the mechanical appliances within the reach of human power, and in spite of them all the sap will rise in the tubes, and run out to the rim of every leaf, and the bud will swell, and the blossom will put forth, and the fruit will mature, because it is the .nature of a good tree so to do. And this process will be repeated year after year; the tree will bud, blossom, and fructuate " without ceasing; " because there is a foundation laid for all this in the root and heart of the tree. In like manner, if the human soul craves intercourse with God; if it is inclined and drawn towards him as its best friend, its support at all times, and its eternal portion; no power in heaven or earth can prevent it from approaching nigh to him. Nothing can separate between a praying heart, and the Hearer of prayer. Neither death, nor life, nor principalities, nor powers; neither height, nor depth, nor things present, nor things to come; are able to preclude and shut off the intercourse between such a soul and its Maker. This has been the strength and joy of God's people in all time. They have been shut up in dungeons, like Paul and Silas at Philippi; but they have found God nearer than ever to them. They have been plunged into earthly trial and sorrow; but this only caused them to take yet greater delight in prayer. They have drawn near to death, and have gone down to the grave; but the ear of their Maker and Redeemer was open and sensitive to their cry. And therefore the people of God pray on, pray ever, and pray without ceasing.

2. But this inclination to prayer may be strengthened by *cultivation*, and the use of means; and it is to this second part of the answer to the question that we direct attention.

It is of great importance to understand the appointed connection between an implanted principle in the heart, and the use of means, and to act accordingly. Because religion is the product of the Holy Spirit within our souls, and consists in a new inclination or disposition, it does not follow that we may neglect those instrumentalities that are adapted to strengthen and develop it. It is indeed true that no human power can originate the principle of spiritual life in the natural man, but after it has been originated by the Spirit of God, it can be cherished and nourished by human faculties aided by divine grace. The flower that hangs in the sunlight in your window contains a mysterious principle of vegetable life which you could no more originate, or call into being, than you could create the planet Saturn. But having been originated by the Maker of all things, you can then supply it with the earth and moisture which its roots require, with the light and heat which its leaves drink in, and can protect it from the frost and the insect, and make it a thing of beauty and of joy in your dwelling. Should this ministry of yours be withdrawn; should you cease to apply to the mysterious germ and principle of vegetable life which dwells in the rose or camellia the appropriate nutriment, it would wane away and finally die out. It would indeed continue for a little while to show its wonderful vitality, by endeavoring to endure the drought, or the sterility, or the darkness, which your neglect had thrust upon it. But there would be a limit to its power of endurance, and that beautiful life which neither you nor the highest angel could summon into being would eventually be quenched in death, by your carelessness.

Precisely so is it with the life of God in the soul of man. The new heart, the obedient disposition, the heavenly affection, the praying inclination—all that is included in that principle of spiritual vitality which is originated in the regeneration—will wane away, without the use of the appointed means of growth in grace. And if we should suppose a final and total cessation of Christian culture in a given instance ; if we could suppose as an actual fact that a renewed person forever ceases to pray, forever ceases to meditate upon the truth of God, forever ceases to discharge any of the duties of a Christian profession ; then we might suppose a final and total cessation of the Christian life within him.

All this applies with force to our subject. The foundation for intercourse with God, which has been laid in regeneration, must be built upon. The disposition to draw nigh to God, which has been wrought in the believer's heart, must be strengthened by cultivation and the use of means. We briefly notice two of them.

In the first place, the Christian deepens and strengthens his inclination to pray, by *regularity* in the *practice* of prayer. The Psalmist says : " As for me I will call upon God ; evening, and morning, and at noon, will I pray, and cry aloud." When Darius the king had made it a capital offence to offer any petition to any god or man save himself, Daniel " went into his house, and his windows being open in his chamber toward Jerusalem, he kneeled upon his knees three times a day, and prayed, and gave thanks before his God, as he did afore time." These holy men observed stated times and seasons of prayer. Man is a creature of habit and routine, and therefore whatever he leaves to the chances of time, place, and opportunity, is very certain to be either ill-performed or neglected altogether. He who has no particular time for winding up his watch will find it very often run down. The man of business who should select no particular hours for his transactions, but should attempt to conduct them at any time in the day or the night, would discover that the world does not agree with him. It is here, that we perceive the fallacy of those who would abolish the Sabbath as a day of special religious worship, upon the specious plea that every day ought to be a Sabbath, because the whole of human life should be consecrated to God. What would be thought of a banking institution that should adopt this theory; that should announce to the public, that inasmuch as it was their desire to accumulate wealth unceasingly, at one time as much as at another, therefore they should set no particular time for banking, but leave the transaction of business to their own convenience, and that of their customers? In the secular world, he will accomplish the most who does not allow his affairs to drag their slow length along through all the hours of the day, subject to accident and caprice, but concentrates them in definite portions of time. And in the religious world, he will make swiftest progress in the divine life who observes times and seasons; upon the principle of the wise man, that there is a time for everything—a time to weep, and a time to laugh; a time for religious duties, and a time for secularities. That man, therefore, will be most likely to make every day a holy day, who makes every seventh day a Sabbath day, as he is commanded to do. And that Christian will be most likely to pray without ceasing, and to breathe through his whole daily walk and conversation the blessed and elevated spirit of heaven, who at certain particular times, like David and Daniel, enters his closet and shuts the door, and prays to his Father who seeth in secret.

Intimately connected with this, in the second place, is the practice of *ejaculatory prayer*. This also tends to deepen and strengthen the believer's inclination to draw nigh to God. Prayer does not depend so much upon its length, as its intensity and importunity ; and hence a few moments of real absorbing address to God, in the midst of worldly avocations, and particularly in the midst of sharp temptations, will accomplish wonders in the way of arming the Christian with spiritual power. Sometimes in a single moment, in the twinkling of an eye, the eye of the believer catches the eye of his Saviour, and glances are exchanged, and the Divine grace flows down in a rill into his heart. It is this direct vision of God, and this direct instantaneous appeal to him, which renders the brief broken ejaculations of the martyr so supporting, and so triumphant over flesh and blood, over malice and torture. There is a power in prayer that is beyond any other power. Reading and meditation are invaluable in their own time and place, but they cannot be a substitute for supplication. The martyr might reflect never so profoundly, and long, upon the omnipotence and wisdom of God, and still be unable to endure the flame and the rack. But the single *prayer :* "Lord Jesus receive my spirit," lifts him high above the region of agony, and irradiates his countenance with the light of angelic faces.

The church of the present day, and particularly those churches in whose membership the reserved English nature prevails, are shorn of much power by an undue suppression of their religious feeling. "My *lips* shall utter praise; my *lips* shall greatly rejoice when I sing unto thee; O Lord open thou my *lips*, and my mouth shall show forth thy praise." Such is the determination, and such the desire of the Psalmist. How frequently does he call upon his tongue, which he denominates the "glory" of his frame, to awake and give utterance to prayer and praise. "Awake up, my glory; awake psaltery and harp." In this, the Psalmist has been followed by the great and devout men who have been called, in the providence of God, to "stand in the gap, and fill up the hedge," in times of great moment to the church. Martin Luther was noted for the urgency and frequency of his prayers, and particularly of his ejaculatory petitions. So easy and natural, nay, so irrepressible was it for him to cry out to God, that even in company with friends, and in the midst of social intercourse, he would break forth into ejaculations. This was often the case in times of trouble to the cause of the Reformation. God was then constantly present to his anxious and strongly exercised soul, and he pleaded with him as a man pleads with his friend.

And this power is within the reach of every believer. In the house and by the way, in the crowd or in solitude, the Christian may whisper in the ear of the Almighty. How marvellous it is that at any instant, and though surrounded by hundreds of his fellow-creatures, a child of God may carry on the most private and secret transaction with his Father who seeth in secret. Standing in the market-place, and hearing the busy hum of men all around him, the Christian can nevertheless hold communication with that Being who is sovereign over all, and take hold of that hand which moves the world. What a privilege is this, did we prize it and use it as we ought. We are not compelled to go to some central point, some Jerusalem or Mecca, to hold intercourse with heaven. "The hour cometh, and now is," says our Lord, "when ye shall neither in this mountain, nor yet at Jerusalem, worship the Father. The hour cometh, and now is when the true worshippers shall worship the Father in spirit and in truth. God is a Spirit." In any section of space, and at any point of time, the ejaculation of the soul may reach the Eternal Mind, and be rewarded by the Hearer of prayer.[1]

This discussion strongly urges upon the Christian, the sedulous cultivation of the spirit of prayer. If he be indeed a Christian, a renewed man, he has already received this spirit. It is not to be originated; but it is to be nurtured and developed. Culture is the great work before are generate person. That holy thing which has been wrought within his heart by the renewing grace of God is now made over to him, to take care of and cherish by God's assisting grace. Cultivate therefore the spirit of prayer and supplication, by uniformity and regularity in private devotions, and by frequent ejaculations to God. Do not be afraid of system and particularity, in this matter of learning to pray. There is little danger of undue

---

[1] "Ejaculations," says Thomas Fuller, "take not up any room in the soul. They give liberty of callings, so that at the same instant one may follow his proper vocation. The husbandman may dart forth an ejaculation, and not make a balk the more ; the seaman never the less steer his ship right in the darkest night. Yea, the soldier at the same time may shoot out his prayer to God, and aim his pistol at his enemy, the one better hitting the mark for the other. The field wherein bees feed is no whit the barer for their biting ; when they have taken their full repast on flowers or grass, the ox may feed, the sheep fat on their reversions. The reason is, because those little chemists distil only the refined part of the flower, leaving only the grosser substance thereof. So ejaculations bind not men to any bodily observance, only busy the spiritual half, which maketh them consistent with the prosecution of any other employment."

formality, in our free Protestant methods. The whole Protestant world might learn something from the Papist, and even from the Mohammedan, in respect to the faithful observance of set times and seasons of prayer. More of conscientious attention to the offices of private and public devotion, in our churches, would beyond all question deepen and strengthen their piety. And were the closet more regularly entered, the habit of ejaculatory prayer more common, the private worship in the family and the public worship in the sanctuary more uniformly rendered, the spirit of supplication, and the inclination to pray, would be developed in a manner that would surprise and bless the impenitent world.

After the death of that remarkable English writer, Sir Thomas Browne, the following resolutions were found in one of his common-place books; and we here cite them, as a specimen of the piety of that seventeenth century which has left the world such a rich legacy of profound and devout literature, and as an example for a Christian man in all time. This thoughtful and God-fearing person resolves: "To be sure that no day pass, without calling upon God in a solemn prayer, seven times within the compass thereof; that is, in the morning, and at night, and five times between; taken up long ago from the example of David and Daniel, and a compunction and shame that I had omitted it so long, when I heedfully read of the custom of the Mahometans to pray five times in the day. To pray and magnify God in the night, and my dark bed, when I could not sleep: to have short ejaculations whenever I awaked. To pray in all places where privacy inviteth; in any house, highway or street; and to know no street or passage in this city which may not witness that I have not forgot God and my Saviour in it; and that no parish or town where I have been may not say the like. To pray daily and particularly for sick patients, and in general for others, wheresoever, howsoever, and under whose care soever; and at the entrance into the house of the sick, to say, The peace and mercy of God be in this place. After a sermon, to make a thanksgiving, and desire a blessing, and to pray for the minister. In tempestuous weather, lightning, and thunder, either night or day, to pray for God's merciful protection upon all men, and his mercy upon their souls, bodies, and goods. Upon sight of beautiful persons, to bless God in his creatures, to pray for the beauty of their souls, and to enrich them with inward graces, to be answerable unto the outward. Upon sight of deformed persons, to send them inward graces, and enrich their souls, and give them the beauty of the resurrection."

Such unceasing supplication as this must result in great spirituality. The growth of a Christian is in nothing more apparent, than in the tone of his prayers. An increasing humility, earnestness, comprehensiveness, conciseness, and heavenly glow in the devotions of a believer, are a sure sign that he is drawing nearer to glory, honor, and immortality—that he is rapidly preparing for a world where every spiritual want will be fully supplied, and where consequently prayer will pass into praise. Therefore, "pray without ceasing," that you may hereafter worship and adore without ceasing.

SERMON XXIV.

THE FOLLY OF AMBITION.

JEREMIAH xlv. 5.—"Seekest thou great things for thyself? seek them not."

MAN is a creature of aspirations. His constant question is : Who will show me any good ? It matters not whether we try him in the highest or the lowest ranges of society, we find him always and everywhere reaching out after something. It is an error to suppose that ambition is confined to the Alexanders and Napoleons of the world. The most retired hamlet has its village aspirants, whose minds and hearts dilate with the same emotions in kind that urged on "Macedonia's madman" in his career of conquest from the Euxine to the Indus, and that stimulated the French emperor through his hundreds of battles from Lodi to Waterloo. To the human eye, there is, indeed, a great difference between the aspirations of a Julius Cæsar and the aspirations of a county politician ; but to the Divine eye there is no difference at all. Mathematicians tell us that all finite numbers are reduced to the same level, when compared with infinity ; that ten thousands or ten millions are just as far from infinitude as ten hundred, or as ten, or as one. So is it in morals. The ambition and aspirations of an earthly monarch, or an earthly conqueror, in the sight of Him who is from everlasting to everlasting,

are just as insignificant as the struggles of a village politician to acquire a village office, or the toils of a millionaire
to add a few more thousands to his treasures.

> "Our lives through various scenes are drawn,
>   And vexed with trifling cares;
>   While Thine eternal thought moves on
>   Thine undisturbed affairs."

If we could but look at human life from the position
of eternity, and measure it by the scale of infinity, we
should perceive that the common distinction which we
make between the great things and the small things of
earth is not a real one; and that all human ambition, be it
that of a king or a peasant, is the same poor and futile attempt of a creature to pass a line which the decree of the
infinite and eternal God has made it impossible for him
to pass. "Men of low degree are vanity, and men of
high degree are a lie; to be laid in the balance, they are
altogether vanity."

The prophet Jeremiah, in the text, recognizes this proneness of man to inordinate and ambitious aspirations, and
warns against it. "Seekest thou great things for thyself?
seek them not." The putting of such a question implies
that this is the common weakness and sin of man. As if
he had said: "Are you one of the common mass of mankind, and is your eye dazzled with visions of glory, or
pleasure? Are you reaching out after an unlimited measure of earthly good? Are you seeking the praise of men,
and not the praise of God? worldly enjoyment, and not
heavenly blessedness? Cease this struggle and attempt
to find solid good in the creature." Let us, therefore, consider some of the reasons for not aspiring after the "great
things" of earth and time; some of the dissuasives from
worldly ambition.

I. The first reason for not seeking the great things of earth and time is, that they will *not be attained*. We do not deny that the energy and perseverance of an ambitious man will accomplish great results, but we affirm confidently that he will never attain what he desires. For his desires are continually running ahead of his attainments, so that the more he gets the more he wants. He never acquires the " great thing " which he is seeking, in such a way as to sit down quietly and enjoy contentment of heart. Alexander, we are told, having conquered all the then known world, wept in disappointment because there were no more worlds for him to overrun and subdue. The operation of this principle is seen very clearly in the narrower sphere of private life. A young man begins life with the aspiration after wealth. This is the "great thing" which he seeks. This is the height of his ambition. We will suppose that he limits the sum which he seeks to one hundred thousand dollars. After some years of toil and economy, he acquires it. But this sum is no longer a " great thing " for him. Now that it is actually in his hands, it looks small, very small. The limit is enlarged, and he aspires to be a millionaire. The " great thing" which he now seeks is one million of treasure. This too is secured, but with the same result. The "great thing" shrivels up again now that it is actually in his possession, and he once more enlarges his limit, only to meet the same disappointment, unless death interrupts him with the stern utterance: " Thou fool, this night thy soul shall be required of thee, and then whose shall those things be which thou hast provided ? "

In this way, it is apparent that he who is seeking great things here upon earth will never obtain them. He is chasing his horizon. He is trying to jump off his own shadow. As fast as he advances, the horizon recedes from him; the further he leaps, the further his shadow falls. His estimate of what a "great thing" is continually changes, so that though relatively to other men he has accumulated wealth, or obtained earthly power and fame, yet absolutely, he is no nearer the desire of his heart—no nearer to a *satisfying* good—than he was at the beginning of his career. Nay, it is the testimony of many a man, that the first few gains that were made at the beginning of life came nearer to filling the desires of the mind, and were accompanied with more of actual contentment, than the thousands and millions that succeeded them.

"As a man thinketh in his heart, so is he." The value of all earthly good depends entirely upon the views and feelings which we entertain concerning it. There is no fixed and unchangeable worth in temporal things, as there is in eternal. Hence that which appeared great and desirable to us yesterday, appears small and undesirable to-day. Like the chameleon, it changes its color according as we bend over it, and cast light or shade upon it. He who loves God and truth, loves an object that is the same yesterday, to-day, and forever. But he who loves wealth, or pleasure, or fame, loves a continually shifting and varying object. God is always great, and always good; and the heart that has made Him its supreme portion never finds Him falling short of its expectations. But he who fixes his affections upon the things that are seen, and temporal, is subject to a constant series of disappointments. As fast as one thing is attained, it proves to be different from what was anticipated, and gives way to another, which in its turn is chased after, and in its turn is flung away in disgust when reached.

We find, then, that a really great thing cannot be secured within the sphere of earth, and sense, and time, because there is no really great thing within this sphere. There are many things that seem great while the struggle for them is going on; but there is not a single thing in the wide realm of creation that is absolutely great. God alone is great. Nothing but the infinite and adorable excellence of God is large enough for the desires of an immortal being like man. Well, therefore, may the prophet say to every ambitious and aspiring man, whether his aspiration reaches out after wealth, pleasure, or power: "Seekest thou great things for thyself? seek them not."

II. A second reason for not seeking great things is, that if they could be attained they would *ruin the soul*. It is fearful to observe the rapidity with which a man's character deteriorates as he secures the object of his desire, when the object is a merely earthly one, and the desire is a purely selfish one. Take, for illustration, the career of that military genius to whom we have already alluded. Napoleon Bonaparte sought "great things." He aimed at a universal empire in Europe. And just in proportion as he approached the object of his aspirations, did he recede from that state of mind and heart which ought to characterize a dependent creature of God. We do not allude so much to outward vices and crimes—though the life of the great captain will not bear inspection in this particular —as to that gradual deadening of the humane emotions, and that Lucifer-like self-exaltation, which transformed the young Corsican of comparatively moderate desires and purposes, into the most grasping and imperious soul that ever lived upon earth. Meekness and humility are traits that properly belong to every finite and dependent creature ; and He who came upon earth to exemplify the perfection of human nature said to all the world : "Take my yoke upon you, and learn of me, for I am meek and lowly of heart." But who can think of meekness and humble dependence upon God, in connection with the character of

Napoleon? On the contrary, we always associate him with those pagan demi-gods, those heaven-storming Titans, who like the Lucifer of Scripture are the very impersonation of pride and ambition. But such a spirit as this is the worst species of human character. It is the most intense form of idolatry—that of egotism and self-worship. It is the most arrogant and defiant form of pride. It would scale the heavens. It would dethrone the Eternal.

The same effect of mere worldly success is seen also in the walks of every-day life. Cast your eye over the circle in which you move, and select out those who are the most greedy of earthly good, and are the most successful in obtaining it, and are they not the most selfish persons that you know? Does not their character steadily deteriorate as the years roll away? They do not become any the less grasping and avaricious, for their success; but, on the contrary, their appetite grows by what it feeds upon. The fact which we have alluded to obtains a remarkable exemplification, in their case. The instant the "great thing" which they have been seeking after has actually come into their possession, it seems a small one; they are not satisfied with it, and enlarge their limits. This intensifies their cravings; and this stimulates them to yet more convulsive efforts. They override everything that stands in their way, and opposes them in the attainment of their projects, and thus acquire an arrogant and exacting temper that renders them hateful and hated.

It is here, that we see the moral benefit of failures and disappointments. Were men uniformly successful in their search after "great things;" did every man who seeks wealth obtain wealth, and every man who grasps after power obtain power, and every man who lusts after fame become renowned; the world would be a pandemonium, and human character and happiness would be ruined.

Swollen by constant victory, and a sense of superiority, successful men would turn their hands against one another, as in the wars of the giants before the flood. There would be no self-restraint, no regard for the welfare of others, no moderate and just estimate of this world, and no attention to the future life. Nothing but the failures and disappointments that so crowd the career of man on the earth, prevents the world from becoming a theatre of contending factions that would ultimately destroy each other. This man is reduced from affluence to poverty, and he is made submissive, and moderate, and reasonable in his temper. That man fails to reach the summit of his ambition, and quietly settles down into a useful and happy sphere of labor. Thus the providence of "God only wise" educates ambitious and grasping man into sobriety, and a judicious estimate of both the great things and the small things of this transitory existence.

III. A third reason for not seeking "great things" lies in the fact, that "great things," so far as they are attained at all in this world, are commonly attained *indirectly*. Saul the son of Kish was sent out by his father to find the asses that had strayed, but he found a kingdom instead. Disappointed in his search for the lost animals, he betook himself to the prophet Samuel for information, and Samuel anointed him king over Israel. He did not obtain what he went for, but something greater and better. This illustrates the manner in which "great things" are generally acquired in this world. They come indirectly.

Look into literary history, and see how this is exemplified. The most successful creations of the human reason and imagination have rarely been the intentional, and foreseen products of the person. The great authors have been surprised at their success; if, indeed, success came to them during their life-time. But more commonly their fame has been posthumous, and their ears never heard a single note of the pæan that went up from the subsequent generations that were enchanted with their genius. Shakspeare and Milton never read a single criticism upon their own works; and to-day they neither know anything of, nor care for the fame that attends them upon this little planet. Wordsworth writes to a friend who had congratulated him upon the estimation in which his poetry was held: "I am standing on the brink of the vast ocean I must sail so soon; I must speedily lose sight of the shore; and I could not, once, have conceived how little I am now troubled by the thought of how long or short a time they who remain on that shore may have sight of me." Speaking generally, the great authors left something so written to after times as men would not willingly let die, not because they aimed deliberately, and with a straining effort, at such a result, but because in the prosecution of other aims—in following their own tastes and impulses, or their desire to be useful to their fellow-men—this result came to them in the providence of God. Said one of the most celebrated of modern poets—one who sprang into notoriety during his life-time, without any preconceived purpose, or any laborious effort to this end—"I woke up one morning and found myself famous."

Look, again, into the circles of trade and commerce, and observe how often great and lasting success comes incidentally, rather than as the consequence of preconceived purposes and plans. The person aimed simply at the discharge of his duties to his family, to the state, and to his Maker. He laid out no plans for the acquisition of a colossal fortune, but endeavored to provide for the present and prospective wants of those dependent upon him, with prudence and moderation. He obtained, however, far more than he calculated upon. Wealth came in upon him with rapidity, and that which he did not greedily seek, and which he never in the least gloated upon with a miser's feeling, was the actual result of his career in the world.

The words of our Lord are true in reference to secular, as well as sacred things: " He that findeth his life shall lose it ; and he that loseth his life shall find it." If we directly seek " great things," we shall fail of their attainment. There are a few exceptions to this general rule, it is true ; but a careful observation of the common course of events will show, that reputation, wealth, and secular blessings generally, fall to those who are not specially anxious concerning them—who pursue the ends of life with wisdom and moderation, and are rewarded by Divine Providence with an overplus of temporal good that formed no part of their original purposes and expectations. The great majority of those, on the contrary, who set up fame, wealth, or pleasure, as their idol, and made everything subservient to its attainment, have been miserably disappointed. They were destined to fail inevitably. For, in case they obtained the glittering object they aimed at, it grew pale and dull in their possession, like that radiant little insect which the child chases in the summer evening, and grasps in his hands, only to find a black and repulsive bug. And in case they failed altogether, in securing the prize which they sought, their anxious and spasmodic efforts after it only left them tired, and disgusted with human life.

Seekest thou, then, great things for thyself? seek them not. They will not come by this method. Seek first of all the kingdom of God, and his righteousness ; and then all these minor things, which the world and the deluded human heart denominates "great things," shall be added unto you. Be faithful to your duties in the family, in the state, and in the church, and then that measure of secular blessings which will accrue to you of itself, will exceed all that you will be likely to attain even by the most engrossing and violent efforts devoted to the sole purpose of obtaining them. If you will lose your life, you shall find it; but if you insist upon finding your life, you shall lose it.

IV. A fourth reason for obeying the injunction of the text is found in the fact, that great *sorrow* springs from great aspirations, when those aspirations are unattained. There is only one species of aspiration that does not weary and wear the soul, and that is, the craving and cry of the soul after God. "As the hart panteth after the water brooks, so panteth my soul after thee O God." The desire expressed in these words of the Psalmist can never satiate, or disgust the human spirit, for the reason that God is the real and true portion, the substantial, eternal good of the creature. But all other aspirations dispirit and discourage in the end. "He that increaseth knowledge increaseth sorrow." The sadness and melancholy of the man of letters is well known. One of the most equable minds in literary history, singularly calm and balanced by nature, and remarkably free from passionate and stormy impulses, confessed at the close of a long life of eighty years that he had never experienced a moment of genuine repose.[1] Humboldt, who had surveyed the cosmos, and who had devoted a long existence to placid contemplation of the processes of nature, and had kept aloof from the exciting and passionate provinces of human literature, said in his eightieth year: "I live without hope, because so little of what I have undertaken yields a satisfactory result." This is the penalty which ambitious minds pay for seeking "great things." There is an infinite aspiration,

---

[1] Goethe: Conversations by Eckermann, p. 58.

and an infinitesimal performance. The hour of death, and the falling shadows of an everlasting existence, and an everlasting destiny, bring the aspiration and the performance into terrible contrast. Most impressively do such facts and experiences in the history of marked men reiterate the prophet's injunction: " Seekest thou great things for thyself? seek them not."

Go down, once more, into the sphere of active life, and see the same sorrow from the same course. Look at that man of trade and commerce who has spent his life in gigantic, and, we will suppose, successful enterprises, and who now draws near the grave. Ask him how the aspiration compares with the performance. He has generally accomplished, we will assume, what he undertook. The results of his energy and capacity are known, and visible to all in his circle and way of life. His associates have praised him, and still praise him ; for he has done well for himself, and for all connected with him. But he writes vanity upon it all. When he thinks of all the heat and fever of his life, all his anxious calculation and toil by day and night, all his sacrifice of physical comfort and of mental and moral improvement, and then thinks of the actual results of it all—the few millions of treasure, the few thousands of acres, or the few hundreds of houses— he bewails his infatuation, and curses his folly. He perceives that great sorrow springs out of a great aspiration, when that aspiration terminates upon things seen and temporal.

Such, then, are the dissuasives to ambition. These are the reasons for heeding the injunction of the prophet, not to seek the great things of earth. They will not be attained, because as fast as they come into possession they lose their value. If they could be attained, they would ruin the soul, by inordinate pride and self-exaltation. So far as they are partially and approximately attained, it is by indirection, and not by preconceived aims and purposes. And, lastly, a great sorrow always springs out of a great aspiration that is unfulfilled.

1. In the light of this subject and its discussion, we perceive, in the first place, the *sinfulness* of ambition. Some speak of a " holy ambition ; " but there is no such thing, any more than a holy pride, or a sanctified avarice. Ambition, as the etymology of the word denotes, is a circuitous method (ambio). It is not the straightforward search after a good thing, simply because it is good ; but it is the roundabout endeavor to obtain a " great thing," for the sake of the personal advantage which it yields. If the student toils after knowledge, not for its own sake but because it brings fame and worldly gain with it, he is an ambitious student. He does not proceed straight to the mark, and acquire learning because it is good in itself, but that he may convert it into a mere means to some ulterior end. If a man seeks religion, not because it is intrinsically excellent, but that his standing in society may be advanced, he is actuated by an ambitious motive. He does not move straight and direct towards the good thing, and choose it for its own pure excellence. It is impossible that such a spirit as this should be virtuous, or of the nature of virtue. On the contrary, it is sinful in the utmost degree, because it is the very essence of selfishness and pride. Such a person employs all the good things, and all the great things, of this world and the next, as mere means for the accomplishment of his private and ambitious ends. It was by this sin, that the angels fell. They were not content with loving God because he is lovely, and obeying law because the law is holy, just and good. They desired to obtain some private and personal advantage, separate from, and over and above the joy, peace, and blessedness of serving God for his own

sake. And the fallen archangel plied our first parents, with the same motive. He promised them that if they would eat of the forbidden tree, they should "be as gods." He wakened in them the feeling of ambition, and by ambition they, too, fell.

2. In the second place, we see in the light of this subject, the complete and perfect *blessedness* of those who are free from all ambitious aims and selfish purposes ; who can say : " Whom have I in heaven but Thee ? and there is none upon earth that I desire besides Thee. Thou, O God, art the strength of my heart, and my portion forever." We cannot find a perfect happiness upon earth, because we cannot find a soul that is perfectly unambitious and unselfish. The best of men will confess that the lingering remains of this Adamic sin, this desire to be as gods, this straining after superiority, are continually stirring within them, and interfering with their spiritual peace and joy. And they long for the time when they shall be satisfied with the Divine likeness; when they shall not be envious in the least of the happiness and the privileges of others ; nay, when they shall not be disturbed in the least to see others placed above them. For such will be the state of feeling in the heavenly world. The spirit of a just man made perfect, who is satisfied from himself because he is satisfied in God, does not envy the exaltation of the angel above him ; the angel feels no pang of jealousy on seeing the cherub higher than himself; the cherub does not begrudge the seraph his glory and joy ; and none of all these have the slightest desire to drag down the archangel from his lofty place in the celestial hierarchy. Each and all of these ranks of happy intelligences know that God is infinitely greater and more glorious than his universe, and in him they all delight according to the measure of their powers and capacities.

And only as this spirit animates the hearts of Christians here below, does the Church resemble the heavenly state. But, alas! Ephraim envies Judah, and Judah vexes Ephraim, and the kingdom of the meek and lowly Redeemer is torn with intestine struggles. And the heart of the individual believer is also torn with an intestine struggle. How difficult it is to obey the injunction of St. James: "Let the brother of low degree rejoice in that he is exalted, but the rich in that he is made low." How difficult to desist from seeking "great things," and in the simple, godly, conscientious discharge of daily duties, seek first of all the kingdom of God and his righteousness, free from all pride and all ambition.

But "to this complexion must we come at last." To this frame of mind we are summoned by our Redeemer, and to this must we attain. Therefore *cultivate* this meek and lowly temper. By prayer and supplication; by constantly remembering that the things which are seen are temporal; by frequent meditation upon the vanity of earth and of man as mortal, and upon the glory and eternity of heavenly objects; by such methods as these, and only by such methods, can we rid ourselves of our pride and ambition, and obey the command of God by his prophet: "Seekest thou great things for thyself? seek them not."

SERMON XXV.

EVERY CHRISTIAN A DEBTOR TO THE PAGAN.

ROMANS i. 14.—"I am debtor both to the Greeks, and to the Barbarians; both to the wise, and the unwise."

THIS is the reason which the apostle Paul assigns for his readiness to go to Rome, or to the ends of the earth, to preach the gospel of Christ which is the power of God unto salvation to every one that believes it. He is a debtor. He *owes* the gospel to the world. But St. Paul was not under any such special and peculiar indebtedness, in this particular, as to make his position different from yours and mine. We are too apt to regard the prophets, and apostles, and martyrs, as holding a different relation to the work of evangelizing the world from that which ordinary Christians sustain; and that therefore the Great Steward will not require of the Church at large such an entire self-sacrifice in this behalf, as he did of the first preachers of Christianity. How ready the sluggish disciple is to conclude that he is not called upon to exercise a self-denial for Christian missions that costs him, and tasks him, merely because he is not himself a missionary. Had he decided to devote his life to preaching the gospel to the heathen, there would then be a special obligation resting upon him; but not having so decided, his relation to the great work of missions, he thinks, is distant and unimportant. Such is the unconscious reasoning of too many within the Christian Church; and hence it is, that the work which is dearest of all to the heart of Christ makes so little progress in the world, compared with the great numbers and the immense resources of the Christian Church.

But there is no distinction of Christians, any more than of persons, with God. All Christians stand upon the same position, in regard to the work of evangelizing the world. They are all of them debtors. Every individual member of the Christian Church *owes* the gospel to mankind. Each and every disciple of Christ must say with St. Paul: "I am debtor both to the Greeks and the Barbarians, both to the wise and the unwise." Let us then in the first place consider the nature and strength of that particular motive to labor for the spread of the gospel which is presented in the text.

The feeling of *indebtedness*, in an honorable mind, is a powerful one. It lies under all the trade and commerce of the world, and is the spring which impels all the wheels of secular business. Men owe one another sums of money, and the endeavor to discharge these obligations makes up the sum and substance of agricultural, manufacturing, and mercantile life. Hence it is, that anything that injuriously affects the sentiment of pecuniary obligation strikes a blow at the pecuniary prosperity of a nation; while everything that contributes to deepen and strengthen this sentiment promotes national wealth. Suppose that by reason of some false theory in morals, or some strong workings of human selfishness, the entire mercantile community should lose its respect for contracts, and promises, and obligations of every kind; suppose that the feeling of indebtedness should die away, and an utter indifference to debts should take its place; what a total paralysis in all departments of trade and commerce would ensue. This is sometimes seen upon a small scale, at some particular crisis. A commercial revulsion sometimes occurs within a certain country, or a certain section of a country, because mercantile honor has declined. Men lose confidence in each other, because they see, or think they see, a lax morality, a false theory of indebtedness, creeping in and influencing their fellowmen; and the consequence is a refusal either to buy or to sell. And thus all the wheels of business are blocked.

But the power of this sentiment is seen very clearly in the instance of the individual. When a high-minded and strictly honorable man has legitimately come under certain obligations, there is a wholesome pressure upon him which elicits all his energies. He is in debt. He feels the responsibility, and acknowledges it. He proceeds to meet it. His time is sacredly devoted to his business. He economizes his expenditures. He engages in no rash or speculative transactions. He keeps his affairs under his own eye, and bends all his energies with sagacity and prudence to the extinguishment of his indebtedness. Never are all the merely secular abilities of a man in better tone, or braced up to a more vigorous and successful activity, than when, under the sense of obligation, he proceeds with perfect integrity to obey the injunction, "Owe no man anything." Like a well-built and tight ship, with no gay display of streamers, but with sails well bent, cordage new, strong, and taut, a skilful pilot at the helm, and a thoroughbred master in command, such a man is a master-spirit. Though the gales increase, and the billows roll, "and the rapt ship run on her side so low that she drinks water, and her keel ploughs air," yet there is concentrated and well-applied energy on board, and she weathers the storm.

But not only does this sentiment of indebtedness constitute a powerful motive to action: it is also a cheerful and an encouraging motive. The species of indebtedness of which we are speaking, supposes the possibility of payment. It implies a proper proportion between the talents and resources of the person, and the amount of his liabilities. In case his debt becomes so vast, and out of all relation to his present and prospective means of extinguishing it, as to render its payment hopeless, then the sentiment of indebtedness operates like an incubus. The proposition to pay a debt as large as that of a nation, like the proposition to lift a mountain, would be paralyzing upon any one man's energies. He could not lift a finger towards the impossible task.

But we are speaking of a kind of indebtedness that stands in practicable proportion to individual ability. And in this reference we affirm, that he who feels the stimulation of such a moderated obligation is under a pressure that strengthens, rather than weakens him. He finds in his very indebtedness a cheerful and encouraging motive to "go forth to his work, and his labor, until the evening." Every hour of faithful effort, every well-contrived plan, all his sagacity, prudence, and economy—the whole labor of the day—tends directly and surely to the extinguishment of the claims that lie against him. Men distinguished in the monetary world have described the sense of satisfaction, nay, the gush of pleasure, which they experienced in the earlier days of their career, from the excitement incident to a gradual but certain overcoming of their liabilities. Though later years brought with them vast wealth, yet they confessed that their earlier years were their happiest—the most marked by energy, a sense of power, and the feeling of buoyant hopefulness.

Such is the general nature and influence of that sentiment to which St. Paul gives utterance, when he says: "I am debtor both to the Greeks, and to the Barbarians; I owe the gospel to the wise, and to the unwise." And we proceed now to apply what has been said, to *the Christian's indebtedness to the unevangelized pagan*.

I. In the first place, every Christian owes the gospel to the pagan, because of the deep interest which Christ takes in the pagan. In the account of the last judgment, we are taught that all neglect of human welfare is neglect of Jesus Christ; that he who cares nothing for unevangelized man cares nothing for the Son of God. Our Lord identifies himself with those who have never heard of his gospel, and represents all discharge of duty to them as discharge of duty to Him, and all dereliction of duty to them as dereliction of duty to Him. When those on the right hand shall ask: "Lord, when saw we thee an hungered and fed thee? or thirsty and gave thee drink? When saw we thee a stranger and took thee in? or naked and clothed thee? Or when saw we thee sick, or in prison, and came unto thee? the King shall answer, and say unto them, Verily I say unto you, inasmuch as ye have done it unto one of the least of these my brethren, ye have done it unto ME." And when those on the left hand shall ask: " Lord, when saw we thee an hungered, or athirst, or a stranger, or naked, or sick, or in prison, and did not minister unto thee? then shall he answer them, saying, Verily I say unto you, inasmuch as ye did it not to one of the least of these, ye did it not to ME." In these remarkable words, the Divine Redeemer indicates his profound interest in every sinful man without exception. Anything that is done for human salvation, in any nation or age, is done for Him. And the awful curse of the merciful Saviour falls upon those who do nothing for human welfare. Jesus Christ compassionates lost men universally, and intensely desires their deliverance from sin. His compassion is so tender, and his desire so strong, that any one who labors to save a human soul from sin labors for Him. He who spiritually feeds, clothes, and medicines any sinner, feeds, clothes, and medicines the Saviour of sinners. Our Lord thus identifies himself with the sinful and lost world for which he died. We have no conception of the immensity of that Divine sympathy and compassion for man which moved the second Person of the Godhead to become the Man of sorrows, and, in the phrase of the prophet, to "take our infirmities and bear our sicknesses." When he was upon earth, the sin and suffering of the children of men immediately and uniformly affected his heart, and we never detect in him the least indication or exhibition of weariness, or indifference, towards human woes and wants. So absorbed was he in his merciful work, that "his friends went out to lay hold on him, for they said, He is beside himself." When, upon that last and sorrowful journey to Jerusalem, he had reached the summit of the Mount of Olives, and the whole city burst upon his view, his eyes filled with tears at the thought of its guilt and misery. Look through the world, look through the universe, and see if there be any sorrow like unto his sorrow—so profound, so spontaneous, so unceasing, so commiserating.

This sympathy and compassion originated partly from his Divinity, and partly from his humanity. As God, he understood as no created mind can understand what sin, and guilt, and hell are ; and as man, he was bone of man's bone, and flesh of man's flesh. The doctrine of the incarnation explains this profound interest, and this entire identification. The Divinity in his complex person gave the eye to see, and the humanity gave the heart to feel and suffer ; and when such an eye is united with such a heart, the sorrow and the sympathy are infinite. As God, the Redeemer was the creator of men, and as man, he was their elder brother; and therefore it is, that he can so unify himself with the world of mankind, as he does in these wonderful utterances which will constitute his rule of judgment in the last great day. "Inasmuch as ye have done it unto one of the least of these my brethren, ye have done it unto *me*. Inasmuch as ye did it not to one of the least of these, ye did it not to *me*."

II. In the second place, every Christian owes the gospel to the unevangelized pagan, because of his own personal indebtedness to Christ. That every Christian is indebted to Christ will not be denied for an instant. There is no claim equal to that which results from delivering an immortal soul from eternal death. Language fails to express the absoluteness of the right which the Redeemer has to the service of his redeemed people. The right to man's service which he has by virtue of his relation as a Creator is immeasurable. To originate a being from nothing, and then to uphold him in existence, lays the foundation for a claim that is complete and indefeasible. And did mankind realize how entirely they belong to their Maker, by virtue of being his workmanship in a sense far more literal than that in which we say that a watch belongs to the artisan who made it; did they feel the force of the fact that God made them, and not they themselves; they would not dare to set up a claim to those bodies and spirits, those talents and possessions which are His. "I have made the earth, and created man upon it; I, even my hands, have stretched out the heavens, and all their host have I commanded. Every beast of the forest is mine, and the cattle upon a thousand hills," saith the Almighty.

But this claim which God as Redeemer possesses upon a human being whom he has saved from eternal death is even greater than that of God as Creator. "Ye were not redeemed with corruptible things as silver and gold, but with the precious blood of Christ, as of a lamb without blemish, and without spot." The Christian Church, many centuries ago, was agitated with the question whether it is scriptural and proper to say that Mary was the "mother of God," and that sinners are redeemed by the "blood of God." The phrases, "mother of God," and "blood of God," were condemned by the Church represented in general council, because those who contended for their use were understood to employ them in a sense inconsistent with the Divine attributes. They were taken to mean that Mary was the mother of *un*incarnate God; and that the blood spoken of was the blood of *un*incarnate God. This is incompatible with the impassibility of the Divine Essence. But the Church was willing to affirm, and did affirm, that the Virgin Mary was the mother of incarnate God, and that the blood spilled upon Calvary was the blood of incarnate God. There is a mother of the God-man, and a blood of the God-man. In this latter statement, the birth and the blood are confined to the human nature of Jesus Christ, while, at the same time, this birth and this blood are infinitely exalted and dignified above the birth and blood of an ordinary man, by the union of the humanity with the Divinity. This makes the sacrifice of Christ more than finite, and more than human. It becomes an infinite and divine oblation. And to indicate this, the Scripture itself employs the phraseology which by a wrong interpretation led to the Nestorian controversy. St. Paul, addressing the elders of Ephesus at Miletus, says: "Take heed therefore unto yourselves, and to all the flock over which the Holy Ghost hath made you overseers, to feed the Church of God, which he hath purchased with *his own* blood." (Acts xx. 28.)

If this language be explained as the Church explained it, by the union of two distinct natures in the one person of the Lord Jesus Christ, so that he is at once truly God and truly man, then it teaches the Christian that he has

DEBTOR TO THE PAGAN.

been redeemed by no merely common and finite sacrifice; that his sin has been expiated by the blood of a God-man, the "precious blood of Christ, as of a lamb without blemish and without spot." And it is this great fact which brings every redeemed sinner under an infinite indebtedness to his Saviour. He has been purchased by the blood of God incarnate. It was this truth that filled the Apostle Paul with such an overwhelming sense of his duty to Jesus Christ. This it was, that made him say: "I am debtor both to the Greeks and to the Barbarians. I owe the knowledge of this great atonement which my Redeemer has made for the sin of the whole world, to every human creature, wise or unwise, high or low, rich or poor." The stupendous fact that God Almighty unites himself with the sinner's nature, and dies in the sinner's stead, lays upon that sinner an immeasurable obligation to live and labor for the same world and the same object for which, in the phrase of the hymn, "God the Mighty Maker died."

We have thus considered the nature of the feeling of indebtedness, and the foundation upon which it rests, with reference to the duty of every Christian to obey the great command of his Redeemer, to preach the gospel to every creature. As to its source and foundation, it springs out of the fact of Christ's deep interest in the salvation of men, and of the believer's personal redemption by the blood of incarnate God; and as to its nature and operation, it is a powerful and a cheerful motive, and principle of action. We now proceed to draw some conclusions from the subject.

1. We remark, in the first place, that every Christian should look upon the work of evangelizing the world as a debt which he literally and actually owes to Christ, and to his fellow-man. He should heartily *acknowledge* this debt,

and not attempt to free himself from it, by explaining it away as a figure of speech.

It is a great honor and privilege to be allowed to labor together with God in anything. When we consider how imperfect and unworthy our services are, it is strange that the Infinite One, who is excellent in working, and who doeth all things well, should admit us into a fellowship of toil with him. Yet so it is. "We are laborers together with God," says the Apostle. If we felt the full significance of this truth, we should need no further motive to self-sacrifice in the work of preaching Christ. The honor and privilege would be enough. But, alas! we do not. And therefore we need to stimulate ourselves to greater activity, by the consideration of our serious and solemn duty in the premises.

"Freely ye have received, freely give." This was the command which our blessed Saviour gave to his twelve disciples, when he sent them out as his commissioned heralds. He had endowed them with miraculous powers—"power against unclean spirits to cast them out, and to heal all manner of sickness and all manner of disease." This endowment laid them under obligation to employ it *faithfully*, and *scrupulously*, in his service. Suppose now that, like Simon the sorcerer, they had attempted to use this supernaturalism for their own selfish purposes; suppose that instead of giving health to the sick, and sight to the blind, freely and without price, they had sold miracles, and taken money for the marvellous cures. How instantaneously would the wrath of the Lamb, the merciful Redeemer who had endowed them and commissioned them, have fallen upon them. But the case would have been the same, had they neglected to make any use at all of their supernatural gifts. By being thus selected by the Redeemer, and clothed with miraculous virtues, they were constituted *debtors* to the inhabitants of Judea. They *owed* these healing mercies to the sick and the dying, and the mere non-use of them would have been a sin and a crime.

Precisely such is the relation which every individual Christian sustains to that power of healing spiritual maladies, and saving from spiritual death, which is contained in the gospel of Christ. Having himself freely received this gospel, he is now under a solemn duty to give it to others. If he should formally refuse to impart the gift; if he should deliberately decry and oppose Christian missions; if he should put obstacles in the way of those who are endeavoring to evangelize the nations; he would of course incur the Divine condemnation. But so he will, if he simply neglects to discharge his indebtedness; if he merely non-uses the precious and the marvellous treasure which has been committed to him in virtue of his own discipleship. That Christian, if we can call him such, who should trust in the blood of the God-man for personal justification in the great day of judgment, and yet never commend this same method of salvation to the acceptance of his fellow-creatures, either himself personally or by proxy through some missionary, would be precisely like that Judas who carried the bag and what was put therein, but who expended the contents upon his own traitorous and worthless self.

We cannot too carefully remember that the work of missions is not an optional matter, for a disciple of Christ. It is a debt. "Woe is me," said St. Paul, "if I preach not the gospel." The "treasure" which "has been committed to earthen vessels" must be made over to those for whom it is intended, or it will prove to be a poison and a curse. It is like the manna which God bestowed upon the Israelites in the desert. So long as they used it, it was the bread of heaven and angels' food; but when they hoarded it, it became corruption and putrefaction in their very hands. If the Church looks upon the gospel, and the preaching of it, as a gift which it has freely received and from which untold blessings have come upon herself, and heartily acknowledges her obligation to impart this gift to others; if she does not regard this evangelizing work as an optional matter, but a most solemn debt to her redeeming God and her perishing fellow-creatures; she will go forward, and by the grace of God fulfil her obligations. But if this sentiment of indebtedness declines in her mind and heart, then she will lapse back into indifference and apathy, and these are the harbingers of a corrupt Christianity, which will be buried in one common grave with Paganism, Mohammedanism, and all forms of human sin and error.

2. In the second place, we remark in view of this subject, that Christians should labor zealously to *discharge* this debt to Christ, and to the world of sinners for whom he died.

In speaking of the influence of the feeling of indebtedness, we had occasion to remark that it is always a stimulus to effort, in case the payment of the debt is within the compass of possibility. Such is the fact in the instance before us. The debt which the believer is to pay is not his debt to eternal justice. That he can never discharge. That is beyond all created power. Christians are not to send the gospel to the Greek and the Barbarian, for the purpose of making an atonement for their sins, and thereby cancelling their obligations to law and justice. That debt Christ himself has paid; and paid to the uttermost farthing.

But this is the debt which you, and I, and every professed disciple of the Lord Jesus Christ owes, and which we *must* discharge. It is the obligation to do here upon earth, in our own little period of time, and our own little section of space, all that in us lies to "preach the gospel to every creature." If the providence and Spirit of God indicate that we are to go in person, then we are to go in person. If the providence of God has forbidden this, but has placed in our hands the silver and the gold by which we can send our representative, then we are to give our silver and our gold, with our prayers for the Divine blessing upon it. One or the other of these two courses must be pursued, in order to discharge our indebtedness to our Redeemer and our fellow-sinners.

And, by the grace of God, this can be done. The labor to which we are called by our Lord and Master is not of that immense, and infinite kind which he undertook when he veiled his deity in our flesh, and sweat great drops of blood under the burden of God's wrath, in our stead. It is that moderate and proportioned species of labor, which consists in giving back to Christ what we have received from him. This is all. We are to provide salvation for the destitute, out of resources which God has first bestowed upon us. If God has given us the requisite mental and moral powers, and the means of education and discipline, these we are to employ in personal evangelistic service, if such be the leadings of his grace and providence. God has given us personal influence more or less, and a portion of this world's goods more or less, and these we are to employ in making the world better. We repeat it; the disciple of Christ is to "give to God the things that are God's;" to pay his debt out of God's own purse and treasury. And therefore it is, we say again, that this indebtedness is not of that infinite and superhuman nature which puts it entirely beyond the reach of a mortal. It is simply to employ, to the best of our opportunity, our talents, our time, our wealth, our prayers, in extending the knowledge of Christ to the whole world. Each and every one of these things comes to us, ultimately, from God. And is it not a deep and selfish sin that refuses, or neglects to employ in his service even a portion of his overflowing bounty, but squanders it upon the pampered and worldly creature?

3. The third and final observation suggested by the subject is, that the faithful Christian will be *rewarded* for his discharge of his obligations to the unevangelized world. In that memorable picture which our Lord draws of the final day, he represents himself as saying to those who have fed the hungry, clothed the naked, and visited the prisoner: "Come ye blessed of my Father, inherit the kingdom prepared for you from the foundation of the world." God rewards his own grace. His people, who in this world have been enabled by him to discharge their duty with measurable fidelity, will be crowned with glory and honor in the next. It is not by an absolute merit that the disciple acquires this immense compensation. He has done what he has, only in the strength of Christ, and therefore his reward is a gracious reward. Hence we find that the faithful disciples are surprised to learn, in the great day, that their imperfect services have been so highly estimated by the Lord and Judge. They cannot imagine that they deserve such an amazing recompense. "*When* saw we thee an hungered and fed thee; or thirsty and gave thee drink? *When* saw we thee a stranger and took thee in? or naked and clothed thee? Or *when* saw we thee sick or in prison and came unto thee?" It will indeed be a surprise, and a joy unspeakable, when the believer, who is deeply conscious of his imperfect services, shall yet hear from the lips of the Infallible One: "Well done, good and faithful servant, enter thou into the joy of thy Lord." But he will hear this plaudit, because God

gives "grace for grace," and by grace the believer is enabled to discharge the debt which he owes to Christ, and to his fellow-men. And he will say with St. Paul, who in our text confesses himself to be a debtor to the Greek and the Barbarian: "I have fought a good fight, I have kept the faith, I have labored more abundantly than they all, yet not I but the grace of God that was in me. Henceforth there is a crown of righteousness laid up for me, and not for me only, but for all who love his appearing."

SERMON XXVI.

THE CERTAIN SUCCESS OF EVANGELISTIC LABOR.

ISAIAH lv. 10, 11.—"For as the rain cometh down and the snow from heaven, and returneth not thither, but watereth the earth, and maketh it bring forth and bud, that it may give seed to the sower, and bread to the eater; so shall my word be that goeth forth out of my mouth: it shall not return unto me void; but it shall accomplish that which I please, and it shall prosper in the thing whereto I sent it."

IT is the duty of the Christian Church to preach the gospel to every creature, because Christ the Head of the Church has commanded it so to do. It follows from this, that every individual member is obliged to contribute to this result, in proportion to his means and opportunities. No one believer is charged with the performance of the whole work. St. Paul was not bound to evangelize the entire globe, but only to preach as far and as wide as he could. The work that is assigned to the Church as a whole cannot be devolved upon a few persons, and no single generation is required to perform the service of all the generations of believers. On the contrary, each and every disciple of Christ has laid upon him a certain portion of this Christian service which he is solemnly bound to render. The command to the single Christian: "Go work this day in my vineyard," is as imperative as the command to the whole Church: "Go preach my gospel to every creature." The entire labor of evangelizing the globe is thus distributed among the generations of Christians, and among the innumerable individuals composing them, and if each one were as faithful in his own sphere and time as was the apostle Paul, this sinful and miserable world would present a far different appearance from what it now does.

Inasmuch as each and every disciple of Christ is thus bound to contribute his share towards the evangelization of the globe, it becomes an interesting and important question, whether the work is *feasible*. May it not be that the Church is attempting too much? The larger part of the world is still pagan, and totally ignorant of God in Christ; and a considerable part of nominal Christendom consists of unrenewed men who are as distant from heaven as the heathen, so far as the new birth is concerned. In comparison with the entire human family, the Church of Christ, as the hymn tells us, is still

> " ' A little spot enclosed by grace,
>   Out of the world's wide wilderness."

How can the Church at large, and the individual Christian, be certain that they are not undertaking a work that is intrinsically impossible of performance? No laborer desires to spend his strength for nought. It was one of the torments of the pagan hell, perpetually to roll a stone up a hill, and just as it reached the summit, perpetually to see it slip from the hands and roll back to the bottom. It was another of the torments of Tartarus, to draw water in a sieve forever and forevermore. These futile labors of Sisyphus, and the daughters of Danaus, are emblematic of that species of effort which cannot succeed, by reason of an intrinsic infeasibility. No man can conquer the force of gravitation. He may resist it, but he cannot conquer it; the stone and the drop of water will eventually fall to the ground, in spite of the most persevering efforts to the contrary. Is the endeavor to preach the gospel everywhere, and instrumentally to convert the souls of all men, a labor of this kind? Is the Church engaged in the toil of Sisyphus? If so, it is work without hope, and

> "Work without hope draws nectar in a sieve,
> And hope without an object cannot live."

Unless the people of God have sure and strong reasons for believing that the enterprise in which they are engaged—the endeavor to put a Bible into every man's hand, and to impress its truths upon his heart—is within the compass of possibility, they ought to cease from their labors. And if, on the other hand, they have in the purposes, promises, truth, and power of God, an infallible certainty of success in this endeavor, then they ought to toil with a hundred-fold more energy, and a hundredfold more courage.

We propose to mention some of the reasons that make it certain that evangelistic labor will succeed; that the effort of the Church to preach Christ crucified will no more fail of its effect, than the rain will fail to water the earth, and cause the seeds that are sown in it to germinate.

I. We argue and derive the certainty of success in evangelistic labor, in the first place, from *the nature of Divine truth*. There is something in the quality and characteristics of the doctrine which we are commanded to preach to every creature, that promises and prophesies a triumph. The word of God is both living, and quickening. This is implied in the figure which the prophet Isaiah employs in the text. "As the rain cometh down from heaven, and returneth not thither, but watereth the earth and maketh it to bring forth and bud, *so* shall my word be that goeth forth out of my mouth." This is the declaration of God himself, who understands the intrinsic nature of his own Revelation; and by it he teaches us that there is no greater adaptedness in moisture to fructify the ground, and germinate a corn of wheat, than there is in Biblical doctrine to renew and convert a human soul.

For the truth which the evangelist scatters upon the printed page, or teaches from his own lips, is *superhuman*. It does not originate within the sphere of man, and man's reason. The Bible contains a mass of information that issues from an *inspired* sphere and circle, and therefore differs in kind from all other books. We know very well the difference between the truths of mathematics, and the truths of poetry. They proceed from two different species of perception. The poet's intuition is so diverse from that of the man of science, that we never confound poetry with science. On the contrary, we know that the one destroys the other; and it has passed into a proverb, that he who is made for a poet is spoiled for a mathematician. From a college of savans, we do not look for a Paradise Lost; and from the "laureate fraternity " of poets, we do not expect a Mécanique Céleste. This inadequately illustrates the immense diversity between Divine Revelation, and human literature. The former issues from the mind of God; from an intellectual sphere infinitely higher than that of the human mind. That inspired circle, within which the Scriptures of the Old and New Testaments took their origin, differed from all other intellectual circles, be they schools of religion, or of philosophy, or of poetry, or of science, by a difference to which that between the mind of a Milton and the mind of a Laplace is only the faintest approximation.

This fact we need to keep in view, if we would see any ground of certainty for the success of the Christian evangelist. Unless he is commissioned to teach something that is superhuman; something that did not take origin within the sphere of earth and of man; something that is not found in the national literatures of the world; he will spend his strength for nought. The apostles of human reason, the inventors of human systems, and their disciples, have labored for six thousand years without radically changing a single individual man, or converting any of the sin and misery of earth into the holiness and happiness of heaven; and if the Christian herald does not go entirely beyond their sphere, and proclaim truths from another and higher world, he will only repeat their futile endeavor. He must teach the word and commandments of God; a higher doctrine than the commandments of man, and a wisdom superior to that of any people, Hebrew or Hindoo, Greek or Roman.[1]

---

[1] The erroneous postulate of all rationalistic Biblical Criticism is, that the Bible is a national literature, and not a Divine Revelation—that the books of the Old Testament are the natural development of the Hebrew mind as the poems of Homer, the dramas of Æschylus, and the dialogues of Plato are of the Greek mind. From this it follows, that Moses, Samuel, David, and Isaiah were not above the level of their nation, but thought, felt, and taught in harmony with the common national sentiment of their day. This view makes the Hebrew *nation* to be the real source of the Old Testament doctrines and miracles (myths); and the Hebrew Bible to be the Hebrew literature. If this be so, the Old Testament is no more infallible than the Vedas, and its antiquated truths may fitly be compared to "Hebrew old clothes."

A recent writer who tries to retain the doctrine of the inspiration of Scripture while surrendering that of its infallibility, adopts a modification of this view. He says that "the nation is *inspired*. This is the primary fact. The inspiration of Moses, Isaiah, or Ezekiel, is the secondary fact." (Ladd's Sacred Scripture I. 117; II. 483.) But this is refuted by the fact, that the history of Israel is that of a continual conflict between the national sentiment and opinions, and the inspired doctrines. The Old Testament Scriptures teach monotheism, the fact of sin and guilt, and promise a spiritual and Divine Redeemer; but the nation, whenever left to its own natural development, substituted in

In this fact, there is great encouragement to diligence and perseverance, upon the part of every disciple of Christ, to proclaim Divine truth in every form and manner possible. Revealed truth is immortal. It can never perish. You may educate a child or a man by the choicest secular methods, and may put him in communication with the ripest lore of the ancient and the modern world; he may become a highly disciplined scholar, and may leave behind him an illustrious name in the annals of literature; but the knowledge which he acquires, and which he transmits, shall all pass away. "Whether there be tongues they shall cease; whether there be knowledge it shall pass away." It ought to extinguish all the proud ambition of a merely earthly scholarship, to consider how transitory is all knowledge that is not divine, religious, and inspired. It is strictly true, that no truth, no doctrine, shall abide for millenniums, shall abide for eternity, but the truth and doctrine of God. Consider Shakespeare for example. This was the most comprehensive, capacious, original, creative intellect that ever inhabited a human body. Take him all in all, he possessed more power of intuition, and of expression, than any other human being; and the addition which he made to the stock of uninspired human literature, and culture, is greater, more original, more quickening and fertilizing to the mind of man, than that of any other author, ancient or modern. John Dryden was within the bounds of moderation, when he pronounced " that Shakespeare was the man who of all mod-

---

their place polytheism, self-righteousness, and an earthly Messiah. Had the nation, like its small circle of "holy men," been "moved by the Holy Ghost," there would not have been these two contradictory systems. The only reason why the Hebrew people did not become a nation of idolaters, was the restraining presence among them of a college of inspired prophets and legislators—a wheel within a wheel.

ern, and perhaps ancient poets, had the largest and most comprehensive soul." But where will the Shakespearian drama be, ten million years from now? Who will read the play of Hamlet, marvellous as it is, in the eternal years of God? Far are we from despising the really grand achievements of the human intellect, in literature, art, and science. They have their function, and appropriate work to perform in the education of the human race. But they are finite, mixed with error, unrelated to the salvation and destiny of the human soul, and therefore transitory. Excepting those elements in them which have been derived from the eternal fountain of truth, and which therefore harmonize with the kingdom of God, they are all of them to disappear, when that which is perfect is come. They are all to give place to that higher intuition, that beatific vision of truth and of beauty, which is in reserve for the pure in heart. And therefore it is, that human art, human science, and human knowledge—all that the fallible and imperfect human intellect has wrought out, in these centuries of dimness and of sin—like

> " The cloud-capped towers, the gorgeous palaces,
> The solemn temples, the great globe itself,
> 　　　　　　　　　　shall dissolve,
> And leave not a rack behind."

But not so, with Divine truth. That species of knowledge which the Christian Church possesses in the Scriptures of the Old and New Testaments, and of which it is the appointed depositary and teacher, has in it nothing fallible, nothing transitory. That Christian disciple, or missionary, who is instrumental in teaching a single human soul, either in America or in Africa, in the ninth century or in the nineteenth, that "God so loved the world, that he gave his only begotten Son that whosoever believeth in him might not perish, but might have ever-lasting life," announces a truth that will be of as momentous importance ten million years hence, as it is at this very moment. Schools of literature have their day, lose their interest, and give place to others that are subject to the same vicissitudes. But Christian doctrines never have their day. They are subject to no fashions. Sin is as real and as hateful now, as it ever was. Hell is as lurid and awful now, as when Satan and his host were hurled into it. The blood of Christ is as precious, the doctrine of the divine clemency is as peace-giving, now, as it was when our Lord said to the sinful woman, "Thy sins are forgiven." Instead of waning in truthfulness and importance, the doctrines of Revelation acquire a deeper truthfulness and a more solemn significance, as the centuries roll away. Those truths relating to God, Man, and the God-man, which the Scriptures have now made the common heritage of the beggar on the dung-hill and the king on the throne; those doctrines relating to human apostasy and human redemption, which the Church is commanded to teach to every creature; are the word of God "which liveth and abideth forever;" they are the immortal seed of a life everlasting.

Here, then, is a ground of certainty that the work of the Christian evangelist will succeed. In lodging the truths of the Bible in any human soul, you are placing something there which is literally eternal; which will have the same value millions and billions of ages from now. No lapse of time can destroy its truthfulness, or its importance. The work which you do when you put the few pages of a tract in the hands of an unrenewed man, and by your prayerful earnestness are instrumental in its being wrought into the texture of his mind and heart, will endure forever. You may build a pyramid; but it will one day be part and particle of the sands that are blown and sifted by the winds of the desert. You may compose an Iliad or a Macbeth; but it will lose its interest, and disappear from the memory of mortals, when they stand before the judgment-seat of God. But if you teach to any human creature the words of Jehovah; if you mortise the law and the gospel into the framework of the human mind; you erect a structure which it is not in the power of man, or of everlasting time, to tear down and destroy.

Not only is Divine truth immortal in its nature, but it can never be expelled from the mind. Teach a child or a man, for example, the true Biblical doctrine of sin; fix it in his mind that God abhors wickedness, and will punish it everlastingly; and you have imparted something to him which he can never get rid of. He may lose sight of it for a week, or a month, or a year, or ten years, but he cannot lose sight of it for eternity. It will sooner or later, and with more than the certainty of a planet's motion, emerge within the horizon of his consciousness, and fill him with terror if he is an impenitent sinner. In imparting to his mind this truth concerning the holy nature of God, and the wickedness of sin, you have imparted to him something like a fatal secret, which will haunt and waylay the soul through all the years of open or of secret transgression. One of the most powerful of modern fictions[1] is founded upon the accidental discovery, by a servant, of a fatal secret belonging to his master. The discovery fills his whole life with fear and apprehension, and drives him to the borders of insanity. He would give worlds, if he had not made that discovery; he would give the universe, if he could forget it. But the secret has come to his knowledge, and he

---

[1] Godwin's Caleb Williams.

cannot erase it from his memory. There is an art of remembering, but no art of forgetting. The secret stays with him and by him like a fiend, and he cannot get from under its black shadow. Are there not on record many instances in which the solemn declarations and warnings of the Divine law, which had been wrought into the mind perhaps in earliest youth, still clung to it, and punished it with fears and forebodings, during the after-life of license and forgetfulness of God? Human knowledge is soon forgotten; the images of the human poet are fading and fugitive as the colors of the frescos in the Vatican; but the knowledge of the Divine law, and the awful imagery of the Scriptures relating to it, are indestructible, and burn themselves into the texture of the soul like the colors of encaustic tiles.

And on the other side of Revelation, all this is equally true. The peace-speaking promises of mercy, the doctrine of the Divine pity, of the forgiveness of sins and the preparation for eternal life—all this portion of Divine truth when once imparted is never again expelled. And when in the years of sin the law makes itself felt, and the transgressor is brought into consternation, the doctrines of grace which had been conveyed to the mind many long years ago by the Christian teacher are all that save it from everlasting despair, and everlasting perdition. And even if this is not the happy result, owing to the inveteracy of vice, or the torpidity of the conscience, or the obstinacy of the proud heart, and the soul goes into the presence of God unforgiven, still the truths of the gospel are not expelled from the understanding. They will be a portion of the soul's knowledge through all eternity; the evidence of what it might have secured, and the index of what it has lost.

II. We argue and derive the certain success of evangelistic labor, in the second place, from the fact that *God feels a special interest in his own Word.*

The Scriptures warrant us in asserting, that God is more profoundly concerned for the success of that body of truth which he has revealed to mankind in the Scriptures, than he is for the spread and influence of all other ideas and truths whatsoever. This is the only species of truth which he personally watches over, and accompanies with a Divine influence. He leaves human knowledge to itself, to make its own way without any supernatural aid or influence from him; but the doctrines of the Bible are not dismissed from his hand with this indifference. We have seen that they have an intrinsic adaptation to the wants and woes of the soul, and that in this particular they possess a vast superiority over all earthly knowledge; but this is not their sole, or their highest prerogative. They are not only related to man, but they are related to the Holy Ghost. From the very depths of the Divine Essence, there issues an energy that adds to the intrinsic energy of Revelation, and makes it a two-edged sword quick and piercing. Powerful as the Word of God is in itself, it would fail to touch and soften the flinty human heart, were it not that God personally watches over it, and effectually applies it. Men go into ecstasies over the discovery of a new fact in science, or a fresh and original creation of the poet and artist. There is joy and pride in all educated circles, when a new addition is made to the literature of the nation, or to the sum of human arts and inventions. But there is no corresponding and equal joy in the Eternal Understanding, at such events. The Deity never becomes thus profoundly interested in a poem or a painting; in the telegraph or the steam-engine. The "wisdom of this world," we are told, is "foolishness" with him. But there is a species of truth, a form of doctrine, in which the entire energy of the Godhead is engrossed, and whose spread and triumph fills him with deep eternal joy. It is that which he has deposited in the Scriptures, and has commanded his people to teach and preach from generation to generation, until the whole world is leavened with it.

This fact is clearly taught in the text. " My word," says God by his prophet, "shall not return unto me void; but it shall accomplish that which *I please*, and it shall prosper in the thing whereto *I sent* it." Here is personal interest, and personal supervision. These doctrines relating to the salvation and destiny of man, are not sent forth from heaven lonely messengers, to make their way as they best can. The third Person of the Trinity goes with them, and exerts an influence through them that is undefinable, but as almighty and irresistible, within its own sphere and in its own way, as physical omnipotence itself. For there is not a human heart upon the globe, whose hardness is impenetrable to the combined operation of the Word and Spirit of God. There is not a human will upon the planet, so strong and stubborn as to be able to overcome the union of the Scriptures and the Holy Ghost.

In this fact, then, we find a second ground of certainty of success for evangelistic labor. You may proclaim all your days, your own ideas, or those of your fellow-men, but you will say with Grotius, at the close of a long and industrious career which had by no means been exclusively devoted to humanistic learning: "I have spent my life in laboriously doing nothing." But if you have passed your days in teaching the unevangelized, and conveying into their dark and blinded understandings the truths of the law and the gospel, you may say, at the close of life, as you sum up your work, with a clearer consciousness than that of the pagan Horace: "I shall not wholly die. I have erected a monument more durable than brass. I have taught the word of God that liveth and abideth forever, to many human souls."

III. A third ground of certainty that evangelistic labor will succeed, is found in the *actual instances of success* furnished by the annals of such labor. Men are continually writing upon the evidences of Christianity, but there is no demonstration like that which proceeds from the practical work of the Church and the ministry, in bringing this religion home to the business and bosoms of men. This was the argument which the Primitive Church employed, to prove to the pagan the Divine origin and power of the new religion. Christianity must be from God, argued Justin Martyr and Tertullian, "because it makes the voluptuous man chaste, the avaricious man liberal, the man of cursing a man of prayer, the implacable enemy a forgiving friend, converts wrath into gentleness, debauchery into temperance, and vice of manifold form into manifold virtue." The fruits evince the reality, and the quality of the tree. There is always great force in a fact. It is the element of reality. Men are realists, and they love reality wherever they find it. In this element, lies the great power of a certain class of poets and novelists. Why is it that Dante, and Chaucer, and De Foe, so impinge themselves upon the minds of their readers, and make the same kind of impression upon them that is made by actually going through the wards of a hospital, or over the acres of a battle-field, or out into the warm sunlight of a June landscape? It is because of the intense realism, the matter of fact, that pervades the poem or the novel. It is a work of the imagination, so far as plot and costume are concerned, but the imagination is employed with such stern and intense truthfulness, that all fanciful and unnatural qualities are purged out, and the result is a product that is veritable like actual life, and actual experience itself. Robinson

Crusoe is the product of the imagination, and yet every reader knows and feels that it is as real as his own daily existence. But when we pass from poetry and fiction, to the very life itself of man—to the tears which we see him drop, to the pain and bereavements which we see him suffer, and to the joys which we see mantling upon his countenance—we understand still better how powerful is plain truth and reality.

Now we find what we may call the realism of Christianity, in the evangelizing operations of the Church. So long as we know the gospel only by book and theory, we do not know it in its most impressive and convincing form. A Church, or an age of the Church, that carries on no missionary work, will be liable to latent and increasing skepticism. The facts and forces of Christianity do not smite upon it, and make the gospel real. Suppose that I have never myself felt the revolutionizing power of Christianity, or have never seen an instance of it in another person: will not the theoretical belief which I may have in this religion be likely to wane away, in the lapse of time ? If a power is not exerted, we begin to doubt its existence. And if an individual or a Church witnesses no effusions of the Spirit, and no actual conversions of the human soul, it will inevitably begin to query whether there be any Holy Ghost, and whether the gospel is anything more than ethics. This has occurred in the history of the Church. The eighteenth century in England was an age of infidelity outside of the Church, and of very inadequate faith within it. And it was because the Christian religion showed little of its power, in visibly converting and transforming the human soul. Men were not actually born again, and it was an easy and ready conclusion that the doctrine of the new birth is fanaticism. And whenever this notion enters either the individual or the general mind, unbelief in the essential and energetic truths of Christianity comes in apace. The same remark holds true of the German Church. Its rationalism, which has exerted so wide an influence, was the consequence of a decline of faith in evangelical doctrines ; and this decline of faith in evangelical doctrines was owing very greatly to the absence of striking impressions from these doctrines. In the age of the Reformation, the popular mind felt the truth of such dogmas as original sin, and forgiveness through atoning blood. These truths evinced their power in thousands of actual instances, and therefore they could not be disputed or denied. But when the energy and fervor of the Reformation period had declined, and men within the visible Church itself lived on from year to year with little or no consciousness of the corruption of the heart, and of the pacifying efficacy of Christ's blood and righteousness, it was no wonder that the dogmatic belief of the Church should change, and in the place of the warm evangelism of Luther, there should rise the cold rationalism of Paulus and Wegscheider.

In the actual success, then, of endeavors to convert the souls of men, we find the striking instances, the matters of fact, the living Christian verities, that brace up our declining faith, and warm our cooling piety. The preacher goes into a destitute town upon the borders of our Western or our Southern country, teaches the condemning law, and proclaims the saving gospel, to a soul steeped in sin. His prayer of faith, and labor of love, are rewarded and crowned with the descent and personal presence of the Holy Ghost. That soul is converted. It undergoes a revolution as great and momentous as that by which Adam fell ; for regeneration is as great a change as apostasy. That fact, that actual exertion of Divine power, is known in the heavens, and the angels rejoice over it ; and it enters into the archives of the Church here upon earth, and exerts an influence. It is another instance of the actual exercise of *personal* power on the part of God the Redeemer, and tends to deepen and strengthen the faith of Christians in that species of power, wherever it is known. But the annals of missions are full of such instances, so that from year to year an intense and mighty Christian realism is issuing out from all evangelizing enterprises, and by a reflex action is refreshing the faith, and consolidating the doctrine of the Churches that set them in motion.

The power of Biblical truth even when not proclaimed by the voice of the evangelist is continually receiving demonstration, from this same source. The records of Bible and Tract Societies are full of instances in which the bare text of Scripture led to the conversion of a human soul. Consider the following. A distributor gave a tract to a young man, accompanying it with some words expressive of a serious and affectionate desire for his salvation. The young man, upon the departure of the missionary, threw the pages into the fire; but as they curled up in the flame, his eye caught the words : "Heaven and earth shall pass away, but my words shall not pass away." As these words turned to ashes in the fire, they turned to fire in his mind. He found no rest, until he found it in the blood of atonement. Now, this was an actual occurrence. It is not a story invented for the purpose of exciting interest in the mind of a reader or a hearer. There is not the slightest mingling of imaginative elements in it. That thirty-first verse of the thirteenth chapter of St. Mark's gospel was thus impressed upon the mind and conscience of a human being, in a certain section of space, and at a certain point of time. The time and the place could have been specified under oath. Lord Bacon, in laying down the rules by which the materials for composing a history should be collected, says: "We would have our first history written with the most religious particularity, as though upon oath as to the truth of every syllable; for it is a volume of God's works, and, as far as the majesty of things divine can brook comparison with the lowliness of earthly objects, is, as it were, a second Scripture." Of this kind are the materials that are collected and edited by the evangelizing associations of the Church; and of this kind is this incident which we have recited. And it demonstrates that there is a converting power accompanying divine truth, similarly as an explosion proves that there is an explosive power in gunpowder. How much more vivid is such an evidence of Christianity as this, than many of the volumes that have been written for the laudable purpose of demonstrating the divinity of the Christian Religion. We by no means undervalue or disparage that fine body of apologetic literature, which the attacks of infidelity have called forth, from the second century to the nineteenth. But we do affirm that it all needs to be filled out, and corroborated, by the actual instances in which Divine truth and the Divine Spirit have exerted their power. When the doctrines of the gospel evince themselves to be mighty, by showing their might, and transforming, by actually producing transformations; when the theory is verified by the stubborn fact; we have the perfection of evidence. This is what the evangelistic agencies of Christendom are doing. By their steady, quiet, oftentimes subterranean labors among the poor, the ignorant, and the vicious of teeming populations, and by the record in their annals of what God has wrought through their instrumentality, they are proving to the doubter and the skeptic that God is personally interested in his own word and watches over it; that there is a secret spiritual energy at work, of which they know nothing.

God is hiding himself from the glare and tinsel of a luxurious civilization, but he is revealing himself to "the poor of this world, rich in faith, and heirs of the kingdom which he hath promised to them that love him." As we look over the surface of society, we do not find the strongest evidence that God is present among his creatures, and is interested in them, in the fact that he is raining down upon them physical happiness and prosperity. He indeed comes near to man in these methods of his providence, and this providential care and goodness should lead to repentance. But the closeness of his proximity to man, is seen chiefly in the operations and methods of his grace. When he says to a soul: "Thy sin is forgiven thee," he comes infinitely closer and nearer to his creature, than when the corn and wine are increased. Nay, how do I know that there is a God; how do I know it with *living certainty;* unless he touches me, and moves me to cry: "My Father, my Heavenly Father?" Carefully scrutinized, there is no argument for the Divine existence and agency in this lower world, that is equal to the very sense of God, and feeling of God, which is granted to a soul when it mourns over sin, and experiences pardoning mercy. "I have heard of thee by the hearing of the ear, but now mine eye seeth thee," may be said of the Christian's conscious faith, as contrasted with the worldling's hearsay belief.

There is no surer evidence that the truths of the gospel are destined to prevail, than the fact that they do prevail. Only as the individual Christian, and the Church at large, feel the influence of the *ocular demonstration* of the power of the gospel, will they know that evangelistic labor is not the spilling of water upon the ground which cannot be gathered up again; is not the eternal drawing of water in a sieve; is not the everlasting rolling of the stone to the verge of the summit, and its everlasting falling back to the abyss.

We have thus argued the certainty that all evangelistic labor will succeed, from the nature of the truth which is proclaimed ; from the fact that God himself watches over and effectually applies it; and from the actual examples of success which fill the annals of the Church. He who teaches, or is instrumental in teaching, the law and the gospel, teaches a truth that is superhuman in its origin and nature, and ineradicable from the rational mind. He who teaches, or is instrumental in teaching, the law and the gospel, teaches the only truth in which the Godhead is profoundly interested, and the only truth which He accompanies with a supernatural energy and influence. And he who teaches, or is instrumental in teaching, the law and the gospel, will see the truth accomplishing its purpose, and doing its blessed work before his very eyes.

From the subject as thus discussed, we infer the duty of great *courage*, and *confidence*, in the work of evangelizing men. We have seen that there is a strong and settled foundation for such a feeling upon the part of the Church. God himself has laid it in promises, oaths, and blood. If, therefore, we would possess it, and feel its inspiriting influence, we must look intently and continually at the *foundation*. We must keep in mind, the superhuman quality of Divine truth, the profound interest of God in it, and the fact that it is making progress and conquests. When an individual Christian is cast down and dispirited by doubts respecting his good estate, we bid him look at the *object* of faith, and not lose sight of his Redeemer in his sight of himself. In like manner, if the Church would be courageous and confident in this immense work of home and foreign evangelization, she must cease to dwell upon the difficulties and obstacles, and look intently and solely at the power and promise of God. Too many Christians, from year to year, contribute of their substance, and even of their labors, and put up supplications for the conversion of the world, in a half-despairing temper. It is their duty; and they perform it with something of the hireling's spirit, who looks longingly for the going down of the sun that the unwelcome task may be over. They forget the almightiness of the Being in whose service they are employed, and whose plans they are carrying out. When that eminent and successful missionary, Dr. Morrison, some fifty years ago, was about to sail to China, the kind-hearted but unbelieving merchant who had offered him a passage in one of his vessels, with good-humored raillery said to him: "And so you really expect to make an impression upon the Chinese Empire." "No, sir, but I expect that God will," was the calm and confident response. In that spirit he labored, and in that sign he conquered. He did not himself see the conversion of the Chinese race; but that sight is as certainly destined to bless the vision of the Christian Church at the time appointed by God, as Enke's or Biela's comet is destined to be a reappearing meteor in the heavens.[1] If the planets are punctual, and dawn upon our vision with certainty and regularity, though we do nothing towards wheeling them in their orbits, think you that the conversion of nations and races for which the promise of God is pledged, and for which the blood of incarnate God has been spilt, will fail? Let us take this lofty, Biblical theory of missions, and we shall be confident and courageous. Look not at the hardness of the human heart, but look at the hammer and the fire that break it in pieces. Look not at the stubborn will and the carnal

---

[1] "Behold these shall come from far; and lo, these from the north and from the west; and these from the land of Sinim." Isa. xlix. 12.

mind, but look at Jehovah who says: "I will take away the stony heart out of your flesh, and I will give you a heart of flesh." Look not with a despairing vision upon the hundreds of millions that are outside of Christendom; upon the tens of millions within Christendom who never open a Bible or enter the house of God; upon the crowded streets and alleys of vast cities, in themselves as horrid and hopeless as the lazar-house which Milton describes—look not at this immense mass of human sin and misery, but look to Him who died for it all, who has power to pardon and purify it all, and who commands you to scatter the good seed of the word broadcast, and trust Him for the harvest.

The same law prevails in the larger sphere of missions, that rules in the individual experience. There must be a ceasing to look at the creature, and an absorbing, empowering looking to the Creator and Redeemer. No sinner obtains peace, until he sees that the Divine clemency is greater than his sins. So long as his sins look larger than the Divine mercy, so long he must despair. Precisely so is it with efforts to save the souls of men. The Church will not be instrumental in evangelizing the globe, unless it believes that God the Holy Spirit is more mighty than man's corruption. So long as the work looks too great to be accomplished; so long as the ignorance, vice, brutality, and apathy, of the sinful masses all around seem insuperable by any power human or divine; so long there will be no courageous and confident labor for human welfare. Not a missionary would ever have gone upon his errand of love, had his eye been taken from God, and fixed solely upon man, and man's hopeless condition. Think you that the apostles would have started out from the little corner of Palestine, to convert the whole Græco-Roman world to a new religion, if their vision had been confined to earth?

Apart from the power and promise of God, the preaching of such a religion as Christianity, to such a population as that of paganism, is the sheerest Quixotism. It crosses all the inclinations, and condemns all the pleasures of guilty man. The preaching of the gospel finds its justification, its wisdom, and its triumph, only in the attitude and relation which the infinite and almighty God sustains to it. It is *His* religion, and therefore it must ultimately become a universal religion.

Go forth, then, to evangelistic labor of any and every variety, with cheerfulness, with courage, and with confidence. And when the vastness and difficulty of the work threaten to discourage, and dishearten you, look away entirely from earth and man's misery, to God's throne, and recall his own word which is settled in heaven : " My thoughts are not your thoughts, neither are your ways my ways, saith the Lord. For as the heavens are higher than the earth, so are my ways higher than your ways, and my thoughts than your thoughts. For as the rain cometh down and the snow from heaven, and returneth not thither, but watereth the earth, and maketh it bring forth and bud, that it may give seed to the sower, and bread to the eater ; so shall my word be that goeth forth out of my mouth : it shall not return unto me void ; but it shall accomplish that which I please, and it shall prosper in the thing whereto I sent it."

Other SGCB Classic Reprints

Biblical & Theological Studies by the faculty of Princeton Seminary from 1912 was published in commemoration of the 100th anniversary of Princeton. Warfield, Machen, Vos, Allis, Hodge Jr., and ten other giants contribute to this timeless book.

A History of Preaching by Edwin Charles Dargan is a two volume hardcover set that is the standard work of its kind in the field of Homiletics. Every pastor, student and teacher of religion should own it.

Homiletics and Pastoral Theology by W.G.T. Shedd expounds almost every aspect of preaching, analyzing its nature, outlining the main features which should characterize powerful preaching. The second part is devoted to the vital subject of Pastoral Theology. Briefer but equally valuable.

The Power of God unto Salvation by B.B. Warfield is the hundredth anniversary edition of Warfield's first volume of sermons. This volume includes a warmly written Preface by *Sinclair Ferguson,* and an Appendix of Four Hymns and Eleven Religious Poems written by Warfield.

Christ in Song: Hymns of Immanuel from all ages compiled by Philip Schaff drew forth the following high praise from Charles Hodge, *"After all, apart from the Bible, the best antidote to all these false theories of the person and work of Christ, is such a book as Dr. Schaff's 'Christ in Song.'"*

The Shorter Catechism Illustrated, from Christian Biography & History by John Whitercoss first appeared in 1828 and passed through many editions. It last appeared in the 1968 edition done by Banner of Truth.

The Lord of Glory by B.B. Warfield is considered one of the most thorough defenses of the Deity of Christ ever written. Over 320 pages of exposition of the designations used of our Lord throughout the New Testament.

First Things by Gardiner Spring is a two volume work setting forth the foundation laid for mankind in the opening chapters of Genesis. Rare and valuable!

The Preacher and His Models by James Stalker is the substance of the Yale Lectures of Preaching from 1891. This gifted Scots preacher uses both the Prophets and Apostles to stimulate modern preachers of the Gospel.

Imago Christi: The Example of Jesus Christ by James Stalker was called by C.H. Spurgeon *"an immortal book."* Our Lord is presented as a model for every aspect of life in this world of sin and misery. Thoroughly evangelical!

The Church Member's Guide by John Angell James was once the most popular book in both the UK and the USA for instructing Christian's in their privileges and responsibilities as members of the body of Christ.

Young Lady's Guide: to the Harmonious Development of Christian Character by Harvey Newcomb sets forth the biblical foundation needed for a young lady to grow to Christian womanhood. A manual for Christian maturity.

Call us toll free **1-877-666-9469**
E-mail us at **sgcb@charter.net**
Visit us on the web at **solid-ground-books.com**

Printed in the United States
28832LVS00007B/135